# AMONG THE GODS

# AMONG THE GODS

*An archaeological exploration of ancient Greek religion*

JOHN FERGUSON

Routledge
London and New York

First published in 1989 by Routledge
11 New Fetter Lane, London EC4P 4EE
29 West 35th Street, New York NY 10001

© 1989 John Ferguson

Printed in Great Britain by
St Edmundsbury Press Ltd, Bury St Edmunds, Suffolk
Photoset by Rowland Phototypesetting Ltd,
Bury St Edmunds, Suffolk

All rights reserved. No part of this book may be reprinted
or reproduced or utilized in any form or by any electronic,
mechanical, or other means, now known or hereafter
invented, including photocopying and recording, or in any
information storage or retrieval system, without permission
in writing from the publishers.

*British Library Cataloguing in Publication Data*

Ferguson, John, *1921–*
Among the gods: an archaeological
exploration of ancient Greek religion.
1. Greek antiquities. Archaeological
investigation
I. Title
938

ISBN 0–415–02953–8

*Library of Congress Cataloging in Publication Data*

Ferguson, John, 1921–
Among the gods: an archaeological exploration of ancient Greek
religion/by John Ferguson
p. cm.
Includes index.
1. Greece – Religion. I. Title.
BL782.F47 1989
292′.08–dc19    88-23942

For
Miranda and Stephen

# CONTENTS

Preface ix

List of abbreviations xi

1 THE RELIGION OF ANCIENT CRETE 1

2 GODS AND GODDESSES 11

3 SANCTUARIES, TEMPLES, AND ALTARS 25

4 PRIESTHOOD 48

5 GAMES AND FESTIVALS 54

6 ORACLES 67

7 HEALING SANCTUARIES 88

8 THE MYSTERIES 103

9 DEATH AND BURIAL 122

10 VOTIVE OFFERINGS 137

11 PRIVATE CULTS 143

12 MAGIC 147

13 POLITICS AND RELIGION 159

## CONTENTS

| | | |
|---|---|---|
| 14 | SOME ISLANDS AND THEIR CULTS | 173 |
| 15 | THE RELIGIOUS LIFE OF ATHENS AND ATTICA | 190 |
| | Notes | 214 |
| | Glossary | 221 |
| | Index | 225 |

# PREFACE

In the last twenty-five years I have been increasingly impressed by the amount that archaeology can tell us about the real thought-world of Greece and Rome. Two factors have particularly influenced this. The first has been the opportunity of travelling in the Graeco-Roman world and seeing things for myself, first as a means of breaking the journey between Nigeria and Britain, and more recently through the good offices of Mr Swan. The second has been the experience of directing an outstandingly able Ph.D. thesis by Dr Miranda Green concerned with an archaeological approach to an aspect of Romano-Celtic religion. Already when I wrote *Religions of the Roman Empire* I was taking far more cognizance of archaeological evidence than, say, T. R. Glover did in his splendid book on the same topic of half a century previously.

As I turn over the pages of the general English-language introductions to Greek religion, such as Gilbert Murray's exciting *Five Stages of Greek Religion*, and even H. J. Rose's *Ancient Greek Religion*, I find that very little use is made of archaeological evidence. Of course there are exceptions, such as A. B. Cook's monumental *Zeus* and Jane Harrison's two seminal books, *Themis* and *Prolegomena to the Study of Greek Religion* (was ever an immensely exciting book given a more unpromising title?). In this book I have tried to concentrate on the archaeological evidence. Plainly it is impossible totally to ignore the literary evidence. To take two obvious examples, Pausanias has helped us to elucidate the archaeological sites themselves, and Eleusis in particular would mean little to us were it not for the *Homeric Hymn to Demeter*. Obviously literary evidence has helped to shape my background thinking, and I do not think that I can be charged with neglect of the literary evidence: witness my *Greek and Roman Religion: A*

*Source-Book* (Noyes Press, 1980), or an article currently appearing in *Museum Africum* on 'Herodotus as a source for Greek religion'. But here I have allowed archaeology to dictate the agenda. There is little reference here, for example, to Xenophanes, Plato, or Aristotle, and that probably means that they scarcely touched the mainstream of Greek religious practice.

The time for writing has been snatched from spare moments among administrative, pastoral, and teaching responsibilities, various forms of voluntary public service, and a determination to find time for the constructive recreations of cricket and music. I have not spent as long in libraries as I would wish. The sites discussed I have almost all visited for myself. Obviously, though, I have had often to rely on the work of others, and I have made acknowledgement of this in footnotes.

I have long given up the search for consistency in transliterating Greek, and unless one is prepared to stomach Aiskhulos, Platon, and Sokrates, it is doubtful whether consistency can be achieved. I have aimed at internal consistency, but may not even have achieved consistency in inconsistency. It is to be hoped that nothing will prove too misleading. If it is remembered that Greek K becomes Roman C, Greek U Roman Y, Greek OU Roman U, and Greek AI Roman AE, it is unlikely that there will be too much confusion. Conventional abbreviations of the names of Greek authors and their works will be found in Liddell–Scott–Jones, *Greek–English Lexicon* and of classical periodicals in *L'année philologique*.

Two special debts of gratitude are due. Lesley Roff has been a personal friend for more than ten years, and remains the best among several outstandingly good secretaries who have helped in the Zoroastrian battle of Order versus Chaos. Here she has produced order out of a more than usually chaotic MS. My wife Elnora and I have explored the classical world together for many years, and she has been a constant encouragement in all sorts of ways; what is more, she produces the best indexes a person could hope for.

John Ferguson<br>
Selly Park<br>
Birmingham

# ABBREVIATIONS

| | |
|---|---|
| *AA* | see *Arch. Anz.* |
| *AJA* | *American Journal of Archaeology* |
| *AP* | *Anthologia Palatina* |
| Ael. Arist. | Aelius Aristides |
| Aeschin. | Aeschines |
| Aeschylus | |
|   *Agam.* | *Agamemnon* |
| Alciphron | |
|   *Ep.* | *Epistulae* |
| Alex. Aphr. | Alexander of Aphrodisias |
|   *Prob.* | *Problemata* |
| *Ann. sc. arch. Atene* | *Annuario della Scuola Archeologica di Atene* |
| Ant. Lib. | Antoninus Liberalis |
| Ar. | Aristophanes |
|   *Ach.* | *Acharnians* |
|   *Cl.* | *Clouds* |
|   *Lys.* | *Lysistrata* |
|   *Plut.* | *Plutus* |
|   *Thesm.* | *Thesmophoriazusae* |
|   *W.* | *Wasps* |
| *Arch. Anz.* | *Archäologischer Anzeiger* |
| *Arch. Delt.* | *Archaiologion Deltion* |
| *Arch. Dr. Or.* | *Archives d'histoire du droit oriental et revue internationale des droits de l'antiquité* |
| *Arch. Eph.* | *Archaiologike Ephemeris* |
| *Arch. Zeit.* | *Archäologische Zeitung* |
| Arist. | Aristotle |

| | |
|---|---|
| Pol. | *Politics* |
| Ath. | Athenaeus |
| Ath. Mitt. | *Mitteilungen des deutschen archäologischen Instituts, Athenische Abteilung* (1876– ) |
| Athan. | Athanasius |
|   De Inc. Verb. |   *De Incarnatione Verbi* |
| Aud. | Audollent |
|   Def. Tab. |   *Defixionum Tabellae* |
| Aug. | Augustine |
|   CD |   *De Civitate Dei* |
|   De haer. |   *De haeresibus ad Quodvultdeum* |
| BCH | *Bulletin de correspondance hellénique* |
| BMC | *British Museum Catalogue of Coins* |
| BMC Bronzes | *British Museum Catalogue of Bronzes* |
| BSA | *Annual of the British School at Athens* |
| BSA Arch. Rep. | *British School at Athens: Archaeological Reports* |
| Bull. Soc. Arch. Alex. | *Bulletin de la Societé Royale archéologique d'Alexandrie* (1898– ) |
| CIA | *Corpus Inscriptionum Atticarum* (in *IG*) |
| CIG | *Corpus Inscriptionum Graecarum* |
| CIL | *Corpus Inscriptionum Latinarum* |
| CQ | *Classical Quarterly* |
| Call. | Callimachus |
|   H. Zeus |   *Hymn to Zeus* |
| Cic. | Cicero |
|   Div. |   *De Divinatione* |
|   Verr. |   *Verrine Orations* |
| Cl. Ph. or Cl. Phil. | *Classical Philology* |
| Clem. Al. | Clement of Alexandria |
|   Protrept. |   *Protrepticus* |
| Cohn-Haft | L. Cohn-Haft, *The Public Physicians of Ancient Greece* (Northampton, Mass., 1956) |
| col. | column |
| Collitz | see *Samml.* |
| Comptes Rend. de l'Acad. d'Inscr. | *Comptes rendus de l'Academie d'Inscriptions* |
| Corinth | American School of Classical Studies of Athens, *Corinth* (1929– ) |
| Dem. | Demosthenes |

## LIST OF ABBREVIATIONS

| | |
|---|---|
| *Denkschr. Akad. Wien* | *Denkschriften der Akademie der Wissenschaften* (Vienna, 1850– ) |
| *Didyma Inschr.* | A. Rehm, *Didyma II: Die Inschriften* (Berlin, 1958) |
| Diog. Laert. | Diogenes Laertius |
| *EG* | *Epigrammata Graeca*, ed. G. Kaibel (Berlin, 1878) |
| *EM* | *Etymologicum Magnum* |
| ET | English translation |
| *Eph. Arch.* | *Ephemeris Archaiologike* |
| *Etym. Magn.* | see *EM* |
| Eur. | Euripides |
|   *Hec.* |   *Hecuba* |
|   *IT* |   *Iphigeneia in Tauris* |
|   *Phoen.* |   *Phoenissae* |
| Eus. | Eusebius |
|   *V. Const.* |   *Vita Constantini* |
| *Explor. arch. de Délos* | *Exploration archéologique de Délos* (1909–61) |
| *F. Gr. Hist.* | F. Jacoby, *Fragmente der griechischen Historiker* (Berlin, 1923– ) |
| *Forsch. in Eph.* | *Forschungen in Ephesos*, Oesterreich archäologische Institut (1906) |
| *Fouilles* | *Fouilles de Delphes* (Paris, 1906–70) |
| fr. | fragment |
| *Griech. Ep.* | *Griechischen Epigramme*, ed. J. Geffcken (Heidelberg, 1910) |
| *GRBS* | *Greek, Roman and Byzantine Studies* |
| *Gr. Vers-Inschr.* | *Griechische Vers-Inschriften* |
| *HTR* | *Harvard Theological Review* |
| *Harpocrat.* | *Harpocration* |
| Hdt. | Herodotus |
| *Hell. Oxy.* | *Hellenica Oxyrhyncha* |
| Herod. | Herodes |
|   *Mim.* |   *Mimes* |
| Herzog | R. Herzog, *Heilige Geschichte von Kos* (Berlin, 1928) |
| Hes. | Hesiod |
|   *Theog.* |   *Theogony* |
|   *WD* |   *Works and Days* |
| *Hesp.* | *Hesperia* |

| | |
|---|---|
| Hesych. | see Hsch. |
| Hipp. | Hippolytus |
|   *Phil.* | *Philosophumena* |
| *Hist. Num.* | B. V. Head, *Historia Nummorum* (Oxford, 1911) |
| Hom. | Homer |
|   *H. Dem.* | *Hymn to Demeter* |
|   *Il.* | *Iliad* |
|   *Od.* | *Odyssey* |
| Hsch. or Hesych. | Hesychius |
| *IC* or *I Cr.* | *Inscriptiones Creticae*, ed. M. Guarducci (Rome, 1935– ) |
| *I Cos* | see *Inscr. Cos* |
| *IG* | *Inscriptiones Graecae* |
| *IG Ant.* | *Inscriptiones Graecae Antiquissimae praeter Atticas in Attica repertas* |
| *IG Ins.* | *Inscriptiones Graecae insularum maris Aegaei praeter Delum* |
| *IGRR* | *Inscriptiones Graecae ad res Romanas pertinentes*, ed. R. Cagnat *et al.* (Paris, 1911–27) |
| *I Magn.* | *Die Inschriften von Magnesia am Maeander*, ed. O. Kern (Berlin, 1900) |
| *I Ol.* | *Olympia 5 Die Inschriften*, ed. W. Dittenberger and K. Purgold (Berlin, 1896) |
| Iambl. | Iamblichus |
|   *De Myst.* | *De Mysteriis* |
|   *In Plat. Tim.* | *In Platonis Timaeum* |
| *Ins. Smyrna* | *Inscriptions de Smyrna*, ed. J. Keil |
| *Inscr. Cos* | W. R. Paton and E. L. Hicks, *The Inscriptions of Cos* (1881) |
| *Inscrr.* | *Inscriptions* |
| *JHS* | *Journal of Hellenic Studies* |
| *J. Int. Arch. Num.* | *Journal international d'archéologie numismatique* (1898– ) |
| *JRS* | *Journal of Roman Studies* |
| *Jahrh. Oest. Arch. Inst.* | *Jahreshefte des österreichischen archäologischen Instituts* (1898– ) |
| Joh. Lyd. | Johannes Lydus |
|   *Mens.* | *De Mensibus* |
| Kern | O. Kern, *Orphicorum Fragmenta* (Berlin, 1937) |

## LIST OF ABBREVIATIONS

| | |
|---|---|
| *Koische Forschungen* | R. Herzog, *Koische Forschungen und Funde* (Leipzig, 1899) |
| Lebas-Foucart | P. Le Bas and P. Foucart, *Inscriptions grecques et latines recueillies en Grèce et en Asie Mineur* (Paris, 1847–77) |
| *LGS* | J. de Prott and L. Ziehen, *Leges Graecorum Sacrae* (Leipzig 1896–1906) |
| *LSAM* | F. Sokolowski, *Lois Sacrées d'Asie Mineure* (Paris, 1956) |
| *Lindos* | C. Blinkenberg *et al.*, *Lindos: Fouilles et Recherches* (Copenhagen, 1902–14) |
| Liv. | Livy |
| Lucian | |
|   *DD Syr.* | *De Dea Syria* |
|   *Philops.* | *Philopseudes* |
|   *Salt.* | *Saltatores* |
| Lycophr. | Lycophron |
|   *Alex.* | *Alexandra* |
| *MAMA* | *Monumenta Asiae Minoris Antiqua* (Manchester, 1928–62) |
| Maiuri | A. Maiuri, *Nuova Silloge Epigrafica di Rodi e Cos* (Florence, 1925) |
| Meiggs–Lewis | R. Meiggs and D. Lewis, *Greek Historical Inscriptions* |
| Michel | C. Michel, *Recueil d'Inscriptions Grecques* (Brussels, 1900) |
| *Milet* | T. Wiegand, *Millet, Ergebnisse der Ausgabungen und Untersuchungen seit 1899* |
| Moretti | L. Moretti, *Icorizioni agonistiche greche* (Rome, 1953) |
| *OGIS* | *Orientis Graeci Inscriptiones Selectae* (Leipzig, 1903–5) |
| *PBA* | *Proceedings of the British Academy* |
| *PGM* | see *Pap. Gr. Mag.* |
| P. Lond. | F. G. Kenyon and H. I. Bell, *Greek Papyri in the British Museum* (London, 1893– ) |
| *P. Osl.* | *Papyri Osloenses*, ed. S. Eitrem (Oslo, 1925– ) |
| *P. Oxy.* | *Oxyrhynchus Papyri*, ed. B. P. Grenfell and A. S. Hunt (London, 1898– ) |
| Page | *Select Papyri* III, ed. D. L. Page (London and Cambridge, Mass., 1950) |

| | |
|---|---|
| *Pap. Gr. Mag.* | *Papyri Graecae Magicae*, ed. K. Preisendanz (Leipzig, 1928–31) |
| *Par. del. Pass.* | *Parola del Passato* |
| Paus. | Pausanias |
| Peek | W. Peek, *Griechische Vers-Inschriften* (Berlin, 1972) |
| *Phil. Woch.* | *Philologische Wochenschrift* |
| *Philol.* | *Philologus* |
| Phot. | Photius |
| Pind. | Pindar |
|   *N.* |   *Nemaens* |
|   *O.* or *Ol.* |   *Olympians* |
| Plin. | Pliny |
|   *NH* |   *Natural History* |
| Plat. | Plato |
|   *Rep.* |   *The Republic* |
|   *Tim.* |   *Timaeus* |
| Plut. | Plutarch |
|   *De Soll. An.* |   *De Sollertia Animalium* |
|   *Flam.* |   *Flamininus* |
|   *Mor.* |   *Moralia* |
|   *Phoc.* |   *Phocion* |
|   *Pyth. Or.* |   *De Pythiae Oraculis* |
|   *Thes.* |   *Theseus* |
| Porphyr. | Porphyry |
|   *Abstin.* |   *De Abstinentia* |
| *Proc. Am. Phil. Soc.* | *Proceedings of the American Philological Society* |
| Procl. | Proclus |
| Ps. | Psalms |
| *RA* | *Revue archéologique* |
| *REG* | *Revue des études grecques* |
| *Rec. IG* | *Recueil d'inscriptions grecques* |
|   *supp.* |   *supplément* |
| Rev. | Revelation of St John the Divine |
| *Rev. hist.* | *Revue historique* |
| *Rev. phil.* | *Revue de philologie* |
| *Riv. Fil.* | *Rivista di Filologia* |
| Robert | L. Robert, *Etudes anatoliennes* (Paris, 1937) |

| | |
|---|---|
| *Rom. Mitt.* | *Mitteilungen des deutschen archäologischen Instituts, Römische Abteilung* |
| SEG | *Supplementum Epigraphicum Graecum* (1923– ) |
| SIG | W. Dittenberger, *Sylloge Inscriptionum Graecarum* (1915–24) |
| *Samml.* | H. Collitz, F. Bechtel, *et al.*, *Sammlung des griechischen Dialektinschriften* (Göttingen, 1884–1915) |
| Schol. | Scholiast |
| Sherwin-White | S. M. Sherwin-White, *Ancient Cos* (Göttingen, 1978) |
| *Sitz. Akad. Berlin* | *Sitzungsberichte der Akademie Berlin* |
| Sokolowski | F. Sokolowski, *Lois Sacrées des Cités Grecques* (Paris, 1962) |
| Soph. | Sophocles |
|   *Trach.* |   *Trachiniae* |
| Sozom. | Sozomen |
|   HE |   *Historia Ecclesiae* |
| Steph. Byz. | Stephanus of Byzantium |
| Strab. | Strabo |
| *Stud. Pont.* | *Studia Pontica* (Brussels, 1903– ) |
| *Sylloge* | see *SIG* |
| *Symb. Osl.* | *Symbolae Osloenses* |
| TAPA | *Transactions and Proceedings of the American Philological Association* |
| Theocr. | Theocritus |
|   *Id.* |   *Idylls* |
| Theophr. | Theophrastus |
|   *Char.* |   *Characters* |
|   *Sign. Temp.* |   *De Signis Tempestatum* |
| Thuc. | Thucydides |
| Tzetz. | Tzetzes |
|   *Chil. Hist.* |   *Historiarum variarum chiliades* |
| Verg. | Vergil |
|   *Ecl.* |   *Eclogues* |
| Xen. | Xenophon |
|   *Anab.* |   *Anabasis* |
|   *Hell.* |   *Hellenica* |
| YCS | *Yale Classical Studies* |
| *Z. f. Num.* | *Zeitschrift fur Numismatik* |

| | |
|---|---|
| ZPE | *Zeitschrift für Papyrologie und Epigraphik* |
| Zeitschr. neut. Wiss. | *Zeitschrift für die Neutestamentliche Wissenschaft* |

# 1
# THE RELIGION OF ANCIENT CRETE

The religion of Minoan Crete was dominated by the figure of a goddess. She is to be seen in figurines of the neolithic period, but her period of greatest authority was the Middle Minoan period of about 1800–1500 BC. She appears in a variety of associations. She is our lady of the animals, the Greek *Potnia Theron*, and may be seen on a seal standing on a mountain between two lions. A well-known ivory statuette shows her with snakes entwined round her arms. The seal reminds us that she is queen of the mountains and of the wild; the statuette proclaims her ruler of the earth and that which lies under the earth. She was the patron of craftsmen: in the cave-sanctuary at Arkalokhori there was both a shrine and a smithy, and this can be paralleled by Lord William Taylour's discovery in the Citadel House at Mycenae of an ivory workshop attached to a shrine adorned with a fresco portraying a female divinity, and by the evidence from Pylos that the bronze workers were *po-ti-ni-ja-we-jo*, 'In Potnia's service'.[1] Athene Ergane took over this work in Greece later (Paus. 1, 34, 3; 3, 17, 4; 5, 14, 3; 6, 26, 3).

The universal domination of the Minoan goddess is eloquently and justly described by Willetts:

> The goddess is represented in a rich variety of associations: with animals, birds and snakes; with the baetylic pillar and the sacred tree; with the poppy and the lily; with the sword and the double-axe. She is a huntress and a goddess of sports; she is armed and she presides over ritual dances; she has female and male attendants. She has dominion over mountain, earth, sky and sea; over life and death; she is household-goddess, vegetation-goddess, Mother and Maid.[2]

It is hard to know whether this goddess is one or many. Certainly she was later known by many names. Britomartis or Britomarpis is thought to mean 'sweet maid' (Hsch. s.v.; *EM* 214, 29; Solinus 11, 8). She was identified by the Greeks with Artemis, but was clearly separate in origin, and retained an independent existence in oaths (*IC* I ix 1) and cult. She was identified with Aphaea on Aegina (Ant. Lib. 40), and the discovery on the Aegina temple site of Mycenaean figurines of bulls, nursing mothers, and other female figures suggests a Cretan connection. Dictynna was also assimilated to Artemis, and to Britomartis. But she was a figure of independent power, worshipped outside Crete at Astypalaea (*IG* XII 3, 189), Athens (*IG* II–III 4688), Las (Paus. 3, 24, 8), Massilia (*CIG* III 6764), Phocis (*IG* IX 1, 5) and Sparta (Paus. 3, 17, 8). She is surely the goddess who holds sway on Mt Dicte. She appears, usually as a huntress, on coins of Cydonia, Lisus, Phalasarna (probably), and Polyrthenia. Ariadne or Ariagne, the princess of myth, abandoned by Theseus but having a sacred marriage with Dionysus, is said to mean 'very holy maid' (Hsch. s.v. *hadnou*). She was honoured particularly at Cnossos where she appears on coins, and there is literary evidence of a sacred dance associated with her (Hom. *Il.* 18, 590–606; Schol. *ad loc.*; Plut. *Thes.* 21; Lucian *Salt.* 49). She is generally agreed to be a vegetation spirit, and her death and resurrection was celebrated on the island of Naxos.[3] Europa was in Greek myth taken by Zeus in bull form to Crete. She appears on early coins of Gortyna and Phaestos, and, rather later, at Cnossos. She is also associated with Tyre and Sidon and one or two other places outside Crete. At Lebadeia there was a cult of Demeter Europa (Paus. 9, 39, 5). It is possible that she came over from western Asia; in Crete she is the goddess at Gortyna. Pasiphae appears in myth as the queen, the wife of Minos; the most famous aspect of the myth tells of her passion for a bull, and the device by which she was enabled to copulate with it. The name was believed in antiquity to mean 'she who shines on all' (Paus. 3, 26, 1) and would represent the goddess as queen of the sky, and naturally the moon. The union of the bull with Pasiphae as the form of a cow would then be the ritual union of sun and moon.[4]

Other goddesses with Cretan associations are more familiar from the Greek pantheon. Eilithyia, goddess of childbirth, is one. The name, which appears in various forms (on Crete most commonly as Eleuthyia) is not Indo-European, and the Homeric poems indicate the Cretan association (Hom. *Od.* 19, 188). Inscriptions and coins alike attest that her worship was particularly concentrated at Lato (*IC* 1 xvi 2, 31; 3, 18; 5, 48; 5, 75; 26, 8; 27, 3, etc.). Eleutherna was presumably named after her. She appears in other cities also. Leto, the divine mother of Apollo and Artemis, originated in Asia Minor; her name has been associated with the Carian *lada* 'woman'.[5] Her independent cult in classical times is stronger in Crete than in mainland Greece. Lato was her town, and she had a temple there (*IC* 1 xvi 5, 21–2). An area of Gortyna called Latosion implies a sanctuary (*IC* 4, 58, 78). At Phaestos there was a local cult of Lato Phytia, associated with puberty ritual (*IC* 1 xvii 1, 18; xxiii 2, 6). Lato appears independently in the oath of the Drerians (*IC* 1 ix 1A 24–6) and in treaty oaths (*IC* 1 xviii 9 c 6). By an ancient tradition Demeter reached Greece from Crete (Hom. *H. Dem.* 123) and it was in Crete that Iasion embraced her in a thrice-ploughed field, a clear link between the ritual sacred marriage and the fertility of the soil (Hom. *Od.* 5, 125–8). In historical times she was worshipped all over Crete, sometimes with Kore. We have seen how Artemis and Athene stand naturally in an organic relationship with the great Cretan goddess; so, of course, does Hera.

The goddess needed a consort, but the male divinity is later in time (he does not appear in the neolithic period at all) and inferior in status. He is a young god, often armed, but for the hunt rather than for war. He is the power of nature which dies and returns. Sir Arthur Evans wrote: 'That his death and return to life were of annual celebration in relation to the seasonal re-birth of Nature is an almost irresistible conclusion.'[6] As Willetts has put it, he represents the element of discontinuity in the vegetation cycle, where the goddess represents continuity.[7] It was Guthrie's guess that his name in the Minoan period was some form of Zagreus, itself an oriental name perhaps derived from Mt Zagron in the regions of Mesopotamia and Persia.[8] Certainly to the Greeks of the fifth century he was Zeus, and Zeus had the title Cretagenes or Cretan-born. In the inscription from Lisus recording a treaty between the mountain peoples and Cyrene, Zeus Cretagenes appears, but he is inferior to Dictynna (*IC* 2 xvii 1). There are naturally many stories of the birth of Zeus; more cities claimed him than claimed Homer; but Crete is prominent among them. Crete is also associated with his marriage, and with his death. It was because the Cretans said that Zeus died that Callimachus called them liars (Call. *H. Zeus* 8ff.).

*The Hymn of the Curetes* in honour of Zeus Dictaeus has come down to us in a fragmentary insription from Palaikastro. The inscription dates from about 300 BC, though the material is no doubt earlier (*IC* 3, 2, 2).

>Hail, greatest of the Youths,
>Welcome, son of Cronus,
>In almighty radiance you have come,
>Leading your divine spirits;
>Come for the year to Dicte
>And joy in this hymn
>Which we strike on the strings,
>Blending with the pipes,
>Standing and singing
>Around your well-walled altar.
>>Hail [etc.]
>
>There, immortal child,
>The Curetes with their shields,
>Took you from Rhea,
>And guarded you with stamping feet,
>>Hail [etc.]
>>. . .
>>. . . of the lovely Dawn.
>>Hail [etc.]
>
>Seasons brought fruit each year,
>Justice gained hold of man,
>Peace who loves prosperity
>Took charge of all that lives.
>>Hail [etc.]
>
>Leap for herds of cattle,
>Leap for fleecy flocks,
>Leap for fields of corn,
>Leap for full houses.
>>Hail [etc.]
>
>Leap for our cities,
>Leap for sea-going ships,
>Leap for young citizens,
>Leap for far-famed Themis.
>>Hail [etc.]

There are some uncertainties of text and interpretation, but the general tenor is clear. The connection of the young god with fertility is explicit.

Dionysus seems in some of his myths to be a doublet of the Cretan Zeus. He was, however, the independent object of worship, especially in the west, where Cydonia, Polyrhenia, and Sybrita all display him on their coins. There is little epigraphic evidence, but a damaged inscription from Eleutherna, datable to somewhere around 500 BC, seems to deal with the cult of the god (*IC* 2 xii 9), and at Praisos there is evidence of a month Dionysios (*IC* 3 vi 7A).

Two other divinities must be mentioned here. Hyacinthus is certainly a pre-Greek name. He is the young god who dies. We do not know much about him in Crete, but there was certainly a month named after him (*IC* 1 xvi 3, 3; 1 xix 3A40) and a festival (*IC* 1 viii 4 a 17). In myth and cult on the mainland, Hyacinthus is associated with Apollo. Apollo is not the god who dies, but he is in other ways the most obvious counterpart to the young god of Crete, and he had associations with the sun as did the young god. He was also associated with flocks and herds, and with vegetation through the laurel.

Among the religious symbols of the Minoan age the stone pillar and the tree are especially prominent. Evans thought them to be related to one another, and the pillar to be an aniconic image of the divine, without assigning any priority between the two symbols, but holding them rather to be associated. Certainly in many parts of the world tree and stone are equally symbols. But where the stone significantly takes the form of a pillar it is perhaps more likely that the column or post cut from a tree retains the sanctity of the tree, as does the stone column substituted for it. Certainly within the palaces it seems that there were single pillars in rooms with no obvious functional purpose, which may be presumed to have been associated with shrines. Sometimes they are marked with the sign of the double axe. Often they are square. They can be seen at Cnossos, Phaestos, Ayia Triadha, Mallia, Zakro, and, outside Crete, at Phylakopi on Melos. In addition columns can be seen as sacred objects on gemstones.[9]

The other symbols which date from an early period are animals and birds. Bird figures occur in the neolithic age. In the Minoan period they are found perched on double axes, columns, and trees, and it is natural to interpret them as indications of a divine presence. In the bronze votive tablet from the cave of Psychro depicting a cult scene, the ring dove perched on a bough can hardly be other than an epiphany of the goddess. Terracotta birds have been found in domestic shrines in Gournia, Ayia Triadha, and Palaikastro, but as they do not appear with any frequency in votive deposits it is probable that they are not votives, but actual reminders of the presence of divine power.[10] Among animals the bull, to which we shall be coming, and the snake predominate. We have already noted the snake in association with the goddess. The snake comes from the earth; it is a power of the dead. But it sloughs its skin and is a power of life. It kills and heals. It belongs to the fertility of the earth, and is a power of blessing, but always awesome. Other animals we have seen also with the goddess as queen of the wild. Otherwise our evidence is mainly from votive offerings. The mountain sanctuary near Palaikastro, for example, produced terracotta oxen, goats, rams, pigs, dogs, hedgehogs, tortoises, stoats, and weasels. Animal sacrifice was also practised; the cave at Psychro produced the remains of cattle, sheep, deer, wild goats, pigs, and dogs. Whether this indicates an early stage of totemism is an unresolved issue of scholarly argument.[11]

The double axe is one of the most familiar of Cretan religious symbols. The symbol appears constantly at Cnossos, on painted pottery and on stucco, on seals, on an altar, or just carved in the stone of walls. Splendid bronze examples can be seen in the Iraklion museum, and elsewhere. Bronze double axes, for example, were found as votives in the cave of Psychro, or the cave at Arkalokhori. As *labrys* the double axe gave its name to the labyrinth. The double axe is usually taken to be an adjunct of a sky god, akin to the thunderbolt, and its prominence dates from the point when the young god is asserting himself over against the goddess.[12]

The bull is another basic symbol from the same period. The bull is obviously a power of male fertility; it was in the form of a bull that Zeus came to Europa, and it was with a bull that Pasiphae found her fulfilment. In this last the bull symbolizes the sun, and it would be generally accepted that this was so. The bull's horns presided in blessing and protection over the walls of the palace at Cnossos. The bull-leaping which we see depicted on frescoes and ivories, by which acrobatic dancers apparently grasped the horns of a charging bull and vaulted lightly with a somersault over its back, was a dangerous religious ritual, an *agon* of a sort, and the huge courts at Cnossos, Phaestos, and Mallia were designed for this purpose.

Sun symbolism is clear on the vases and in other artefacts. This is true even in the pre-palatial period. A neolithic pottery box from the cave of Eilithyia has a lid engraved with an eleven-pointed star in a circle. One of the whorls has the form of an eight-spoked wheel, but as it antedates spoked wheels, it seems to be a straightforward sun symbol. Among the polychrome vases from Palaikastro one has sunflowers, and variants on the sunflower or wheel pattern are found on sealstones from the tombs of Messara. From the proto-palatial period the necropolis at Mallia yielded a magnificent sunflower vase. Many other vases of the period have flowers of a circular pattern, not least from Cnossos and from the Kamares cave. On some the floral pattern has a large red centre, and on one vase we can see the sun symbol being transformed into an octopus with tentacles swirling round a red centre. This is the period when bull figurines, and bronze double axes, begin to proliferate. The sunflower motif is seen at its finest in the neo-palatial period in faience. The large centre is surrounded by twenty-one small petals; there may have been more. One of the most important vases comes from the temple repository at Cnossos. It has on it three sun-birds. The body is the sun; head, wing, tail, and legs are added. Three circular suns lie between each pair, and spiral patterns adorn the neck of the vase. Circular flowers continue among other floral patterns. Concentric circles and spirals betray their origin. The octopus is now recognizable, but one suspects a double symbolic function covering sea and sky. On the great storage jars the patterns are elaborate. Double axes sprout among leafy reeds. One has a circular flower, with sixteen petals, set in an enclosing circle, on its stem. Circular flowers float in the background. Some superb vases emerge from the tombs at Isopeta and Cnossos. One has two intersecting double axes within two concentric flowers surrounded by swirling petals; the impression of an eight-spoked wheel is misleading. Zakro produced star symbols and swastikas.[13]

Ritual gestures can be identified on votive terracottas and bronzes, sealstones, and other records, although it is impossible to disentangle the exact meaning of each. One of the most frequent shows the right hand to the forehead. Another, found in many forms, shows both arms raised, sometimes in front of the body, sometimes outspread. A common pattern has both arms horizontally across the chest, sometimes with hands to armpits, sometimes with arms not touching the body and fists clenched. Another pattern shows the right arm raised diagonally across the chest. The position of the left arm varies. In men, but not in women, it may similarly cross the chest; or it may drop below the other and parallel to it towards the belly; or it may simply be held at the side. One exceptional figure has the left arm extended sideways and the right akimbo. Women sometimes hold their hands under their breasts.

One of the most exciting religious discoveries dates from the end of the Old Palace period. It was found at Anemospilia on the lower north slopes of Mt Juktas. It has been identified as a three-roomed shrine with a surrounding wall. In one room, presumably used for storage, were quantities of pottery. In the centre room were the remains of a wooden statue with separate clay feet. In the third room the body of an 18-year-old lay on a low platform, transfixed by a magnificent ritual blade of bronze decorated with a boar's head. Three other bodies, one of a man with a fine signet ring and a cylinder seal of agate showing a man in a boat, one of a woman, and the third unidentifiable, were also found. It looks as if this was an example of human sacrifice to ward off impending catastrophe, which none the less descended on the keepers of the shrine (*BSA Arch. Rep.* 1979–80).

Evidence of ritual can be gleaned from occasional representations. A series of sealstones show the goddess standing on a mountain between two lions receiving the adoration of a worshipper, arguably the king in person. The Chieftain Vase from Ayia Triadha is difficult to interpret. Three men carrying hides, perhaps but not certainly stylized shields, are under the leadership of a man wearing a neck-ring and bracelet, and carrying a sword and lustral sprinkler, but himself in a subordinate attitude to the dominant young ruler. Most probably it represents the ceremonial presentations of ox hides to the king after a sacrifice.[14] The bronze votive tablet from the cave of Psychro shows a ritual scene; it is probably to be dated to the Late Minoan I period. There is a worshipper on the right, a sacred tree in the centre with the sun and moon in the sky. To the left are horns of consecration with an epiphany of the goddess in the form of a bird on a sacred bough. *The Hymn of the Curetes*, late as it is in its present form, must represent a very early practice. It involves music, singing and dancing, surely re-enacting the clashing shields and stamping feet, and at the last leaping high in sympathetic magic for well-grown animals, tall fields of corn, and general prosperity. Another visual document of some importance is the sarcophagus from Ayia Triadha. This is a limestone coffin, plaster-covered and painted. At each end a goddess is portrayed in a car, drawn by griffins or horses. On one side a woman in ritual garb is making an offering on an altar. There is a shrine with bulls' horns and an olive tree, and a double axe with a bird on it. Behind her a piper is leading three women to an altar on which is an ox ready for sacrifice; two calves are under the altar. The other side has two scenes. At one end women are pouring liquid into a receptacle set between double axes; their ritual is accompanied by a musician with a lyre. At the other end three men are carrying votive offerings, figures of a boat and of animals, to the dead man who is depicted standing outside his tomb. The whole can be dated to about 1400 BC. Plainly we have here sacrifice and votive offering, some belief in the survival of the dead, and a belief in the presence of the divine symbolized by the double axes, the bird, and the bulls' horns.

In general, apart from cave shrines and some mountain sanctuaries, separate religious buildings were rare in the Minoan period. Religion and life were integrated with one another, and the palaces were themselves religious centres. At Cnossos the sign of the double axe recurs continually. The horns of consecration adorned the walls to the south. The wall-paintings frequently depict sacral scenes. The great courts were for religious ceremonies such as the bull-leaping or some of the holy dances associated with Ariadne, Pasiphae, and others. The so-called Throne Room has every appearance of a cult-room. Small shrines and lustral basins abound throughout. It has been cogently argued by Evans and Nilsson that the king was a priest-king, and Minoan rule a signal example of sacred kingship.[15] The arguments are partly indirect, but sealstones show a votary adoring the goddess, perhaps in a representative capacity, the Chieftain Vase the Ayia Triadha sarcophagus, and the so-called priest-king relief from Cnossos seem to show a sacral ruler at work, and there are indications within the palaces to suggest rituals performed by the ruler.

In his profoundly original book *The Earth, the Temple and the Gods* (1962, [2]1969), Vincent Scully successfully shows that the horns familiar from the palace walls at Cnossos are also found on mountains with which the palaces, which are sacral complexes, as well as administrative centres and royal residences, are aligned. He suggests an identification with either the female cleft or a pair of breasts, or, sometimes, raised arms or wings. Sometimes the alignment is with a cone or single peak rather than the double peak. Either is associated with the cult of the mother goddess. In other words the landscape itself is part of the religious context of the sacral palace. This is true of Cnossos where the alignment is with Mt Juktas, not along the great court, but further west where an altar and a cylindrical wooden column stood, this last representing the presence of the goddess. Similarly the palace at Phaestos looks towards Mt Ida. That at Mallia looks towards Mt Dicte. All these mountains have cave sanctuaries.

Scully claims something similar for the Mycenaean palaces on the mainland, most obviously for Mycenae itself, situated as it is between two peaks. As the approach road sweeps right towards Mt Zara, the Lion Gate dominated by the column which represents the goddess echoes the mountain's conical shape. The fortress at Tiryns is aligned with Mt Euboea. The shrine in Nestor's palace at Pylos is aligned with the great conical bulk of Mt Mathia to the south: here there is a further point. The tholos tomb of the Lord of Pylos also echoes the shape of the conical mountain. Scully asks pertinently whether this does not identify the lord with the consort of the earth mother. On Crete they showed the tomb of Zeus. Does this make the ruler almost one with Zeus? Scully has a further suggestion of some interest, that the flat Mycenaean roofs might have been used as a kind of viewing platform for sacral purposes.

# 2
# GODS AND GODDESSES

The name of Zeus, from the Sanskrit *dyaus*, evokes the bright sky. He is the sky and he lives in the sky. He controls the weather. He is the High God far beyond that, Father of gods and men. He is naturally portrayed as a dignified, powerful, awesome, bearded figure. The thunderbolt is his emblem of power. The eagle, soaring into the sky, itself the king of birds, often accompanies him. One early representation (about 650 BC) was on a bronze cuirass from Olympia, now lost, portraying the encounter between Zeus and the young immigrant Apollo.[1] Often he is shown in conflict with a monster whom we may dub Typhon, whose human image sometimes ends in a horse's body, sometimes in intertwining snakes' tails. In a fragment of a column-krater of Lydos datable to about 560 BC in the Acropolis museum at Athens we can see a Victory or Nike accompanying a figure wielding a thunderbolt. He is no doubt striking down a Titan as he is on the west pediment of the Temple of Artemis at Corfu. A number of vase paintings show him, grasping the thunderbolt, in the seemingly more innocent pastime of pursuing a young lady – except that she is probably Semele and the thunderbolt represents the power which will eventually blast her. On one the god has lowered the thunderbolt and is carrying it in his left hand, on another she has actually escaped on to the shoulder of the vase, a unique effect.[2] The figure of the god nude with the thunderbolt at the ready is common to a number of small bronzes of the early fifth century. Usually there are signs of the eagle perched on the outstretched left hand. One highly stylized early version from the seventh century was found on Mt Lykaion.[3] A similar type appears on some coins of Olympia datable to the middle of the fifth century, and perhaps portraying a statue which Pausanias saw at Olympia carved by an Aeginetan named Aristonous and presented by Metapontum (5, 22, 5). The tremendous bronze statue rescued from the sea at Artemisium, and one of the glories of the national museum at Athens, may represent Poseidon but is more likely Zeus; the parallel with a red-figure lekythos in the Bibliothèque Nationale in Paris is very close. By about the middle of the century the portrayals become robed.

The other main type shows the god seated upon a throne. One such, from Mt Lykaion, datable to the second half of the sixth century, shows him thus (though the throne is lost) with thunderbolt at rest in his left hand, and a sceptre resembling a shepherd's crook in his right. In the fifth century he appears on the federal coinage of Arcadia enthroned with eagle in his right hand and sceptre in his left.[4] A remarkable cup in the Louvre shows the god seated on his altar swathed in a cloak while his eagle flies towards him.[5] But the greatest of all conceptions of Zeus enthroned was produced by Pheidias as the chryselephantine statue for the temple at Olympia. The statue has long vanished, though Pheidias's workshop has been discovered. It was, however, carefully described by Pausanias (5, 11). The god was seated on an elaborate throne with a wreath on his head, a golden Victory in his right hand and a staff in his left with his eagle perched upon it. Representations of the statue appears on coins of Elis but they are of course totally inadequate in giving any real idea of it because of the difference of scale. A marble head, now in Boston, of great nobility, dating from the fourth century, is thought to be an early copy. It was this statue which Quintilian said 'added something to revealed religion' (12, 10, 9).

Of the numerous cult-titles of Zeus, one of the most interesting is Zeus Hypsistos; Theos Hypsistos and just Hypsistos are also found. The oldest datable votive inscription comes from Edessa, the old capital of Macedonia, from the early second century BC (*Arch. Delt.* 8, 1923 (1925) 268). Zeus's eagle appears on one stone, and it looks as if this is a true Greek cult with special reference to Macedonia. It was an obvious enough cult-title for a sky-god; as an epithet it was applied to Zeus by Pindar, Aeschylus, and Sophocles, and it is only surprising that it did not appear earlier as a cult-title. In the Hellenistic age it proved a convenient equation with the mountain-Baalim of Syria, and (without Zeus) was used of the Jewish Yahweh. But it was not eastern in origin. It is found widely enough in Greece, at Athens, Thebes, Corinth, Argos, Olympia, Thessalonica, to name a few sites, on the islands of Corcyra, Imbros, and Delos, and in Asia, at Miletus, where there was a priest and interpreter, and in Mysia with a cult society. In Lydia and Phrygia a large number of altars were dedicated to Theos Hypsistos, but it is noteworthy that at Thyateira a votive eagle was found. Of particular interest is the record of a guild of Zeus Hypsistos in Egypt, probably in Philippopolis, with provision for a monthly banquet in the sanctuary of Zeus; the papyrus, which is a copy of an earlier record, can be dated to the 60s BC.[6]

Zeus's consort Hera – the name means 'our Lady' – had her supreme homes in Argos and Samos. The sacred marriage between Zeus and Hera, a union of sky and earth, also represents the fusion of two cults. It is, curiously, seldom depicted in sculpture, perhaps being more apposite to drama. An archaic wooden relief showing the divine couple, found in Hera's sanctuary on Samos and datable to the seventh century, is unfortunately lost, but a photograph survives.[7] A more sophisticated representation is found on a metope from Temple E at Selinus, now in the national museum in Palermo. Zeus is seated, and raises his right hand to touch his consort's left as she gently unveils herself. A power of earth, such as Hera was, had a ritual bath, symbolic of the soaking of the earth by rain. This is now thought to be portrayed on the Ludovisi throne in the national museum in Rome. It shows the goddess emerging from the water assisted by two nymphs. If this is the right interpretation it may have originated in the sanctuary of Hera at Argos; it has been attributed to Polycleitus. Polycleitus made the great cult-statue showing the goddess enthroned with a staff in one hand, and pomegranate, symbol of fruitfulness, in the other, and with a cylindrical crown, or polos, on her head. The statue is represented on coins of Argos. Classical representations of the goddess show her with an oval face, large eyes, and a small mouth with full lips and a serious expression behind the apparent serenity. In later representations she is accompanied by the peacock, a symbol of immortality.

Pallas Athene suggests a double origin by her double name, the warrior daughter of Zeus, and the goddess of Athens, bearing a pre-Greek name, and with the owl as her emblem. Her motherless birth from the head of Zeus was a favourite theme of sixth-century art, and may be seen even earlier on an amphora from Tenos moulded in relief. The scene appears on bronze strips in Delphi and Olympia designed for shields. Athene was regularly depicted with spear and crested helmet, and sometimes shield, wearing the aegis, a goatskin fringed with snakes and bearing the Gorgon's head upon it. An exquisite stele from the Acropolis at Athens shows her leaning upon her spear contemplating a stone, with head bowed; she is usually thought to be mourning the Athenian dead. Pheidias made two famous images of her for the Acropolis at Athens. One is generally known as the Promachus, though the justification for this is not as large as it might be. It was a freestanding statue with a spear in the left hand which could be seen gleaming in the sun from out to sea. Some bronze statuettes are thought to be replicas of this. The other, the Parthenos, was the cult-statue for the Parthenon, a work of gold and ivory. The goddess had a helmet with curious monsters worked on it. She was finely robed with the aegis. Her spear was in her hand and her shield at her side, and she was accompanied by a figure of Victory (Paus. 1, 24, 6–7). Late replicas survive, one from the Piraeus; they are on a small scale and shudderingly horrid; the original must have impressed by its size. Athene was also the patron of crafts: we see her, for example, on a red-figure vase from Berlin modelling a horse. The olive was another of her symbols, her gift to Athens, and to humanity, and appears on her coins.

A particularly interesting record of Athene in action will be found in the temple chronicle of Athene Lindia from Lindos in Rhodes. This dates from 99 BC, and gives the account of four epiphanies of the goddess. The first is dated to 490 BC, the second cannot be precisely dated, the third comes from 305–304 BC, and the fourth is too fragmentary to be comprehensible. The first dates from the expedition of Darius's admiral Datis. The citizens were crowded into the acropolis, under siege, and short of water, and were contemplating surrender. Athene appeared to one of the magistrates in his sleep, and told him to keep up his courage; she would ask her father for water. When he woke he checked and found that they had water for five days. He asked Datis for five days' truce, saying that Athene had gone to invite her father's help; if it did not arrive, they would surrender. Datis roared with laughter, but next day there was a colossal thunderstorm over the acropolis, and not over the Persian supplies. The second epiphany had to do with a suicide within the temple. The goddess appeared to the priest and gave him instructions about purifying the place. The third epiphany was to a former priest named Callicles, at a time when the city was under siege by Demetrius Poliorcetes, telling him to go to one of the magistrates named Anaxapolis and tell him to go for help to Ptolemy of Egypt. At first he did nothing, but the epiphanies continued for six successive nights, and in the end he acted (*Lindos*, II Inscriptions No. 2). Athene seems to have had a propensity for epiphanies, for a decree in honour of a historian Syriscus up in the Tauric Chersonnese commends him for his account of her epiphanies (*Samml. d. gr. dialektinschr.* III 1, 3086).

Phoebus Apollo is another complex figure, with his double name, a double tradition of origin from the north and the east, and his two great shrines at Delphi and Delos. This most Greek of Gods was not Greek at all. We have already seen Zeus meeting him as he advances with his lyre accompanied by some girls, perhaps the Hyperboreans from the far north. He is a young god, a god of culture and of music. We see him with the lyre again on a seventh-century amphora from Melos meeting his sister Artemis. He is a god of healing, but also a god of destruction, associated somehow with the sun which both scorches and gives life. A favourite and fearful myth, often in art, shows how he and his sister annihilated the children of Niobe. At Delphi he was the god of prophecy. Coins show him seated on the omphalos which represented the navel of the world; vase paintings show him wrestling with Heracles for possession of the sacred tripod. A wonderful cup at Delphi has been supposed to depict the god, but perhaps shows a victorious lyre-player, crowned with a bay-wreath, pouring a libation to the god who has inspired his victory, while the god's own prophetic raven perches opposite. The finest of all portrayals of the god, however, is not at Delphi and not in one of the god's own temples, but in the temple of Zeus at Olympia, where in the west pediment which portrays the battle between Centaurs and Lapiths he stands majestic and impassive above the strife, his bow lowered in his left hand, his right hand outstretched in imperious gesture. This is one of the greatest of all representations of numinous power.

His sister Artemis is the earth mother under another guise, the power of nature in the raw. As earth mother she remains a goddess of fertility. But she resisted the dominance of Zeus and the male gods of the Hellenes by becoming virgin.

She is the old Minoan–Mycenaean Lady of the Beasts, the *Potnia Theron*. In this capacity she meets Apollo on the amphora from Melos, or appears on the chest of Cypselus in Olympia, winged and dangling two lions from her hands, an awesome sight. On one white-ground lekythos she is feeding one of her brother's swans. A marvellously strange archaic representation on a fountain from Cameiros shows her threefold, each with a lion below her feet as she holds its tail. From the same town came gold relief figures of the goddess, now in the

British Museum. Another statue from Rhodes shows her with a polos on her hand and a lion in each hand, held by the tail. We see her on a seventh-century Boeotian amphora (now in Athens) with arms outspread above two fierce animals with spiralling tails. Above are two birds, and there are swastikas around. Even at Ephesus we see her on a bronze hydria, with wings outspread, sheltering and surrounded by animals. She is often portrayed as huntress, with bow and arrows. Like Apollo she can be gentle or destructive. One of the metopes from Temple E at Selinus shows her destroying Actaeon through his own hounds; he had happened upon her naked. She appears on vases shooting down Niobe's daughters. Though to the Greeks she, like Athene, was virginal, her many-breasted statue at Ephesus shows her in a different guise. A particularly fine version of this has recently been found in the sanctuary of Hestia Boulaea at Ephesus, a magnificent twice-lifesize statue of the goddess with towering headgear incorporating grotesque animals, which guarded the entrance to the sacred hearth. Another, half the size, may have stood in the council chamber, and there are indications that small replicas were mass-produced. The normal interpretation of the protuberances is that they are breasts, but Meuner has shown that they form part of the outer garment (*Röm. Mitt.* 19 (1914) 200ff.), and Miltner has argued that they are eggs (*Anatolia* 9 (1958)), and Seiterle scrota of sacrificial bulls (*Antike Welt* 10, 3 (1979) ). One way or another, they symbolize fertility.

On the whole her temples reveal her as the power of the wild. At Sparta she enjoyed one of the oldest rectangular temples, on a marshy site near the river Eurotas. Here Spartan boys went through their tests of toughness at the altar. The earth mother chooses a hollow, but the wild mountains tower above. On the slopes of Ithome in Messenia her temple is in wilder scenery; so too at Calydon. At Sicyon the approach to the temple (oriented due east) commands a view of the goddess's domain of wild mountains: the temple itself looks over to Acrocorinth. At Stymphalia, where the birds, which are sometimes associated with her on vases, were sacred to her, the mountain itself is named Mt Artemision and her temple is deep-set in its gorges. Sometimes she commanded the seashore, at Munychia below Athens, at Cape Artemision in Euboea, at Aulis, where Iphigeneia in myth was sacrificed, at Loutsa, and at Brauron on the coast of Attica.

The shrine of Artemis on Thasos produced some interesting light on the goddess in that the local pottery was contained within the precincts. Its output was prominent in the seventh century BC and lasted until about 570 BC when superior wares from Corinth and Athens put the local potters out of business. Their work was genuinely local, though later they engaged in poor imitations of the Attic style. They continued successfully for centuries with terracotta figures. It is curious to find this work under the patronage of Artemis: we are reminded not to make our categories too narrow. Artemis herself is represented in a charming archaic bronze statuette, once a mirror handle. A large number of votives, mainly from the seventh to the fifth centuries, were found within the precincts, the most interesting being a gold headband with rosettes and figures of griffins and lions. The cult continued into Roman times, and the sanctuary was restored by one Epie in the first century BC (*BCH* 1959).

Just as Athene appeared at Lindos so we have records, *c.* 207–206 BC, of epiphanies of Artemis Leucophryene ('of the White Brow') at Magnesia-on-the-Maeander some fourteen years previously. The oracle was consulted and the general result was an injunction to the Ionian states to honour Apollo Pythius and Artemis and to treat the territory of Magnesia as sacred and inviolable (*SIG* [3]557).

Hermes seems to be in origin the spirit of the cairn, the stone-heap which guides travellers in mountain country: the linguistic argument has been challenged but the argument from function remains. The vertical stone in the middle of the cairn was later elaborated and equipped with head and male sex-organ; they were found at crossroads, boundaries, city gates, and house doors, and revered as protectors and bringers of luck. There is an excellent example from Siphnos in the national museum at Athens. As well as those which have survived they can be seen on vases. Hermes is the protector of travellers and a traveller himself, the messenger of the gods, and the guide of the dead as of the living. We see him characteristically with sandals (sometimes winged), a hat, and the herald's staff, twined with snakes. A low relief in the Villa Albani at Rome shows him leading Eurydice to Orpheus. A beautiful brooding youthful figure from Boston shows him meditating on the fate of souls. He is a shepherd's god: a sixth-century bronze statuette, also in Boston, shows him with high boots and round hat with a ram under his arm, and in one form he becomes the prototype of the Good Shepherd. As a god of the mountains he was patron of bandits and thieves, and a thief himself. A splendid black-figure hydria in the Louvre shows him as an infant having stolen Apollo's cattle. He was a trickster god, and very popular.

Ares was god of war, and was understandably unpopular. Statues of him are rare. On vases he appears as the bearded soldier, standing by, for example, at the birth of Athene. His affair with Aphrodite was wittily told by Homer. We see them together on vases. On a seventh-century amphora from Naxos they are driving a chariot; on a fifth-century cup in the British Museum they are feasting. The most famous sculptural representation of him is the Ludovisi Ares from the national museum in Rome. Here he has laid aside his armour and become the lover; a little putto plays at his feet. The Greeks liked to think of him tamed.

Aphrodite is the goddess of sexual power. Her name is perhaps Phoenician. She has some likeness to the Phoenician Astarte. A Cypriot coin of the Roman imperial period shows her temple at Paphos, decidedly Phoenician and un-Greek in style, and inside no image but a conical betyl. Aphrodite is another of the forms the great mother goddess took for the Greeks. Like Artemis she was a mountain goddess. Literary evidence records how Anchises promised to make her 'an altar in a prominent place on a high peak' (Hom. *H. Dem.* 5, 10–3) on Mt Ida near Troy. Acrocorinth was another of her mountain homes; she had a temple on the summit, and another, not yet discovered, under its shadow. Here were the talented and expensive temple prostitutes. At Athens she was found on the slopes of the acropolis commanding a view of Mt Lycabettus, on the hill at Kaisariani near the sacred spring, on a high point of the pass from Athens to Eleusis along the Sacred Way. At Troezen her temple stands by a tremendous mass of rocky formations. At Eryx in Sicily the mother occupied the height of the mountain: the Greeks called her Aphrodite, the Phoenicians Tanit, the Romans Venus. The Greeks thought her name meant 'foam-born' and her birth from the sea appealed to some of the minor artists of the fourth century and later. Her moulded figure emerging from a shell, supported by Erotes and surrounded by flowers, can be seen on an oil flask in Boston. In a fanciful terracotta figurine in the British Museum the two halves of the shell appear as wings. A famous painting by Apelles showed her emerging from the sea. Some sculptor decided to render this three-dimensionally and the result was the lovely Benghazi Aphrodite from Cyrenaica, now in Philadelphia, where she is seen wringing out her hair in long plaits. Her island shrines on Cyprus and Cythera and her prominence in the great port of Corinth suggest that she came from overseas. She is associated too with birds, principally the dove, a bird as mythically amorous as it is actually quarrelsome. Coins of Cyprus show the doves over her shrine. A terracotta figurine from Cameiros, datable to about 540 BC, now in the British Museum, shows her still, impassive except for her archaic smile, holding a dove to her breasts in her left hand. She has other birds too. She is often riding upon a swan, as on a red-figure lekythos in the Ashmolean, perhaps because she is a spring goddess and comes with the swans in springtime. A magnificent cup by the Pistoxenus painter in the British Museum shows her riding on a goose. The dolphin is hers, and she often rides it. So too is the goat, creature of sex. She was carved by Scopas riding on a goat for her temple at Elis. That is lost but we see her holding a goat on a terracotta relief from Gela in the Ashmolean. One of her titles was Epitragia (*IG* III 335).

Mostly, however, Aphrodite inspired Greek sculptors to the supreme effort in portraying the perfection of feminine beauty. Such was the famous Aphrodite of Cnidos, by Praxiteles. The original is lost, but the type is known to us from numerous copies and imitations. She was shown ready for the bath, with a pitcher of water at her side: the Vatican Aphrodite is a good example. The original is said to have borne the marks of physical ravishment. The round temple in which the goddess was displayed so that she could be admired from all sides has recently been discovered – appropriately enough, by Miss Love. Aphrodite Kallipygos – 'lovely-bottomed' – was one of her titles. This can be seen in a late copy, now in Naples, of a statue where she leans back to admire her rear view. The concept is contrived, but we may not say that it has become merely secular. Sometimes she admires herself in a mirror – or in the shield of her lover Ares, as in the Aphrodite of Capua. One reconstruction of the Aphrodite of Melos (Venus de Milo) in the Louvre would give her a mirror. Another type shows her with her arms masking – but also drawing attention to and revealing – her breasts and sex-organ in the *Venus pudica* attitude; such are the Medici Venus in the Uffizi and the Capitoline Venus – both Graeco-Roman copies of Hellenistic originals. A famous third-century statue by Doedalsas showed her crouching at the bath; there are many copies, a fine one in Rome from Hadrian's Villa, and another in Ostia. The loveliest of all variants of this, so lovely that it has become a masterpiece in its own right, is a little statue in Rhodes from the first century, rare in its undamaged state, showing her separating the strands of her hair as she crouches. Finally we should mention the superb head of the Bartlett Aphrodite from Boston, one of the most marvellous portrayals of feminine loveliness.[8]

Aphrodite was married in a Beauty-and-the-Beast myth to Hephaestus, the ugly, lame smith-god, with a pre-Greek name and associations with Lycia and Lemnos, the very spirit of petroleum fire. He had his temple in the smiths' quarter in Athens, where it remains nearly complete; but we have no notion of the cult-statue. In early representations he was young and beardless; later he became a powerful, mature, bearded workman. We might have expected the smiths to have depicted their patron in the metals in which they worked. Most of our pictures of him are from vases, and incidental to the god himself: he is seen forging the arms of Achilles. One of his myths the vase painters enjoyed: his return to Olympus after exile. We can see this on Attic red-figure vases, for example, in the Louvre or in Munich.

Poseidon was god of the sea, and his temples often stood close to the sea. At Mycenaean Pylos he was more prominent than Zeus. Poseidonia (Paestum) in Italy was named after him and he appears on the coins. His image is close to that of his brother Zeus: indeed in some ways he seems almost a double of Zeus: his emblem is, however, the trident or three-pronged fish-spear, rather than the thunderbolt. Monuments of him are surprisingly scanty: a large bronze, unfortunately armless, from about 480 BC, dredged from the sea, declares itself to be the god. He is tall and kindly, and was perhaps holding the trident and a dolphin.

Demeter was the earth mother or corn mother, and her mysteries at Eleusis were one factor in developing her cultic representation. At Hermione mystic sacrifices in a stone circle (Paus. 2, 34, 10) must go back to the Stone Age. In the central Peloponnese and at Camarina in Sicily many terracottas have been found, votive offerings at her shrines, showing the goddess with a pig in her arms. Near Marathon a clay pig from the early neolithic was found (*Ath. Mitt.* 71, 1956, 24), perhaps from an early form of the cult. She is often shown with her daughter Kore, or Persephone, giving the gift of corn to mankind: there is a good example on a red-figure vase in the British Museum. Perhaps her supreme image for worship is that of the *Mater Dolorosa*, mourning the loss of her daughter. Such is the exquisite veiled Demeter in the Louvre, and above all the Demeter, now in the British Museum, from the sanctuary of the Underworld Deities in Cnidos, an anonymous masterpiece of skill and sensitivity.

The twelfth member of the Olympic pantheon was Hestia, goddess of the hearth. Not merely was she the goddess of the hearth; she was the hearth. So her dwelling place was the hearth in every home, and the public hearth, represented by an altar, in every prytaneum. She was especially honoured at Delphi, where her hearth was the common hearth of Greece, indeed of the world. Her temples, like her hearths, are liable to be circular. She has little mythology, and for this reason and because the hearth is her being she is seldom given visual form by artists, though there were famous statues of her at Olympia and Paros. She does not seem to appear on coins.

Hestia was the Cinderella of the Twelve, and was ousted by the arrival – or return, since his name has been identified on a Linear B tablet – of Dionysus. He was a god of nature in the raw, of vegetation and of wild animals, of ecstasy and inspiration, and above all of wine.

One particularly important discovery was that of an early cult-figure of Dionysus found at Brusa. The face is unfortunately damaged. The god is wearing a short pleated *chiton*, and carries a thyrsus in his left hand and a wine cup in the other. Bunches of grapes frame the head. The god is accompanied by snakes, by an unidentified figure wearing a fawnskin, with thyrsus and grapes, and a satyr. The figure is typical of those found to the north-east of Türkomen-Däg, and suggests a revival of the cult from the highlands of Phrygia. His earlier portrayals show him bearded and middle-aged: he so appears on a coin of his favoured island of Naxos, where he found his bride Ariadne, and where they made excellent wine. Later he is depicted as young, even effeminate, as in a rather revolting statue from the Villa Albani. His natural accompaniments are the ivy wreath, the thyrsus or staff ending in a spray of leaves, the vine and grapes, a wine cup, a fawnskin or pantherskin. His companions include the gross Silenus, sometimes riding on an ass, satyrs and maenads, and wild animals of all sorts. On a sixth-century black-figure vase in the Rhodes museum he is riding a bull, sitting sideways, looking back, wreathed and draped with vines.

There were many myths about him. His mother Semele was blasted by the glory of Zeus, and the child with which she was pregnant sewn into Zeus's thigh. The birth from the thigh is shown on a fifth-century Attic red-figured lekythos in Boston. Hermes with caduceus in one hand and thyrsus ready in the other is watching with interest. In a bas-relief in the Vatican the child is jumping from the thigh into a cloth which Hermes is holding for him. Another myth told how he was kidnapped by pirates. But the mast of their ship burst into vine leaves and clusters of grapes, and the pirates jumped overboard and were turned into dolphins. A splendid sixth-century cup by Exekias, now in Munich, shows the god alone in the vine-masted ship with the dolphins all around. The god is often portrayed with Ariadne, as on a red-figure vase in the British Museum, or in the Villa of the Mysteries at Pompeii, or on many sarcophagi of the second century AD. There is a sadly damaged but otherwise magnificent Hellenistic relief of a Dionysiac sacrificial scene in the Rhodes museum. A slim, beautiful woman is leading a male goat, resisting, towards an altar. A second woman is divesting herself of a veil. A satyr dances vigorously. Two divinities appear in the clouds.

In some areas the pantheon was distinctly odd by normal Greek standards. Lycia, for example, acknowledged the Twelve Gods of Lycia. The centre of this cult was Comba (the modern Gombe), a city barely mentioned in the ancient literary sources. Of the twenty or so dedications to the Twelve, between one-third and half come from this neighbourhood. They are consistent in form, comprising a stone slab, with a double relief: above, the Twelve divided into two groups by a single central god, below, twelve seated animals, probably dogs, divided by a central standing male figure, with a standard inscription 'To the Twelve Gods by command'. The upper central figure is usually male but occasionally female; in the latter instance it is certainly Artemis of Comba; in the former almost certainly the father-god; there is in fact one inscription 'To Artemis, to the Twelve Gods, and to their Father'. The Twelve Gods normally appear in tunics; in one exceptional relief they are carrying shields; the presence of the dogs suggests that they are gods of hunting. The crudity of the reliefs suggests a date of the third century AD, but the cult is far older, as the so-called obelisk at Xanthus, a pillar-tomb in honour of a dynast, whose statue stood on top of it, has an important inscription from the fifth century BC recording among other things that the stele was dedicated to the Twelve Gods.[9]

On Delos the Twelve were organized in triads. We know from an altar dedication that one triad was Zeus, Athene, and Hera, and many think that another was Apollo, Artemis, and Leto. About the others we can only guess. One might well be Demeter, Kore, and Zeus Eubuleus (equivalent to Pluto-Hades). The other would probably be Poseidon, Aphrodite, and Hermes, none of whom could easily be omitted.[10]

## GODS AND GODDESSES

After the great gods the figure most portrayed in religious art was undoubtedly Heracles, the divine son of Zeus, persecuted by Hera and protected by Athene, whose labours, imposed on him by hatred, were none the less seen as a service to mankind, and whose other adventures were beyond counting. As early as the eighth century he is portrayed on a funerary vase in the Ceramicus fighting the Nemean lion, a favourite theme throughout the centuries. On another of the same period in Copenhagen he is dealing with the Stymphalian birds. A bronze tripod in Olympia, from about 700 BC, shows him wrestling with Apollo for the Delphic tripod. The Stymphalian birds, the Erymanthian boar and the Ceryneian hind are among black-figure scenes in the British Museum. One of the metopes from Temple Y at Selinus shows him wrestling with the Cretan bull; one from Temple C shows him with the Cercopes, the imp-like bandits whom he hung upside down, one from Temple E shows him killing an Amazon. The other metopes from this last temple show Athene killing a giant, the marriage of Zeus and Hera, and Artemis setting the hounds on Actaeon. Heracles was accepted in their company. Temple C was in fact dedicated to him, and several hundred seals depicting him were found there. A sixth-century frieze from the temple of Assos shows him shooting Centaurs. In archaic bronzes he is often depicted as an archer. He was prominent at Delphi, wrestling with Apollo over the tripod in the pediment of the Siphnian treasury, labouring in the Athenian treasury and in the late frieze which decorated the theatre, shouldering his bow as Eurystheus cringes in the cauldron in a bronze statuette. A coin of Byzantium shows him as a child strangling the snakes which were sent against him. His most famous statue was a bronze showing him with club and lionskin, standing at rest. It has been attributed to Myron, and is known to us from copies, such as the statuette in Boston. Another, attributed to Lysippus, shows him gross and exhausted; we know this from the Farnese Hercules in Naples.

For Athenians Theseus was the counterpart to Heracles, and the temple of Hephaestus showed his exploits, as did the Athenian Treasury at Delphi. His killing of the Minotaur is often depicted, as on a sixth-century Attic black-figured hydria in Boston, or in a red-figure vase in the British Museum, or in a sculptural group in the Villa Albani.

A few other divine figures should be mentioned. Helios, the sun god, does not appear much outside Rhodes, where he was the patron god of the island. His head with long locks of hair blown by his passage through the sky, and rays emanating from it, appears on coins of Rhodes. Eos, the dawn goddess, is shown on vases in pursuit of Cephalus (who has no time for anything but hunting and Procris), or mourning her son Memnon. Cybele, an earth mother from the wild mountain ranges of Asia Minor, often wears a turreted crown, and is seated on a car drawn by lions or on a throne attended by lions. Sometimes she bears a whip with knucklebones as a symbol of power. Asclepius is a grave, bearded physician with healing snakes in attendance. Sarapis was an invention of the Ptolemies. His cult-statue was supposed to have been brought from Sinope on the Black Sea, but no one knows what it was. He appears as a Zeus-like figure in majesty but with the kindly grace of Asclepius as well; indeed the three were mystically one. Another divinity prominent in the Hellenistic Age was Tyche, Fortune. She was capricious, and the epitaph of one Phileremus identifies her as a tyrannical autocrat. But she had her good side too. As Agathe Tyche she is Good Fortune, and in a remarkable relief in Copenhagen she is wife to Zeus the Fulfiller. She was regularly invoked, even in consulting the oracle at Dodona. Tyche also was the protectress of cities. Beyond all these were immense numbers of local gods, heroes, and nymphs.[11]

# 3

# SANCTUARIES, TEMPLES, AND ALTARS

The oldest sanctuaries in which we can trace continuity of holiness from the Mycenaean period are perhaps five in number.[1] On Delos a well-constructed building of the period lay under the later temple of Artemis; it was isolated from other buildings and contained valuable deposits. There is some evidence from pottery that the area was in use during the Dark Ages. There are two other apparent sanctuaries of the same period, but without evidence of continuity. At Delphi nearly 200 figurines of a goddess – perhaps the earth goddess – have been found under the later sanctuary of Athene Pronaia, and some more under Apollo's temple. Evidence of continuity here is less strong, though there is tenth-century pottery. But in the area of Apollo's temple there seem to have been houses; it is the other site which was more probably continuously sanctified. The sanctuary of Hera on Samos has produced buildings and pottery from the Mycenaean period, though there is no evidence of religious use; but in the Dark Ages a sequence of animal figurines which must be votive deposits begins. At Amyclae near Sparta a sanctuary of the Mycenaean period is attested by the figurine of a goddess and a fragmentary animal votive. There is a gap of a century in the archaeological evidence, which is renewed by a magnificent collection of proto-Geometric pottery, clearly votive offerings. Despite the gap, continuity is here assured in a curious way. In classical times there were sanctuaries here to Apollo and Hyacinthus. Hyacinthus is not a Greek form and represents a pre-Greek deity. The fifth example is on Ceos at Ayia Irini. Here there stood a small, fifteenth-century shrine in which were found some terracotta statues of unusual quality. This was damaged by an earthquake, and the temple was remodelled and elaborated. For a period the main activity focused on two larger rooms to the south-west, but by the tenth century had reverted to the inner sanctum. In the classical period the sanctuary was sacred to Dionysus, and as the god's name has appeared on a Linear B tablet from Pylos, it is at least possible that it was always his.

There are one or two sites which are known to have been sanctuaries in the Mycenaean age, and to have been sacred later, but where evidence of continuity is conspicuously lacking. Such is the cave of Pan in Attica where archaeology provides no evidence for the whole period between Mycenaean and classical times, or the sanctuary of Apollo Maleatas at Epidaurus, where the gap is less striking, covering the Dark Ages. Amyclae reminds us not to press the argument from silence overmuch. Perhaps we can assume some permanence with Maleatas. It does however look as if the cave of Pan was rediscovered, though the local peasants may have maintained its holiness with perishable offerings.

In some other sites we have evidence of continuity from the Dark Ages into classical times. With these we can be reasonably certain that the same deity continued to be honoured. Such are the sanctuary of Zeus near the top of Mt Hymettus, the temple of Artemis Orthia at Sparta, the temple of Athene at Cameiros on Rhodes, and probably the sanctuary of Olympia where the earliest votive bronze caldrons may go back to the tenth or ninth century.

We know little of these holy places. The Dark Ages did not go in much for permanent stone buildings. This is not to say that there may not have been buildings which have perished without trace or been swept aside. At Ceos we have definite evidence of a building. A cave is a natural covered enclosure. But we may reasonably suppose that most sanctuaries were open to the sky; there are clearly examples from Ayia Triadha in Crete and Ayia Irini in Cyprus. Further at Samos the earliest temple is firmly datable to the eighth century. Before that there was an open space with altars.

Caves were shelters and homes to primitive man, burial places at the same time and later, and sanctuaries. Cave sanctuaries have probably been most fully explored in Crete. The cave of Miamu shows in its stratification the development from residence to burial ground. At Pyrgos hundreds of burials were found with stone images, bronze weapons, and over a hundred Early Minoan vases.

Numbers of caves show from the votives that they were sanctuaries. One near the top of Mt Juktas had terracotta animals. The cave at Arkalokhori was a major sanctuary in Minoan times, and gold and silver objects were found there. The cave of Psychro also, which contained an offering table, had its glory in the Late Minoan period. The cave at Phaneromeni had offerings from the Late Minoan period through to the Roman. Four miles east of Iraklion near the river Karteros, a cave was found which may be referred to in *The Odyssey* (19, 188) as belonging to Eilithyia, goddess of childbirth. Here there is evidence of a break in cult and its revival in Roman times.

The Kamares cave on Mt Ida, with which the palace at Phaestos is aligned, was plainly a holy place, and cannot have been a dwelling because of the snow. As well as bronze objects grain was found here. The cave was probably sacred to the mother goddess. It was ousted from its pre-eminence by the cave of Zeus, or the Idaean cave, where there were remains of animal sacrifices, rich votives including a bronze drum, weaponry, and numerous animal figurines, and an inner secret shrine suggesting initiation and mystery. Another cave on Ida, near Parso, was in classical times sacred to Hermes. The cave of Lera in west Crete produced sherds from the neolithic to the Byzantine period, as well as lamps, figurines, and reliefs. Graffiti on the sherds show that in classical times it was sacred to Pan and the Nymphs.[2]

In general the same pattern holds good on the mainland of Greece. A few caves seem to have been used only in the Stone Age. One such is the Franchthi cave in the Argolid, where a late-neolithic painted terracotta female figure suggests a cult. Another is the cave of Dero (Mani) with a remarkable neolithic marble head of an idol; here there are indications that the mouth may have been blocked by an earthquake. But the Maroneia cave in Thrace was in continuous use from neolithic to Byzantine times, first as a dwelling, then as a shrine, and finally as a refuge.

The Corycian cave in Phocis is of particular interest. It was inhabited from neolithic times and produced from that period pottery both crude and painted, terracotta figurines, and flint and obsidian figures. The offerings extended from late Mycenaean times to the third century BC, with a strange gap from the eleventh to the seventh century. The majority of the offerings came from the latter period. There were hundreds of aryballoi and other pots, thousands of figurines, animal and human, of Attic, Boeotian, or Corinthian ware, and 16,000 knucklebones, some with a hole drilled through them, and some with a letter or the name of a god or hero inscribed on them. Other interesting finds included a sixth-century Attic plaque, painted, with satyrs and maenads, a marble statue of Pan, and a bronze statuette of a squalling infant with his right hand on a tortoise, presumably Hermes. This last is interesting by reference to the dedication of the Parso cave. The Corycian cave was sacred to Pan and the Nymphs.

Equally interesting is the grotto of Pan, Apollo, and the Nymphs on the slopes of Hymettus above Vari in Attica. There is a spring within the cave, a rock-cut altar of Apollo Hersus, and some crude but fascinating rock-cut carvings, one showing a figure at work with a hammer and chisel, one a seated goddess, and one a lion's head. Votive reliefs were also found of the fourth to third centuries BC, one showing Pan playing on the syrinx, and another depicting Hermes with the nymphs. There were offerings of coins showing use from 600–150 BC and again in the fourth century AD. The most interesting feature of this cave, however, is the rocky wall dividing it into two. A charming story told how Plato's parents left him on Mt Hymettus while they went to make offerings to Pan, Apollo, and the Nymphs, and returned to find a swarm of bees above the lips that were to be honey-sweet. It seems that Plato's family had an estate hereabouts. He himself must have known this cave, and this rocky division gave him the idea of the cave in *The Republic*, where there is a similar low partition.

There is another cave of the nymphs on Mt Pentelicus. Here the evidence for cult extends from the fifth century BC to the second century AD. Votives include reliefs, clay lamps, terracottas, and a plastic vase depicting a winged female.

Many other sacred caves are to be found throughout the Greek world. Sometimes, as at Claros, they are oracular. Sometimes we have evidence of sacred caves from other monuments. Thus on a coin of Magnesia-on-the-Maeander a bull is being driven to the mouth of a cave, and kneels in readiness for sacrifice. In the museum at Cos there are two reliefs of the Graces from the same site. One shows them dancing as Pan peers over a rocky wall. The other shows them standing. In the foreground is a small unidentified figure in a cave.

Zeus as a sky god arrogated to himself the tops of mountains.[3] Many of his cult-titles are associated with the names of such peaks – Atabyrius on Rhodes, Heliconius on Helicon, Cithaeronius on Cithaeron, Idaeus in Crete, Hymettius, Parnethius, and Anchesmius in Attica, Athoius on Athos, Cynthius on Delos, and many others. Some titles refer generally to his liking for mountains – Acraeus,

Epacrius, and Coryphaeus for instance. Only exceptionally was there a temple. Usually there would be an altar, for annual public and occasional private sacrifice. Sometimes the altar was accompanied by a statue. On Ida there was a permanent rock-cut altar. The acropolis of Pergamon is here of particular interest. The Great Altar of Zeus lay on a small plateau well below the summit. But on the highest point there are traces of a square structure, which was probably the original altar. Sometimes the mountain is the throne of Zeus. This is clear on coins of Thessaly referring to Zeus Acraeus (*BMC Thessaly* 19) or Cyrrhus in Syria referring to Zeus Kataibates (*BMC Galatia* 133 pl. 17, 4). He also appears reclining on a mountain on some vases, and on the famous relief of Archelaus in the British Museum. Rock-cut thrones have been found on numbers of peaks in Asia Minor. Some go back to the Hittites. One of the most remarkable is on a precipitous crag on Mt Sipylus above the ancient Magnesia and the river Hermus. On the island of Chalce near Rhodes is a double throne, inscribed to Zeus and Hecate. Sometimes a temple was added later. A good example is the late temple on Mt Cynthus on Delos. An inscription runs 'To Zeus Cynthius and Athene Cynthia, Apollonides, Theogeiton's son from Laodicea, dedicated the *kataklyston* when Aristomachus was priest, Nicephorus acolyte, during the administration of Quintus of Azena' (*Guide de Délos* 150). Unfortunately we do not know the meaning of *kataklyston*. Today Ayios Elias, the prophet Elijah, has ousted the god.

There is a model discussion of the sanctuary of Zeus on Mt Hymettus.[4] The sanctuary lies in a hollow near the summit. It is fairly simple, consisting of enclosure walls, open-air altars and a pit for offering. Sherds with dedications identify it as a sanctuary of Zeus. On one he is called Zeus Semius, but it is at least possible that this is the sanctuary of Zeus Ombrius known from Pausanias (1, 32, 2), Zeus as a rain god; Hymettus was recognized as an indicator of approaching rain (Theophr. *Sign. Temp.* 1, 20, 24; 3, 43). The offerings, which were especially prominent in the late Geometric period and in the seventh century, would accord with this, consisting mainly of pottery open in shape. Zeus as a weather god was naturally concerned with agriculture, and in Attica the Diaisia and Dipoleia remained important festivals. The rise of Demeter and of local agricultural heroes would account for the decay of the sanctuary. But Zeus remained a weather god in one aspect. Plutarch (*Mor.* 158E) calls Zeus Ombrius an important agricultural deity; Marcus Aurelius cites a prayer in which the Athenians called on Zeus for rain for the crops (5, 7); Alciphron records offerings made in Attica in time of drought to Zeus Hyetius (*Ep.* 2, 33). This continuing faith is enough to explain the sporadic continuation of individual offerings at the shrine.

As to Zeus Semius, the title is not found elsewhere, though on nearby Parnes there was an altar to Zeus Semaleus; offering was also made there to Zeus Ombrius and Zeus Apennius (averter of evils). Near this second altar were found large numbers of Corinthian aryballoi and 3,000 iron daggers, as well as animal remains and bronze ornaments: these may have to do with Zeus averting evils. Zeus Semius or Semaleus presumably gave a 'sign' of approaching bad weather. On Hymettus Zeus was also worshipped as Epacrius (*Etym. Magn.* s.v.; Hesych. s.v.; *SEG* 21, 541), plainly on a peak, though not necessarily *the* peak. He also had a statue as Zeus Hymettius (Paus. 1, 32, 2), a cult-title not clearly found elsewhere.

On top of the Oros on Aegina stood a sanctuary of Zeus Mantellanius. Excavations have revealed the sanctuary with the altar on a wide platform on the heights. This was a major sanctuary with wider connections than weather prophecy, but not necessarily excluding this last. On Mt Lykaion in Arcadia was a famous peak sanctuary of Zeus Lycaeus. Here too there was a wider purview, though we know that the priest did pray for rain in time of drought (Paus. 8, 38, 4), and indeed used a form of sympathetic magic, stirring the dust with an oak branch so that it rose and fell to earth as rain. Here archaeology has revealed a flat circular platform with an immense pile of burnt offerings in the centre, dating from the fifth and fourth centuries. On a spur of Mt Geraneia above Megara was a sanctuary of Zeus Aphesius. Excavations have revealed a temple, altar, and other buildings. Pausanias took the title to mean 'releaser of rain' (1, 44, 9). The extent of the remains again shows a wider use of the sanctuary; the *Etymologicum Magnum* gives the meaning 'Saviour'. On Mt Pelion Zeus Actaeus had a sanctuary. One of the rituals, by which men wore sheepskins in the height of summer, suggests rain magic, the fleecy skins being fleecy clouds. Excavation has added no significant information. The greatest shrine of Zeus as a rain god elsewhere on a mountain is outside Sardis on Mt Tmolus, where he was worshipped as Zeus Hyetius (Joh. Lyd. *Mens.* 4, 48). Zeus Hyetius was further worshipped at Argos (Paus. 2, 19, 8), in Trophonius's sanctuary (4, 39, 4), Cos (*Inscr. Cos* no. 392), and Rhodes (*Annuario* 8–9 (1925–6)

321 no. 21). Zeus Ombrius is known from Elis (Schol. Lycophr. *Alex*. 160), Corinth (*IG* 4, 1598), and the Athenian agora (*Hesperia* 12 (1943) 72–3 nos 19–21; 37 (1968) 291 no. 32).

A few other mountain sites in Attica have associations with Zeus. Mt Anchesmos had a statue of Zeus (Paus. 1, 32, 2); Anchesmos was perhaps Tourkovouni which has a sanctuary on its northern peak, with Geometric sherds. In central Attica exploration has revealed places of offering on Megalo Mavrovouni, Pani, and Meranda; in southern Attica on Keratovouni and Attic Olympus; in western Attica on Kerata. In all cases eighth- and seventh-century remains predominate.

Outside Attica may be mentioned Mt Apesas, by Nemea, said to be sacred to Zeus Apesantius (Paus. 2, 15, 3) with traces of an altar; Mt Arachnaion, by Epidaurus, where Zeus and Hera had altars where offerings for rain were made (Paus. 2, 25, 10), and altar foundations with offerings can be seen; Mt Coccygion in the Argolid with an altar of Zeus (Paus. 2, 36, 2) of which no trace remains; Mt Cithaeron, sacred to Zeus (Paus. 9, 2, 4), with a wooden altar long since vanished; Mt Helicon with an altar of Zeus (Hes. *Theog.* 4), perhaps but not certainly to be identified with the rectangular structure on the east peak; Mt Oche in Euboea, with a cache of sherds; Mt Olympus, where exploration has revealed a late sanctuary of Zeus Olympius; and Mt Zeus on Naxos, called in antiquity the mountain of Zeus Melusius (*IG* 12, 5, 48), with an area for sacrifice.

Here then we have some important matters of definition. A sanctuary is a holy place. The basic meaning of the Greek word *temenos* or the Latin word *templum* is not the same as 'temple' in our usage; it indicates an area cut off or marked off for religious purposes. In Cyprus, for example, a typical sanctuary was an open court, surrounded by a wall, and enclosing one or two small cult-buildings and an altar. Such an area might be a mountain top, or a cave, or a grove of trees, or a spring and its surroundings, or a promontory, or a chasm in the earth, or an unusual rock or other geographical feature, or a place where lightning has struck or a meteorite fallen or some other awesome occurrence has taken place. Often we cannot discern why one place is regarded as holier than another. An altar is a place for making offerings to a deity. If the deity is a sky-being or regarded as living 'above' (in a three-tiered universe) then the altar is normally an elevated surface, often, though not necessarily, of stone. If the deity belongs to the underworld, the place of offering is naturally a pit or trench; these are not usually called altars, but their function is similar. The two sacrifices were distinguished by name, *thysia* to those above, *enagismos* to those below. Congregational worship in the ancient world usually consisted of a gathering in the open air around an altar. It should be remembered that for a people who did not regularly eat meat, a festival at which an animal or several animals were sacrificed was an occasion for feasting. An old legend, an aetiological myth, told how Prometheus tricked Zeus into accepting the bones disguised with fat and leaving the good meat for humans (Hes. *Theog*. 535ff.). When temples were built, the altars remained outside, usually in front of the temple. Here worshippers congregated. The temple was the deity's home; the cult-statue represented his or her presence; only the attendant priest or priestess went in and out, though individual worshippers might be allowed to approach with their offerings, and, in a more sophisticated age, there was a religious or aesthetic desire to see some of the great cult-statues.

Sanctuaries might have regulations of their own. At Athens it was forbidden to collect timber or firewood from the sanctuary of Apollo Erisathaus, on pain of a fine of fifty drachmas for a free citizen or a punishment of fifty lashes for a slave (*SIG* ³984). At Ialysos in Rhodes we have regulations governing the sanctuary associated with the temple of Alectrona. No horse, mule, donkey, or other beast of burden may enter the precinct. No one is to tread the holy ground in shoes made of pigskin or to introduce anything else associated with pigs. Any offender must purify the precinct. Anyone introducing sheep must pay a fine of an obol per animal. The law was engraved on marble and set up in three separate places. The sanctuary of Men Tyrannus at Laurium was founded by a slave named Xanthus, who laid down carefully on his own authority the nature of pollution which would prevent people from entering the holy place, and the length of time needed for cleansing (*CIA* III i 73–4). At Amorgos in the late fifth century the council resolve that no one is to light a fire in the precinct of Hera or the Lyceum on pain of a fine of ten drachmas to Hera (*LGS* II 95). About a century later an addition is made refusing all strangers admission to the sanctuary (ibid. 96). From Chios from the early fourth century we have a council resolution to the effect that there is to be no pasturing of animals or dumping of manure on the sacred groves; it is evident from the wording that excrement is regarded as a pollution. At Pergamon we have from about 130 BC regulations of the temple of Athene Nicephorus. Men and women who have had sexual relations with their lawful spouses are not precluded from entering the temple on the same day, but sexual relations with anyone else involves a delay of twenty-four hours and ritual washing. Contact with the dead or with a woman in childbirth similarly involves a delay of twenty-four hours, except in the case of attendance at a funeral when simple purification by lustration is sufficient (*SIG*$^3$ 982). Regulations from Lindos from the Roman period call for purity of hand and mind. Then follow curious limitations. Eating cheese involves a day's delay, bears or goats two days, abortion or contact with a dead kinsman forty days. Lawful sexual intercourse requires only lustration and unction (*SIG*$^3$983). In Lydia in the Roman period a woman named Antoria put up an inscription declaring that she had been visited by Apollo of Boza with punishment for daring to enter his sanctuary in dirty clothes. When she had recovered she confessed her sin and had the record of it publicly displayed (*Arch. Zeit.* 38 (1880) 37).

An altar is a raised place, in early days perhaps of earth, and later usually of stone. The great altar of Zeus at Olympia was simply formed of the ashes of previous sacrifice. For the altar was the place where the offering of the people was made to the god, where the god received the offering of the people, and which thus was the point of communion between god and people. The altar regularly stood in front of the temple in the countryard of the sanctuary.

Altars of this kind were usually rectangular, sometimes square, very occasionally circular (there is one at Didyma). They became more elaborate as time went on. Even in early days in the district around Corinth altars were decorated with triglyphs and plain metopes: such were discovered at Perachora, in Corinth, at the sanctuary of Hera above Argos, and at Argos.

In the Hellenistic age altars became independent monumental constructions. One is to be seen at Syracuse; it dates from the third century BC and was dedicated by Hiero. The monumental quality was formed by extending the normal rectangular form of altar to an incredible length of 194.95 m. The most elaborate of all such altars was the great altar of Zeus at Pergamon. It stands on a nearly square platform (36.44 × 34.2 m). A great flight of steps rises up the west side. A colossal series of high-relief sculpture showed the battle of gods and giants in wild barbaric power. Above was an Ionic colonnade. A central court, its walls decorated with a relief of the story of Telephus, contained the sacrificial altar. The altar was never completely finished. It dates from the second century, and, for all its impressive quality, is a piece of imperialistic megalomania.

In a careful study of Greek altars,[5] Constantine Yavis identifies five different forms of sacrificial apparatus from the Mycenaean period, the first three of which are paralleled from Minoan Crete. These are: sacred stands with concave sides, which are represented on gems, plaques, and models, and on the Lion Gate at Mycenae, though none actually survives; roadside shrines, known from signet rings, though a wall-bench of undressed stone slabs was found at Asine (*Arch. Anz.* 42 (1927) cols 378–80); and hearths, like those at Berbati in the Argolid. Besides these there is evidence of ceremonial fires in tholos tombs; and walled pits at Mycenae and Tiryns.

When we come to the Geometric period we note that sacrificial altars are determined by functional considerations. We have noted the distinction between altars which look up and altars which look down. The former particularly are determined partly by the desire to do honour to the divinity, and to provide an appropriate focus for worship whether in public or in the home, partly by the need to have a surface apposite to the offering, whether large public burnt offerings of animals or simple domestic libations and offerings of fruit or cake. Formally, altars have been divided into twenty-five types, which can conveniently be reduced to seven: hearth altars; ceremonial; monolithic; stepped monumental; colossal; well altars and sacrificial pits; arulae or altars too small for a sacrificial fire.

Hearth altars (not domestic hearths which might be so used) belong largely to the pre-classical period. Good examples occur in the temple of Apollo at Dreros in Crete from the eighth century, or the little temple of Heracles on Thasos. The only certain example from the later period is an early Hellenistic hearth altar at Lato in Crete, measuring $2.5 \times 1.5 \times 0.45$ m in height (*BCH* 27 (1904) 216–19), though one is known from Cos in the temple of Hera by an inscription (*JHS* 9 (1888) 327–31).

The ceremonial altar is a straightforward cubical structure. These are the original altars at the east end of temples, sometimes antedating the temple itself as in the sanctuary of Hera at Samos or the sanctuary of Artemis at Ephesus. In the sanctuary of Athene Nike on the Acropolis at Athens, a ceremonial altar existed in the sixth century, with perhaps an even earlier one below. A new marble altar was set on the same site when the temple was built. Ceremonial altars sometimes have a deep depression in the centre, usually when dedicated to deities of the underworld: there is a good example in the sanctuary of Demeter and Kore at Acragas.

Monolithic altars are found in cubical or cylindrical form. They will often have had a metal fire pan on top. Sometimes the cubical altars are flat-topped, sometimes volutes provide a frame for the top of the altar. The earliest date from the sixth century. The earliest cylindrical altars were found in Miletus. Later the types become more various and are often endowed with relief sculpture, for example bulls' heads (bucrania) with festoons of garlands; no fewer than nineteen of these were found on Delos. Hexagonal and even octagonal altars are sometimes found. Monolithic altars were often carved. A fine archaic example from Gela shows Heracles killing Alcyoneus.

Stepped monumental altars comprise broad steps leading to a platform on which is built a long monumental altar. These occur first in the first half of the eighth century, and, with growing prosperity, and the desire to give increased honour to the god or goddess, they became an impressive feature in conjunction with the larger temples. As the temple of Hera at Samos increased in size, so did the altar become more monumental, eventually reaching a length of 38.7 m. A much simpler early example is the altar outside the temple of Hera at Olympia. This is 5.9 × 3.8 m, perhaps with two or three steps. The date is uncertain, but it is not later than the seventh century. In the later period there was a large altar, datable to the mid-fifth century, outside the temple of Hera at Acragas, 29.8 × 10.6 m. The largest known is the Great Altar of Hiero II at Syracuse. This is so huge that it does not precisely conform to any one type, measuring 194.95 × 20.85 m. The base itself rises to a height of 2.055 m. A small group of stepped altars have the steps along the shorter side. These are from the Hellenistic and Roman periods; one is in the sanctuary of the Egyptian gods in Priene, another is a large altar (23.6 × 6.6 m) by the river Eurotas at Sparta.

Well altars and sacrificial pits are naturally associated with powers of the underworld. There are numbers of them in the sanctuary of Demeter and Kore at Acragas, and, interestingly, in the sanctuaries of the Cabeiri on Samothrace and at Thebes.

The small altars or arulae, of stone or terracotta, were presumably portable, a fact which creates some difficult problems in relation to ritual. The large majority are Hellenistic, and come from Magna Graecia, but forty are known from Thera and thirty-five from Olynthus.

A holocaust is an offering in which nothing was left for the worshipper. Such was normally offered to deities of the underworld, perhaps because of the awesomeness of their being and the danger of touching offerings dedicated to them, or to the mighty dead, for the same reason, and because they were thought to need the food and be jealous if they did not receive it; or occasionally to the gods above in dire circumstances when a strong constraining power on the forces of nature was needed, as in the occasional records of suggestions of human sacrifice. In general, as suggested above, sacrifices to the gods above were shared with their human worshippers, as in the Delphic Theoxenia, where the god was guest rather than host (he might be either). No doubt there was some idea of communion, not necessarily articulated. There is some ambiguity about offerings to heroes. It is often stated that they were treated as the dead and that the offerings were not shared, but there are certainly exceptions to this. A hero may be ambiguous between a dead figure from the past and a faded god, but some, like Theseus at Athens, were certainly regarded as historical, and yet not given holocausts. So with the Salaminians' offerings: Iolcus received a holocaust, Eurysaces and others seemingly not (*Hesp.* 7 (1938) 1ff.). Sacrifices offered to Paralus were distributed (C. Michel, *Rec. IG supp.* 1517). Melampus was treated as a god (*IG* VII, 219; the reading *theou* must be right). A law of Myconos indicates participation in the sacrifices to Archegetes (*SIG* 1024, 39ff.).[6]

The temple in Greece was a product of the eighth century.[7] Temples of that period are based on three patterns of house-building in use at the time. The simplest is square or rectangular with a stone bench for offerings at the back. This can be seen in the temple of Hera on Delos, and, elaborated with a porch, in the temple of Apollo Delphinius at Dreros in Crete. The second pattern is a long hall, usually with a narthex, and ending in an apse. Such houses were found in the east, as at Smyrna, and in Greece itself, as near Asine or at Lefkandi. The temples, however, except for one at Antissa on the island of Lesbos, seem to be confined to the mainland. An early example was dedicated to Hera Acraea at Perachora; it was small, about 8 × 5 m. A clay model of a temple found here shows the general pattern, complete with porch. There are two excellent examples at Eretria in the sanctuary of Apollo Daphnephorus. One is very old, and has been called the bay-hut. Stone foundations and clay column-bases remain; the superstructure must have been of wood. A reconstruction by P. Auberson looks much like the Perachora model, porch and all. Adjoining this, but not aligned with it, and replacing an unfinished building, is a *hekatompedon* or hundred-footer, five times as long as its width, with a row of columns to support the roof, and an apse at the end. It is the biggest of all apsidal temples. An altar with a sacrificial pit stood outside the front. It is not quite aligned with the temple, which suggests that it is older. Other apsidal temples have been found at Mycenae, Solygeia (near Corinth), and perhaps Eleusis.

The third type of temple may be called a *megaron*, a long rectangular hall. One of the earliest is the temple of Apollo at Thermon, 21.4 × 7.3 m. It seems to have incorporated a pre-existing sacrificial pit. It was unusual in having external wooden roof buttresses. The date is uncertain; pottery deposits suggest the tenth century, but it may be later. The future of temple architecture lay with the *megaron* pattern.

Greek temples were constructed with a wide variety of orientations – Dinsmoor commented that they boxed the entire compass – but four-fifths of the known examples are aligned roughly towards the east, and it seems that they were generally set to catch the rising sun on the festal day of the divinity to whom they were dedicated. This itself is an important fact reminding us that the heavenly bodies retained their power in the religious life of Greece. A temple on Euboea acknowledged its goddess under the cult-title Artemis Facing-East (Prosoea). This also helps to explain the phrase in Aeschylus:

> gods who face the sun,
> now if ever let your eyes shine
> as you receive the king
> (*Agam.* 519–21)

In the temple of Apollo at Bassae, perhaps because of the lie of the ground, the orientation of the temple is approximately north–south, but there was a side door in the eastern wall to enable the proprieties to be observed and the god to look out at the rising sun.

Crete has produced some interesting temples from the Geometric period.[8] At Dreros there was a stone-built temple of the first kind 10.9 × 7.2 m. The cult-statues of hammered bronze show one god and two goddesses. As a temple of Apollo Delphinius is recorded in a late inscription (*I.Cr.* 1, 85 no. 1); these have been identified with Apollo, Artemis, and Leto. The most interesting feature of this temple is the presence of a central hearth for sacrifice within the temple, apparently below an opening in the roof to take out the smoke, a table for offerings, and an altar with two sacrificial knives and a lot of goats' horns, reminiscent of the famous altar on Delos.

At Gortyna there is a larger temple (16 × 13.65 m) also with a corner bench for offerings and a central lined sacrificial pit; it dates perhaps from the late eighth century, though the excavators placed it earlier. It has some puzzling unexplained interior rooms. At Prinias two seventh-century temples also have internal sacrificial hearths and benches for offerings. This is unusual elsewhere in Greece; we must remember the Cretan cave-sanctuaries where worship was naturally within the cave.

Hera is the earth mother. One of the earliest Greek temples was the temple of Hera Acraea at Perachora near Corinth, excavated by Humfry Payne. The sanctuary is set under the cliffs which give the goddess her cult-title. A small terracotta model gives us some idea of the temple, with a high gabled roof, curving slightly from rooftree to walls, a simple rectangular shrine with two pairs of columns *in antis*, facing east, with a small apse. This may be as early as the ninth century. Hera was the goddess of the cliffs and the sanctuary was enfolded within the surrounding cliffs.[9]

The Argive Heraeum is a site of peculiar sanctity and antiquity. It is also spectacular, standing as it does on the slope of Mt Euboea commanding the view over the plain to the citadel of Argos and the bay beyond. Like the other sanctuaries it is enclosed within encircling hills and claims the body of the earth. According to the myth Zeus came to Hera in the form of a cuckoo here and ravished her (Paus. 2, 38, 2). The sanctuary goes back to the Mycenaean period. Legend ascribes the original temple to Dorus, the eponymous ancestor of the Dorians. It stood on a rectangular terrace: the masonry of the retaining walls suggests an eighth-century foundation. In the second half of the seventh century this was replaced by a temple which occupied the whole terrace. Below, on a second terrace, was a hall for offerings and an open space for cult practices. Of this date or earlier are the foundations of an altar, no doubt the earliest holy place, and the point of Homer's reference to Argos as one of Hera's favourite sanctuaries (*Il.* 4, 51–2). In 423 the upper temple was destroyed by fire, and a new one built on the lower terrace, forming a less effective spectacle for those coming up from the plain, but offering a magnificent view from the old terrace, taking in temple and landscape. Here, perhaps more than anywhere, we can be certain that the siting took account of the whole environment.[10]

At Olympia Zeus reigned. But Hera's temple was older. The present remains belong to the seventh century. Before the fifth-century temple of Zeus was built it was dedicated to Zeus with Hera. But two earlier temples lie under the present one, and the very fact that Zeus took Hera alongside him may lead us to think that the oldest of these belonged to the earth mother. It was inevitably a simple building with no surrounding columns and a pediment at one end only, a simple box-enclosure. Furthermore, the temples of Zeus and Hera are not quite parallel. They incline towards one another. They speak of reconciliation, of the *hieros gamos*, the sacred marriage.[11]

Hera had a great sanctuary on the west coast of Italy at Paestum, the ancient Poseidonia, set in a wide coastal plain. There are two temples, one from the mid-sixth and the other from the mid-fifth century. These are of the Doric order, and are singularly impressive. Although some 35 m apart they form a complex set against a backcloth of hills from the sea, and sea from the hills. These, and indeed the other temples of Paestum, speak of the all-embracing power of the earth mother. But the two temples are different. The older is broad, strong, and heavy, pressing down to earth; the later is Doric architecture at its highest, balanced and harmonious, and masterful in the careful treatment of columns. Scully quotes Louis Kahn as saying 'Paestum marks the great event in architecture when the walls first parted and columns became.'[12]

Hera was an earth mother, but she might encounter the sky god on the mountain tops. So the two highest peaks of Euboea are associated with Hera rather than Zeus. On Mt Dirphys she was Dirphya. Mt Oche bears a name which speaks of sexual union. The holy marriage has associations with Euboea. Sophocles called a nearby island 'bridal Elymnion' because it was associated with the marriage (Schol. on Ar. *Peace* 1126). High on Mt Oche stood a ceremonial cult-house of the sixth century, or earlier, with a single door, two windows, and a low roof.[13]

On Delos Hera had her sanctuary on a high terrace solidly constructed. The original foundation went back to the early seventh century; the cella was slightly trapezoidal and contained a table for offerings. A magnificent collection of votives from this temple was discovered, small seated figures of Hera, terracottas of various kinds, including a sphinx, masses of orientalizing and Corinthian vases, and a limestone dove. It is thought that the temple had a colonnade in wood. It was replaced at the very end of the sixth century by a Doric temple. The altar stood outside the south front.

The sanctuary of Hera on Samos was of primeval antiquity, and certainly antedated the coming of the Greeks. It was set on low-lying, marshy ground, rather like the sanctuary of Artemis at Ephesus, and this makes it clear that we are dealing with the great mother goddess of Asia Minor. The temple is sited opposite a gorge or cleft in the hills and commands a spectacular view over Mt Mycale in Asia Minor. In this sweeping, commanding position the earth mother is asserting her imperial claims. There was, interestingly and unusually, a sacred tree, called the Lygos. Here was the older sacral point, and sacrifice was offered before it.

The earliest temple has been dated as early as 800 BC, though it may be a little later. It was of mud brick on stone foundations, and was long and narrow (32.8 × 6.4 m) with wooden columns down the centre supporting the roof: it parallels ancient house construction, though it is twice as long as any human habitation, being a true *hekatompedon*, like the one at Eretria. The central columns must have seriously masked the view of the cult-statue, even though this was set off-centre. This was later expanded by a surrounding portico of wooden columns. There was no precise parallel in previous architecture. It will have provided protection for the mud-brick wall, and at the same time added to the already impressive spectacle. Its effect must have been to mask the temple as an enclosure, and to integrate it more closely with the space around. It was unusual in that there were five columns at the front so that one was aligned with the roof supports. In front of the temple naturally stood an altar, and there was a simple entrance to the sanctuary.

This simple temple was soon replaced by a more elaborate one, a stone building with terracotta roof-tiles. The line of wooden supports was no longer needed with more advanced architectural techniques. The entrance to the sanctuary was made more elaborate; the sacred tree was given its own enclosure; a large portico was built to the west; and the sanctuary was enriched with treasuries and offerings. Herodotus (4, 152) tells us of one dedicated by the explorer Colaeus, a bronze caldron upheld by three human figures twice lifesize and adorned with griffin heads; this has not survived. A ritual bath by the mouth of the river Imbrasus was provided for the annual bathing of the goddess.

The sixth century saw a colossal expansion of the temple, reflecting economic prosperity and imitating the monumental scale of Egyptian sacred building. The altar was not moved, so that to increase the size of the building involved diverting the river and reclaiming marshland. The platform for this new temple was approximately 105 × 53 m. Now there were eight columns along the front, and double rows along the sides. These were beautifully carved, of the Ionic order, set in moulded bases, and rose to a breath-taking height of 12 m. The temple was nicknamed the Labyrinth, after an Egyptian temple (Hdt. 2, 148). It was built by Theodorus, who was both a practical inventor and a theoretician, and Rhoicus.

This temple succumbed to fire in about 530 BC, and was razed and replaced by the dictator Polycrates with an even larger successor. The new plinth actually measured 111 × 54.4 m.

The oldest 'image' of the goddess was a block of wood, we are told (Clem. Al. *Protrept.* 4, 46). This was replaced, perhaps at the same period as the modification of the old temple, by a wooden image carved by one Smilis. This is reproduced on Samian coins of the Roman imperial era.[14] The statue was naturally archaic in style, somewhat rigid, wearing a long robe, high headgear, and a veil leaving the face free. Her arms were held out stiffly from the elbows, trailing two fillets. Another archaic statue found on the site, dedicated by one Cheramyes, has the arms in a different position and therefore does not represent the cult-statue. It was higher than the earlier plinth, with ten steps. Now there were three rows of columns at the front of the temple. It is certain that the entablature was far lighter in every sense than in the Doric order prevalent on the mainland: John Cook once offered the contrast between Perpendicular and Norman as a parallel.[15] The offering of statuary must have been impressive: a fine sixth-century marble kouros from the sanctuary has recently been discovered (*BSA Arch. Rep.* 1980–1, 41). But the vast conception was left unfulfilled, the cella unroofed, the peristyle uncompleted. Development continued through the Hellenistic and Roman periods, but was never completed.

The altar was, with the tree, the first holy place, the nucleus as it were, and the earliest stone altar, about 2.4 × 1.2 m, goes back to about 1000 BC. It was enclosed in more and more imposing structures until about 550 BC when the seventh altar, the so-called Rhoicus altar, was built, actually measuring about 36 × 16.5 m, on a colossal scale. Only the altars at Syracuse and Pergamon surpassed it in size.

This was a sanctuary of Hera, but other divinities shared in it, Hermes and Aphrodite, Apollo and Artemis. Artemis, the Great Mother as she was known across the straits in Asia Minor, had in fact a large shrine alongside her sister goddess.[16]

In Asia Minor Artemis was especially honoured at Ephesus, Magnesia-on-the-Maeander, and at Sardis. At Ephesus the sanctuary lies outside the city. Like the sanctuary of Hera on Samos it is on low-lying, marshy ground. Both speak of an ancient earth mother living in the folds of the earth. Pausanias says that the foundation was pre-Greek and due to the Amazons. Traces of early buildings have been found in the marshland. The evidence is not clear, but there was perhaps a sanctuary without a temple. A cache of treasures was found at this level. The first temple dates from the late seventh century. This was a simple house of the goddess of which virtually nothing remains. In the middle of the sixth century this was replaced by a huge temple to which Croesus of Lydia contributed (his name appears on a dedication now in the British Museum). The Ephesians aimed to upstage Samos. They drew Theodorus from there to solve their structural problems. They sought greater elaboration, more obtrusive richness, using marble instead of limestone. The temple stood on a huge ($115.14 \times 55.1$ m), low platform, approached by two steps. It faced west, and had eight columns along the front and perhaps twenty-one along the sides. The spacing of the columns at the front was irregular, and they were matched by nine columns at the rear. There were a number of other eccentricities. The number of flutings on the columns varied between forty, forty-four, and forty-eight; the capitals too varied one from another. There seems to have been an inner room behind the cella. Little survives, but the fragments of mouldings and capitals indicate the almost baroque excesses.

It is not certain that the sixth-century temple even reached completion. It was destroyed in 356 BC by the arsonical Herostratus, who achieved a dubious immortality similar to that of John Martin's brother who set fire to York Minster; better to confine one's extravaganzas of destruction to paint. This was replaced in the time of Alexander by the largest temple of classical antiquity, one of the Seven Wonders of the ancient world. The platform, appreciably higher than its predecessor, measured $127 \times 73$ m, the dimensions of the temple being $104 \times 50$ m. It was octastyle, with eight columns in front and at the rear in each row, and dipteral, with two rows of columns all round. There were 100 of these in all, and they were about

1.83 m in diameter at the base. If they were tall in proportion their height must have been 16.9 m.[17] This great monument has almost utterly vanished.

The famous cult-statue is preserved for us in many copies. It is often described as many-breasted, and this may be a correct interpretation. But it is right to leave a question mark against it, partly because the breast-like excrescences seem to be part of the costume rather than of the body beneath, and partly because they have been interpreted as symbols of sacred animals. Clearly, whatever the truth in detail, this goddess was a fertility power, and represented as such.

The sanctuary of Artemis at Magnesia gave her the cult-title Leucophryene (white-browed). The temple was designed by Hermogenes of Priene, and belongs to the second century BC; it was admired by Strabo and Vitruvius. The sanctuary plan is orderly and simple: an open court surrounded on three sides by Doric colonnades, so that there was a sense of walls enclosing space rather than of space enclosing a building. The temple was of the Ionic order with a peristyle, on a raised plinth, tall and imposing. In front is the altar and the ceremonial entrance.

The Doric order with its fluted columns, rounded capitals, triglyphs (stones marked by three vertical bars) in the entablature, and general solidity, almost certainly has its origin in wooden structures, though some have argued that Egyptian stone temples were the parents. But the triglyphs certainly seem to have replaced the end of a wooden beam.

Vitruvius says that the Ionian cities built a Doric temple to Panionian Apollo, and that they were the first to devise the proportions of the Doric order (4, 1, 5). He also says that these proportions express the true character of the male body (4, 1, 6). Not all Apollo's temples were Doric; Didyma was Ionic and so was Naucratis.

One of the early Doric temples was at Thermon in Aetolia replacing the early hall. It had a long, narrow *naos*, without a porch, though we can trace the gates on either side of a central column. There was a back porch. The walls were of mud brick, and some terracotta facing survives. There were five columns at front and back and fifteen along the sides. The metopes were painted with mythological creatures, including Gorgons, and rosettes. There was a pediment at the front only. This temple, dedicated to Apollo, dated from about 620 BC and was restored the following century.

There was another early temple to Apollo with the cult-title Laphrius at Calydon, and a sister temple to Artemis Laphria. These both had painted terracotta metopes, and both were crowned with images of the Gorgon. We become aware of the power on the religious imagination of such monsters as the Gorgon and indeed the Sphinx which also appeared on the temple of Artemis. They must have been protectors of the temples and terrors to evil-doers.

At Corinth we can see Apollo as the representative male. Acrocorinth is sacred to the mountain mother under the guise of Aphrodite. The great Doric temple of Apollo, dominating the city from a slight eminence, stands in obvious dialectic with it. It is interesting that, as Scully observes, there is no entasis in the columns which stand firmly, defensively upright.

The finest of the early Doric temples is the temple of Hera (originally Hera and Zeus) at Olympia. The earliest temple here dated from the eighth century and had no peristyle. The surviving temple is to be dated to about 600 BC. It had six columns at front and back and sixteen along the sides, the proportions being unusually long (4:11 instead of the more classical 3:7). The columns were originally of wood, and were replaced piecemeal as need demanded, as the variety of the surviving columns show. The distance between the columns also implies a wooden superstructure, and this is confirmed by the absence of any appropriate stone survivals.

A unique temple of Apollo under the cult-name 'Epicurius' or 'Helper' stands high in the mountains of the Peloponnese at Bassae, 'the Glens'. It was designed by Ictinus, architect of the Parthenon. It surely antedates the Parthenon, and is probably to be dated to the mid-fifth century BC.

The temple is orientated north–south unusually. The outer order is Doric, and the temple is peripteral hexastyle with fifteen columns along the flanks. The pronaos was shut in by a metal grille. The cella is decidedly curious with a side entrance to the east, and with five pairs of semi-columns projecting from buttresses. Four pairs have Ionian capitals, the most southerly have Corinthian capitals, and a single Corinthian column standing in between. This will have been the earliest known Corinthian capital, and it seems that these three columns and the side-door mark off the area of the cult-statue facing east. Another exceptional feature is the continuous frieze which ran round the interior of the cella: it depicted battle scenes between Greeks and Amazons, Lapiths and Centaurs.

It is not needful to examine the architectural details of different temples. The temple would normally have a porch (*pronaos*) or narthex. The inner chamber (*naos*) was the god's own room. The cult-statue stood there looking out eastward, and this would be all the worshippers saw in normal circumstances. As the interior was usually dimly lit, the moment when the rays of the rising sun fell full upon the divinity must have been precious indeed. Often there was a room behind for the priest. Here too the temple treasures were kept in safety. The porch at the back (*opisthodomus*) was also used as a store.

The pediments and metopes, and later the continuous frieze, became the scenes of appropriate sculpture. The great archaic temple of Artemis in Corcyra had on its west pediment a terrifying figure of the Gorgon with her offspring, Pegasus and Chrysaor, and two attendant leopards. At Selinus in Sicily the metopes of temple C showed heroic scenes of conflict, Perseus with Medusa, Heracles with the Cercopes, and so on. The marvellous temple of Aphaea, a local goddess on the island of Aegina, datable to the very beginning of the fifth century, had on its pediments scenes from the Trojan War in the presence of the goddess Athene. The temple of Hephaestus at Athens was long called the Theseum because of the sculpture dealing with the exploits of the Athenian hero.[18]

Shrines of the heroes are of particular interest. One of the finest was discovered at Trysa in Lycia, a site so remote that it achieves no mention in ancient literature. The remains discovered include parts of a fifth-century city wall, a temple, perhaps, to judge from inscriptions, dedicated to Zeus or Helios, some water cisterns, a number of tombs, and the heroon. This took the form of an enclosure, rather less than 20 m square, surrounded by a wall 3 m high. In the centre was a rock-cut sarcophagus. The wall was covered with reliefs from heroic legend, now in Vienna: the Trojan War, the exploits of Theseus, the battle between Greeks and Amazons, the battle between Centaurs and Lapiths, the Seven against Thebes, and others. The whole dates from the fourth century BC.[19]

There is no need to pursue the story of the temple through the Hellenistic Age. The pattern was established. The Corinthian order, first discerned uniquely at Bassae, but not otherwise known until it appears in the round tholos within the precinct of Athene Pronaia at Delphi, now becomes more prominent, although it does not displace the other orders. There is some experimentation, some variety, some striving after effect. The religious principles remain unchanged.

One sanctuary of the Hellenistic Age must be mentioned. This is the Great Altar of Zeus at Pergamon. It dates from the second century BC. It stood on a colossal platform measuring about 36.5 × 34 m at the base. It carried a solid wall on three sides. To the west was a flight of between twenty and thirty steps leading to the altar. This was covered by a vast curved canopy or baldachin which may be seen on a coin of the Roman Imperial period (*BMC Mysia* 152 pl. 30, 7), as can two statues of zebu cattle flanking the steps at their foot, and statues of deities above the colonnades on the wings of the altar. The celebrated frieze round the outside showed the battle of the gods and giants. This was the art of kings not of citizens. It was an affirmation of the programme of the monarchy, Greek culture against barbarism, and an invocation – or rather an assertion – of divine blessing on that programme. It is not surprising that the idea was imitated on a smaller scale, at Priene in honour of Athene Polias and at Magnesia in honour of Artemis Leucophryene – nor that the author of the last book of the Bible called it 'the seat of Satan' (Rev. 2:13).

Some temples preserved their sanctity as churches. One, which has none the less perished, was the temple of Aphrodite at Aphrodisias. When it was turned into a Christian basilica the cella was dismantled and the stones reused for the walls of the church. The preservation of the temple of Hephaestus in Athens was due to its adaptation as a Christian church, perhaps as late as the seventh century, with the addition of an apse. There were further changes in about AD 1300. It remained in use as a church under the Turks. The Parthenon too was turned into a church under Justinian. Athene might not have disapproved of her fane being dedicated to Santa Sophia or Holy Wisdom. It was the metropolitan church of Athens. Here, however, the Turks turned it into a mosque, using a Byzantine bell-tower as a minaret. At Acragas the temple of Concord was preserved as a church. At Syracuse the old temple columns can be seen within the structure of the modern cathedral.

In *The Earth, the Temple and the Gods* Vincent Scully has made a number of points about the siting of temples in the classical world. First, most are oriented to the rising sun, and even, as Dinsmoor has shown, towards the rising sun of the deity's feast day in the actual year of the temple's dedication.[20] Second, the altars relate to the total grasp of the sacral landscape. Third, some temples, especially on mystery sites, provide an enclosure for the deity – almost creating a cave. Fourth, some temples provide an inner landscape, especially some of the Ionic order. Fifth, some temples, Doric especially, form a sculptural unity. Sixth, there is some tension as temple building develops, between standardization and the religious needs of a particular site. Finally, there are changes in the general balance as time passes and new attitudes emerge.

# 4
# PRIESTHOOD

There was no priestly caste in Greece, although some priesthoods were hereditary. Religious business was in fact political business, and religious matters took priority in the business of the state (*IG* II ²107; 212). The priest or priestess was in general a state official, charged with the performance of certain religious observances on which the wellbeing of the whole state, or some component part of it (such as a phratry), was deemed to depend. A priest or priestess never had a general competence; (s)he was always the minister of a particular deity in a particular sanctuary. The ritual observances were handed down by tradition; in every other way the officiant was responsible to the political authority.

No special qualifications were needed for the office of priest or priestess. They were normally, if not invariably, expected to be of citizen birth. We know that this was true at Athens, a particularly exclusive community (Dem. 59, 1369), except perhaps for foreign cults with their own priesthood, like that of the Thracians in Piraeus (*Jahrh. Oest. Arch. Inst.* 5 (1902) 127). It was also true of the service of Hera at Amorgos (*SIG* ²565). At Halicarnassus the priestess of Artemis Pergaea had to be of citizen birth on both sides for three generations (*SIG* ²601). There are occasional indications that manual workers should not be priests. This is stipulated for the priesthood of Asclepius at Chalcedon (*SIG* ²594). Aristotle wanted all priests to be landed gentry (*Pol.* 4, 1329A). Physical defects might rule out a candidate (*SIG* ²594). Occasionally physical beauty is insisted on, as with the boy chosen to be priest of Zeus at Aegae (Paus. 7, 24, 4). There were no intellectual tests, and not much concern for moral probity, though notorious sexual licence might be a bar, as might blood-guiltiness; yet one suspects that the issue is pollution rather

than ethical judgement. Priesthoods sometimes demanded virginity –
so Poseidon at Calauria (Paus. 2, 33, 3), Athene at Tegea (8, 47, 3),
and Heracles at Thespiae (9, 27, 6) – or alternatively at least chastity
during office, like Artemis Hymnia in Arcadia (8, 5, 12) or Heracles
Misogynus in Phocis (Plut. *Pyth. Or.* 20). Ge at Aegae would not
accept a priestess more than once married (Paus. 7, 25, 13). Athene,
virgin herself, might have a married priestess (*IG* II 550), just as
Aphrodite, who was certainly not a virgin, in Sicyon demanded
virginity in her priestess and chastity from the temple attendant
(Paus. 2, 10, 4). Although in general gods had priests and goddesses
had priestesses, this was not an absolute rule: Poseidon might have a
priestess (Paus. 2, 33, 3) and Athene a young male priest (8, 47, 3).
There were regulations about age, but they were particular, not
general. It was not uncommon for office to be held by boys up to the
age of puberty or girls up to the age of marriage. At Cos we have
records of minimum ages of 10 and 14 for different priesthoods (*LGS*
II i 133; 135). Some priestesses had to be elderly.

Some priesthoods were hereditary, some were filled by election or
appointment. Some were for life, others for a fixed term of years.
Priesthoods were sometimes purchased. We have an example from
Halicarnassus (*SIG* $^2$594), and a long list from Erythrae of sales of
priesthoods with titles, prices, purchasers, and guarantees: Hermes
Agoraeus fetches the highest price (*SIG* $^2$600). A late record deals with
the sale of the priesthood of Asclepius at Chalcedon. Candidates must
be physically in perfect condition, and eligible for public office. They
are not allowed to canvass in advance. Vicarious purchase is not
permitted except on behalf of a son. The money is to be paid in two
instalments, with a sales tax. The price on this particular occasion,
including tax, is 5,038 drachmas 4 obols. The priest cannot take office
until full payment is made (*SIG* $^2$594). As one of many examples of
hereditary priesthood we may take the priesthood of Asclepius at
Mytilene (*IG* XII ii 102). Sometimes the rules of hereditary succession were inordinately complex. From Halicarnassus we have a list of
twenty-seven priests of Poseidon in which the succession passes in
order of seniority from brother to brother, then to the sons of the first
brother in order and the sons of the rest in order, then to the grandsons
(*SIG* $^2$608). In some cities, as we know from Rhodes and Sicily, the
eponymous archon was always a priest.

The duties of the priest of Asclepius at Chalcedon are spelled out.
He must open the temple daily, and see that the portico is kept clean.

He must care for the temple building and its contents. He was expected to deal with the customary sacrifices. At festivals he was expected to wear a wreath and attend the public banquets. He had the use of the open space in front of the sanctuary except when the city of Chalcedon was using it officially (*SIG* ²594). Similarly we have details of the responsibilities of the priestess of Artemis Pergaea at Halicarnassus. This was a life appointment. She had to keep the sanctuary in due order, but was not responsible for the administration of the treasure deposited there. She had to perform sacrifices both for the state and individuals. Every new moon she had to make a ritual act of placation on behalf of the city. Once a year she was entitled to take up a collection – though not a house-to-house one – to provide income for herself (*SIG* ²601). The temple-law of the Amphiaraon at Oropus spells out the special duties of prayer over a sacrifice and the proper organization of the sacrificial offerings (*LGS* II i 65, 26). The priest was responsible for the decent and orderly conduct of his sanctuary, and might be empowered to lay down by-laws to endure this (*SIG* ² 592, 24). Sometimes it is specified that he has an assistant or *neocorus* in his tasks (*SIG* ²589, 6). At the Amphiaraon the assistant was permanently in residence, but the priest had to be there for at least ten days each month, and might not leave the sanctuary unvisited for more than three days in the winter months. The priest could impose fines upon offenders in the sanctuary, to be paid in his presence. If in attendance he was required to say the prayer over the public sacrifices, and over all private sacrifices except at festival time. He received the skins of all victims, and the shoulder portions except from private sacrifices during the festival (*SIG* ³1004).

Priests were not normally salaried, though the priestess of Athene Nike at Athens was an exception (*SIG* ²911). In some cases there was the right of taking a street collection (*SIG* ²601; 666), though that seems to have been an eastern custom. No doubt the priest had some rights from the temple endowments. The perquisites at sacrifices public and private will have been significant, sometimes, but not always, including the skins (*SIG* ³1004). At Chios a priest is recorded as receiving for himself the first portions of entrails, shanks, knees, tongues, two double portions of meat, Hermes cakes, and the offerings of which anyone makes burnt sacrifices, the right to participate in all banquets, and one-twelfth of a gold stater on the occasion of official banquets (Sokolowski 77). The priestess of Nike mentioned above had the skins among other perquisites. There were also fees paid by private individuals; they were fairly nominal and no doubt designed to cover incidental expenses, but the priest may have managed a small rake-off (*SIG* ²591; some worshippers pay a lump sum of five obols). The right of free public meals must have been a considerable saving; so must tax exemption (*SIG* ²592, 20; Sokolowski 77).

Some privileges were accorded to priests *ex officio*. One of the most familiar is the right to special seats in the theatre. In the theatre of Dionysus at Athens the seats are labelled accordingly. The priest of Dionysus naturally has the place of honour, but many other priesthoods are accorded reserved and special seats. The same can be observed less extensively in other theatres, at Oropus, for instance. Sometimes priests might be accorded special places in processions. Exemption from military service was a normal aspect of priesthood.

The practical, economic, and prestigious importance of priesthoods is to be seen in the record of a dispute over religious prerogatives between two branches of an aristocratic family, the Salaminioi. The priesthoods concerned are those of Athene Sciras, Heracles at the Ferry, Eurysaces, Aglaurus, Pandrosus, Curotrophus.[1]

Priests may be specially honoured by the states they served. A decree from Athens awarded a wreath to the priest of Zeus Soter for the responsible energy with which he had offered sacrifices for the council and people. Sometimes the reasons for the honour are less strictly religious. Gaea, a priestess of Hera at Aphrodisias, was honoured for entertaining the people to sumptuous banquets, providing generous supplies of oil for the public baths, and introducing contemporary music into the musical and dramatic contests. Her reward was an inscription in her honour and the title 'Chaste Life-Priestess of the Goddess Hera and Mother of the City' (*CIG* 2820). Similarly Phaena, priestess of Demeter at Mantinea, was honoured for her munificent endowments and magnificent entertainments alike before, during, and after her term of office, including a promised testamentary endowment. Her liberality, however, was directed to her fellow-priestesses and liturgical duties. She received the right to be invited to all ceremonies of the goddess, as well as seeing her virtues engraved in marble for posterity (Lebas-Foucart II 6 p. 215 no. 352 i). The Athenians allowed a priest of Asclepius and Hygieia to record his own name as restorer of the temple at his own expense (*CIA* II i 419 no. 489b). At Ilium a priest gave the city 15,000 drachmas to endow a yearly sacrifice (*CIG* 3599).

A wide variety of religious offices are known to us from inscriptions. The most general term is *hiereus* or *hiereia*, priest and priestess. Many temples simply had a single officiant. But some had large staffs with specialized functions. The *loutrophorus* and *hydrophorus* carried the holy water. At Eleusis the *hierophantes* 'revealed the holy things' to the initiates; the *daduchus*, as his name implies, bore the torches. In the worship of Hecate the *cleidophorus* carried the key. The *hierokeryx* was a herald announcing the ritual. The *cosmeteira* was responsible for adorning the image of a goddess. In oracular shrines a *mantis* or *prophetes* might proclaim the word of the god. In some sanctuaries there was special terminology. The child-priestesses of Artemis at Brauron were bears; her priestesses at Ephesus were bees. The term *neocorus* originally meant the sweeper-out of the temple, but it became more exalted with the passage of time. The *diaconus* (our 'deacon') was responsible for some of the chores. Temple slaves were called *hieroduli*. Sometimes, as at Andania, we read of *hierothytai* with responsibility for the sacrifices, and *rhabdophori*, whose task was to keep order at the festival. At Smyrna the Mysteries of Dionysus involved a *theophant*, who must have had to do with divine epiphanies (*Ins. Smyrna* 17).

We have excellent information about the organization of the Asclepieion in Athens.[2] The staff was headed by a priest, elected annually, assisted by a *zacorus* (senior attendant), who became more prominent in the Roman period. There were four junior staff, two men, a sacristan, and a fire-bearer (*pyrphorus*), and two women, a basket-bearer (*canephorus*), and a bearer of holy secrets (*arrephorus*). The post of physician was sometimes held by the priest or *zacorus*, but might be held by others. The sacrifices were carried out by a board of officials, and a board was appointed annually to record and check the offerings. At Epidaurus we hear of a priest, fire-bearer (*pyrphorus*), torch-bearer (*daduchus*), *zacorus*, and a *mageirus* or sacrificer, and at Cos a *neocorus* (temple-assistant) was in charge of the sacrifices. In Crete there was a *hiarorgus* or performer of sacred acts, who takes the place of the normal priest (*Philol.* 1896, 587). Among minor attendants we know at Pergamon of a *thyrorus* or janitor (Ael. Arist. 477, 15–16).

Similarly on a marble tile found in the temple of Zeus at Olympia we have a list of the staff of the sanctuary for Olympiad 188–9 or 28–24 BC. They include *spondophori* (libation bearers), *manteis* (prophets), *cleiduchi* (key-holders), *auletes* (musician), *exegetes* (interpreter), *cathemerothytes* (maker of the daily sacrifice), *grammateus* (scribe), *oenochous* (wine-pourer), *epispondorchestes* ('dancer of the libation'), *xyleus* (woodcutter), *stegonomus* (house-accountant), and *mageirus* (sacrificer) (*SIG* 1021).

Priests and priestesses are occasionally portrayed in art. There is a splendid statuette of a priest from Ephesus, at present in Istanbul's archaeological museum. It dates from the early sixth century. He wears a high hat, a long embroidered robe with a belt, and a long necklace which he grasps in both hands. In the Antalya museum is a priestess of Aphrodite, with a shell at her waist and a necklace of diamonds and rectangles. Sometimes it is difficult to be sure whether the one portrayed is the divinity or priest or priestess representing the divinity. There is an interesting example in a relief in the Carl Milles collection at Lindingö near Stockholm. A male figure with bare feet, wearing an ankle-length chiton with a cloak, is pouring a libation onto an altar. He carries a bunch of grapes in his left hand. The altar is garlanded. On it is an offering of fruit, and a goat's head. At the back of the altar stands a half-size Priapic herm, with bearded head, ithyphallic, and holding a cornucopiae. The relief is almost certainly from the Roman imperial period. On the face of it, it would seem to show Dionysus offering a libation to Priapus, but there are serious objections to one god receiving a sacrifice from another. Artemis is once or twice shown kindling a sacrifice, but not as honouring another deity. It is far more likely that we are seeing the priest wearing the emblems of his god.[3]

# 5
# GAMES AND FESTIVALS

The sanctuary of Zeus at Olympia was originally a sacred grove: Pausanias tells us that that is the original meaning of Altis. The grove measured 200 × 160 m. It must from an early date have been enclosed by a sacred boundary, but this has left no trace; it may have been a slit trench, or a set of wooden stakes, or even of holy trees. In the fourth century BC it was replaced by a stone wall.

We should probably assume that this was originally a shrine of the earth mother. It lies, cradled in the bosom of the land, under the conical hill known later as Kronion, the hill or tomb of Kronos. The oldest of the temples was on the site of the temple of Hera, not that of Zeus. It is said to have been a shrine of Zeus with Hera, which suggests that Zeus has usurped a sacred place of the mother. But, whatever its origins, Zeus certainly took over, and the sacral centre was the altar of Zeus, built up not of stones but of the ashes of sacrifice. The name Olympia dates from Zeus's takeover.

From 776 BC the Olympian truce began. It is hard to know at what point the celebrated games started: traditionally from that date. But the association of the sanctuary is with another semi-divine figure, the hero Pelops, whose myth includes a memorial games. The Pelopion, a five-sided enclosure containing a hillock, a grove, and an altar to the hero, is a key-building. It has been noted that a line drawn across the sanctuary from the north-west entrance to the south-east touches the corners of the two great temples and passes right through the hero's shrine. It was evidently regarded as his tomb; Pindar says that 'his tomb is thronged about at the altar where many strangers pass' (*Ol.* 1, 102–5). A great many bronze and terracotta votives were found within the shrine. But another heroic association was with Heracles, the legendary founder of the festival (Pind. *O.* 2, 3; 3, 21; 11, 64). The original running track was presumably within the sanctuary; at Isthmia too it lay by the temple. Stadia of the sixth and fifth century began within the sanctuary but extended outside it. From one of these we have a blue-black marble seat reserved for Gorgos of Sparta, who looked after the interests of citizens of Elis in Sparta. The surviving stadium, wholly outside the sanctuary, dates from the fourth century. The chariot-racing must at all times have been outside.

The great temple of Zeus was built by Elis between the end of the Persian War and 458 BC. It was at the time the largest temple of mainland Greece, 64.12 × 27.68 m. The larger temple of Zeus at Athens was begun but left at foundation stage. The Parthenon was deliberately enlarged to surpass Olympia. Zeus's temple was Doric, with eighty-four columns (six rows of thirteen) of a coarse conglomerate, rough with seashells, and covered with white stucco. The front pediment at the east showed the chariot race between Pelops and Oenomaus. The other pediment, with less obvious relevance, showed the conflict between Centaurs and Lapiths. Pirithous, king of the Lapiths, was, as Pausanias argued, a son of Zeus, and his ally Theseus was a descendant of Pelops: but probably we are right in seeing these allusions as less important than an act of thanksgiving for the triumph of civilization over barbarism.

The cult-statue was chryselephantine, by the Great Athenian sculptor Pheidias. The statue was one of the Seven Wonders of the ancient world. It was colossal; they said that if the god stood up he would take the roof with him. We have noted Quintilian's view that it deepened the understanding of religion.

According to Nikolaos Yalouris, the site was already sacred in the second millennium BC. Apsidal houses have been found. He suggests that there will have been memorials of Pelops and Oenomaus, and a sacred olive tree. This is speculation, and it is hard not to think, equally speculatively, that there was a holy place of the earth goddess. In the Dark Ages and the Geometric period (1100–700 BC) he suggests that there were in addition altars to the mother of the gods, Zeus, Hera, and perhaps Hestia, and by the end of the period a stadium. From 200 BC we are on firmer archaeological ground. We can now add the temple of Hera, the *bouleuterion* outside the sanctuary to the south, and the *prytaneion* near the north-west gate incorporating the altar of Hestia, a small temple to Eilithyia, goddess of childbirth, and the treasuries where the states deposited their offerings. By 400 BC the temple of Zeus was established and the main geography of the buildings firm. A noteworthy addition was the statue of Victory by Paeonius. The inscription records its dedication to Zeus by the people of Naupactus and Messenia as a tithe from their enemies. It is thought to have been dedicated in 421 BC. It is one of the masterpieces of ancient sculpture. It shows the goddess, one breast bare, alighting; her diaphanous drapery, swept backwards by the movement, clings delightfully to her right side and right leg revealing the contours of the body beneath. Also in front of the temple it became customary to set the statues of victors and chariots dedicated by them.

The treasuries stand on a terrace to the north of the sanctuary, east of the temple of Hera. They mostly date from the sixth century BC and are difficult to identify. Of the twelve all but two are from states outside the Greek mainland. The oldest belonged to Gela, and incorporated terracotta plaques imported from Sicily. Other Sicilian towns were Syracuse and Selinus; Sybaris and Metapontum from Magna Graecia were also represented; Epidaurus from up the Adriatic coast; Cyrene from Africa; and, across the Aegean and beyond, Samos and Byzantium. The mainland states were Megara and Sicyon. There is some doubt which is which, and one is unassigned. We know that Syracuse offered the spoils won at Himera in 480, and that Myron of Sicyon commemorated his chariot victory in the games with gifts so weighty that the floor had to be strengthened.

A place of festival competition requires a great deal more than the sanctuary itself can provide. To the west, between the sanctuary and the river Cladeus, stand a great gymnasium, one wing of which was a covered running track, and, beyond, a palaestra surrounded by a water channel. Next comes the priests' house with eight rooms around a central court, adjoining a circular heroon with an altar of earth and ashes inside. The impressive remains of a Byzantine church overlie the workshop of Pheidias when he was producing the great statue; tools, chips, moulds, and a cup with his name were found here. Adjoining this are the baths; the present remains are Roman, but there was a swimming pool of the fifth century BC here and even earlier baths. Beyond again is the *leonidaion*, a luxury hotel for distinguished visitors. Many of these buildings date from the fourth century.

The *bouleuterion*, as indicated, originally lay to the south outside the sacred precinct, which was extended to incorporate it. It consisted of a square hall with apse-ended wings. Here stood the altar where the athletes took their oaths. In the south-east corner a fourth-century building surrounded by a colonnade was demolished to make room for a palace to accommodate Nero on his visit; a lead water pipe has been found with the inscription NER AVG. Beyond, baths were later added.

The sanctuary had a vaulted tunnel leading to the stadium. Just outside this stood a row of twelve Zanes, bronze statues of Zeus dedicated from the fines imposed on cheating athletes. The stadium, in its fourth-century form, would accommodate 40,000 people, which gives some idea of the scale of the festival. One of the strangest features of Olympia is that it has no theatre, unlike all or almost all other sacred sites, where large numbers of people congregated.[1]

We know a good deal about the events which took place on the central three days of the festival. On the second there were chariot races and horseraces in the morning and the pentathlon in the afternoon (discus, javelin, jumping, running, and wrestling); on the third, footraces; on the fourth, wrestling, boxing, the all-in-wrestling known as *pancratium*, and the race in armour. But it must never be forgotten that this was a religious festival, proclaimed in the spring by three sacred heralds, marked by a sacred truce, inaugurated by a solemn swearing-in ceremony before Zeus of the oath and by prayers and sacrifices, climaxed by the procession round the Altis and sacrifice of a hundred oxen on the morning of the third day, and ending on the fifth with the procession of victors to the Temple of Zeus to be crowned with wreaths of wild olive. Such at least is the most plausible reconstruction on all the evidence. Something of what it meant can be seen in the dedications – a jumping-weight from about 500 BC celebrating the victory of a Spartan named Acmatidas in the pentathlon without a contest, or a charming bronze statuette of a runner in the starting position with the words 'I belong to Zeus' scratched on his thigh – or some of the coins issued from Gela or Rhegium to celebrate victories by their rulers.[2]

But what was the religious significance of the games? Here we are on speculative grounds. Some scholars would say 'little or nothing'. This is to underestimate the extent to which religion permeated the fabric of society, certainly at the time at which the games were said to start, in 776 BC. Others have said 'Well, it was really just fun. The spectators enjoyed it; so would the gods.' That may have truth in it, but it seems inadequate. We should at least consider the link between games and death, as in the funeral games of Patroclus, where there is certainly a contest in excellence, that his surviving things may go to the best person – and that may be directed by the divine powers including the spirit of the dead man. We should also consider the *agon* or contest as representing the struggle between death and life, chaos and order, evil and good, darkness and light, winter and summer, night and day, and all the other dichotomies with which human beings are faced. It is represented in Greek myth by gods and giants, Greeks and Amazons, Lapiths and Centaurs, Heracles and various pests, Theseus and the Minotaur, and numerous other conflicts. There is a kind of sympathetic magic in the enactment of such contests in other fields, especially where the best man – by definition – wins.

The second of the great festivals, also every four years in the third year of each Olympiad, was the Pythian at Delphi. We know nothing of the origin or early history of these. They were said to have been reorganized in 582 BC. Previously there seem to have been musical competitions, appropriate to the god of music, and the main event was for a hymn to the lyre celebrating the conflict between Apollo and the snake Pytho. Flute-playing and singing to the flute were added, and in 558 lyre-playing. The mountainous site is a decidedly unpromising one for athletic activities. In early days the athletics programme took place in the plain below. The events were similar to those at Olympia. The horseracing and chariot racing could never have found a venue on the mountainside and must always have been held where now the olive groves teem. We have no idea of the exact locations.

The practice grounds were later placed on the eastern site, to the west of the sanctuary of Athene. Even so they could be fitted in only with ingenuity. On one terrace is a covered running track parallel to an open-air track, for practice in all weathers. On a lower terrace stands the palaestra, a square courtyard with sides 13.6 m surrounded by a colonnade, and a circular cold bath 1.8 m deep and 9 m in diameter, with an early form of shower available in the retaining wall behind. The hot baths are a Roman addition.

A suitable site for the stadium was found in about 450 BC. It meant climbing nearly 100 m above the temple where there was a sufficiently level open space. The pillars adorning the entrance are of Roman date. The track was 175 m long, a length known as a Pythian stade. There was room for seventeen or eighteen runners. The west end, unlike that at Olympia, was curved in a semicircle. On the north the seats were carved in twelve tiers out of the rock; to the south six tiers were artificially constructed. The whole seated 7,000 spectators. Sir James Frazer commented, justly, 'A more striking scene for the celebration of national Games could hardly be imagined.'[3]

We have already visited the sacred site. It must have been surrounded by accommodation for the visitors, and the enterprises of the local trades people. There was no doubt plenty of camping out in August. We do not know the details of procedure at Delphi. We can be sure that there were sacrifices, probably both preliminary and as a culmination to the festival. The main ceremony was naturally a procession up the Sacred Way to the temple of Apollo. We may reasonably assume that there the victors were crowned, with bay leaves culled by a boy whose parents were still alive.

There were two other recognized national festivals. These were more frequent than the others and carefully co-ordinated with them. The Isthmian festival took place in April, followed by the Olympian or Pythian in August, and the Nemean in July of the following year. Such at least was the practice in the third century BC (*Philologus* 37, 1ff.), and there is no reason to suppose that any change had been introduced from the inception. To put it slightly differently: in any Olympiad there would be a sequence of games at Olympia, Nemea, Isthmia, and Delphi, followed by Nemea and Isthmia again; or again, starting from the Olympia or the Pythia, it was possible to share in all four festivals in the course of twenty-five months. They were in fact called the circuit (*periodos*), and a victor in all four was known as a circuit victor (*periodonices*).

The Isthmian festival was celebrated on a low plateau on the isthmus of Corinth, in honour of Poseidon. No doubt there was an ancient local festival here. It achieved panhellenic status in 581 BC, the year after the reorganization at Delphi. The coincidence is too striking to be accidental, and there must have been either co-ordination or emulation. It has been argued that it was the most populous of the great festivals, by reason of its accessibility, and the proximity, here alone, of a major city (Corinth). Archaeological evidence does not confirm or deny this. We know little about it. There was of course sacrifice to Poseidon. Events celebrated in song by Pindar are chariot racing and the pancratium, but the stadium shows that the normal races were held. The prize was a wreath of 'dry celery', we are told, marking it off from the 'fresh celery' at Nemea.

The festival was in honour of Poseidon and held in his sanctuary, but there were different traditions about the foundation. One of the most persistent was that Ino jumped into the sea a little further up the coast, with her child Melicertes in her arms. A dolphin brought the body of the boy to shore on the Isthmus. There was a famine at the time, and the Corinthians received an oracle to the effect that the famine would cease only when the boy received proper burial and funeral games were held in his honour. A second oracle declared that to prevent a recurrence of the famine the games should be held in perpetuity. This was done, and the boy received the new name Palaemon, the wrestler, and was honoured as a sea divinity. The name was also attached to Heracles. So here too we have the association of the games with funeral rites, and Heracles cropping up, however indirectly, Heracles, whose life was one of contests. The Athenians, characteristically, attributed the institution of the games to their own hero Theseus. Other stories attributed them to Sisyphus or to Helios.

The sanctuary has suffered sadly from the ravages of time and the depredations of Byzantine military engineers. The famous Isthmian Wall, a military fortification, runs to the east and north of the sanctuary. In origin it belongs to the third century BC, but the visible remains mostly belong to the age of Justinian and his general Victorinus, as does the colossal Byzantine fortress in the north-east corner. It is in these that the remains of the sanctuary buildings are to be found, but they are beyond recovery.

The site was dominated by the Temple of Poseidon. There was an archaic temple on the site which had succumbed to fire; a holy-water stoup from this can be seen in the museum in Corinth. It was replaced in the fifth century by a Doric temple, peripteral hexastyle, with thirteen columns along the side. There is little to be seen today; Oscar Broneer, who excavated it, said that 'the casual visitor will marvel chiefly, perhaps, at the thoroughness of its destruction'. We know from historical evidence that this suffered from fire in 394 BC and had to be reroofed (Xen. *Hell.* 4, 5, 4). The most exciting discovery relating to the temple was a huge statue, which formed part of the cult-statue of the temple which showed Poseidon with Amphitrite.

A major building of the later, Roman period was the temple of Palaemon. The foundations of this can be traced. We know that it had a circular open colonnade of eight columns which is depicted on Corinthian coins of the second century AD. This temple raises some curious questions. There was a complex water-supply system on the plateau, and the temple was built over part of this. It has been suggested that it had fallen into disuse, and its purpose was not understood; it was thought to be Palaemon's grave. It is however difficult to think that there was no shrine for Palaemon within the sanctuary from the first. What is fairly certain is that it was not here. The original stadium ran from north-west to the south-east. It seems to have been abandoned early in the fourth century BC, and the south stoa was built over it. The remains however are fascinating. There is a pit from which shallow grooves radiate along the surface of the triangular pavement. It is evident that this was part of the starting mechanism. The starter stood in the pit holding cords leading to all the starting gates. He could thus simultaneously open all the gates. The later stadium lies to the south-east in an open space in the hills hollowed out by a river. It was in use from about 390 BC to the destruction of Corinth by the Romans in 146. It was just under 200 m in length, with the starting line at the open end of the little valley. It was oriented, according to the lie of the land, at right angles to its predecessor.

Other remains within the sanctuary include a fourth-century theatre, where roof-tiles were discovered with the name of Poseidon or with a dolphin and trident, and a bath-building of the Roman period. We are told that in classical times the sanctuary was framed by a row of pine trees on one side and of statues of victorious athletes on the other. Neither can be seen today, though there are plenty of pine trees in the hills round about.

Nemea used to be an exquisite site with sweet-scented shrubs all around. Pindar describes it as 'beneath the shady hills of Phlius' (Pind. *N.* 6, 45), and we know that it was in origin a sacred grove of cypresses, long since vanished. The desire to explore the site has stripped it of the shrubs, and it is today a somewhat bare open tract. The games as a panhellenic event date from 573 BC. Nemea, like Olympia, does not lie near a major city-state, and the festival was administered by the little village of Cleonae up until 460 BC when Argos decided to take it over.

The foundation has the clearest legendary associations with Heracles, who killed the Nemean lion here, and instituted the games in commemoration. But an alternative story, perhaps with political overtones, attributes the foundation to Adrastus, a hero or demigod from Argos. He is said to have killed the snake which killed Opheltes, left alone by his nurse Hypsipyle. The Tomb of Opheltes was a feature of the sanctuary though the mound which used to be so identified has been shown to belong to the Christian period. The probably authentic site has recently been identified by a bronze statuette of a baby boy found nearby (*BSA Arch. Rep.* 1979–80, 25). So here too in the legendary origins is a conflict with a snake (as at Olympia), a funerary celebration, and the ubiquitous name of Heracles in a contest of his own.

Pindar celebrated winners of the chariot race, pancratium, boys' wrestling, boys' pancratium, boys' pentathlon, double footrace, wrestling. We note the predominance of boys' events, which were found at Olympia but took a relatively minor place there. The competitors seem to have come from a relatively circumscribed area of the Greek world, Athens and Aegina, Argos and the Peloponnese, and a few of the islands; there were few from Magna Graecia, though Chromius of Aetna won the chariot race, probably in 474. The prize at Nemea was a crown of wild celery; this appears on a coin of Argos of the Roman period with the inscription NEMEIA.

At Nemea the main feature of the site is the temple of Zeus. Its present form dates from the middle of the fourth century BC. It is Doric, but the columns are unusually slender, and the temple less long than usual in proportion to its breadth. It is peripteral hexastyle with thirteen columns along the sides. The capitals in the inner colonnade were Corinthian. There was a secret inner chamber or *adyton*, reached by some rough steps. It was preceded by an early sixth-century temple, perhaps with an entablature of wood, and vividly painted ridge acroteria. There was a huge altar in front of the temple, long, narrow, and not easy to parallel. Other remains include a palaestra with baths attached. A pentagonal enclosure some 35 m wide was unroofed with trees and altars, perhaps the shrine of a hero: from the fifth century we have ashes of sacrifice, dozens of miniature and full-size drinking-vessels, lead curse-tablets, coins, and a few statuettes (*BSA Arch. Rep.* 1980–1, 12). A large rectangular building appears to have been a hostel or hotel. One of the stones reused in repairs during the Roman period bore an honorific inscription to Pheidon of Cleonae for his four victories in the pancratium, a remarkable achievement. Other apartments were found to the north of the sanctuary. One of the most interesting features of the site was a tunnel leading to the stadium. The architectural features of this seem derived from Persia. Athletes scratched their names here, and it was perhaps used for locker rooms; we know the boxer Telestas, because he was at Olympia in 340. There were fixtures in the doorways from a rope or chain, and holes in the walls perhaps held clothes. Admirers scratched KALOS ('handsome', 'gorgeous') against some of the names.

Three hundred coins and six finger-rings were found near the entrance. It is thought that these might have been thrown by admirers and never collected. This tunnel was later used as a hideout by the Christians during the Slavic invasion of AD 580 (*BSA Arch. Rep.* 1978–9, 12–13). The stadium itself is much eroded (ibid. 1980–1, 12). The venue for the games seems to have been shifted to Argos in about 270 BC.

These four were recognized as the great panhellenic festivals, though it is not easy to see why they were singled out from a multiplicity of other festivals which remained local. Probably Olympia had the primacy, which is recognized in the historical traditions. The Pythian games owed their success to the reputation of the oracle. The Isthmian and Nemean games were perhaps developed through the patronage of Corinth and Argos. Sparta and Athens played no part in this. Since her revolution – whenever that was – Sparta had withdrawn from such activities. Athens had not reached her position of later dominance, and – whatever date we place on Solon's reforms – was in economic turmoil. So the Panathenaea, though probably founded at much the same time, never achieved the international reputation of the others. It *was* panhellenic; at least we know of a wrestler from Argos achieving first prize (Pind. *N*. 10, 35), and we can suppose that there was a great influx into the city from other parts of the Greek world. We know too that in the fifth century, during the period of the Athenian empire, dependent states were expected to participate in the festival, at least by sending a suit of armour and an ox as an offering (*IG* I $^2$45 etc.). Some of the competitions, however, seem to have been open to Athenians only, and were organized on a tribal basis. One of these was the regatta, in which a prize was given to the victorious tribe 'for the feasting' (*SIG*$^3$ 271). In addition to the normal athletics events, horseracing and chariot racing, there was a contest in the Pyrrhic dance, a war-dance in armour, perhaps to be seen in a relief from the Acropolis, a curious contest in physical fitness (*euandria*), a torch race, and a whole series of musical events. The athletic events were in three classes, for boys, beardless youths, and adults. The stadium lay approximately where the modern stadium stands. From the fifth century the musical events were held in the Odeon of Pericles. The chariot racing was away from the city towards the coast, and the regatta in the bay.

One of the great united festivals was the Panionia, which brought together the twelve scattered settlements of Ionian Greeks along the coast of Asia Minor to honour Poseidon Heliconius. It was held at a sanctuary on the promontory of Mycale between Samos and Miletus. Old Sir William Gell claimed to have found the word Panionia twice on stones built into a church hereabouts. Archaeology unfortunately cannot tell us the original date of the cult. The precinct has been identified, and a large altar 20 m long and council chamber have been found, but they date only from the sixth century. Certainly the peninsula was occupied from some time in the second millennium; it is at least possible that the Ionians took over a preexisting cult. The temple of Poseidon has disappeared without trace. The priest was always a young man from Priene, appointed with the title 'king'. One of the features of the festival was the sacrifice of a bull which gave a good omen if it roared at the moment of despatch. It does not seem that there were games attached to this festival; indeed it was more important as a political gathering at which politically binding resolutions were taken (Hdt. 1, 141; 1, 170). Diodorus (15, 49) seems to think that the festival was transferred to the neighbourhood of Ephesus. This is almost certainly an error, contradicted by Strabo (14, 639). There was another united festival at Ephesus, in honour not of Poseidon but Artemis, to which the Ionians came. This was an annual festival. It had political as well as religious significance. It went back at least to the fifth century BC, and surely beyond. We know that there were special sacrifices to Artemis, and that there were games and contests (Hesych. s.v. Ephesia).

Strabo compares the gathering of the Ionians for the Ephesia with the gathering for the Delia. This was a quadrennial festival in honour of Apollo on the island of Delos. It certainly went back to the eighth or seventh century, as the Homeric Hymn testifies (3, 146–55) in which the Ionians are depicted as gathering with their children and shy wives, and delighting the god by their boxing and dancing and singing. Participants came from the islands, the coastal towns, and, from an early stage, from Athens. We shall take a closer look at the cults of Delos later. For the moment we can concentrate on the areas associated with the festival. The sacrifices will have been offered in the great sanctuary of Apollo. Although we know of a temple of Artemis going back into the Bronze Age, we know of no such temple of Apollo. There must have been an early temple. The oldest, not much before 500 BC, is the so-called Porinos, though some granite substructures may relate to an earlier temple. From the mid-fifth century the focus was probably the Great Temple (still quite small), peripteral hexastyle with thirteen columns at the sides. As we move north from there we pass the sanctuary of the Twelve Gods, and move between the terrace of the lions and the Sacred Wheel-Lake. Beyond this are two palaestras, known as the Granite Palaestra and the Lake Palaestra. Both date from the second century BC but have underneath them the foundations of earlier buildings. In the Lake Palaestra was found a magnificent bronze head, broken from a statue, perhaps of a victor solemn in thought at the transience of human glory. Beyond these practice grounds is a vast open space bounded to the west by an archaic wall. Here must have been the hippodrome for horse- and chariot-racing. Beyond that on the left it is strange to pass so close to the Archegesion, the sanctuary of the mysterious Anios, the demigod founder of the city of Delos, dating from the early sixth century, and comprising a long building with small rooms (called in inscriptions 'The Houses') and a courtyard with a round sacrificial altar; strange, because foreigners were forbidden to enter. A fine archaic *kouros* was found here, and numerous vases and sherds with the name of Anios. Next comes a large gymnasium which we know from an inscription was founded in the third century. Beyond this is the stadium with a *xystus* or covered track alongside to the west, and a street to the east with houses on the far side, one of which contained an altar covered with religious paintings. It is interesting that the synagogue is not far away. We do not know of Jewish competitors here, though we do elsewhere, and as early as the third century there were victors at Delos from the Phoenician cities of Byblos and Sidon.[3] The musical events will have been held in the theatre.

In the Hellenistic Age, though the victor in the circuit of the four great festivals is still found (*CIA* III add. 758a; II 3, 1319, 1323), other lesser festivals are more frequently mentioned in the inscriptions. Records from Attica alone refer to festivals all over the Greek world, the Eleusinia (where we know of a chariot-victory at an earlier period: *CIA* I 419), Amphiaraa, Trophonia, Heraclea in Thebes, Dionysia, Thargelia and Naa in Dodona, Delia, Soteria, Ephesia, Claria, Iliaea, and from the Roman period, Thesea, Epitaphia, Hephaestea, Charitesia at Orchomenus, Hadrianeia, Eusebea, Capitolea and Panhellenia (*CIA* II 3, 1302; 23; III 107–28). So many were the festivals that a man of Tegea could claim forty-three victories (*CIG* 1515). We know of festivals in Macedon and Thrace, Thessaly and throughout mainland Greece, Sicily, Massilia, Corcyra, Cyprus, Rhodes, Cos, Chios, Delos, Icaria, Naxos, Paros, Tenos and Thera,

Cyrene, and the cities of Asia Minor. This immense proliferation of festivals was designed to attract people from other states. We should not be too cynical about these. No doubt the people of Oberammergau do benefit economically from the influx of visitors for the Passion Play, but this does not mean that they are insincere in their religious dedication. An example of the new institutions is the four-yearly Actia inaugurated by Augustus in honour of Apollo at Nicopolis to celebrate his victory at Actium. There were horse-racing, wrestling, musical contests and sea-fights. This was probably a restoration and elaboration of a festival at the old temple on the promontory. Even in its ruined state the theatre remains impressive; the site of the stadium lay hard by. Within the Byzantine walls Augustus's odeon, built for the festival, has been delightfully restored. This festival was given the title 'Sacred', and ranked with the four panhellenic festivals. It was imitated elsewhere. Hierapolis, for example, had its Olympia, Pythia, and Actia. Many more examples could be taken. Athletic and musical prowess had become a matter of individual professionalism rather than civic pride. But it was still exercised in the context of a religious festival, and in those religious festivals the new cities took their pride.

# 6

# ORACLES

Dodona is a site of great beauty, an upland valley nearly 2,000 feet above sea-level, harsh in winter, radiant in spring.

Here stood an oracular sanctuary of Zeus of great antiquity. Here, as the exploration of the sanctuary has shown, was a sacred place whose sanctity goes back long before the coming of the Hellenes, since the accumulation of pottery, stone axeheads, and later bronze axeheads and knives goes back to the middle of the third millennium BC and almost certainly represents votive deposits. Zeus, like Apollo at Delphi, took over from an older occupancy, an oracle of Earth. Archaeological evidence further shows that Zeus was here associated not with Hera, the great mother goddess of the Argive plain, but with his older consort Dione, who had her own shrine. Priestesses were involved as well as priests.

In *The Iliad* Achilles prays for Patroclus:

> Lord Zeus of Dodona, Pelasgian, living far off,
> ruler of Dodona's harsh winters; around whom the Selloi live,
> your spokesmen, sleeping on the soil, never washing their feet
> (16, 233–5)

The reference to the Selloi, sleeping in contact with the Earth, with their curiously unpleasant ritual obligations, as spokesmen or interpreters, suggests an oracle, and in the *Odyssey* (14, 327–8; 19, 296–7) this is explicitly mentioned as associated with an oak tree. So too in Hesiod: 'He went to the oak-grove of Dodona, where the Pelasgi live' (fr. apud Strab. 7, 327). A more extended passage runs:

> There is a place Ellopia with ploughland and meadows in plenty,
> rich in flocks of sheep and shambling cattle.

## AMONG THE GODS

> The men who live there have copious flocks and herds,
> themselves uncountable, tribes of mortal men.
> There on its frontier is built the city of Dodona.
> Zeus loved it and appointed it to be his oracle
> and in honour among men . . .
>                      . . . they lived in the hollow of an oak.
> From there humans carry away prophecies of all kinds –
> anyone who comes and questions the immortal god
> bringing gifts, and accompanied by good omens.
>                      (fr. apud Schol. Soph. *Trach.* 1167)

'They' are doves. The presence of doves as part of the oracle accounts for the shrine of Aphrodite which exists among the ruins, for doves are sacred to her. Heracles was also here and had his shrine; he was the legendary ancestor of the kings of Epirus. Sophocles makes him say, as he nears his death:

> I will show later oracles coming
> to similar conclusions, matching those of old.
> When I went to the grove of the Selloi who live in the hills
> and sleep on the ground, I wrote them down.
> They came from the many-voiced oak of my father.
>                      (*Trachiniae* 1164–8)

His shrine gave up a rich deposit of bronze votive gifts.

The sanctuary was long without monumental buildings. In the fourth century BC the particular sacred oak was set in a small courtyard which also enshrined a small building which was the house of the God (*Arch. Delt.* 16, 4–40). It was perhaps because of souvenir hunters, as the sacred palm tree on Delos was damaged by scraping, that the sanctuary was enclosed. Now perhaps caldrons which rang in the wind were replaced by a statue given by Corcyra, a bronze of a boy with a whip, ending in knucklebones, which rang against a caldron. It is not clear whether the oracle was given by the rustling of the oak leaves, the murmur of doves, or the sound of the caldron.

It was the Hellenistic Age, and particularly the reign of King Pyrrhus in the early third century BC, which saw the spectacular buildings, the great theatre, 10 m wider than Epidaurus, the stadium, and the council chamber. Scully has an important imaginative analysis of the site. The treasuries are organized in an arc around the temple, irregularly, completing, dynamically not statically, the circle of the valley. The arrangement of the buildings complements the natural scene, and speaks of wholeness, the wholeness of sky and earth; it reflects the sacred marriage, the *hieros gamos*.

Archaeology has unearthed for us a series of lead tablets extending from the fifth to the second century BC and recording questions put to the oracle. The first, which dates from the terrible civil strife of the fifth century, is political, as is the second, but most are personal.

> God. Good Fortune. The people of Corcyra communicate to Zeus Naos and Dione their desire to know which god or hero they should invoke and honour with sacrifice to ensure the blessings of concord.

There is tragic pathos here, which adds to the pages of Thucydides.

> The commonwealth of . . . ask Zeus Naos and Dione whether it is safe for them to join politically with the Molossi.

> God. Good Fortune. Evandros and his wife communicate a request to Zeus Naos and Dione. Which god, hero or spirit should they invoke with prayer and honour with sacrifice to secure present and permanent prosperity for themselves and their household? [*Answer*] Evandros.

The response is obscure. Has he to make up his own mind, or sacrifice to an eponymous ancestor, or sacrifice to the son of Hermes and the nymph Themis or Nicostrate?

> Would it be good and profitable for me to purchase for myself the house in town and the plot of ground?

> God. Good Fortune. Antiochus asks Zeus and Dione about his own health and that of his father and sister. Which god or hero is it best and most valuable to honour? [*Answer*] He should go quickly to Hermio.

Hermio is perhaps Hermes, but there may be deliberate ambiguity.

> Cleutas asks Zeus and Dione if there is any profit for him in rearing sheep. [*Answer*] From rearing sheep.

> God, Zeus, Dione will he do better to go off to Alyzea? [*Answer*] Live where he is and hold on.

> God. Fortune. Aeschylinus asks Zeus Naios and Dione whether it would not be better for him to sail to Adria to the Tisates. [*Answer*] No.

Good Fortune. Shall I meet success as a merchant if I follow my own flair for gain, decide on my own course, and use my navigational skills?

Lysanias asks Zeus Naios and Deona whether the child Annyla is carrying is his or not.

Agis asks Zeus Naos and Dione about the blankets and pillows which . . . has lost. Could they have been taken by an outside burglar? [*Answer*] Agis. (*Rec. IG* 843–51)

In the last answer it is not clear whether the oracle is charging Agis with the theft, or implying that he must do his own detective work. There are many other queries. Genoton asks about marriage, Anaxippus whether he can hope for a son from his present wife, Leontius about his son's health. There is a question about the kidnapping of a slave and another, obscure because of the jargon, about some chicanery in horseracing. In general these oracular questions bring home to us the ordinary life of ordinary people.[1]

Delphi, with its temple of Apollo, is the best-known of the oracular sites of mainland Greece. It is a numinous place, high above the gorge of the Pleistos, whose silver ribbon trails its way among the thickly clustered grey-green olives. Above tower the Shining Rocks, the Phaedriades, two precipices some 300 m high guarding the heights of Parnassus, roseate and imposing. It is an earthquake-riven area, and the cleft which divides the west from the east, the Bear Gorge, where the waters of Castalia flow out, continues down to the valley beneath.

Apollo, as we have noted, was a latecomer. The site of his temple was occupied in the Mycenaean period, but the remains are purely secular and domestic. Indications are found of religious usage elsewhere in the sanctuary, including a limestone libation vessel in the form of a lioness's head (*Fouilles* V 3; *BCH* 59 (1935) 528ff.).

By tradition this was a sanctuary of Earth (Ge).

> First of the gods in this my prayer I honour
> Earth, the first prophetess, and, after her, Themis,
> second to sit in her mother's oracle,
> tradition says. Then in the third place,
> willingly and not constrained by force,
> another child of Earth received the seat,
> the Titaness Phoebe. She gave it as a birthday gift
> to Phoebus, who takes his name from hers.
>
> (Aeschylus, *Eumenides* 1–8)

Some of the myths, represented often enough on vases, are more violent, and tell how Apollo had to conquer the shrine by killing the monstrous snake Pytho, who 'ministered the oracle of Earth' (*chthonion*: Eur. *IT* 1248), and had to do penance for his sacrilegious act.

Archaeology goes far to confirm this picture. In the first place, a goddess, in classical times Athene, had her sanctuary at Delphi, and it was of great antiquity, going back to the Bronze Age. It was on a lower level than the sanctuary of Apollo, and on the other side of the gorge of Castalia. One puzzling feature is that its use as a sanctuary seems to antedate the sacredness of the other site. Possibly this reflects the intrusion of Apollo upon an older cult. Athene's sanctuary is on a narrow terrace. The oldest surviving temple dates from the seventh century; it was twice restored, for the site is subject to landslide.

Secondly, we should expect that in the Mycenaean period a goddess would be worshipped, and an area so reft with chasms is a natural place to worship the goddess Earth.

Thirdly, one of the most obviously sacred places in the sanctuary is a towering rock which lies above the Sacred Way a little below Apollo's temple. This is traditionally called the Rock of the Sibyl, and it is said that the Sibyl used to give oracles from there.

Fourthly, the very fact that a prophetess gave the oracles suggests that Apollo was not the original oracular power, for elsewhere his ministers are priests, except at Argos where the cult was probably an offshoot of Delphi. Further, on a well-known red-figure vase of about 440 BC we see a stylized representation of a consultation, in which the priestess is named not Pythia but Themis.

Fifthly, the omphalos, the sacred stone which marked the navel of the world – for Delphi was believed to be the centre of the world – was typical of the sacred stones associated with the goddess of the Minoan–Mycenaean period. The stone actually found had the name of Ge scratched on it.

For the process of consultation we have to combine literary and archaeological evidence. The oracles were given by a priestess seated on a tripod, as we see her in the cup referred to above, where a veil or hood covers the back of her head, her dress flowing down to her ankles, and she sits, slightly bowed, with a laurel twig in her right hand and a bowl in her left. Some myths we can dismiss. There was no chasm with vaporous fumes to create a state of ecstasy. No such chasm exists under Apollo's temple, and the limestone and schist which surround Delphi do not emit such gases and cannot have done so. Laurel is certainly closely connected with the oracle, but there is no suggestion before the second century AD that the priestess chewed laurel leaves; she is not doing so on the vase; and although there is a little prussic acid in some varieties, she would not have been put into a state of ecstasy by such consumption, and a worthy modern scholar who carried out the experiment remained uninspired. She was not inspired by drinking holy water. Castalia is associated with poetic not prophetic inspiration. Another spring, Cassotis, rose just above the temple, and plunged underground. Pausanias (10, 24, 7) said that the waters of this emerged within the temple to give her inspiration, but archaeology shows that they did not do so. Ecstasy can be induced simply by meditation. One wonders however what the bowl in her hand was for. It may have been to pour a libation to the god, but it might have contained a substance giving off fumes, or even water to produce a mirrored hypnotic effect.

We can then recover something of the process of consultation. The enquirer came, in Plutarch's time only on nine days of the year, one each month and none in the winter (Plut. *Mor.* 292D; 398A). The priestess cleansed herself in Castalia (Schol. Eur. *Phoen.* 224) and was purified further with a preparation of barley meal and laurel leaves (Plut. *Mor.* 397A). At the pool today, though the cuttings are old, the scene has changed. A low wall, now broken down, with spouts in it, separated the channel from the basin. The water flowed from right to left in the channel. The priests now took a goat before Apollo. If it trembled the day was auspicious, and it is said that they encouraged trembling by sprinkling it with cold water (ibid. 435B; 437B; 438A). The goat was sacrificed next, presumably on the great altar before the temple. The priestess now entered the sanctuary. It is likely but not certain that she entered an underground chamber. There are indications of such a chamber with no other obvious use. At Aegeira on the other side of the Gulf of Corinth there was an oracle of Ge where the priestess used to descend into a cave (Paus. 7, 25, 13; Plin. *NH* 28, 147). Such a supposition might help to explain some accounts of her descent. She would then emerge and take her place on the tripod, as we see on the cup referred to, now taken up into the god or momentarily ready for this. The tripod was the god's seat, as we see in some reliefs; she is thus one with him. It is likely, again from reliefs, that the tripod was surrounded with laurels. A block from the floor of the shrine with three holes in a triangular pattern indicates the place of the tripod (*AJA* 37, 208). The enquirer was also required to take a lustral bath, and offer an expensively bought sacred cake at the altar outside. He – or she – was then admitted in due order to the temple; on the vase we see him – or the prophet on his behalf – standing before the priestess. He put his question to the prophet who put it to the priestess. Her answer was interpreted by the priests, often in hexameters, and available in writing if wanted. We have records of other means of response, but this was the usual pattern. No permanent record of enquiries and answers, such as were found at Dodona, has survived at Delphi. This means inevitably that, dependent on literary sources, we hear more of the great political consultations than about enquiries from private individuals, though we should not forget that when in Euripides's play Creusa arrives at Delphi the young temple attendant asks her 'Crops or children?' (Eur. *Ion* 303), a fair indication of the expected topics. We have however in a verse inscription an elaborated account from the fourth century BC of a private consultation. A mother had evidently been through terrible traumas in pregnancy and had a series of miscarriages. She consulted the oracle, who encouraged her, telling her to dedicate her child's hair when born. According to the inscription she had an easy pregnancy and eleven months after the consultation in a gentle labour gave birth to a child named Delphis. Three years later she had another child whom they named Pytho (*Fouilles* III 1, 560). In another inscription we learn of a private enquirer who was told to attend the Pythian games (*BCH* (1882) 88), but we do not know why.[2]

A visit to the site is an evocative experience. The modern visitor sometimes regrets the crowds – but with them he is seeing it with the hordes of people who must have been there for the sacred days of consultation. For the oracle we can concentrate on the western site, not forgetting, however, the waters of Castalia. The beginning of the Sacred Way lay at the bottom of the sanctuary, in the south-east corner. In front of the gate is a large paved square flanked by Ionic porticoes and shops where, we may assume, religious tokens were available for sale. Five steps lead up to the Sacred Way which is 4 m or so in width; the present paving dates from Roman times. On either side are records of public gratitude, to the right the base which carried a bronze bull dedicated by Corcyra to celebrate a miraculous draught of fishes about 480 BC. Beyond is a large rectangular recess of unknown purpose, and in front of it the base which carried statues of nine gods and heroes of the Arcadians in honour of their victory over

Sparta in 370–369, and a base with an inscription indicating that it carried a statue of Philopoemen. On the other side the Spartans put up a huge monument for their victory over Athens in 404. Beyond, ironically, were a Trojan Horse given by Argos to celebrate a victory over Sparta, an offering of sixteen statues by Athens in memory of Marathon, and another offering from Argos. Next we come to two exedrae, one on each side, also dedicated by Argos. Beyond these, to the left is the base of an offering from Taras in south Italy, to the right a square niche covered with records of decrees.

We now come to the treasuries of the several cities, where were stored smaller offerings and important records. To the left is the treasury of Sicyon, dating from about 500 BC, but replacing an older building which had been adorned with the archaic metopes whose remains may be seen in the museum. The treasury of Siphnos was intended to surpass the others in splendour; they had their own gold mines to draw on. The northern frieze which fronted the Sacred Way showed the battle of the gods and giants. The others showed the Judgement of Paris, the Trojan War, and an uncertain theme. The treasuries on the other side are now scarcely discernible. One may have belonged to Megara, one to some Aeolian state. At this point, 'the Crossroads of the Treasuries', the Sacred Way sweeps sharply uphill to the right. Straight ahead the road continues to the west gate, passing the treasury of the Thebans and the almost totally destroyed treasury of the Boeotians. Above, to the left of the Sacred Way is the treasury of the Athenians, built with a tithe of the spoils from Marathon out of marble from Paros, and excellently reconstructed. It was placed on a terrace with a triangular extension which carried some of the booty for all to see. The inscription, 'The Athenians dedicate to Apollo the spoils of the Medes after the Battle of Marathon', is a third-century copy of the original. The metopes of the treasury showed heroic scenes involving Heracles and Theseus. The walls were covered with over 150 inscriptions, some honorific decrees, some relating to special embassies to Delphi, and, most interestingly, two hymns to Apollo with the musical notation interlineated in Greek letters. Behind are the minor remains of the treasury of Potidaea, and the treasury of the Etruscans. Opposite are the treasury of Syracuse (celebrating their victory over Athens in 413 – another confrontation) and the treasury of Cnidos (an early foundation), and, far beyond to the east, the treasury of Cyrene. The rich treasury of Corinth lay somewhat higher, and beyond it lay two treasuries totally destroyed.

We are coming towards one of the especially sanctified points. But first, above the treasury of the Athenians is the *bouleuterion*, the meeting place of the Council of Delphi, significantly within the sanctuary, as is the *prytaneion*, which lies over to the east. Above the council chamber is the sanctuary of Ge-Themis, marked by its rocks, especially the Rock of Prophecy associated with the Sibyl, and by a cleft in the earth. Behind stood a column dedicated by the island of Naxos and carrying a sphinx. Now the Sacred Way crosses the *halos*, or threshing floor, a large level open space for the enactment of sacred drama. Above we can see the dignified stoa of the Athenians erected in gratitude for the victory over Persia. A fine archaic inscription proclaims: 'The Athenians dedicated the portico, the arms and the figureheads captured from the enemy.' Behind this again is the extraordinary polygonal wall of the temple terrace, built of large stones whose curving surfaces fit perfectly in a complex jigsaw. In the second and first centuries BC and the first AD this was covered with more than 800 inscriptions on a variety of topics including records of the manumission of slaves.

The Sacred Way climbs steeply along the east front of the temple platform. Hereabouts were a large number of rich dedications, some of the more extravagant coming from the kings of Pergamon. Notable are the site of the Tripod of Plataea where a tripod with a central column of intertwining snakes, inscribed with the names of the allies at Plataea, carried a golden caldron. The remains of the snake column stand in the Hippodrome in Istanbul, and some of the names are still discernible. Another evocative base, dedicated by Rhodes, carried the chariot of the sun god Helios. This also was removed by Constantine for his new capital and looted from there by the Venetians in 1204. A careful comparison of the cuttings on the statue base with the horses on St Mark's in Venice suggests a perfect match. Yet another base carried the acanthus column with the three dancing girls, now in the museum, dedicated by Athens in 335–325 BC. The dancers have been supposed to be Thyiads, honouring Dionysus, who guarded Delphi during the winter months, or the three daughters of Cecrops. Other dedications came from Sicily for their victories over Carthage. Over to the east lay the Stoa of Attalus, a late addition to the sanctuary, and a somewhat strange one, since it was allowed to break the line of the sanctuary wall.

Now we are at the great temple itself. In the forecourt stands a large altar dedicated by Chios to celebrate its deliverance from the

Persians. It is of some interest in that its alignment is not precisely that of the temple; it must have followed the alignment of the previous altar which followed the alignment of the previous temple. Inscriptions read 'The Chians this altar to Apollo' and 'Delphi granted the right of promanteia to the Chians' – that is precedence in consultation after the local authority. More offerings stood round about. They included a huge statue of Apollo 15.5 m tall and a bronze palm tree with a gold Athene dedicated by Athens to celebrate the victory at Eurymedon. They also included an equestrian statue of Prusias II of Bithynia and a statue of Eumenes II of Pergamon. These reflect changing religious values, since the Hellenistic monarchs had a semi-divine status. They also reflect the power of money, since they were generous benefactors. The temple remains impressive with its re-erected columns towering above the desolation of bases without their superstructures. Complete it must have dominated the complete scene. It was of the Doric order, peripteral hexastyle, measuring $60 \times 21.8$ m with fifteen columns along the sides. Among its predecessors according to tradition were legendary shrines of laurel, wax, and bronze. Archaeology can record only the immediate predecessors, also Doric. The first built in about 650 BC was destroyed by fire in 548. A new temple was built in about 510. This was supported by a panhellenic collection; the final construction work was carried out by the Alcmaeonid family, in exile from Athens. The pediments, whose remains are in the museum, showed the battle of gods and giants, and the epiphany of Dionysus. Earthquakes destroyed this in 373, and a rebuilding on the same foundations was not completed till about 330. This time the pediments showed the epiphany of Apollo at one end and his partner Dionysus at the other. There were no carved metopes, the spaces being hung with shields captured from the Persians in the Persian War and from the Gauls in 279 BC.

The Delphic oracle played its part in the establishment of common moral principles throughout Greece, and our literary sources associate the shrine with the precepts 'Know yourself', 'Avoid excess', and the mysterious letter E, whose significance is unexplained. An inscription from in front of the temple shows more comprehensively the morality inculcated ($SIG\,^3$1268):

> Help friends. Control anger. Avoid injustice. Acknowledge religion. Control pleasure. Watch luck. Honour forethought. No oaths. Love friendship. Grasp learning. Pursue repute. Praise virtue. Act

justly. Return favours. Cherish friends. Avoid enemies. Cultivate relatives. Shun evil. Be accessible. Guard property. Oblige friends. Hate violence. Be gently-spoken. Pity suppliants. Educate sons.

Fulfil your capacity. Be kind to all. Exercise authority over your wife. Do well by yourself. Be affable. Give timely answers. Work with a good reputation. Repent mistakes. Control your eye. Guard friendship. Consider the time. Act promptly. Dispense justice. Practise harmony. Despise none. Keep secrets. Respect those in power. Trust time. Do not indulge in small-talk. Worship the divine. Accept opportunity. Dissolve enmity. Do not glory in your strength. Accept old age. Use what is beneficial. Speak words of good omen. Be ashamed of a lie. Shun enmity.

In the area above the temple the most significant structures are the shrine of Dionysus, the rectangular exedra which can be identified by an inscription as dedicated by Craterus in thanks that he saved the life of Alexander the Great in a lion hunt, the offering of Polyzalus of which the famous bronze charioteer formed a part, and the splendid fourth-century theatre.

In our picture of Delphi we cannot ignore literary sources. The guidebook of Pausanias in particular is essential for identification. Plutarch, who was a priest here and loved the place, wrote widely about it. We have evidence from historians and dramatists and poets. But it all must be tested by the evidence of our eyes. Delphi was an oracle. It was more than an oracle. It was a prime centre for the worship of Apollo. It housed one of the great panhellenic festivals. But it was an oracle first and foremost, and the complexity of the site gives us some idea of the complexity of a successful oracle, and the ramifications of Greek religious emotion. The oracle shows the cardinal importance of two emotions – anxiety and gratitude. Without anxiety the oracle would hardly have any being. But it was gratitude which covered the sacred site with treasuries and statues and other offerings. Nothing is stranger at Delphi than the number of offerings in gratitude for the victory over the Persians, when we reflect that the oracle was charged with medizing – going over to the Persian side. Yet the more impressive offerings were here rather than at Olympia. We also have the sense of the god as protector. Important records are safe in his keeping.[3]

Not far from Delphi was the oracle of an oracular god named Trophonius. This is mentioned in the fifth century by Euripides (*Ion*

300) in a dramatic context centuries earlier. Our main source of information is Pausanias (9, 39, 5–14), who personally consulted the oracle, though his account is not necessarily valid for the earlier period. According to Pausanias the enquirer had to spend a number of days in a building dedicated to the Good Spirit and Good Fortune, engaging in purificatory ritual and offering sacrifices. The final sacrifice was of a ram offered over a pit (and therefore an offering to powers of the underworld) with an invocation of Agamedes, Trophonius's legendary brother. If all was propitious he was escorted to the sacred river Hercyna for a ritual washing and anointing, then to two springs, drinking the waters of Forgetfulness and the waters of Memory. He was then shown an ancient image. Dressed in ritual garments he now went to the shrine, descending by a ladder into an underground vault. This was merely the anteroom to the true shrine, a cave reached by a narrow aperture at floor level. Grasping two barley cakes kneaded with honey in his hands he thrust his feet through the aperture and waited. Suddenly he found himself whisked through. The answer to the oracle was given sometimes in words, sometimes through spectacle, after which he returned the way he came, needing a period of recuperation before leaving. All enquirers had to dedicate an account of the response given them: unfortunately none of these has survived. The oracle has been identified.[4] It is situated outside Levadhia on the slopes of Mt Ayios Elias. On the left bank of the river spring the waters of Memory; there are votive niches in the rock. A narrow passage leads to the Waters of Forgetfulness. The temple was perhaps sited where the chapel of the Panayia stands; inscriptions referring to Trophonius have been found there. Higher up a fourteenth-century fortress contains ancient stonework. The oracle is thought to have been under the summit where there are the remains of a circular subterranean construction. It is altogether a beautiful and awesome place.

    On the west coast of Greece in Epirus the river Acheron and its tributary the Cocytus flow out into a harbour long silted up, by the town of Ephyra. Here stood an oracle of the dead, excavated by Sotiris Dakaris from 1958. The site is mentioned by Herodotus as among the Thesprotians.

    Underground, below the exact middle of the sacred compound, lies a cave, which was believed to belong to the world of the dead. From the presence of Mycenaean pottery and a Mycenaean tomb within the sanctuary this was clearly a sacred place of high antiquity. It was in this shrine that Odysseus is supposed to have consulted the dead seer Teiresias about his return to Ithaca. Statuettes of Persephone date from the seventh century BC, and some black-figure sherds of the sixth century, attest the archaic shrine, associated with a rock and a cave. The present remains, a vast rectangular structure 62.4 × 46.3 m, bare and sinister outside, and originally pyramid-shaped, are Hellenistic. They enable us to discern the process of consultation. The inner sanctum can be reached only by entering from the north, passing round three sides of a square, zigzagging through rooms with traces of iron grilles and finally coming in from the south. Rooms to the north, dark and windowless, but with hearths, beds, and washing facilities, may have been used for incubation in the hope of oracular dreams, or purificatory rights. Thirty-seven storage jars were used for food, and sulphur which could have given an eerie light. The enquirer entered the enclosure from the north side, and turned left to a series of rooms where he was ritually cleansed, ate special foods including beans containing hallucinogenic elements (traces of these have been discovered), and slept. His time was spent in darkness or near-darkness. He might remain there for days. When he was ready to proceed with the consultation (having been, as we might say, softened up) he threw a stone to a heap already there: this was familiar magic to resist hostile magic. He then sacrificed a sheep over a hole in the ground. We know from various sources that the victim will have been black, and will have had its throat cut from underneath. Bones and charcoal have been found in a trench of this kind. He then made a further offering of barley flour, lupin seeds, and honey in vases with a broad opening: some of these have been found. Now he moved, no doubt in something of a trance, along tortuous corridors to the place of consultation. A little before the inner sanctum were the remains of broken jugs, perhaps to pour libations for the dead to devour, and deliberately broken for their sinister associations. This room had very thick walls. Underneath it was a subterranean chamber in which blocks and pulleys were discovered. Plainly these were used to facilitate appearances and disappearances. The enquirer poured libations to Aidoneus, Lord of the Underworld, and Persephone. We can imagine awe-inducing sounds, perhaps even the barking of Cerberus, the emergence of phosphoric apparitions, a ghostly voice answering the enquiry. Lucian gives a parody of a similar oracle in Mesopotamia. Final destruction was by a raging inferno of fire.[5]

Apollo had other oracles on the mainland. One was at Thebes, where his temple, known as the Ismenion, was set above an ancient oracular cavern. It is fairly clear that here, as at Delphi, the god has usurped the powers of the earth mother.[6] The temple at Corinth was also oracular, and was associated with a sacred spring whose babbling sound was translated into oracular responses.[7]

Apollo had his oracles in Asia too.

At Didyma, within the territory of Miletus, the Sacred Way from the port of Panormus was lined with lions and sphinxes, tombs and statues. Some 100 m from Apollo's temple was a sacred grove. A monumental altar 8 m in diameter stood 9 m in front of the temple, adorned with Medusas and lions' heads; there were three other plinths for offerings.

We have plenty of information about the oracle at Didyma. Pausanias says that it antedated Ionian colonization: presumably then Apollo took over, as at Delphi, encouraged by the accidental resemblance of the Anatolian name to the Greek for twins. Inscriptions go back to about the seventh century BC. The Pharaoh Necho made a dedication here. Darius reminded one of his satraps that Apollo had always told the Persians the truth. The legendary founder of the oracle was Branchus, and the hereditary priesthood rested with the Branchidae, efficient but autocratic. They sold out to the Persians, and escaped to the river Oxus. Legend said that a century and a half later Alexander, who had a flair for historical drama, executed their descendants. Historians doubt it, but it is not impossible.

In about 330 Miletus built a new temple, one of the largest in the Greek world. Strabo wrongly calls it the very largest (it is smaller than Artemis at Ephesus or Zeus at Acragas) but it is twice as large as the Parthenon, aligned northeast–southwest with dimensions 117.5 × 60 m, with a foundation of seven steps, and a front ceremonial stairway of thirteen. The temple is dipteral with two rows of twenty-one columns along the sides, and two of ten columns at front and rear. The columns are Ionic, and are the tallest known in Greek architecture, surpassed only by the Corinthian columns at Baalbek in the Roman period. The temple was in fact never fully completed. For this reason it is unusual among Greek temples in showing changes of style (like a Gothic cathedral), the decoration extending from Pergamene to late Roman. Especially noteworthy are the corner capitals in the peristyle with bulls' heads and heads of Apollo in place of the normal Ionic volutes. The *pronaos* is spectacular, with a magnificent roof: the great cella was unroofed.

The architecture helps us to understand the process of consultation. The client would go to the *chresmographeion* or office, a small hypostyle room, 15 × 8 m, about 1 m above the *pronaos*. From there two lateral doors led to vaulted passages leading to the underground *adyton*, a large ornamental court a little over 4 m down, measuring 53.5 × 25 m with a frieze of scrolls, griffins, and lyres in a style which was archaic for the period when this was carved. The clients remained in the room off the *adyton*. The priest and acolytes went down the passage to the holy place. There was a prophetess with a spring which was covered with an Ionic *naiskos*, and exhaled sulphurous vapours. She gave the oracular response; the priests translated it into recognizable Greek, usually in verse, and proclaimed it from a balcony.[8]

At Didyma we have two early responses, both from the sixth century BC, recorded in inscriptions, and published by Th. Wiegand and his colleagues and successors in *Milet*. We have lost the question and occasion in both cases. It seems likely that both were official consultations by the city of Miletus. In the first the answer, in prose, runs 'It will be better and more good for him who obeys, the contrary for him who disobeys.'[9] The response is formulaic, is paralleled from Delphi, and must indicate the god's approval of a law, perhaps cultic. The other response,[10] in verse, incorporates regulations for the cult of Heracles. Women are not to enter the sanctuary. There is to be no eating of greens. The response includes fragmentary regulations for sacrifice.

Another early consultation, about 600 BC, came from young men who were worried about piracy as a profession. The oracle, rather like Gilbert's Father Paul, told them 'It is right to do as your fathers did.' Herodotus has a curious story of Pactyes of Lydia who took asylum from the Persians at Cyme. The Persians demanded extradition. Cyme consulted the oracle which said 'Give him up!' One Aristodicus asked for a confirmatory consultation involving himself. The god gave the same answer. Aristodicus started driving away all the birds from the temple. A voice called 'Most impious man! How dare you act so? Driving away a suppliant from my temple!' He replied 'Mighty Lord, if you care so much for suppliants, why tell Cyme to surrender them?' 'As a punishment for asking an impious question, so as to destroy you; then you'll know it's wrong to ask the oracle whether to betray those who put confidence in you.' This was reported back. Unwilling to risk the anger of the Persians or the destruction threatened by the god, they sent Pactyes off to Mytilene.

Another consultation is recorded in an inscription in the theatre at Miletus. There was an industrial dispute, and strike action was threatened by the building-trade workers. The oracle was asked to arbitrate and told the city to make proper use of building technique, call in an expert, and sacrifice to Athene and Heracles, deities of skill and hard work.

After this there is a gap, but we have a number of records from the third century. A letter of Seleucus II (*Didyma Inschr.* 493 ll. 3–5) tells us that his predecessors have received favourable oracles from the gods. In 228–227 BC the Demos of the Milesians ask about the application of Drerians and Milatians from Crete to be admitted to the citizen body. The answer, in verse, runs 'Receive the support of settlers in your city; for it is better . . .'. There are two other similar questions with answers damaged or lost (*Milet* 1, 3, 33 f 11–14, g 1–4 cf. 1, 3, 33 g 11–2; 1, 3, 36 a). In 225 BC the Demos had received a proposal from a cult association honouring Artemis Boulephorus Sciris about the conduct of her festival, and inquired whether this will win the goddess's approval and so benefit the Demos. The answer is lost but must have endorsed the proposals (*Rev. phil.* 44 (1920) 290; Michel 480). The declaration that Antiochus III should rule with harmony, found in Iasos, probably came from Didyma (Michel 4676). So did the assertion that the city and country of Teos should be sacred and inviolable, found in Crete (*I. Cr.* 1, 19, 2), and the turning of the Didyma festival into a panhellenic occasion, recorded in Cos (*SIG* 590). In about 180 BC Miletus is told to make a treaty with Heracleia-by-Latmos (*Milet* 1, 3, 150; *SIG* 633).

These are political consultations. Not all were such. In about 100 BC, Lochus the son of Lochus, in response to a lost question, is told to 'dedicate it to Apollo of Delos lord of Calymna' (*Inscr. Cos* 60). In about AD 150 Alexandra, priestess of Demeter Thesmophorus, asks why the gods have not given evidence of their power since she became priestess; is this auspicious? The response, in verse, is fragmentary. It declares that the gods are with humans, and make their will known. The priestess is told to honour the mother and daughter, the goddess who produced grain and ended savagery; the appropriate service is in silence and tranquillity (*Didyma Inschr.* 496). In about AD 100 an unknown enquirer asks about building a gymnasium and bath, and seems to be told to incorporate an altar (*Milet* 1, 9, 345). A few years later the builders of the theatre at Miletus ask questions about the arches and vaults, and are sensibly told to call in an expert (*Sitz. Akad. Berlin* (1904) 83). A little later an athlete from Alexandria, Appheion Heronas, asks how to turn in a good performance and is told in verse to pray to Phoebus, Sarapis, and Nemesis (*Milet* 1, 7, 205a 9–11). At much the same period a certain Carpus asks about fulfilling his vow to Sarapis, to be told 'Immortals delight in the honours coming from the good will of mortals' (*Milet* 1, 7, 205 b 4). The oracle, as Robert has shown, was of major importance in the early third century AD (*Comptes Rend. de l'Acad. d'Inscr.* 1968, 568–99; 1971, 597–617).

Finally we may note two consultations by a prophet named Damianus in the reign of Diocletian. In the first he asks permission to found an altar of Kore the Saviour, his ancestral goddess, in the sanctuary, and is told to do so. He then asks for a special epithet for the goddess, and is told to call her 'gentle' (*meilichos*).[11] Apollo shows a notable concern for Demeter, whom he calls Deo.

At Didyma the priest of Apollo was an annual appointment, and he was called *prophetes*. This does not necessarily mean that it was he who was believed to receive the god's direct inspiration. A *prophetes* is not a *mantis*, and at Delphi the *prophetes* was the presiding figure, but it was the Pythia who gave the divine responses. At Didyma there is some literary evidence of a woman seer,[12] though we cannot be certain that it is right.

Evidence of the games at Didyma is provided by a relief of *c*. 160 BC, which has been interpreted as a dedication to the Muses by one of the victors: it is a relief sculpture (now in Istanbul) and shows on the upper level a nymph, Demeter, and Kore, Artemis, Apollo Citharoedus, Leto, and Zeus, a woman, and a water-nymph, and on the lower the nine Muses, Pan, and a writer (*BSA Arch. Rep.* 1978–9, 74; *AA* (1972) 87–105).

Claros is another oracular shrine of Apollo, brilliantly excavated by Louis Robert. At times the oracle appears to have been delivered from a cave in the hills above. The dedications in the lower sanctuary are mostly late, but include a late archaic kouros. There was also found within the sanctuary a column in honour of Quintus Cicero, a sundial dedicated by an aedile, and a decree of the Ionians on asylum at Colophon. The surviving temple dates from about 300 BC and replaced an earlier one. It is of the Doric order, 46 × 24 m, with five steps, and six columns along the front, eleven at the sides. On the steps and the front columns are inscribed lists of consulting delegations, from places as far away as Olbia, Britain, Rome, Sardinia, and North Africa. Before the temple stands a huge altar with two sacrificial tables, one to Dionysus and one to Apollo – an interesting parallel to Delphi. Fragments of the cult-statue group, of Apollo (seated with a laurel), Artemis, and Leto, have survived. Artemis Claria, depicted (as we know from coins) as Artemis Ephesia, had her own Ionic temple nearby.

Literary sources tell us that there was a male prophet, that he descended into a cave by night, drank water from a holy spring, and then prophesied. Excavation revealed this *adyton* under the cella of the temple in a state of excellent preservation. About 12 m from the temple front in the *pronaos* two narrow staircases go down, one to the north, the other to the south. Four sizeable steps lead into a gallery on either side, and these unite into a single corridor, low and narrow (1.65 m high and 0.65 m wide), which changes direction sharply no less than seven times, but leads under the centre of the temple. The first room, an antechamber, contained an omphalos of blue marble, 0.65 m tall. This outer room was reserved for the officials, who included, as we know from inscriptions, as well as the prophet (an annual appointment), Apollo's priest (who held office for life), the thespoid who versified the responses (another life appointment), and official secretaries. From here a low passage about 3 m long leads to the inner sanctum. The entrance was marked by a low step, and was probably shut off by a curtain. The inner room was narrow and vaulted. Here was the sacred well; the excavators found it and tasted it; contrary to the evidence of the elder Pliny, it was pleasant enough to sample, though they do not record any special inspiration. No inscription preserves any questions or responses.[13]

One of the more interesting oracles of Apollo is at Sura in Lycia, not far from Myra. The temple of Apollo Surius is quite small, and stands on the edge of marshland. The inner walls are covered with inscriptions, oddly directed not to Apollo, but to the local divinity Sozon, and in one instance to Zeus Atabyrius. However we have nearby a row of stelae cut from the rock with a list of officials of the cult. The site on the marsh's edge is at first curious, until we see it in relation to the oracle, which used fish as augurs used birds. It happens that we have four accounts of this. Pliny (32, 17) says that there was a spring; the fish were summoned three times on a recorder. Food was thrown to them, and their acceptance of it was favourable, their rejection unfavourable. Plutarch (*De Soll. An.* 23) says that the interpretation was based on the movement of the fish. Polycharmus (Ath. 8, 333–4) records a whirlpool by the seashore. The client has two spits with ten pieces of meat on each. He throws them in; the pool wells up with seawater; fish appear as if by magic, and the interpretation is based on the species of fish (implausibly said to include whales). This is broadly confirmed by Artemidorus. The marshland was, of course, sea in ancient Greek times; the spring of Apollo can be seen and there are other freshwater springs which will have created a swirling effect in the seawater. There seems to have been a similar oracle at Limyra (Plin. 31, 22); we might suspect a confusion of names were it not that the oracle is attested by coins.[14]

A curious oracle is to be found at Olympus in eastern Lycia. Two tombs are inscribed with letter oracles in which the reply is believed to have come from the ancestor.[15]

We have a number of questions to an oracle in Egypt ranging over some centuries. Here is one from the first century AD:

> My Lord Sarapis, the Sun, my Benefactor. Is it right that my son Phanias and his wife should refuse to enter into agreement with his father, and should contradict him and not offer a contract? Give me an answer which agrees. Goodbye. (*P. Oxy*, 1148)

It is not only the oracle which is capable of ambiguity. The cunning questioner has been ambiguous. An answer which agrees is an answer which agrees with the truth, an answer agreeable to the questioner, and an answer which recommends agreement. From the next century we have:

> To Zeus the Sun, Almighty Serapis and his fellow-gods. Nike wants to know whether it is profitable for me to buy from Tasarapion her place Sarapion also called Ganon. Grant me this. (ibid. 1149)

From about AD 300, we have a whole string of questions which reflect the deteriorating economic situation.

72  Shall I receive the gratuity?
73  Shall I remain in the place where I have been posted?
74  Am I going to be sold?
75  Am I going to make any profit from my partner?
76  Am I permitted to make a deal with the other man?
77  Am I to be reconciled with my son?
78  Am I to get leave?

79 Shall I receive the money?
80 Is he alive overseas?
81 Is it going to be a profitable deal?
82 Are my goods to be distrained?
83 Shall I find a buyer?
84 Am I able to bring off what I have in mind?
85 Am I to end up in the gutter?
86 Shall I become a refugee?
87 Shall I be appointed ambassador?
88 Am I to be appointed to the council?
89 Is my escape to be intercepted?
90 Am I going to get a divorce from my wife?
91 Have I been poisoned?
92 Am I going to get my rights? (ibid. 1477)

It will be noted that these oracles were consulted by all manner of people, men and women, slave and free, rich and poor, humble and powerful. The questions about high office do not arise from ambition; at this time high office was a grave financial responsibility.

The most notable of the Egyptian oracles was the oracle of Zeus Ammon in the Oasis of Siwah. Amen-Ra was originally the god of Thebes in Egypt. Ra, the sun god, was invoked as a ram on the walls of the royal tombs of Thebes, and Amen-Ra was portrayed with ram's horn and addressed as 'King of the Gods'. Contact with the Egyptians led the Greeks to identify him with their own Zeus as Zeus Ammon. But as Zeus had a different title in Thebes itself it is likely that he received the title with special reference to the sanctuary at Siwah. This must have taken place in the sixth century BC or earlier, since the cult had spread to Laconia by that period, and to Cyrenaica by the end of the century, when the god's head appears on coins.

Unfortunately, the oasis is difficult of access; even in antiquity it was exceptional to make the journey more than once (Arist. fr. 99 Rose 1494 1 7ff.). From 1792 some intrepid travellers have left reports. The oasis is 29 m below the level of the Mediterranean. It has lagoons which overflow in winter and dry up in summer leaving precious and holy deposits of salt, of which the name 'sal ammoniae' still reminds us. There are also some thirty springs of fresh water, one of which, today called Ain el hamman (perhaps a relic of an ancient name) is marked out by an ancient wall as a place of special sanctity, and is clearly the spring known to ancient authors as the Fountain of the Sun (Hdt. 4, 181 etc.). The oasis naturally is a place of trees. Silius

Italicus, admittedly with poetic freedom, speaks of oaks there (3, 688–91). There is no trace of them today, but it is not impossible. The name gum ammoniac reminds us also that plants could be introduced, with healing properties. It is a place of birds also. Herodotus tells the story that Dodona and Siwah were founded as oracles simultaneously by two doves from Thebes. Wild doves are still found at Siwah. There were two temples on the site. The smaller was in a precinct perhaps 20 × 19 m, and was built of limestone. The larger stood on the Acropolis, and was an impressive structure; it was built or restored by Akoris in the early fourth century BC. Both temples were covered with hieroglyphics but the ritual texts tell us nothing of the oracle. In the upper temple, however, there was a secret passage about 0.6 m broad leading to a platform looking down upon the waters of a spring; this must be the sacred spring within the temple which Diodorus says was used to purify offerings to the god (17, 50). Quintus Curtius, in his account of the consultation by Alexander (4, 7, 20–2), gives a clear picture of the two levels, saying that both were groves. Unfortunately he is less clear about the oracle, which he says was situated at the upper level; but he also says that when a question was asked the sacred image was taken out in a golden boat in the lake formed by the Fountain of the Sun. Diodorus gives a similar picture. The cult-statue is taken on a golden barge by twenty-four priests while women sing hymns.

How the god's will was discerned remains uncertain: it was presumably either the stirring of the water, or the movement of the leaves in the grove, or the sound of the sacred birds, or possibly direct prophetic inspiration from the journey with the god. Herodotus declared that the oracular usages at Thebes in Egypt and Dodona were similar (2, 58).

Ammon had oracles elsewhere, notably at Aphytis in northern Greece (Steph. Byz. s.v.) where his head appears on the coinage.[16]

# 7
## HEALING SANCTUARIES

The greatest healing sanctuary of mainland Greece is at, or rather a few miles outside, Epidaurus. Here there was an ancient cult of Apollo, and a sanctuary and altar to Apollo Maleatas from the seventh century BC have been found on the hill above the theatre, with a Mycenaean altar underlying. In the sixth century dedications appear jointly to Apollo and Asclepius; Apollo retained the first sacrifice, but by the fourth century Asclepius had virtually ousted the older god. This was his special sanctuary; his birthplace was claimed for these hills rather than for Thessaly, and from here spread to Athens, Asia Minor, and North Africa.

The theatre is spectacular, but those eager to see it sometimes get their priorities wrong. The reason for the site seems to be contained in an ancient well 55 feet deep and dating from the sixth century BC, which was incorporated for ritual reasons within the holy buildings when these were constructed in the fourth century. The water has an alkaline content.

The adjacent temple is small, about $10 \times 20$ m with six columns at the ends and eleven along the sides, of the Doric order and datable to about 420 BC. A stele gives details of the building. The architect was Theodotes; the building was 4 years 8½ months in construction, at a cost of between 23 and 24 talents. The director of sculpture was Timotheus, though others executed the work to his designs. The doors were of ivory. The cult-statue was made of gold and ivory by Thrasymedes of Paros. Pausanias tells us that the god was seated with a staff in one hand, the other over the head of a snake, and a dog at his side (2, 27). Two marble reliefs were discovered showing the statue.

The great altar of the god lay to the south of the temple, not at the end.

Close to the temple is the tholos, built in the middle of the fourth century by Polycleitus the Younger, grandson of the famous sculptor; he was also architect of the theatre. Only the foundations of this circular shrine remain *in situ*, in the form of six concentric walls. The building was about 24 m in diameter. It had an outer portico of twenty-six Doric columns of stuccoed poros. Inside were fourteen Corinthian columns of marble with exquisitely carved capitals with a little bluebell peering out from the volutes. The pavement was of marble, chequered in black and white, the ceiling elaborately coffered, the high roof flanked with lion-head gargoyles and crowned with a floral decoration. The building was known as the *thymele* or altar. Its function is unknown. It has been suggested that it enshrined a sacred spring which later dried up; that it housed a pit for the sacred snakes; that it was a place for special offering by the priest-doctors.

To the north of tholos and temple is the *abaton* or *encoemeterion*, the place of incubation where the patients slept in the hope of healing experiences in their dreams. The total length is about 70 m; the western portion is in two storeys, and owing to the slope of the ground the upper storey carries on the line of the eastern section. Some of the benches survive. Here were found tablets with records of divine healing. With some we can see medical science at work. Sometimes the treatment seems to be psychological or spiritual. Some, like the account of Cleo, it is impossible to credit; yet one asks how ever such a record came to be kept.

> God. Good Fortune. Healings of Apollo and Asclepius.
>
> Cleo was pregnant for five years.
>
> She had been pregnant for five years, went in supplication to the god and slept in the sanctuary. Immediately after leaving, once outside the precincts she bore a son, who immediately after birth washed in the spring and went round with his mother. In her good fortune she had inscribed in her thank-offering: 'Do not wonder at the size of this tablet, but at the greatness of the god. Cleo bore in her womb the burden for five years, slept in the sanctuary and was made whole . . .'
>
> Ambrosia from Athens, blind in one eye.
>
> She came in supplication to the god, but as she walked round the temple she laughed at some of the cures as implausible or impossible, with the lame or blind restored to health by seeing a vision in

sleep. She slept in the sanctuary and saw a vision. She thought the god stood over her and said that he would make her well, but she must present a silver pig as a thank-offering to the temple, as a record of her ignorance. With these words he made an incision in her diseased eye and poured in a salve. When day broke she came out cured . . .

Euphanes, a boy from Epidaurus.

He was suffering from gallstones and slept in the sanctuary. He thought the god stood over him and said 'What will you give me if I cure you?' He answered 'Ten knucklebones.' The god laughed and promised to help him. When day broke he came out cured. (*SIG* $^2$802)

Other cures are of equal interest. A naughty boy named Aeschines climbed a tree to peer into the *abaton*, fell and damaged his sight; he became a suppliant and was healed. The god or his representative, sometimes described as a handsome man, pours a salve into ailing eyes, applies ointment elsewhere, massages stomach or head, extracts a lance-head by surgery, lances an ulcer, simply gives medicine, even in one case compounding a hair restorer. In one amusing episode the god's action was indirect. A boy stole Nicanor's crutch in broad daylight. Nicanor chased after him and found that he was fit. Sometimes the god used animals, usually snakes, sometimes dogs; in one unique record a gout sufferer was bitten by a goose and healed. A good dream-cure relates to a man with a stone in his penis, who dreamt he was lying with a pretty boy and ejected the stone in the process. Sometimes the epigraphic record offers us a cautionary tale. A blind man received his sight, refused to pay, and was struck blind again until he should pay. One man, cured of facial scars, sent his fee by a friend who stole the money. But the thief had occasion to come to the god with a similar affliction. The god took down the other man's bandage and laid it on the face of the false friend, and he went on with the other man's scars in addition to his own. Another amusing episode records a lady named Ithmonice who asked to conceive a girl. The god said 'Do you want anything else?' 'No' she replied. She became pregnant, but could not give birth; the pregnancy lasted, according to the record, for three years. So she went back, and the god pointed out that she had all she asked for, but as she had returned he would grant her birth too. Another story with a happy ending tells of a sceptic named Caphisius who wondered why the god did not heal

Hephaestus's lameness. The god caused him to be thrown from his horse and lamed as a lesson. After earnest pleas he was healed.

One long inscription from Epidaurus, dating from the second century AD, is a statement by Marcus Julius Apellas from Idrias and Mylasa. According to this the god sent for him because of his digestive upsets, and on his journey to Aegina (presumably at another shrine) told him to keep his temper under control. On arrival at Epidaurus he was told to cover his head against the rain, to eat bread and cheese and celery with lettuce, to bathe unattended, to jog, to drink citron juice diluted, to bathe and have a rub down, followed by a walk, to swing, to cover his body with sand, to walk barefoot, to rub wine into his body and then have a warm bath, tipping the attendant to make an offering to Asclepius, Epione, and the goddesses of Eleusis and to drink milk with honey in it. He prayed for a quicker cure and had a vision of being rubbed with salt and mustard; this must have been in the course of incubation. The priest told him he was healed and must make a free-will offering; however, he still rubbed himself with salt and mustard, and the priest, or the god (if so, there was a further incubation) touched his right hand and right breast. He records two more slightly curious episodes. In one he had his hand burned in the course of a sacrifice, but it healed swiftly. In the other the god told him of a prescription for a headache. He had no headache then, but one ensued. He also gargled. The god told him to write down the treatment. He did and went home healed and grateful (*SIG*$^3$ 117).

The courtyard of the healing sanctuary may have been used for some kind of cult-drama. In the Roman period this was formalized, and a theatre built in the court.

The healing sanctuary is the essence of the site. We can rejoice in the perfection of the theatre, in the stadium which lies just outside the sanctuary proper, in the gymnasium and palaestra, in the hotel, in the baths of different periods, in the sanctuaries of Themis or Aphrodite, or Artemis or the Egyptian gods, in the ceremonial entrance and Sacred Way. All this brings back to us the popularity of the Festival of Asclepius every four years – the theatre holds 14,000 – and the popularity of the sacred place. It is for healing that it exists.

At Corinth the shrine of Asclepius lies a little to the north of the theatre, outside the city wall and adjacent to a spring. It seems that Asclepius took the sanctuary over from Apollo, since a fragment of a vase has been found with the inscription 'I belong to Apollo'. There was at one stage a simple temple and lodging accommodation. This was replaced in the late fourth century BC by a large rectangular walled *temenos*, with the *abaton* to the west, and a colonnade to the north. There was a ritual piscina near the entrance, and an altar for offerings. The new temple was on the site of the old; on either side were perhaps snake pits. To the west of the *abaton* at a lower level lay a pleasant courtyard, adjacent to the spring, and with three luxurious dining-rooms under the place of incubation. Corinth has not produced inscriptional records of gratitude comparable to those of Epidaurus, but it has produced a collection of terracotta limbs of unparalleled extent. The excavator reckoned that they amounted to ten cubic metres. They include at least 125 hands, nearly as many feet, numerous legs and arms, 65 female breasts, sometimes singly, sometimes in pairs, 6 heads, 35 penises. Although there are numerous ears, it is strange that there are only two eyes. Mostly we can only guess at the complaint, but one hand does show an abnormal growth. Breasts may be offered in thanksgiving for a birth rather than necessarily indicating a breast complaint. The whole is an impressive record of gratitude.[1]

In Athens the sanctuary of Asclepius lies under the south face of the Acropolis. The god, as we know from other sources, was brought to Athens because of the plague of 430–427 BC, but he was not given a precinct of his own until 418 BC when the sanctuary was dedicated by Telemachus of Acharnae.

At Athens the healing god was introduced from Epidaurus during the lull in fighting in the year after the Peace of Nicias (420 BC). We have an account of the development of the sanctuary which was established on the south slope of the Acropolis.

> The god arrived during the Great Mysteries, and was escorted into the precinct at Eleusis. From his home he called for his snake to come in a chariot; Telemachus welcomed him. Hygieia was in the company. So the sanctuary was founded in the archonship of Astyphilus, son of Cydantides. In the archonship of Archias the heralds prevented the work from going on by laying claim to some of the property.... In the archonship of Teisandrus the gateway was built of wood and the remainder of the sacred furnishings installed. In the archonship of Cleocritus the planting was done. He personally paid to have the decoration of the whole precinct finished. (*IG* II $^2$4960 = *SIG* $^3$88)

The dates are 420–419, 419–418, and, after a lacuna, 414–413 and 413–412. There is not a great deal to see of the sanctuary today, but the remains have been the subject of a careful study (*BCH* 73 (1949) 316–50). In the fourth century the precinct was moved further west. Both the old precinct and the new contained a spring once sacred to the Nymphs, and above the terrace in the cliff face was a cave containing another spring, a healing sanctuary from prehistoric times.

The sanctuaries as constructed incorporated a temple and altar, and also a stoa for the practice of encoemesis or incubation, the dream cure. Votive stelai or offerings were affixed to the steps of the stoa, to columns or walls. Many of these have been found; sometimes the tablets show the part of the anatomy treated.

In addition to this we have records of the temple inventories, starting in 341 BC. They include such dedications as a gold ring, a silver crown (ominously described as 'missing'), a bronze wine jar, a marble conch shell, a silver libation bowl, a silver cup, a cloak, a wooden chair, a caldron, a tripod, crystal seals, jasper gems, body scrapers, a flute, a pillow, and gazelle knucklebones. Meletus dedicated a silver heart and a small emblem of a snake on a plaque; we may presume that this indicates the cure of some sort of heart disease. Model eyes and limbs, often gilded, are recorded; those are the usual thanksgiving for cure. Sometimes it is the whole face which appears (*IG* II $^2$1533). At Athens we can discern a particular interest in eye complaints, and nearly half of the votive offerings of model parts of the body consists of eyes. It is hard to know whether this represents an expertise in the sanctuary, or a complaint to which the Athenians were for some reason particularly prone. Next in frequency is the torso, which may represent a wide variety of internal complaints; and after that legs, ears, and hands. Breast, face, mouth, and sex organ are also found several times, and head, feet, fingers, knee, jaw, teeth, and even heart; one woman offered two hearts.

Asclepius had another sanctuary in the port town of Piraeus. This produced a magnificent votive relief, early in date (about 400 BC) showing the god, attended by the goddess Hygieia, actually in the process of treating a sleeping patient.

Later the site was occupied by a church dedicated to the healing saints Cosmas and Damien: such is the power of continuity in religion.

The island of Cos is associated with the name of Hippocrates, and the development of scientific medicine. But science is not to be set in sharp contrast with religion, and it is certain that the association of Cos with medicine goes back beyond the fifth century. An inscription from the early fourth century (*SEG* 16, 326; *BCH* 80 (1956) 579ff.) shows that the physicians of Cos were members of a guild or *koinon* and called Asclepiadai, a form of name which must date back to the archaic period, and that membership was jealously guarded as a matter of birth. Late sources (*Suda* s.v.;[8] Tzetz. *Chil. Hist.* 7, 155ff.) give Hippocrates doctors for his father and grandfather, and his great-uncle Aeneos, a rare name, is perhaps, though not certainly, commemorated on the acropolis at Athens (*IG* 1 $^2$1019). From the earliest that we can trace, medicine was the province of Asclepius.

The great Asclepieion dates from the late fourth century BC, a century or so after Hippocrates. It lies on a hill slope, looking north-east towards the city, some 2½ miles distant, and beyond to the coast of Asia Minor, and well supplied with water. The precinct grew from small beginnings to monumental grandeur. From the first, however, it was devised in three terraces. The lowest of these offered the ceremonial entrance in the centre of a covered portico. The middle terrace was a place of peculiar holiness and healing. It contained a small Ionic temple identified by an inscription with the shrine of Asclepius, and a monumental altar, placed centrally and dominating the terrace. This seems to have taken the place of an altar privately dedicated to the slightly miscellaneous collection of Halios, Hamera, Machaon, and Hecate, Machaon being a semi-divine healer (*Arch. Anz.* (1903) 191). Near the temple was a small building with two rooms, which must have had some sacred purpose, perhaps as an *abaton*. Foundations of a second contemporary temple have been found, presumably (though there is no direct evidence) dedicated to Apollo. A covered porch open to the north contained statues. The water supply was controlled by a spring-house at the back and draw wells at the front of the terrace. The upper terrace contained a sacred cypress grove, and was surrounded on three sides by a portico. It is quite uncertain how old this was. It was dedicated to Asclepius and Apollo Cyparissius (Herzog 12), a unique example of this cult-title for the god. But Apollo slipped into the background, and by the Augustan age Asclepius had sole possession. An early epigram found on the upper terrace refers to the healing deity Paeon (*BCH* 73 (1949) 361ff.)

The site remained basically unchanged for a century and a half. In the second century BC the upper terrace was developed in a monumental baroque conception. In the centre a large ornate temple was constructed, built of marble rather than of limestone, with a platform 18.793 × 33.28 m. Two halls stood one on each side, and a colossal stairway led up from the middle terrace. The middle terrace itself was equipped with a more grandiose altar. The enhanced reputation of the Asclepieion is shown in changes in coinage. From the middle of the century Asclepius replaces Heracles on coins of Cos, and, on the reverse, the coiled snake takes the place of the emblems of Heracles.

Mithradates did no harm to the site, but Turullius, Antony's admiral, cut down the sacred cypresses to build ships for Actium. After the battle Turullius was executed on the site of the grove he had desecrated. There was damage through earthquake in about AD 142, and this occasioned some rebuilding, notably a new temple on the site of the presumed temple of Apollo. Down on the lower terrace baths and toilet facilities were added, and a hotel nearby. Prosperity continued, as a coin hoard from the fourth century demonstrates. We know of disastrous earthquakes, however, in AD 469 and AD 554. At some point a Christian monastery was established on the site, but the date is quite unknown.

Curiously there is some uncertainty about the relationship between the school of medicine, which traditionally practised in the city of Cos, and the religious sanctuary. We do not have records of cures such as survive at Epidaurus, though we know from Strabo (374) that they did exist, so we do not know how far they used scientific medicine, and how far spiritual methods. The site was plundered in antiquity and yielded little by way of votives, though some marble and terracotta representations of ears, genitals, and breasts survive. A number of decrees honouring doctors have been found in the Asclepieion, but this does not mean that they were closely associated, as the sanctuary was a general repository of public decrees. We do have one record of a doctor dedicating his medical equipment in the Asclepieion (Cohn-Haft 30), and a well-known doctor of the Roman Imperial period, Xenophon, court physician to Claudius and Nero, improved the water supply to the Asclepieion (pipes have been found stamped with his name), and, as an inscription records (*Arch. Anz.* (1903) 193–4), donated a library.

A late mosaic shows Asclepius arriving at Cos by boat, and indeed there is no other way he could arrive. It seems probable that he came from Tricca, and the Coans of the third century BC certainly believed this (Herod. *Mim.* 2, 95–8), though Epidaurus has its claimants. The earliest sanctuary lay a little to the north of the modern town (*BSA* 52 (1957) 120–1). The state-cult, it has been argued, dates only from about 350 BC, and it is from the third century that Asclepius begins to take the primary place in the religious life of the island. A cult-calendar from the early third century already includes sacrifices for Asclepius and Hygieia (*Inscr. Cos* 401). Hygieia elsewhere is Asclepius's daughter, and Epione his wife, but in Cos Hygieia always takes precedence, and their roles may be reversed.

The public cult included an annual festival which incorporated a curious ceremony of the Renewal of the Staff. In 242 BC the Great Asclepieia was inaugurated as a panhellenic festival every four years. There were sacrifices of oxen to Asclepius and Apollo Cyparissius, and of heifers to Hygieia and Epione, a magnificent procession to the cypress grove, and musical, athletic, and equestrian competitions (*OGIS* 42).[2]

The third of the great sanctuaries of Asclepius (with Epidaurus and Cos) to survive in something of its ancient glory is that at Pergamon. It lies outside the city to the south-west. It is of particular interest because the great doctor Galen practised here, and the religious hypochondriac Aelius Aristides, who had an almost mystical devotion to Asclepius, was a frequent visitor. It was set on the site of an older shrine to some female deity. A magnificent Sacred Way leads at an angle to the ceremonial entrance. This opens into a rectangular courtyard, 130 × 110 m, surrounded on three sides with porticoes, and enclosing the sacred well and two other healing springs, in whose waters tiny turtles now thrive. One of these was used for mud baths. The building for incubation was also within the courtyard, though nothing survives except foundations. So too were three small shrines. Interestingly some burials were found within the sanctuary. Most exciting is an underground passage from the middle of the courtyard, by the well, to a large circular building in the south-east corner. Various explanations of this have been offered – access to the sacred well in bad weather, a cool refuge in a hot summer, a corridor for the secretive carrying out of the dead, something to do with the priests effecting an unexpected epiphany of the god. The building with which it communicates is also mysterious; it has been called the hospital, from the number of washing places. There were two storeys. Between this and the entrance is another round building. This was the main temple, of Zeus Asclepius. On the far side of the entrance stood a library. In the north-west corner of the courtyard is a delightful theatre of the Roman period, seating some 3,500. In the south-west corner are latrines, those for the men being somewhat more sumptuous than those for the ladies.[3]

The Asclepieion on Delos is situated apart from the main area of residence, business, and religion, to the south of the island, on a sandy promontory overlooking a peaceful bay. It is in a wholly ruinous condition, but we can discern some of the characteristic features: a ceremonial entrance, courtyard, encoemeterion, temple of the god, and record office, for votive offerings and the records of cures.[4]

At Gortys in Arcadia a sanctuary of Asclepius was explored. It was firmly identified by tiles stamped with the god's name. Here the interesting feature is the presence of a bath in addition to the usual temple and *abaton*.

In the Rhodes museum there are excellent statues of Asclepius with a snake along his staff, and Hygieia with a snake in her right hand eating off a patina held in her left.

Asclepius had a shrine of particular importance at Lebena in Crete. We do not know whether the cult was introduced from Epidaurus or Cyrene or Cos. The oldest buildings associated with Asclepius seem to date from the third century BC, but they replaced earlier buildings, suggesting a pre-existing healing sanctuary to a local god. The temple was restored somewhere about 100 BC (*IC* 1 xvii 6).

Asclepius was honoured elsewhere in Crete. He had a temple at Itanos in the east (*IC* 3 iv 3; 7). Aptera in the second century BC expressed their gratitude in his temple on Cos for the services of one of their doctors (*IC* 2 iii 3); a statue of Hygieia survives from the same city. There were temples at Cnossus, at least in the Roman period (*IC* 1 viii 49), Olous (*IC* 1 xxii 4 A 1), perhaps also Pylorus (*IC* 1 xxv 2) and Gortyna (*IC* 1 xxv 4, 239–40). A dedication survives from Lasaea (*IC* 1 xv 3), and a particularly important one from Chersonesus (*IC* 1 vii 5). The Cretan Arcadians celebrated the festival of the Asclepieia (*IC* 3 iii 1 B 9) as early as the third century BC.

But Lebena was predominant, and, as at Epidaurus, inscriptions tell us a good deal about procedures. Thus Demandrus of Gortyna was operated on for sciatica in his sleep by the god (*IC* 1 xvii 9). Diodorus somehow was cured of defects of vision in both eyes during his sleep and offered two statues in thanks (*IC* 1 xvii 24). An unnamed woman gave thanks for the healing of a finger ulcer by the application of the grindings of a shell mixed with ointment of roses, and application of a compound of oil and mallow (*IC* 1 xvii 19). Poplius Granius Rufus was coughing blood atrociously. The god told him to fast and chew rockel, to take Italian wine mixed with pepper, starch, and hot water, powdered ashes specially consecrated, consecrated water, resinated egg, moist pitch, honey and iris, boiled quince and wind purslane mixed, and a fig with ashes from the altar (*IC* 1 xvii 17). He came again for shoulder trouble, and was given a complex poultice (*IC* 1 xvii 18).

In all this we can see the normal practice of ritual preparation, leading to incubation in the course of which, in the patient's semi-drugged state, the priest representing the god applies surgery or other medical techniques, or recommends herbal or similar remedies, or simply uses the patient's faith.

There was a great shrine of Asclepius at Pautalia, now in Bulgaria, once the main settlement of the Dentheletai. Here are found medicinal springs whose temperature can rise to 75°C. A small portion of the Asclepieion has probably been unearthed. It was on a monumental scale; one room was 19.5 × 11.5 m; another is marked by remarkable vaulted hypocausts. There are a number of relics of the cult. The coins show a snake coiled and sometimes haloed, and a ritual egg. One ritual marble egg has been found. Another interesting discovery was a collection of iron knives. One view is that they were sacrificial knives thrown into the spring after being used; this custom prevailed well into this century.

Asclepius seems to have been prominent in what is today Bulgaria even without healing springs. He was often identified with the Thracian horseman, the mysterious riding figure who appears so often on monuments of the classical period in the Balkans, and is sometimes identified with Apollo or one of the Dioscuri. At Philippopolis there seems to be the record of an Asclepieion in an early-third-century frieze portraying in high relief eight deities associated with health, Iaso (goddess of health), Panacea (daughter of Asclepius), Telesphorus (a small hooded figure), Asclepius (with rod and snake), Hygieia, Epione (Asclepius's wife), and Machaon and Podalirios (Asclepius's sons). By a spring (but one without medicinal properties) near the modern village of Batkoun, another sanctuary of the god has been discovered. This was evidently a shrine of some prominence, as it has yielded nearly 200 inscriptions in Greek or Latin, often associated with altars or relief sculpture, as well as over

100 sculptures without inscription. The sculptures vary from a magnificent marble torso, perhaps imported, to a powerful head of the god in a style more redolent of local folk art. Another shrine was evidenced at Odessus on the coast, by an altar and other material relating to Asclepius and Hygieia.[5]

We have a number of regulations for sacrificial offerings associated with Asclepius. The first comes from Epidaurus and is dated to about 400 BC:

> Sacrifice a bull to Apollo, and another bull to the gods to share his temple. Sacrifice these on Apollo's altar, and add a hen to Leto and another to Artemis. The god's portion is fifty litres of barley, 25 of wheat, 4 litres of wine and the leg of the first bull. The officiants are to take the other leg. The precentors are to receive one leg of the second bull, and the guards the other with the intestines.
>
> Sacrifice a bull of Asclepius, and another bull to the gods, and a cow to the goddesses who share his temple. Sacrifice these with a cock on Asclepius's altar. Asclepius's portion is fifty litres of barley, 25 of wheat, and four litres of wine. One leg of the first bull must be offered on the altar of the god, and the other is for the officiants. The precentors are to receive one leg of the second bull, and the other.... ($IG$ IV $^2$1, 40–1 = $SIG$ $^3$998)

The second, a little later, comes from Piraeus:

> Gods! These are to be the preliminary offerings: three wheat-cakes to each of the following – Meleas, Apollo, Hermes, Iaso, Panacea, the Dogs, the Huntsmen. ($IG$ II $^2$4962 = $SIG$ $^3$1040)

The third comes from Erythrae in Boeotia, and is datable to 380–360 BC:

> When the city sacrifices to Asclepius, the first sacrifice is offered by the city for everyone. At a festival a private individual may not make the first sacrifice, though he may do so at any time during the rest of the year in accordance with the stated regulations. Those who sleep in the sanctuary, when they sacrifice to Asclepius and Apollo after incubation, or when they dedicate the portion of their sacrifice after prayer and sacrifice, are to sing this paean three times over Apollo's altar. 'Hail Paean, O hail Paean, hail Paean, o hail Paean, hail Paean, o hail Paean, Lord Apollo, spare the youths....' (E. J. and L. Edelstein, *Asclepius* I (Baltimore, 1945), no. 521)

It is interesting to compare this evidence with some evidence from western Europe.

At Essarois in the Côte d'Or near the source of the river Cave, there is a sanctuary to Apollo Vindonnus and Apollo of the Springs (*CIL* 13, 5644–6). There are two similar but disconnected stone shrines replacing a wooden temple. Pottery and coins are partly Gallic, partly Roman from the late Republic and early Empire. Large numbers of offerings, now in the Musée de Chatillon, show that Apollo Vindonnus, in his association with the springs, had acquired the character of a healing god. They include stone carvings of legs, arms, and torsos, and thin bronze plaques of eyes and breasts. Many of the offerings show deformities of limbs, genitals, or eyes. There is an interesting collection of infants in swaddling clothes, and a single stele showing five women's heads grouped together.

At Chamalières in the Puy-de-Dôme, near Augustonemetum (Clermont-Ferrand), was discovered a mineral spring, with no engineering of any kind. More than 5,000 wooden ex-votos from the first centuries BC and AD were found, originally stacked round the natural basins and then fallen in. Mostly they are representations, life-size, of legs and arms, or other sections of the body (sometimes draped); some are splints; there are some statuettes and busts (classical or classicizing in style), and some painted plaques. The finds are in the Musée Bargoin in Clermont-Ferrand.[6]

Another healing sanctuary, not dedicated to Asclepius, is to be found at Oropus by the border between Attica and Boeotia. This was dedicated to the legendary Amphiaraus, seer and healer, who had taken part reluctantly in the expedition of the Seven against Thebes, and had been miraculously preserved from death by the intervention of Zeus, and swallowed up into the earth.

Amphiaraus had an oracle near Thebes (Hdt. 8, 133–5), but it was transferred to the site of a healing spring near Oropus, and in the Hellenistic and Roman periods was much frequented.

The remains show a temple, without a colonnade, with a statue base and a fragment of a colossal statue. The altar stood outside in a kind of theatral area for spectators. Below was the sacred spring, from which pilgrims used shells to drink.

Further along is the stoa or dormitory for incubation, with separate sections for men and women. Some of the sleeping benches survive. The patient sacrificed a ram and slept on its skin. The offerings of those healed have survived, sometimes with inscriptions, proclaiming their gratitude, sometimes with statues, sometimes with models of the part healed.

The offerings at Oropus suggest a degree of specialism in the medical concerns of the sanctuary. There are literally dozens of model breasts, presented by males, suggesting a particular expertise in diseases of the chest and lungs. Other parts of the body found are, face, hand, or sex organ, but they are few by comparison. But this was not merely a healing sanctuary, and other offerings include bowls and baskets, scrapers, lamps, masks, and figures of Victory. Coins were thrown into the sacred spring.

We happen to have the regulations controlling the priest's duties. He had to exercise responsibility during the winter months, though his assistant, the *neocorus*, was in permanent residence. The priest was responsible for the direction of the *neocorus*; he was also responsible for behaviour in the sanctuary. Anyone coming for healing had to pay an initial sum which was at some point raised from one drachma to nine obols of silver. Before they went for incubation the *neocorus* had to display their names and cities on a noticeboard. The regulations stipulate what can be deduced from the remains, that the men and women were to have separate areas, the men to the east of the altar and the women to the west (*SIG*$^3$ 1004).

As with other healing sanctuaries, a theatre was attached to the shrine, and a festival held every four years with dramatic, musical, and athletic competitions.

Among the statues attested by inscribed bases are Ptolemy IV and Arsinoe, Sulla and his wife, L. Mummius, and Brutus, Caesar's assassin.

There were other healing divinities too. In Sicily they might invoke Artemis Lye or the Mothers, at Lindos or Miletus Artemis Oulia and Apollo Oulios (*CIG* 2566). Hecate is called on to save (*IG Ins*. I 958), and eastern divinites such as Men (*BCH* 20, 75) or Cybele (*CIA* III 134). The admirable Micythus, who spent a great deal of money on his son's health, made offerings at Olympia 'to all gods and goddesses': nothing like making sure (*IG Ant*. 532).

At Nysa there was a healing sanctuary of Pluto close to a ravine on the road to Tralles in the village of Acharne. Strabo gives an account of it (14, 650). The sanctuary centred on a cave called the Charonion. Here it seems that the priests practised incubation on behalf of the patients, though sometimes the patients were taken to the cave and left there without food. For all others the place was forbidden. There was a curious ritual at festival time by which a bull was taken up; it was then released, but collapsed of its own accord. The Charonion has not been found, but the nearby stream is sulphurous, and that too would help to account for the sanctuary. The temple of Pluto and Kore has been excavated, and has some curious features. It is built on a north–south orientation with the entrance at the north. It is a peristyle temple, with the typical six columns along the front but, unusually, twelve along the sides. It has two parallel walls running the whole length of the temple and dividing the cella. No satisfactory explanation of these features has been offered. We have some details from the first century BC relating to the administration of the temple (*SIG*$^3$781).

# 8

# THE MYSTERIES

The most famous of all the sites of mystery-cult in the ancient world was Eleusis. The legend is evoked in the long Homeric *Hymn to Demeter*:

> I am beginning a hymn of the dread goddess, Demeter of the
>   lovely hair,
> and of her neat-ankled daughter, whom Aidoneus
> kidnapped and ravished, a gift from farseeing thundery Zeus.
> (Hom. *H. Dem.* 2, 1–3)

It is amply illustrated by the monuments of all periods. The rape of the corn maiden by the god of death but also of wealth (Pluto) can be seen, for example, on a sarcophagus in the Uffizi, or on a fragmentary terracotta plaque from Locri in the museum in Reggio Calabria, and often elsewhere.

The hymn tells of her grief, so movingly portrayed in the Demeter of Cnidos, her wanderings with lighted torches in her hands. The torch-bearer was to play an important part in later ritual. We see him leading the initiates on an amphora in the Eleusis museum. On a votive tablet in Eleusis Kore holds two torches. In the hymn, Hecate, the underworld goddess, meets her with a lamp and tells her what has happened (l. 52). On the Niinnion tablet, a votive of about 400 BC, either Hecate or Kore is carrying torches high as she presents the initiate to Demeter, and the young god Iacchus, personification of the mystic cry, is torch-bearer in another scene.

Demeter wandered till she came to Eleusis, and met the daughters of Celeus at the well. She accompanied them home, but refused wine, and asked them to mix barley meal, water, and mint; this was the sacred potion. She was set to nurse the boy Demophoon, whom she sought to make immortal by placing him in the fire, but the mother understandably intervened. Demeter revealed herself and demanded a temple and altar on a rising mound above the Callichorus spring, where her rites would be fulfilled.

Now she laid a blight on the land, and Zeus to placate her called the god of the underworld to release her daughter, but gave her pomegranate to eat so that she would have to return. The goddesses were reunited, and Demeter relented so that corn again clothed the land. Then she taught her mysteries to Triptolemus and others:

> Blessed among men on earth is he who has seen these things.
> But he who is uninitiate in the holy rites, who has no lot in them,
> does not enjoy a like fate when he lies in death beneath
>   broad-spreading darkness.
>
> (ll. 480–2)

Much in this hymn is aetiological: that is to say, it is offering a rationale in myth for the places and practices which were historically known. We can see that the hymn has to do with two connected religious elements. One is the fertility of the earth. It used to be said that the period of barrenness when Kore was below ground was the winter. But the description of drought is far more applicable to the Mediterranean summer. So more recent views associate the descent of Kore with the storage of the seed corn in pots underground during the summer after the spring harvest preparatory to the autumn sowing. The author of the hymn, however, seems to parallel Kore's sojourn underground with the presence of the seed in the earth after the winter sowing preparatory to the spring harvest (l. 455). Parallel with the springing of new life from the ground is the promise of new life from death for initiates. This is implicit in the story of Demophoon – Demeter can grant immortality if she is allowed to – and in the closing promise. Cicero said of the ceremonies 'We have gained from them the way of living in happiness and dying with a better hope' (*Laws* 2, 14, 36). 'Glorious indeed', cried an initiate, 'is that mystery vouchsafed by the blessed gods, for death is no ill to mortals, but rather a good' (*Eph. Arch.* 5 (1885) 150).

The site itself as it appears today is a ruinous amalgam of different periods. The Sacred Way approaches the sanctuary as it must have done from time immemorial. Outside are three of the earliest survivals: the well, which appears in the myth as the Callichorus spring; a cave, sacred to Pluto, one of the gates of Hades; and the site of the original altar. But the adjacent temple to Artemis and Poseidon is Roman, as are the two triumphal arches, or what is left of them, the elaborate outer propylaea, and the less imposing inner propylaea. The outer propylaea stands on the corner of the sanctuary wall of sixth-century date, which enclosed the acropolis; it was of polygonal masonry. In the fifth century the sanctuary was expanded, and the new wall met the old at the same point. There was a further expansion of the south-east corner in the fourth century. Beyond the sanctuary wall to the south lies a stadium, and, interestingly, a Roman Mithraeum.

Within the expanded enclosure stands the great telesterion or hall of the Mysteries. The earliest building here was a megaron of the second half of the second millennium BC, a simple house with porch and two columns, presumably the first house of Demeter. The period 1100–700 saw some terracing, and the house was replaced by a circular structure. In the early sixth century this was superseded by a larger oblong hall; the change may tentatively be associated with Solon. Towards the end of the century in changes certainly to be associated with Pisistratus this was rebuilt in fine stonework in a larger and square form. The roof was held up by some twenty columns; tiers of seats were set around three of the sides, and in the south-west corner there was a storehouse for sacred relics. This was destroyed in the Persian invasion. The archaeological evidence gives general support to the tradition that Cimon began a new and larger hall. After his ostracism in 461 Pericles took up the work. He enlarged the precinct but built a slightly smaller hall than Cimon had planned. The roof was supported by forty-two columns, arranged in six rows of seven.

What happened here? The answer is that we do not know. The stones are dumb, and our literary sources do not tell us. For a mystery was not to be divulged, and we are told that Aeschylus was nearly lynched for an alleged betrayal of the secret, Alcibiades was condemned *in absentia* for profaning the Mysteries, Andocides narrowly escaped death for the same cause, and Livy (31, 14) tells of two strangers who wandered into the sanctuary, not being initiates, and were executed. So we can only speculate. One thing only is certain. There was no mystic leading of initiates along subterranean corridors with sudden apparitions, as if in the underworld. There are no subterranean chambers, and the hall itself did not have the mechanical devices needed. It is likely that there was a dramatic re-enactment of the myth, spectacular and quite frightening, the restoration of the Maid to the Mother with revelry of torches and musical ballet, and a gong sounding at the name of Kore. There may have been a sacred marriage encouraging the fertility of the land – we are told of the antiphonal cries of *hye* – *kye* ('rain' – 'conceive') (Procl. *In Plat. Tim.* 293C; Hipp. *Phil.* 5, 7, 34). It is interesting that cut in the stone of a well by the Dipylon Gate in Athens are the words 'O Pan, o Mēn, be joyful, beautiful nymphs rain, conceive, overflow' (*BCH* 20 (1896) 79). The sloping rock which is visible in the hall is thought to have played some part in this. The climax was a visual revelation (*epopteia*) of sacred objects in a brilliant light which must have involved reflectors. This included ancient cult-statues, but the climax of the climax was almost certainly an ear of corn, perhaps in gold. At some point there was a communion in cereal and barley wine. 'I have fasted. I have drunk the barley wine. I have taken things from the sacred chest, tasted them' (or 'done my task') 'and replaced them first in the basket then in the chest' (Clem. Al. *Protrept.* 2, 21, 2). There was some kind of identification with the goddess of the grain. The emperor Gallienus commemorated his initiation by putting GALLIENAE AVGVSTAE in the feminine on his coins (*Z.f. Num.* 38 (1928) 188).

From various sources, mainly literary, we can reconstruct the progress of the Great Mysteries which took place in Boedromion (our September) at the time of the autumn sowing. On the day before the festival (the 14th) the sacred objects were brought from Eleusis to Athens in cylindrical receptacles (*cistai*), such as those carried by the Caryatids in the smaller Propylaea at Eleusis. We have inscriptional evidence about the organization of transport (*CIA* IV 385 d p. 104 ll. 17–20; SIG $^2$2, 587, l. 42). The objects were taken to the Eleusinion in Athens, which has been identified between the agora and the acropolis (*Hesperia* 8 (1939) 207ff.). The first day (the 15th) included a proclamation and invitation. The second (the 16th) was known as 'Seawards, initiates' from the call to purification. The third (the 17th) was perhaps the day of the official sacrifice, but the evidence is not clear. The fourth (the 18th) was called the Epidauria or Asclepieia, and brought the healing god into the ceremonies. The fifth (the 19th) was the great procession back to Eleusis. Stones marking the road to Eleusis have been found (*Athenaion* III 598). A general impression of the procession can be gleaned from the relief carving which supported the votive statue of Nunnius Nigrinus. The sixth (the 20th) was a day of fasting, and of the main sacrifice at Eleusis, leading to the night and day of initiation (the 21st). The eighth (the 22nd) included libations to the dead. The ninth (the 23rd) was the day of return. This ended the festival: on the 24th the council heard an official report on it.

Two major inscriptions deal with the cult-regulations. One is to be dated to the middle of the fifth century BC. The first part, which is in a fragmentary state, deals with penalties for impiety. The second part establishes the timetable for the sacred truce which operated during the festival, whether the Lesser Mysteries or the Greater. For the former the truce was from the middle of Gamelion all through Anthesterion till Elaphebolion 20; for the latter from the middle of Metageitnion through Boedromion until Pyanepsion 20. The truce was binding on all city-states using the sanctuary, and is a good example of the power of religion over politics, since Eleusis was not established as one of the great panhellenic sites, and owed its reputation intrinsically to the Mysteries. The third part gives some information about financial and other arrangements affecting the people administering the festival. The sacred herald received half an obol each day from each initiate, the priestess of Demeter an obol – these are for the goddesses – and 1,600 drachmas were set aside for expenses. The noble families of the Eumolpidae and Kerykes (Heralds) received perquisites from the sacrifice; on pain of a severe fine they were not to initiate anyone under age. The Eumolpidae bore responsibility for orphans. The Athenians were given control of drafts on the sacred treasury. And so on ($IG$ I $^2$6).

Later in the century, at an uncertain date (448, 422, and 418 are all possible) there is a decree making provision for the support of the sanctuary through the first fruits of grain (the gift of Demeter) from Athens and the allies, with voluntary contributions invited from those outside the League. Provision is made for the sacrifices: an ox with gilded horns as the first victim; barley and wheat to each of the two goddesses; an unblemished victim to each of Triptolemus, Pluto, Kore, and Eubulus; an ox with gilded horns to Athene. There follows a prayer for blessings on those who offer their first fruits to the goddesses and do not act unjustly towards the Athenians, Athens, or the goddesses, and no doubt (for the inscription is incomplete) maledictions on others ($IG$ I $^2$76).

Artistic remains tell us a little more. We know that there were votive statues in the courtyard, and (to judge from bases) in the telesterion itself. One inscription tells us that a priestess named Satyra has been granted the right to set up a painted portrait of herself in the Temple of Demeter and Kore, a privilege granted to other priestesses (*Hesperia* 11 (1942) 265–7). It was strongly argued by Otto Kern on the basis of his study of reliefs that the cult-group itself showed Demeter seated on a cylindrical chest with Kore standing by her (*Ath. Mitt.* 17 (1892) 125–42). The oldest representation of the goddess to survive at Eleusis dates from the early fifth century. It shows her seated on a throne with a sceptre in one hand and ears of wheat in the other. Her hair is loose; this is therefore the *Mater Dolorosa*. A young woman is approaching with lighted torches. It is hardly Kore, for there is no joy. It might perhaps be Hecate approaching with unrecognized good news. From much the same period is a fragment of pedimental sculpture representing a girl running away – perhaps one of Kore's attendants at the time of the rape. Somewhat later, about the middle of the century, is the Grand Relief of Eleusis, a masterpiece of relief carving. It shows the goddesses, fully draped, with a young naked boy between them, receiving an ear of wheat. This is usually interpreted as Triptolemus receiving the gift of grain. Metzger has shown conclusively that this is not so: the boy is the *pais aph' hestias* (the boy from the hearth: that is, of Athens), a young aristocratic boy chosen for initiation at public expense to receive the blessings on behalf of the state (*RA* (1968) 113ff.). Triptolemus may be seen often enough in vase painting of both the black-figure and red-figure periods. He also appears on a fragmentary relief at Eleusis, dedicated by a priest named Lacratides: this however is much later, about 100 BC. It shows the priest and his family as votaries. But the fragments are difficult of interpretation. Demeter is seated with Kore before her with lighted torches and a bearded Pluto with sceptre standing near. But two divinities marked god and goddess also appear and it is hard to see who they are if not Pluto and Persephone as rulers of the underworld.

The other major art work is the painted plaque from the early fourth century dedicated to the goddesses by Niinnion. There have been different interpretations.[1] The painting is divided into two planes by a faint white line, and it is not certain whether it should be interpreted as one scene or two. It may be taken as assured that the plaque does not reveal any undivulged secret; we can be seeing only symbolic portrayals. It seems that there are two scenes. The upper shows an Ionic temple which never existed at Eleusis. It must therefore be the Lesser Mysteries at Agrae. Kore with torches is leading initiates to the seated Demeter. In the lower, from the Greater Mysteries, Iacchus with torches is leading initiates again to the goddess. The initiates may include Niinnion herself. The earthenware vessel or *kernos*, comprising a multitude of small cups for seeds of different kinds, can be seen in the procession.

A number of vase paintings and sculptures have to do with the mythical initiations of Dionysus and Heracles. On a few other representations we can add a detail or two about the proceedings. We can see an initiate wearing a myrtle wreath. A girl initiate is carrying a water-basin for purification. Some initiates carry pigs, sacred to Demeter, and offered on the second day in purification. Votive statuettes of pigs have been found, and the pig appears on coins of Eleusis (*Hist. Num.* $^2$391).[2]

The Eleusinian Mysteries were famous throughout the Greek world. Demeter and Kore had local Mysteries elsewhere, and this should not be forgotten. The sanctuary of the goddesses on the north slope of Acrocorinth has rockcut steps suggesting a theatral area for ritual drama.

A particularly exciting discovery was that of gold plates from Magna Graecia, dating from the fourth or third century BC, found buried in graves, and giving instructions to the souls of the dead. The use of the precious, gleaming metal shows alike the importance of the documents and the promise of a brighter life than might be expected in the darkness of the grove or of Hades.

> You will find within the halls of Hades a spring on the left
> and close to it a white cypress standing.
> Do not go near this spring.
> You will find another, cool water pouring
> from the Lake of Memory. Guards stand in front of it.
> Say 'I am a child of earth and starry heaven,
> but my race is of heaven. You know this for yourselves.
> I am parched with thirst and perishing. Quick, give me
> cold water pouring from the Lake of Memory.'
> Then they will freely allow you to drink from the sacred spring,
> and thereafter you will reign with the other demi-gods.
>
> (Kern, 32a)

> Queen of the dead, I come from a pure people,
> and you, Eucles, Eubuleus and the other immortal gods.
> For I claim to be of your blessed race,
> but fate and other immortal gods overpowered me
> .................. the flash of lightning.

I have flown out of the sorrowful, weary wheel,
I have come with speeding feet for the crown of my desire,
I bury my head in the lap of Our Lady, the Queen of the dead.
'Blessed and happy one, you shall be a god, a mortal no longer.'
(ibid. 32c)

These are usually treated as Orphic, but Gunther Zuntz in *Persephone* has pointed out that there is nothing to connect them directly with Orpheus, and not very much indirectly. It is true that Dionysus was worshipped in the guise of a kid, and that the suckling of a kid has some part in the Dionysiac Mysteries at Pompeii. But Zuntz rightly says that the emphasis here is on Persephone, who is 'Our Lady, the Queen of the Dead', and that there is plenty of evidence of honour to Persephone in Magna Graecia. It was after all in the fields of Enna that Pluto seized her for himself, and at Acragas the earliest sacred site, perhaps antedating the founding of the colony, was the sanctuary of the chthonic powers. Eucles ('the fair-famed') is her consort Pluto, and Eubuleus ('excellent in counsel') appears in a hymn as her son. These tablets then represent secret instructions to the soul of an initiate of some mystery-cult associated with Persephone. The alternative choices are a commonplace of such instructions all the world over; so are the formulae to gain admission to blessedness. The white cypress is a puzzle; it looks as if the tree of death has been mystically transformed into a tree of life. The 'sorrowful, weary wheel' suggests a belief in reincarnation. The equation of divinity and immortality is a Greek commonplace: it is even found in the Greek Christian tradition as when Athanasius boldly declares of Jesus 'He became man that we might become god', perhaps meaning not much more than 'He became mortal that we might become immortal' (Athan. *De Inc. Verb.* 54). 'I am a kid fallen into milk' is an expression of rebirth.

The Mysteries of the Cabeiri on Lemnos were of respectable antiquity, and though they never achieved quite the prominence of the corresponding rites on Samothrace, they form an important cult which won the devotion of non-Lemnians from Athens and elsewhere, who might become associate members, take official responsibilities, and make generous financial contributions to the operation. The initiates seem to have formed a close-knit fellowship; inscriptions, going back to the fourth century BC, speak of 'the Assembly of the Initiated',[3] or, still more pointedly, 'the Equally-assessed [*isoteleis*] and People of the Initiated'.

## THE MYSTERIES

Samothrace has been brilliantly excavated and expounded by the Lehmanns. It was settled by Greek colonists about 700 BC; they were (dialect suggests) Aeolian, from Lesbos or the nearby mainland, and their chief divinity was Athene, who appears on silver coinage of the sixth century. It was in the sixth century that the ancient sanctuary of the Great Gods up in the mountains began to develop formal buildings. These developments continued into the fifth century, but then for a century or more Samothrace, subject to Athens and scarcity in resources, was too poor do to much in developing the sanctuary despite its reputation attested by the initiation of Herodotus and Lysander and references in Aristophanes and Plato. It was the patronage of the royal house of Macedon which led to the great structural building from the middle of the fourth century. Here, we are told, in a moment pregnant with history, Philip II saw Olympias, princess of Epirus, fell in love with her and subsequently married her and fathered Alexander on her.

In the sanctuary at Samothrace, situated in a hollow of the mountains, it was natural to worship a mother goddess. She was there from time immemorial, certainly before the coming of the Greeks, as her most ancient rock-altar proves. Her name was Axieros. The Greeks thought of her as Demeter, or Hecate, or Aphrodite with a non-Greek cult-title Zerynthia. She can be seen on coins, enthroned between lions. It may be that Aphrodite Zerynthia is represented by some three-breasted statuettes found in a late tomb. The mother was worshipped on outcrops of rocks which served as altars, and her power was passed on to worshippers, and sometimes dedicated back to her, in the form of iron rings worked from her sacred lodestones.

Her consort was called Cadmilos or Casmilos. He was a god of fertility, portrayed as ithyphallic. The ram was sacred to him and he carried a sacred stave (*kerykeion*); these emblems may be seen on bronze coinage. It was natural for the Greeks to see in him their Hermes.

Two divinities of death were associated with the sanctuary. Their local names were Axiocersos and Axiocersa, and they were portrayed as a bearded male and a young female with a peculiar slim headdress. The Greeks identified these with Pluto or Hades and Persephone or Kore.

Finally there were two young divinities, depicted in bronze as nude and ithyphallic. Their symbols were snakes and stars, which appear on a silver ring, now unfortunately lost. In later times they were identified with the Cabeiri. Susan Cole has shown in an important study that these belong properly to the region of Halicarnassus, and were not original to the Samothracian sanctuary. The Samothracian pair were perhaps Dardanus and Aetion, legendary founders of the Mysteries, with pre-Greek names. The Greeks identified them with the Dioscuri. They were especially regarded as guardians of sailors.

It should be said that Susan Cole holds to a pattern of three at Samothrace, a trinity of Axieros, Axiocersos, and Axiocersa, with Cadmilos a cult-name of one of the others, and a second trinity of Electra (here the mythical mother), Dardanus, and Aetion.[4]

Admission to the Mysteries was open to all, Greeks and non-Greeks, men and women, children and adults, slave and free. In this Samothrace was quite unlike, say, Eleusis. Furthermore, although there was a great annual festival, which may survive today in the festival of Ayia Paraskevi on 26 July, initiation might take place at any time, as we know from the evidence of inscriptions. As usual, the secret of the Mysteries has been well kept. We know that the main rites took place in the dark. The sanctuary is equipped with stones pierced to support large torches; torches appear frequently on the monuments; and there is a proliferation of clay lamps with sacred monograms, suggesting that every initiate carried one. Initiation was in two stages; after the first the initiate became a *mystes* (a mystic initiate), after the second an *epoptes* (one who has seen). We know that initiates were enlightened about the inner meaning of the statues, symbols and religious objects associated with the sanctuary, and learned about Heaven and Earth. There was presumably a visual revelation in the higher stage, and may have been some sort of sacred drama. We have literary evidence of confession of sin, a feature unique in Greek religion. We know from a statue that initiates wore wreaths on their heads, women with a scarf over it. Archaeology furnishes plenty of evidence of ritual banqueting and drinking in the sanctuary. The initiates received protection against storm at sea, in the form of a purple cummerbund and more general protection in the iron rings already mentioned. It is likely that there was also promise of blessings in the afterlife; though this is not directly evidenced, it is implied in a relief showing heroes in the land of the blessed.

The sanctuary covers some 50,000 square metres, and was never formally enclosed. If we approach it from the north we come first to a large fort of the Byzantine period which overlies some indeterminate Hellenistic buildings. Nearby stands a building built in marble in the third century BC by a woman of Miletus; a square room, entered by an Ionic porch, is flanked by two smaller rooms. The purpose is unknown. Further along the same terrace is a building for ritual meals, 22 m in length, with three rooms. South of this is a curious niche with a huge lintel and a relieving triangle: it is pseudo-archaic and must have served a ritual purpose. Beyond this lay the theatre; it was totally destroyed by twentieth-century depredations. It has a curious feature. The orchestra was cut by the ravine which divides the site into two, and must have been covered over by wooden boarding. Beyond this again stood a fountain with a pool where stood the statue of Nike – the Victory of Samothrace – now in the Louvre. She seemed as if alighting on the prow of a ship. The crest of the sanctuary was demarcated by a huge stoa, the largest building of all, 104 m in length; the builders had to raise the ground level at the north end by as much as 5 m. It incorporated a number of monuments.

The older part of the sanctuary lay to the east of the stream. At the north end is the hall of initiation or Anactoron, on a site going back, from the pottery found there, to the sixth century BC, though now dated to the Roman period, and standing in parts to a height of 3–4 m. The interior measures 27 × 11.58 m, and was entered by three doors on the long western side. It had an earth floor and was never paved. At the north end was an inner sanctuary reserved for initiates; a notice from Roman times forbidding entrance to the uninitiated may be assumed to be a replacement of earlier notices. Cuttings in the walls of the main hall indicate beams to support grandstands. The hall incorporated a pit with a sacred stone at the bottom to receive libations. At the south end of the hall a small building was presumably a sacristy. It contained records of initiations. In its present form it dates from the 280s BC, but it replaced an earlier sacred house. Next to the south comes a *tholos* or rotunda dedicated by Queen Arsinoe to the Great Gods in the 280s, with an outer diameter of more than 20 m, the largest closed ancient Greek circular building known. It was designed for sacrificial and official gatherings of the state representatives during the great summer festival. However, it was built over the foundations of an earlier precinct now dated to the early fourth century, but incorporating early rock altars. Just outside this to the south lies a sixth-century rock altar; from literary references it is thought to be the altar of Hecate Zerynthia. Then, in the very centre of the sanctuary, comes a sacred precinct. This was a very ancient sacrificial area, and a hearth of the seventh century and early relics of sacrificial offerings have been found, as well as a slightly later pit for offerings to the dead and more elaborate hearth. In about 340 BC an elaborate entrance was built, perhaps by the great sculptor Scopas and perhaps at the expense of Philip of Macedon. It was of the Ionic order and had an archaizing frieze of dancing girls and musicians. There is a speculative view that this open-air precinct was the scene of ritual drama. To the south again is a complex of three sacred places, the hall of votive gifts, built about 540 BC, behind it a rectangular structure containing a monumental altar, and, alongside both, the building called the Sanctuary or *hieron*, a long narrow hall, some 40 m in length, culminating in an apse. This is thought to have been the scene of the second or higher initiation, by night, as the torch-holders show, with a space for a preliminary ceremony outside, presumably the confession and purification which preceded entry into the sacred place.

Finally over to the east lies a ceremonial entrance dedicated by Ptolemy II in the 280s, a circular theatral area of the fifth century BC where five concentric steps allowed a limited number of spectators to view in the round a central spectacle, and a building dedicated by Alexander the Great's immediate successors Philip III and Alexander IV.

The buildings of the sanctuary are of peculiar interest for anyone wishing to trace the details of this aspect of Greek religion, but nothing can match the awesome quality of the setting, in its upland hollow among the trees and shrubs dominated by the mountain peak. From further off, with the higher mountains showing, the island is even more awe-inspiring, 'a savage place . . . holy and enchanted'.[5]

Susan Cole has made an exhaustive study of all references to the Samothracian gods outside Samothrace with a full appendix of the archaeological evidence, and another forming a prosopography of the Samothracian initiates. Many of them are personal dedications, but there are references to priests of the Samothracian gods in Olbia, Tomis, Dionysopolis, Istros, Chalcedon, Delos, Rhodes, Carpathos, and Mylasa. At the last three it was an annual appointment; at some others the appointment was for life. At Dionysopolis and Tomis the worshippers were called *mystai*. There were temples of the Samothracian gods at Odessus, Callatis, Istros, Delos, Ephesus, Stratonicea, and Philadelphia. It is not clear that the Mysteries were celebrated at any of these sites; they may have been doing no more than maintaining the link and honouring the worship.

## THE MYSTERIES

One of the most important inscriptions relating to a mystery religion refers to the Mysteries of the Cabeiri at Andania in Messenia. It can be dated to 91 BC. The mystery (*telete*) is to be performed by a dedicated group of both sexes chosen by lot from the citizens. After selection the sacred company must swear an oath that they will conduct the offices reverently and in due order on pain of a fine of 1,000 drachmas. During the festival they are charged with the care of the sacred books and their container. The attire, both male and female, is meticulously regulated. Shoes must either be of felt or formed from the skins of sacrificial victims. No gold ornaments must be worn. The men are to wear laurel wreaths, the women white hats. The women may not have transparent clothes; the married women are to wear an Egyptian tunic and a cloak, the maximum cost of which is prescribed. The procession is to be headed by a benefactor named Mnasistratus, followed by the priest and priestess of the deities, the president of the Games, the sacrificers, and the musicians. Then come the holy virgins escorting the caskets of the Mysteries, and the women and men chosen for the sacred office, followed by the sacrificial victims. All those attending the festival are expected to camp out, but the initiates have a sacred precinct which no uninitiated person may enter. Camping is to be simple, and limits are placed upon expenditure. During the sacrifices and Mysteries there is to be silence on pain of beating and exclusion. The finances of the festival are controlled by a board of five commissioners, with severe penalties for peculation. Any profits are to go into the state treasury. The sacrifices are considerable: two white lambs beforehand; a ram of the appropriate colour for purification; three piglets for the purification of the theatre; a hundred lambs for the *protomystae*; in the procession, a pregnant sow for Demeter, a 2-year-old pig for the Great Gods, a ram for Hermes, a boar for Apollo Carneios, and a sheep for Hagna, a local nymph. There is careful regulation of the contract for supplying these. A register of musicians is to be kept by those responsible for the sacred office. They also deal with crime during the festival, and with selecting a place for a market for the crowd of worshippers, though its operation is superintended by the appropriate civic authority. The sacrifices are followed by a banquet attended by those originally selected for the offices, the priest and priestesses of the Great Gods, the priestess of Apollo Carneios, Mnasistratus and family, the musicians, and some other religious officials. After the festival those chosen make a full report.[6]

What this exciting document does not tell us, naturally, is anything about the Mysteries themselves; they were a strict secret. The *hieroi* and *hierai* chosen by lot received these within the sacred precinct. It is clear that the heart of the mystery lay in something revealed, brought in within a sacred chest, and opened to the initiates. The priest and priestesses of the Great Gods must have controlled the ceremony. The *hieroi* and *hierai* were initiated, not as individuals but on behalf of the state. It is interesting to note the public interest and enthusiasm surrounding the ceremony from those who had no part in it except vicariously.

Another centre of the Mysteries of the Cabeiri lay near Thebes. Occupation extended from the archaic period to the Roman era. The site, fully excavated in 1956–69, is not easy of interpretation. A temple and theatre both focus on a central altar, showing that here there was certainly a cult-drama. Two water basins are connected with lustration and purification, and three round buildings have cultic significance. At the edge of the sanctuary three rectangular halls are arranged to enclose a courtyard. There was a grove of Demeter Cabeiria about a mile away. The vases from the Cabeirion show curious caricatured scenes with birds and winged griffins and ithyphallic pygmies. The pygmies seem to represent the lower aspects of human nature, and the winged birds the power of elevation.[7]

The Orphic mysteries create some problems. Orpheus was a legendary musician who charmed the animals, rescued or failed to rescue his wife from death, and was torn to pieces by Maenads. His story impinges on that of Dionysus, of whom he appears in some ways as a doublet. We know of practitioners of Orphic initiation in the fifth century BC, but it is less certain that passages in Empedocles, Pindar, and Plato should be fathered on the cult. Much of our knowledge dates from the Roman period when we have some eighty hymns addressed to various deities, belonging to a cult-society, possibly in Pergamon. This was certainly involved in initiation and the promise of bliss, but it is possible that it was very local, though the hymns gained a wider currency. We know of an associated myth. Dionysus was killed and eaten by the Titans. The heart was rescued and a new Dionysus born from it. The Titans were destroyed by Zeus's thunderbolt. From their ashes emerged mankind, Titanic in body, Dionysiac in soul. Man's aim then is to purify himself of his Titanic element till he becomes divine instead of mortal.

From a late period we have some material remains associated with

Orphism. In Modena there is a relief which shows Phanes, a young Orphic god of light, within an oval, the cosmic egg, with the four winds blowing round it. Above the winged god the creation of heaven and earth is represented by two hemispheres with flames rising from them. Around the oval are the signs of the zodiac. The god has the sceptre of Zeus, the face of Helios, the hoofs of Pan; he is man and beast; he is all gods. Round him is coiled a snake, with rich symbolism: the path of the sun through the zodiac as well as all the power of death and life.

We also have some remarkable bowls associated with an Orphic cult. One has no recorded provenance. The outside represents the cosmos, round, and supported on twenty-four columns, with the four winds as trumpeters. The circles on the base of the bowl represent the movement of the spheres. Quotations from Orphic hymns are inscribed on the base. Inside the bowl a winged snake twines round the cosmic egg, which is protected by fiery flames. Around are sixteen worshippers, nude, nine female and seven male, with a variety of gestures. The scene is one of mystic revelation pointing to rebirth. This was a sacramental bowl; as the worshippers drank the scene was revealed.

Another bowl was found near Pietrosa in Romania. It was made of gold, and has now been destroyed for its metal. In the centre a goddess sat on a vine-encircled throne with a chalice, surrounded by animals including one human figure. Then, more elaborately, are sixteen figures. There was Orpheus as the musician in glory, and Orpheus as fisherman drawing the initiate to him. Around the bowl, as in the Villa of the Mysteries, extended the pattern of initiation. The initiate bore the pine cone of life, and the torch of light in the presence of the raven of death and darkness, paused in reverence before Demeter and Kore, was blessed by the powers of fortune, carried a begging bowl before two torturers with whips in the presence of the raven of death, and was welcomed into new life and the presence of Orpheus with the staff of wisdom and the basket of abundance.[8]

We are best informed of the Mysteries of Dionysus during the Hellenistic and Roman periods. We have for example an account of the introduction of the orgia of the god at Magnesia-on-the-Maeander, perhaps from the third century BC, although we have only a copy of the original. A storm split open a tree and revealed an image of the god. The Delphic oracle told the people to build a temple to him, institute a priesthood, import Maenads and form *thiasoi* or

Bacchic companies (*I. Magn.* 215). In the third century from Miletus we have regulations controlling the initiation and subsequent practices, toning down the wild hunts and tearing apart of wild animals, and trying to ensure that there were no private extravagances (*LSAM* 48). A century or two later we have from Miletus a gravestone with an epigram in honour of a priestess: 'She led you to the mountain, and introduced the holy rites for all our city' (Peek I 1344). From Methymna we know of an all-night festival for Dionysus, seemingly for women (*IG* XII 2, 499). From Seleuceia on Calycadnus we have from the second century BC a dedication to Dionysus leader of the Bacchants, and the mystics (*Denkschr. Akad. Wien* 44, 6 (1896) 104 no. 183). In Pergamon we know of all-night festivals, one at least of which was for women.[9] These Mysteries continued into the Roman period. We hear of mystic initiates from Lerna (*IG* IV 666), Panamara in Caria, where there was a deliberate policy to introduce Mysteries available at any time (*BCH* 51 (1927) 123ff.), Thebes (Peek 694) and Athens (Peek 1024); the last refers to a 7-year-old initiate. We have interesting lists of officials of these mysteries, which include priest, deputy priest, archibacchus, holy children, steward, scribe, iobacchus, oxherd, chorus-master, chorus-leader, silenus, papa, hierophant, garland-bearer, basket-bearer, milk-bearer, archmystic, and many others.[10] As usual, the mysteries themselves are closely guarded. We have however a scene of Dionysiac initiation from a sarcophagus in the Villa Medici. In the background a temple can be seen. In the centre is a nude woman, her dress fallen about her knees with a basket in front of her holding a garland. To her right as we look is the initiate, veiled *cap-à-pie*, seemingly a woman, guided by a man with a thyrsus. Behind him, dimly seen, is a bearded man. Further to the right another woman, also with her dress fallen below her waist, is leaning on a garlanded herm with a tree behind her. In the foreground is a fallen basket of fruit. On the other side a seated woman holds up a platter of fruit with one hand while stirring with the other a krater into which a servant is pouring the holy drink. Behind them a veiled man is carrying a basket (*liknon*) containing a covered phallus; this is often to be seen in Dionysiac representations. Elsewhere on the sarcophagus Dionysus is depicted finding Ariadne. Plainly then the initiate is being guided blind, for it is a mystery. The mystery has to do with fertility, with the phallus, and fruit, and wine. And this is the power of life over death, as the touch of the god stirred Ariadne, left to death by Theseus, into new life.

# THE MYSTERIES

The most powerful witness of Dionysiac initiation is the series of frescoes covering the walls of a room in the villa of the gens Istacidia on the outskirts of Pompeii, in the area of Greek settlement around the Bay of Naples. Those who approach the inner chamber do so through a small ante-room or vestibule where the paintings are symbolic but not systematic. The figures in order, but in no special relationship to one another, seem to represent Ariadne abandoned, a Bacchante with raised hand, a dancing Bacchante, a young dancer, an old Silenus, and, in a second sequence, an old Silenus, a young satyr (missing), a priestess, and a dancing faun. All speak indirectly, mysteriously, of the god.

On entering the room the worshipper faces the figures of Dionysus and Ariadne presiding over the whole ceremony. Along the walls, brilliantly painted against a bright vermilion ground, twenty-seven figures enact the drama of initiation. The lady of the house, perhaps the president of the community, sits immobile and impassive, watching it all. An initiate with head veiled and hand on hip in a ritual attitude stands listening while a naked boy reads the liturgical formulae under the guidance of a seated matron. A pretty maid, whose gently swelling belly betokens a pregnancy of symbolic import, passes from this scene to the next carrying a tray of ritual offerings from the initiate to an officiant seated with two attendants at a table; there is a libation or lustration in process, and the table may signify a ritual meal. From here we pass to the Mysteries proper, shown directly and symbolically. A fat Silenus is playing the lyre, a young Pan is fluting, a charming boyish Panisca is offering her breast to a kid; we remember another mystic formula 'A kid I am fallen into milk'. But all is not sweetness and light. Initiation has its awesome side. Next we see a woman starting back in horror. It is not clear exactly why; perhaps that is part of the mystery. She may be playing a role in some divine drama; she may be horror-struck at one of the scenes on her left: the startling appearance of the lower nature; the awesome presence of the god and his consort; the unveiling of the colossal phallus; or the flagellation. Or perhaps as the neophyte of flesh and blood walked round, and the torchlight fell on this figure, she had the feeling of fear for herself. Next comes a curious scene. A satyr is peering into a bowl held by a Silenus with averted head. Behind him another Silenus holds up a grotesque mask. There is little doubt about this scene. The satyr expects to see his own image and he sees this apparition reflected instead. The satyr already represents our lower nature; this is a parable of what our lower nature becomes if it is not curbed and transformed. On the far side of the divine pair a kneeling woman is unveiling a phallus, the power of life. Next a great winged figure is wielding a rod. Various interpretations of this figure have been given. I earlier thought it was Telete, the very power of Initiation; now I think Nilsson is right, and the closest parallels are with Dike, the spirit of Justice. There is no certainty. The victim is the initiate, her fine robes fallen off, her hair rumpled, a gown of penitence loosely worn, her head in the lap of a comforting woman while another looks anxiously on, her back bared to the blows which are the test of endurance, the ritual death, and at the same time the touch of new life. And now the ordeal is over. The initiate throws off the penitential gown, picks up the scarf on which her head was pillowed, and clashes cymbals as she engages in a great dance of resurrection. Finally we see a preparation for a mystical marriage parallel to that of Ariadne. The whole is a unique record of a profound experience.[11]

How many other rooms in private houses were set aside for Dionysiac mysteries we cannot say. To take one possible example, at Thessalonica in 1964 there was discovered a floor mosaic showing the sleeping Ariadne discovered by Dionysus and his rout. Among the smaller panels is depicted the scene of Ganymede and the eagle. Both these show the touch of immortality on mortality, and one cannot help wondering whether the room was in fact a cult-room (*BSA Arch. Rep.* 13 (1966–7) 15–16).

Another document relating to mysteries of Dionysus is an inscription from Smyrna, dating from the second century AD, probably from the sanctuary of Dionysus Briseus on the outskirts of the city, and setting out some of the prescriptions of the Mysteries. It is written in hexameter verse:

SET UP BY MENANDER'S SON . . . THE THEOPHANT
All you who enter the precinct and shrines of Bromios,
abstain for forty days after exposing
a young child, for fear of divine wrath:
the same number of days for a woman's miscarriage.
If death and doom overshadow one of your household
keep away from the forecourt the third part of the month;
If pollution come from another's house
through a dead body, stay apart for three days.
Do not approach the altars of our Lord in black clothes.
Do not begin the sacred feast until the dishes have been blessed.

Do not serve an egg at the sacred meal in the mysteries of
   Bacchus.
Refrain from burning the heart on the holy altar.
Abstain from mint . . .
and the abominable root of beans . . .
Tell the initiates about the Titans . . .
It is not right to use reeds as castanets . . .
on the days on which initiates offer sacrifices . . .
or to carry . . .

(Ins. Smyrna 17)

The priest's name is lost, but he is called a theophant; this suggests that the Mysteries included an apparition of the god. The inscription is defective and in parts obscure. The respect for children is noteworthy; elsewhere we know of a child initiate in the Dionysiac Mysteries, who died aged 3 years and 2 months. The absence of prohibition of those who have had sexual intercourse is worth noting; evidently the worship of Dionysus was more permissive than some cults. There are, naturally at this late period, signs of assimilation of similar cults, the Orphic (the Cosmic Egg, and the myth of the wicked Titans, and the importance of the heart), and the Pythagorean (abstention from beans).

# 9

# DEATH AND BURIAL

In the Mycenaean Age of Greece our earliest records of the disposal of the dead, dating from the Middle Helladic period (roughly the first part of the second millennium BC) show two related patterns, a simple shallow pit, just sufficient for a human body on its side, and the most elaborate cist-grave lined with stone slabs. Normally a single vase was interred with the body. The famous Grave Circles of Mycenae are in fact an elaboration of the cist-grave. Here the burials were in shafts with a pebble floor, and sometimes space enough for several interments, the shafts set within a circle. The dead were accompanied with rich offerings, and sometimes had gold masks set over their faces, seemingly in emulation of Egyptian practice. The site known as Grave Circle A was holy enough to be incorporated within an extended defence system. Inside or outside the walls it looks as if the ancestors were protecting the approach to the citadel.

The great *tholos* tombs or beehive tombs go back into the Middle Helladic period, though at Mycenae itself they are somewhat later. Their origin is uncertain, but it is possible that they represent the preservation of an archaic form of house-building, elaborated to provide the House of the Dead. The finest are huge chambers approached by a magnificent corridor or dromos. Unfortunately only at Pylos has the tomb escaped the robbers. There four of the burials were placed in storage, accompanied by rapiers, daggers, arrowheads, caldrons, bronze pins and other implements, and fragments of a gilded wreath. In one example there is evidence of horses being sacrificed. Other burials were in pits, the last body of all being laid out in the middle of the tomb with a dagger, an arrowshaft, a bronze bowl, a mirror, an oil flask, a bronze awl, and a female figurine. Chamber tombs are similar to but less elaborate than the *tholos* tombs. The inner chamber is sometimes round, sometimes square, or rectangular with rounded corners. Broken cups in the dromos suggest the practice of libation. All these tombs were family tombs, reopened as needed. But despite their great elaboration, there is no indication of a cult of the dead.[1]

One other fact we know about the attitude to death at this period is that there was a mourning ritual. A characteristic posture from slightly later artistic representations, as on the great Geometric jar in the national museum at Athens, shows mourners with their hands laid on their heads; it can be taken as certain that clay figurines from the Mycenaean period, found at Perati in Attica, Kamini on Naxos, and Ialysos on Rhodes, and figures in a similar posture painted on sarcophagi from Tanagra in Boeotia, represent mourners.

We thus have a complex nexus of beliefs. The dead are laid in the earth, or in houses built for them. They are accompanied by offerings, presumably for their use in the afterlife. The sheer elaboration of the tombs suggests the lasting importance of their condition. The position of the tomb suggests that the dead have a protective function over the living. On the other hand there is no evidence of continued cult, and no evidence of any fear of the anger of the dead at the reopening of their places of rest.

Towards the end of the Mycenaean Age and in the period immediately following cremation becomes more widely practised. In the early period it is always associated with chamber tombs, always side by side with inhumation, and the ashes are placed in vases or left on the floor of the tomb. In the early Iron Age necropolis on the island of Salamis three cremations have been found; each time the burning took place elsewhere, and the ashes were set in a neck-handled amphora within a circular stone-sided pit. The fact that cremation and burial are found in such close conjunction is difficult to interpret religiously.

Within the Dark Ages (roughly 1125–900 BC) the main change is from multiple burial to individual burial, with the exception of Crete, Messenia, and Thessaly. Cist graves and pit graves naturally begin to predominate, as they are most appropriate to individual burials. We cannot be certain of the reasons for this major change. Some scholars would, reasonably enough, attribute it to movement of peoples.[2]

At Athens the Ceramicus, or potters' quarter, was used for burials outside the city walls from about the twelfth century BC to the fifth AD.

Early graves were unmarked or marked by a stone or pot. In the later Dark Ages Athens saw a major swing towards cremation, which largely replaced burial for adults. The ashes were placed in an amphora and set neatly in a pit. But the change was not absolute, since children were buried in cist tombs, and infants were placed in large pots.

In the early Geometric period (roughly 900–700 BC) this trend at Athens continued.[3] It has proved possible to reconstruct some of the rites. A soldier's ashes were buried with his sword bent and made useless in this world, though not necessarily in the next. Spearheads, an axe head, a javelin head, knives, bits for horses, and a whetstone were placed in a cloth in the grave beside him, together with an oil flask and three wine cups. Plainly, life was expected in some sense to go on. A woman was cremated on the Areopagus. While the cremation was taking place the mourners feasted and threw their cups on to the pyre. Her remains were set in an urn, and this was buried with some of her personal possessions, pins and brooches, a knife, beads, and a spindle whorl. Sometimes the place of interment was marked by a large pot to receive libations, and we can trace an early example where the base was pierced to allow the libation to seep through to the urn below. As the century continued we find evidence of increasing prosperity. Most remarkable is the grave of a rich lady whose ashes were set in a splendid amphora, and whose existence in the tomb was brightened by a necklace with more than 1,000 faience discs (perhaps an import from the Asian coast), elaborate gold earrings, ivory seals and amulet, gold rings, other rings, bronze brooches, thirty-four vases of high quality, and a remarkable clay chest surmounted by five model granaries.

In the following century the Athenians moved increasingly towards inhumation, first for women, and by 750 cremation had again virtually died out. The reasons for the change are not clear. Of considerable interest are two inhumations at Eleusis datable to about 800 BC. Their personal ornaments were gorgeous, especially their gold lunate earrings. One of them had a faience figurine of the Egyptian goddess Isis, who was identified with Demeter by the Greeks. It is possible that the women were priestesses of Demeter. Usually in the burials which came to predominate an adult was laid on the back with legs extended and arms to the side.

Elsewhere, in the Argolid or around Corinth, for example, inhumation remained the regular practice throughout the period, most commonly in cist graves, with knees flexed, accompanied by tools or ornaments, though in the Argolid there was an increasing tendency to use vast jars of coarse pottery even for adult burials. In the north the *tholos* tombs continued for family burials. There is one curious exception at Halos in Thessaly, where sixteen cremations were found, ten of men and six of women. The pyres were placed on the bare ground, and the pottery and ritual offerings placed on the pyres with the bodies. At the end of each ceremony the pyre was covered with large stones, and finally all sixteen were covered with a mound of earth. Tumuli covering cremations have also been found on the island of Naxos. At Pithecusae, the colony of Chalcis in Italy, archaeological evidence suggests that the pyre was quenched with wine before the ashes were moved and covered with a tumulus.

On Rhodes, cremation, except of children, was the normal practice, followed by the burial of ashes. Animal bones suggest a feast in honour of the dead, or a holocaust to the dead. In the graves at Ialysus were found vases, real and miniature, two pepperpot vases of helmeted heads, votive figures, a number of bronze objects, miniature bronze figurines, and jewellery (rings, brooches, and necklaces). An unusual number of the vases portray monsters. Sirens, acknowledged spirits of death, appear on one vase, and there is also a terracotta siren. An orientalizing black-figure vase of about 600 BC shows a funerary couple between sphinxes. Another vase shows a seated figure between two standing winged female figures, harbingers of death not of victory. One cup has a winged spirit of death in its bowl. These are clearly all made for the graves, and they indicate that death was regarded as awesome and fearsome.

The Greeks had a tradition of celebrating the death of heroes with funerary games. The most familiar example in literature is provided by the games for Patroclus in Book 23 of *The Iliad*. It is hard to be sure of the religious significance of the contest, and Homer gives no indication. Perhaps there is something in the struggle of the contestants representing the struggle of life with death, in which excellence wins. Or perhaps there is a substitute for human sacrifice involved. Or perhaps it is simply a spectacle to give pleasure to the dead man. Certainly it is a release of tension for the living. Some scholars suppose that the Olympic Games were in origin funerary games for Pelops, and the other Panhellenic festivals claim a similar origin. Funerary games appear on some early works of art, the chest of Cypselus at Olympia, the throne of Apollo at Amyclae, the François vase now in

Florence and the Amphiaraus vase in Berlin. The first games we hear of commemorating a firmly historic figure are recorded by Hesiod (*WD* 654–9), in honour of Amphidamas of Chalcis, killed in the Lelantine War. But from about 700 BC into the fifth century we have archaeological records of funerary games in the form of tripods, caldrons, and other bronze vessels which were prizes, and are often inscribed with the name of the dead man. These mostly come from the Greek cities north of the Isthmus of Corinth and their overseas colonies, like the bronze bowl from Cyme datable to about 500 BC and won at games in honour of a certain Onomastos.

By the end of the seventh century in Athens it became customary to honour the dead with elaborate marble monuments, figures of young men or young women or oriental extravaganzas such as a sphinx. Sometimes these take the form of a stele or a narrow slab of dressed stone, carved in low relief or painted, with figures of athletes or soldiers, or old men with a staff, with a simple inscription, the whole often surmounted with a capital and a palmette, sphinx, or other motif. Sometimes the grave was marked by sculpture in the round, most frequently *kouroi* or young men standing, sometimes *korai* or young women, sometimes riders on horseback, sometimes seated figures. The famous square base from the Ceramicus showing sporting activities perhaps once carried a seated figure. Solon was in fact constrained to limit funerary expenditure.

In the classical period in Attica inhumation and cremation both continued. Tile graves, formed by leaning larger roof-tiles against one another in a protective tent over the body, became more frequent. Children were now placed in stone sarcophagi or clay tombs. Objects buried with the dead are various, even allowing for perishables which have disappeared. Eggs were at all times placed in graves; the survival of the modern Easter egg may serve to remind us of the egg as a symbol of life beyond death. Personal possessions are buried with their owners, especially toys with children. Mirrors and strigils are found. Curiously not very much jewellery has appeared, though there is some clay imitation jewellery. Pottery is frequent, and graves of the classical period have as their most characteristic offering the white-ground oil flasks, known generically as *lekythoi*. They are covered with a white slip, and show allegorical scenes often representing the power of Death directly or indirectly (as through Hermes, the guide of the dead, Charon, the ferryman of the dead, or Hypnos, the power of sleep), mythological scenes, domestic scenes, and scenes of parting or mourning. These were obviously made for burial in the tomb, presumably to contain the oil which the deceased would need for light, food and cleanliness in the afterlife. This fact makes it hard to evaluate whether other pottery buried with the dead was part of the normal household ware accompanying the owner, or made for the occasion. This could be of importance in evaluating some of the paintings. The sexual and phallic scenes on some Attic vases take on an altogether different connotation if they were made specially for the tomb, when they surely speak of the power of life even in death. The most one can say is that some pottery in tombs shows signs of previous use – as with children's feeding bottles buried with children – and some does not. It should always be remembered that the vessel was interred primarily not as a work of art but as a container of wine or oil to refresh the deceased. There are a few objects in tombs of different kinds. Notable are miniature arms with fingers and thumb extended but closed in what is probably an apotropaic gesture. Several are sometimes found in a single grave.[4]

An important text coming from Paros and known as *Marmor Parium* (*IG* XII (5) 444 + 315 *Supp.* 110) gives details of sumptuary legislation imposed on Athens by Demetrius of Phalerum in 317–316 BC, which among other things limited expenditure on death ceremonies. Although he held power for a limited period only, his legislation lasted, and elaborate monuments do not reappear until the second century. Inhumation is commoner than cremation in the Hellenistic period. Grave goods remain much the same. They are on the whole more modest than earlier though leaves and wreaths of gold foil now appear.

After death the body was made ready for the *prothesis* or laying out, probably in the courtyard of the home.[5] Eyes and mouth were ceremonially closed, and the body was washed, anointed with oil, and dressed in white – sometimes in wedding clothes (Peek 1238, 3) – and laid on a bier, the head garlanded, feet towards the door. This last has been a normal precaution all over the world to ensure that the dead walk in the right direction. A cypress bough outside warned of death within; a lustral bowl stood by the door to cleanse those within from the pollution of the corpse. The lamentation or wake was of great importance in the archaic period, and appears frequently on vases and plaques; in the fifth and fourth centuries it appears less. The women of the family gathered round the bier. The father received the guests. The men processed in with ritual gestures. The most commonly represented gesture is beating the head or tearing the hair with both arms raised. There was keening and singing to the wailing of a flute.

After the time of Solon the *ekphora*, or funeral procession, took place on the third day after death at Athens; this seems to have become general. Before Solon the procession was extravagant, as we can see depicted on a number of eighth-century vases in Athens. Expenditure and emotional expression were alike thereafter restricted, but a Berlin black-figure vase shows the pipe accompaniment to the *ekphora* and an Attic vase by the Sappho painter shows the women lamenting while the body is laid in the grave. Fifth-century legislation from Delphi banned keening during the procession but permitted it at the grave (*LGS* 74C). Third-century legislation from Gambreion in Asia Minor laid down the proper wear for mourners, white or dark for men, dark for women, and forbade the rending of clothes (*LSAM* no. 16).

Ceremonies of offerings at graves were made on the third, ninth, and thirtieth days, and after one year. But the third, ninth, and thirtieth days after what – death or burial? This has been a matter of scholarly argument, but in a careful examination of the inscriptional evidence Freistadt has made a strong case for the former, in which case the *trita* will have taken place immediately after burial.[6] The scene at the tomb has been admirably reconstructed by Margaret Alexiou in her excellent book *The Ritual Lament in Greek Tradition*. As she rightly says, the literary evidence, though copious, is vague, and must be reinforced from inscriptions, vase paintings and other archaeological sources. Attic white-ground *lekythoi* are especially valuable for portraying the scene at the tomb. The mourner offered a lock of his hair (*LGS* 93A; Peek 428; 1157; 1422; 1970). He then poured a libation with a prayer, and made the sacrifice of milk and honey, water and wine, celery, funeral cakes, and fruits, often with the killing of an animal over a trench, and sometimes leaving musical instruments, clothes, and other material offerings. The illustrations suggest that this was a relatively private affair carried out by a few members of the inner family. Lamentation was loud, gestures violent.

> Her aunt ran up and tore her robe
> Her mother ran up and began beating her breast.
> (Peek 1159, 9–10)

Legislation from a number of places forbids burial within the precincts of temples (*LSAM* no. 83; *SIG* 3, 1221; 3, 1227). The motive for this legislation is not wholly clear. Bringing the departed into the presence of the immortal gods may have been taken by the mourners as pointing to new life, but to the priests as an act of pollution. It is possible too that in some cases the family hoped that the dead one might receive worship and the status of a demigod.

The cult of the dead is prominent all over Asia Minor, but nowhere more clearly than in Lycia. Early tombs of the classical period abound. The earliest are perhaps the pillar tombs, a Lycian speciality. They are formed by a rectangular pillar on a base, with the tomb proper at the top surmounted by a capstone: they can be seen, for example, at Xanthus or Sidyma, and the famous Harpy Tomb at Xanthus is a combination of sarcophagus and pillar tomb. The temple tombs are carved in the rock in imitation of a temple façade with, inside, a simple chamber incorporating benches for the dead. The tomb of Amyntas at Telmessus is a particularly fine example; there is another at Cyaneae. The house tombs are similarly carved out of the rock, but in imitation of a house rather than a temple; there is an excellent example, surmounted by a pointed 'Gothic' arch and bulls' horns above, at Pinara. The most striking of all is the painted tomb at Myra, decorated with eleven lifesize figures in relief, painted in red, blue, yellow, and purple. Some of these are very striking: a bearded man drinking; the same person dressed for a journey; a veiled servant-girl carrying a casket. Finally, there are the distinctive Lycian sarcophagi, with a second grave chamber in the base for the dead man's servants, the grave chamber, and an elaborate lid, often with the pointed Gothic moulding, the sides being frequently decorated with sculptural scenes.[7]

Something of attitudes to death can be gained by study of stelai and other grave reliefs, including sarcophagi, though we must always remember that the most elaborate monuments appertain to rich families, and that the poor have left few memorials behind them.

There are a number of interesting memorials in the Rhodes museum. The commonest of all grave markers was a round stone adorned with bulls' heads and festoons. This was a standard pattern of altar, and the decoration need be no more than a conventional religious symbol, speaking of sacrifice and festival, though if we press the imagery further it has to do with life and fertility. A few large sarcophagi are pedimented. Here the tomb is clearly the house of the dead. One depicts a horseman killing a panther. The hunt is a common scene on sarcophagi; an exceptional example is the so-called

Alexander sarcophagus in Istanbul, portraying Alexander on a wild-animal hunt. It is hard to know what the symbolism conveys. Certainly that life is a struggle. The sarcophagi show the victory of humans over the wild forces, as the battle sarcophagi show the victories of gods over giants or Greeks over Amazons. But does this indicate victory over death? Or does it tell of the temporary victories of life, with the panther of death lying in wait when your reactions are slower? Or is there a covert allusion to Attis, divinized after his death in a hunt? In the Rhodes example there is a bird sitting on a tree, perhaps the herald of death despite the triumphs of life.

One grave shows a shrine with a trophy and a snake entwined around the breastplate. This seems to speak of victory and a healing power greater than death. Another funerary monument shows a flower in the shape of a vase with a snake again wrapped round; this certainly contains symbols of life.

Many of the stelai show scenes of parting. Timarista in death says goodbye to her daughter Crito (smaller than she). A damaged stele shows a couple standing and embracing. Often the couple clasp hands, usually with one seated and one standing; in one example both are standing. Sometimes the stelai show scenes from life, often with a touch of poignancy. A veiled seated woman is putting something into – or taking something out of – a box held by her standing attendant. A soldier contemplates the helmet he will use no more. Two unusual scenes are particularly complex and difficult of interpretation. In one a nude male is leaning on a herm. Hermes is wearing Heracles's lionskin. On the far side a boy is standing with hands clasped. We can only guess. Hermes was the guide of the spirits of the dead, but Heracles was the one who went to Hades and returned, who wrestled with Death and gave life to Alcestis. There seems here to be hope and faith. One plaque is more difficult because incomplete: another slab is missing. We have a large animal, a horse, contemplating a small lionlike animal across an altar. Behind the smaller animal is a boy with a gesture repelling the horse. In the background are four more children and four adults. Perhaps the boy is dead, the horse of death has come for him, and he and the young lion are challenging death, while the family watch. But does this mean that the boy lost the struggle for life, or that beyond the grave he has defied death?

From Cos museum we may exemplify two other common motifs. One (104) shows the dead man on a ship. This may be no more than the image of the life that is gone, since all the islands will have had numerous people working at sea. But it may represent the common image of the voyage to the Isles of the Blest. This is represented on sarcophagi by the appearance of dolphins and other sea creatures, and sometimes simply stylized in wavy lines. The other motif is the necrodeipnon or banquet of the dead. One (111), which is particularly intransigent of interpretation, shows to the left a seated woman, with a bearded male figure with cornucopiae and snake, to the right a seated goddess, wearing a *polos*, with a shield on her shoulder, a child on her lap, and a patera in her right hand. Below this scene, perhaps in the underworld, is a bearded male with his right hand raised. Here it looks as if the dead man is sharing, at least in awareness, in a celebration in which the human and divine alike participate.

In the Ceramicus area of Athens the most striking monument is that of Dexileos. It is a monument of Pentelic marble showing a young cavalryman charging down and about to transfix a prostrate enemy. The inscription reads 'Dexileos, son of Lysanias, of the deme of Thoricus. He was born in the archonship of Teisander, he died in the archonship of Eubulides in Corinth, of the five knights.' This dates his lifespan to 414–394 BC; he died in battle. The monument commemorates his exploit without any other hope of immortality. Another noble monument honours Aristion. Above him stands a Siren, spirit of death, in an attitude of mourning presumably regretting that she has to lay the hand of death upon one of such promise. The young man is portrayed with a strigil in his left hand; a slave half his size looks sorrowfully up at him. Most beautiful of all is the stele of Hegeso. The dead woman sits fingering an ornament from a box held by an attendant. It is hard to say what this conveys; the very unrhetorical normality makes it more poignant. Also moving is the stele of Ctesileos and Theano. She sits; he stands looking down sorrowfully at her, hands clasped in front of him. He is mourning for her, but the inscription makes clear that both are dead. Mostly the stelai bear no trace of hope. But among the tombs are shrines in honour of deities, Hecate, naturally, as goddess of the underworld, but also Artemis Soteira (Saviour) with two attendants (or cult-titles: it is not clear), Ariste (Best) and Calliste (Loveliest). Here is a cult of a Saviour-goddess, though perhaps only for the living to pray for their own safety as they inter their dead.

Epitaphs – genuine epitaphs and not clever literary conceits – tell us something about beliefs, though we must remember that anyone who has an inscribed tombstone is unlikely to be among the poorest of the poor.[8]

There is one unusual early verse, not strictly an epitaph, about the Athenians who died in battle at Potidaea in 432 BC. This declares that the dead were undone at the gates of Potidaea, and that the ether has received their souls, the earth their bodies (*IG* I² 945). The ether is the luminous upper air in which the gods live, contrasted with *aer*, the mist and cloud of the lower atmosphere. Not infrequently the Greek sailors must have seen Mt Olympus from the sea with a line of cloud part way up and the upper part in brilliant sunshine, the lower in cloud and dark. The philosophical–scientific picture of the universe seems to have been a sphere surrounded by some mysterious form of mind-stuff or soul-stuff or life-stuff, which permeates the upper portions as ether. In the verse the human soul or *psyche* reverts to the ether. This is not necessarily a picture of personal immortality, as a hero among the gods, say, or a star. It may indicate something more like absorption in the infinite, and the annihilation of individuality accompanying a concept such as the Buddhist nirvana. It is somewhat strange to find this concept in a public expression of sorrow for those who have died in battle.

Sometimes in epitaphs we encounter a clear belief in immortality, though none is before the fourth century BC, and it is important to remember the incredulity of Glaucon at the very suggestion (Plat., *Rep*. 10, 608D). Such is, from Alexandria.

> I am undying, not mortal. – Marvellous. Who are you? – Isidora.
> (*Bull. Soc. Arch. Alex.* 27 (1932) 53)

From Rome:

> Here lies Parthenis, ageless and immortal. (*EG* 634)

From Rhodes:

> The halls of heavenly Zeus hold me. Apollo transformed me,
> and took me immortal from the fire.
> (*IG* XII (1) 142, 3–4)

From Corinth:

> So Hermes escorted me to the holy abode of the blessed,
> see that virtue is honoured on earth too.
> (*Corinth* 8, 1, 130, 5–6)

From Laconia:

> In truth the gods raised her to Olympus
>   as confidante to Cypris,
>   servant to Athene, or attendant on lovely
>   Artemis, power of archers and childbirth.
>
> *(IG* V (1) 960, 7–10)

Sometimes the deceased is given divinity. In one late example from Mesembria the relief and the inscription identify the dead woman with Hecate (*Jahrh. Oest. Arch. Inst.* 26 (1930) 2, 122). A young man from Cnossos is described as enthroned alongside the hero Idomeneus (*I. Cr.* 1, 8, 33, 9–10). On some, though not all, epitaphs we should interpret the word 'hero' as an immortal demigod (e.g. *Ath. Mitt.* 56 (1931) 122, 9–10 from Smyrna).

The tomb as the home of the dead represents a more constrained future. An inscription from Amorgos, datable to the seventh century BC, shows a father, Pygmas, offering his dead son Deidamas a home. There is a charming example from Smyrna:

> Others have their money. I, Hermianus, worked with paper.
> In old age I have this underground tomb,
> I yearned for it, I valued it, I built it, preferring it
>   to riches. And in my death I love it.
>
> *(EG* 309)

Another example from Smyrna speaks of the tomb as the dead man's dwelling for the rest of time (ibid. 236). As the tomb is the eternal home of the dead, continued libations and offerings were made there, and many epitaphs speak of this. An inscription records that a bull was sacrificed for the Megarians who died in fighting the Persians, from the fifth century BC continuously to Christian times (ibid. 461). An Athenian on his tomb asks for libations (ibid. 120, 9–10). Flowers were laid on tombs, then as now. Probably they were originally red flowers, as blood surrogates. In general they speak of life and spring as the rebirth of the year. It is even more poignant when the flowers are planted and grow from the dead body, though here the thought is rather that the dead life continues in the flowers rather than in the tomb (ibid. 194, 7 from Astypalaea; 547a, 1–6 from Carales; 548, 3–4 from Nîmes). A more curious and clearer example of belief in life within the tomb comes from Thyatera where the dead woman, a priestess, calls her tomb an altar and offers to make oracular responses from it (Robert 129–33). We may notice also that a number of inscriptions treat the tomb as a sacred place, and lay a curse on any who disturb it; we can cite an example from as early as the seventh century BC from Rhodes (*IG* III, 1473).

Sometimes, however, the honour of the tomb seems to be precisely because it is a memorial. It is parallel to the literary conceit of the immortality of fame. The phrase 'for memory's sake' recurs constantly. A husband sets up the image of his dead wife as 'an everlasting reminder of her virtue' (*Stud. Pont.* 273). Once the tomb is called an 'evermemoried memorial' (*IG* IX (2) 252). A particularly clear example of the contrast between death and memory comes from Athens:

> Callisto, earth hides your body in her bosom,
>   but you have left your friends the memory of your virtue.
>                                                          (*EG* 56)

Some epitaphs stress the contrast between death and life without making explicit whether there is any belief in an ongoing existence of some shadowy sort. Often these simply attribute death to the Fates or Fate, Death or Hades, a spirit or *daemon*, Malice (*Phthonos*) or Fortune (*Tyche*); these deadly powers are often called bitter or hateful or malignant. A quite large number of genuine epitaphs accept the traditional Homeric picture of the underworld, 'the terrifying city of Hades (ibid. 565, 4), 'laughterless Tartarus' (ibid. 575, 2), and Charon, Cerberus, and the divinities of death. One wife, from Rome, however, sees Acheron as a place where she can sing her husband's praises (ibid. 559, 3–4), though we find ourselves wondering whether it was the husband who composed the epitaph.

Sometimes there is a strong sense of bitterness at what has been lost, an expression of injustice, almost of rebellion. Here are two examples. The first belongs to the fourth century BC and comes from Halicarnassus. The first line is missing.

> I lie here in the alien dust of Thuriea.
> Eucleitus, the first cause of his mother's mourning,
>   died at eighteen.
>   After him she wept for Theodorus aged twelve.
>     Alas for those who pass unjustly below ground.
>                                                          (Peek 748)

Closely similar in sentiment is one from Cottiaeum, seven centuries later. It is a long sensitive epitaph. Here are a few lines.

> Ammia, my clever daughter, how did you die so early?
> Why so quick to die? Which of the Fates caught you?
> Before we dressed for the bridal garland in the marriage-chamber,
> you left your home and your sorrowing parents.
> Your father, your dear mother, your whole country wept
> for your untimely unmarried youth.
> (*EG* 372, 26–31)

In these lines there is no necessary disbelief in a life beyond. But there is no belief either. The parents are feeling their own loss; but they are also feeling that the dead have been deprived of the joys of life. There is clearly no consolation of hoped-for bliss. At most there is agnosticism. The writers know what has been lost and have no effective belief beyond that.

Some epitaphs, mainly late (a significant fact in itself for earlier belief) indicate sheer disbelief in any life beyond death. Such is one from Athens, perhaps as early as 300 BC, though this is unusually early. 'I grew from earth and have turned to earth again' (ibid. 75, 3); or again from Eretria: 'I lie like stone or iron without sensation' (ibid. 513, 2); or, a late epitaph from Lydia: 'This is the end of living, the conclusion of life' (*Denkschr. Wien. Akad.*, phil.-hist. Kl. 53 (1909) 151).

A dead man from Astypalaea advises his friends not to make useless offerings at his grave: 'the dead share nothing with the living' (*Griech. Ep.* 209). Occasionally the expression seems Epicurean:

> Traveller, do not pass by my epitaph.
> Stand and listen, and go away a wiser man.
> There is no boat in Hades, no ferryman Charon,
> no janitor Aeacus, no watchdog Cerberus.
> All of us beneath the ground in death
> have become bones and ashes; there is nothing beside.
> I have told you the truth. On your way, traveller,
> or you will think that even in death I talk too much.
> (*EG* 646)

Sometimes this nihilism takes the form of the popular view of Epicureanism, wrongly attributed to Epicurus, 'Eat, drink and be merry, for tomorrow you die'. 'Sport, luxuriate, live: you are bound to die' (ibid. 362, 5); 'Laughter, desire, wine, sleep – these are men's riches. The life of Tantalus is for the gloomy' (*SEG* 4, 104); 'I have what I ate, I have lost what I left. Philistion's right. That's life' (*IGRR* 4, 923).

In all this there are two points to remember. One is that, as Dr Johnson put it, 'In lapidary inscriptions a man is not upon oath'.[9] The other is that the human capacity for holding two incompatible beliefs simultaneously is almost infinite.

# 10

# VOTIVE OFFERINGS

The deciphering of Linear B and the discovery of fresh texts has enabled us to identify records of offerings to divinities in the Mycenaean period. The record in its full form records the date, the god to whom the offering is made, the place, the offering, and the festival. Some of these records come from Cnossos, others from Pylos. At Cnossos Dictaean Zeus receives offerings of oil; and a number of deities receive honey, a goddess Eleuthia, the Lady of the Labyrinth, and all the gods. Other offerings include the other foodstuffs regularly used for the purpose – barley, figs, flour, and wine. Another offering seems to be an aromatic, though some have interpreted it as a woollen garment. At Pylos there are offerings to Poseidon (conjoined once with the Two Queens), Zeus, the Son of Zeus, Hera, the Divine Mother, the Clan Ancestor, Hermes, the Two Handmaidens, the Lady of Aswos, the Lady of Upo, Iphimedeia, the Dove-Goddess, Potnia, the Thirsty Ones (perhaps the dead), and one or two others. The main offering is oil, sometimes rose-scented, cyperus-scented or salvia-scented. Other offerings include gold cups and gold bowls, she-goats, wheat, barley, and figs. One gigantic offering does not name the recipient. It includes barley, cyperus, flour, olives, aromatics, figs, an ox, rams, ewes, he-goats, she-goats, a pig, sows, and wine.[1]

The eighth century saw a great upsurge in prosperity in the Greek world, and this was matched by an increase in the richness of giving to the gods. It was the same age which saw the beginning of temple architecture in place of open sanctuaries. We may compare the great Perpendicular churches of the wool boom in Britain. We may suspect a certain amount of interstate rivalry, one city rivalling another in the endowment of its sanctuaries.

The largest number of votive offerings at this period are in the form of pottery. But the pottery was used as a container or carrier. The gift was what lay in or on it. Jugs and vases will have contained libations, trays will perhaps have carried fruit; a beautiful tray with an eight-spoked flower wheel and swastikas painted on it was found in the sanctuary of Hera at Samos. These containers were ritually broken; they had been used for the service of a divinity and should not be restored to normal human use. Occasionally, however, pottery is found of a less utilitarian kind. At Tegea some miniature pots, decorated in the geometric style, were found (*BCH* 45 (1921) nos 232–42); such dedications become common in the archaic and later periods. At Corinth Hera Acraea received pottery shaped in the form of cakes or doughnuts. Painted rectangular plaques are more widely spread. They were made in Attica and the Argolid, and have appeared on the Acropolis at Athens, in the sanctuary of Hera in the Argolid, and in the sanctuary of Apollo on Aegina.

Personal possessions are often dedicated to a divinity. In the Dark Ages we know of these mainly from interments. Now they are more frequently presented to a god or goddess. These include jewellery of all kinds, pins, and brooches. It is not surprising that goddesses are the chief recipients, Hera, Athene, Artemis, and Aphaea (the goddess of the temple on Aegina), though gods may receive them too. Usually these are treasured possessions, but sometimes their size and ornamentation are such that they must have been specially made as a votive for the goddess; a human can hardly have worn a pin 0.82 metres long! Other personal possessions include arms and armour, increasingly as war prevailed in the Greek world.

Figurines in bronze and terracotta were similarly made specially as votives. Often they represent the god or goddess, and sometimes it is possible to trace on a single site the development of representation from crude slips of clay jammed together in a vaguely anthropomorphic shape to figures moulded in the natural contours of the body.[2] At other times the figurines may depict the worshipper and be a form of self-giving. In the sanctuary of Demeter and Kore on the north slope of Acrocorinth, and in other similar sanctuaries, it is hard to know whether the terracottas of a female figure with a pig represent the goddess or the worshipper. In the sanctuary at Bitalemi in Sicily, identified by a graffito as sacred to Demeter Thesmophorus, the many votives include terracotta figurines of Demeter-Cybele with her lion, and mothers with children in their arms or on their shoulders (*BSA*

*Arch. Rep.* 1966–7, 42). Figures of bulls, deer, goats, sheep, cocks, and the like are substitutes for sacrificial animals. It has been argued that horses show the votary boasting of his status; we should not however forget the horse as a symbol of divine power. Bronze beetles are sometimes found. Beetles were a pest, and the dedication must be an invitation to destroy the pest or a thanksgiving for deliverance from it.

In Cyprus large numbers of terracottas have been found which were made as votive offerings at sanctuaries. Such dedications were so important that the larger sanctuaries had their own terracotta workshops. The figures were of all sorts, shapes, and sizes. Human figures predominate, but model or actual ritual vessels and incense burners are found. The techniques vary. The mould reached Cyprus from Syria in the eighth century, and it was perhaps from Cyprus that it was introduced to mainland Greece. Even in the archaic period there are plenty of moulded plaques and figurines; others are hand-modelled or turned on a wheel. The artistic styles parallel those of contemporary vases. The anthropomorphic figures are occasionally those of a divinity, like the ramheaded enthroned god from Meniko or the goddess enthroned between winged sphinxes from Ayia Irini, or the goddess with a tall hat and arms raised high from near Palapaphos. Mostly they represent the worshipper, directly or indirectly. In some they are actually portrayed bringing their offerings; a lovely broken head of unknown provenance, of a woman carrying a vase, may belong to this group also. Some show the offerer as a soldier or on horseback or at his or her daily work or standing at ease. Some portray scenes from rituals, like the figures from Apollo's temple at Kourion who are donning bulls' masks, or the lyre player, of unknown provenance, who is actually seated in a square shrine. The figures vary in height from about 10 cm to lifesize. It is a reasonable generalization that they represent the offerer's self-giving.[3]

Perhaps the most remarkable single hoard of offerings was that found at Amyclae and dedicated to some chthonic god. Over 10,000 items were found in all, ranging from the Geometric to the Hellenistic period, but predominantly of the seventh and sixth centuries. They include vases of all sizes, terracotta figurines and bronzes. Most interesting are a series of terracotta plaques portraying a wide variety of scenes: acts of worship, horsemen, soldiers, domestic scenes. On one a child is holding a jug, and a seated figure is holding a cantharus from which a snake is drinking. On another a male figure is seated, while a standing woman holds a pot with a snake rising alongside it. The chthonic element is clearly expressed.

Among the more elaborate votive offerings are specially carved reliefs offered to heroes. Rouse has classified these in three groups: scenes of ritual, scenes of feasting, and scenes of the hero's activity.[4] Among the first group are Laconian reliefs. A fine example from Patrae shows the hero enthroned with a female figure behind. Nine worshippers of all ages are bringing a ram in offering. Behind, a shield is hanging, and a horse is peering in through a window. The scenes of feasting are not very different from those on some grave memorials, understandably enough. But the votive nature of the hero reliefs can be seen in their appearance in the Asclepieion in Athens and the Amphiaraon at Oropus. One example from the Piraeus is interesting, similar to the Patrae relief, even to the horse's head, except that this time the hero is reclining with a drinking horn. In the third group we often see the hero riding or hunting.

Among the most remarkable artefacts specially made for votive dedications are bronze caldrons set on a tripod. These were familiar domestic objects, but for dedication to a divinity they were enlarged and elaborated almost beyond recognition. The finest group of these comes from Olympia.[5] They are often decorated with abstract or floral ornament, occasionally showing figures in relief, and with humans or animals on the handles or supports.

An unusual bronze dedication was found in the region of Panticapaeum, a sixth-century bronze work of uncertain purpose, a stand or a handle of some kind, offered to Ephesian Artemis by a worshipper named Son (*BSA Arch. Rep.* 1962–3, 47).

Victory in war naturally produced substantial offerings, some of which we have encountered at Delphi and elsewhere. The Athenians gave regular offerings to Zeus Tropaeus in front of trophies ceremoniously erected at Marathon and Salamis to commemorate those victories (*CIA* II 467; 471). In the Acropolis Museum are helmets, shields, lances, and swords, some of which are inscribed with Athene's name, and which must date from Marathon or thereabouts. A tablet at Dodona pertains to spoils gained from the Peloponnesians, perhaps in the sea battle off Aegina in 460 BC (*IG Ant.* 5); some of the spoils may have gone to Delphi (*IG Ant.* 3a). Spearheads from Thurii were dedicated at Olympia by the Tarentines (*IG Ant.* 548), as were arms captured from the Spartans by Methone (Collitz III 4615). Sometimes the dedications were made by individuals (*IG Ant.* 564).

Large quantities of armour have been found as dedications at Olympia, Delphi, Dodona, and Athens, or are referred to in dedications (*CIA* I, 117–75). Rouse lists dedications of a tithe of spoils of war from Apollonia, Athens, Branchidae, Crete, Mantinea, Megara, Boeotia, and Sparta; at Delphi by Athenians, Caphyes, Cnidians, Liparians, Spartans, and Tarentines; at Olympia by Cleitorians, Eleans, Messenians, Spartans, Thurians.[6] Sometimes models were dedicated, such as the marble model of a shield in Cos (*I Cos* 66–7) or the bronze chariot offered by Athens for victories over the Boeotians and Euboeans (*CIA* I 334; IV 1, 334a cf. Hdt. 5, 77). Sometimes the spoils went into whole buildings, such as some of the treasuries at Delphi.

Something similar was true of athletic victories. Great glory accrued to victors in the panhellenic games, and sometimes practical benefits (such as free meals) from the state they represented. In games other than the four great festivals the prizes might be of considerable value, like the jars of oil in the Panathenaea, or the bronze cuirass at Argos (*CIA* III 116), or the tripod which appears on vases (e.g. Berlin 1655; 1712) or on a plaque from Corinth. It was natural that the victors should give gratitude for divine aid. Sometimes they gave up their prize, as the rhapsode Terpsicles who dedicated his tripod at Dodona (*IG Ant.* 502), or the musician Leonteus, who gave his prize at Sparta to the goddess Orthia (Collitz III 4501), or the athlete who dedicated his prize strigil, which may be seen in the British Museum (*BMC Bronzes* 326). Sometimes the organ of victory was offered, like the huge stone at Olympia which tells us that Bybon threw it over his head with one hand (*IG Ant.* 370); so with discuses, jumping weights, horse-trappings, and the like. Masks from victorious plays were offered, as we know from Teos. Reliefs show them hanging in rows, though we cannot be sure that these reliefs were not a substitute offering. Sometimes victors might dedicate their own statues, like the boxer Euthymus (*I. Ol.* 144) or the wrestler Milo (*I. Ol.* 264). Sometimes they offered bronze representations of athletic activity. Sometimes the thanks are given to the god; Aeschyllus of Argos won the foot-race four times and the race in armour three, and gave thanks to the Dioscuri in the form of a relief depicting them (*IG Ant.* 37).

We have already discussed some of the offerings found in the healing sanctuaries. The thanksgiving might be a sacrifice, of a pig (*BCH* 2, 70) or a cock; no part of the offering might be taken away (*IGS* 1, 235), at any rate in some sanctuaries. Rouse classifies the offerings under four headings.[7] First, there are images of the deliverer – Asclepius himself, sometimes called simply 'the Saviour', or Hygieia, or a snake: a woman from Megalopolis gave a silver snake weighing 25 drachmas (*CIA* II 836, 66). Secondly, there are images of the person healed, sometimes, with children, given by the parents (*CIA* II 1500). Under this head may be taken images of the limb healed. Thirdly, there are images of acts of healing, or associated ritual acts, such as the offering of sacrifice or a ceremonial banquet. The rest are classified as miscellaneous: slippers (*CIA* II 766 l. 30) or a cloak (ibid. l. 18), a leather flask (ibid. l. 33) or a pillow (ibid. l. 35). We remember the boy at Epidaurus who offered knucklebones, and the sceptical woman who was told for her folly to give a silver sow.

We must not forget that many offerings will have been perishable and will have left no trace. Such are offerings of flowers and fruits, milk, cakes, oil, cheese and fish, honey, wine. We have plenty of literary references to the practice, not least in the sixth book of the Palatine Anthology, and the pastoral romance of Longus, but earlier also, and this is confirmed in inscriptional evidence, as in the offering of grain to Cybele (*SIG* $^2$377). Sometimes the offerings were first fruits; we have, for example, records of offerings of first fruits of grain (*CIG* 484; *CIA* IV 2, 834b), oil (*CIA* IV 1, 27b), the produce of the seasons (*IG Ins*. III 436); we do not know what proportion was deemed appropriate. Another perishable offering was hair, offered at puberty and in time of crisis, often to a river god, but also to other deities, such as Zeus, Apollo, and Hygieia. The hair is a living part of the person, and it is a form of self-offering. There are pleasing records of the dedication of a child's hair (*CIG* 2391–3), an inscription from Paris (*CIG* 2391), or a carving of hair in relief, presumably as a record of the offering, from Thebes in Thessaly. Many other offerings, of cloth and wood and other perishable materials, have vanished. Clothing was certainly dedicated (Eudocia 656; *AP* 6, 282), and we should remember that our collection of children's toys is not representative.

# 11

# PRIVATE CULTS

*Phrateres* means brothers, but in classical Greek it had ceased to bear its literal meaning. The phratry survived as a kinship group. Its relation to the geographical deme is highly unclear, though it seems that membership of a deme was compulsory for all citizens, membership of a phratry was probably not. It is not even clear what was the function of the phratry. In the fourth century they kept a written record of their members (*SIG* ³921), and they may have been able to provide important evidence in cases of disputed succession or disputed citizenship (Dem. 39, 5; 57, 46), but they were of course subject to the courts of law (Dem. 39, 4; 40, 11; 44, 41–2). Their one certain duty was religious, to celebrate the Apaturia (*SIG* ³921), which was the great state family festival at which in addition to rites involving the living, the dead were also commemorated.[1]

A phratry had at least a semi-official standing though it was in essence a kinship group. One of the most important inscriptions in this regard relates to the regulations of the phratry of the Demotionidae. It dates from the early fourth century, and was found at Deceleia in Attica (*SIG* ³921). It was put up by Theodorus, priest of Zeus Phratrius, and he was careful first to record his own perquisites of meat, wine, flour in the form of a pancake, and money at time of sacrifice. The resolution recorded was carried at a meeting of the phratry. All members are to vote immediately on new candidates, and deadlines are established for future elections. The elections are a serious religious business, carried out under the auspices of Zeus Phratrius. Appeals against non-election are permitted, with a heavy fine if the appeal is not upheld. There is careful scrutiny to ensure that true kinship is maintained. When children are introduced witnesses must swear 'I testify that this child is the legitimate son of the man introducing him, born of a lawful wife. I swear by Zeus Phratrius that this is true. If this oath is true, may all good come to me; if false, the reverse.' The name of the father, his deme, the grandfather on the mother's side, and his deme, must be registered with the president and published on a white board in the shrine of Leto. There is provision for two sacrificial offerings, the *meion* offered by the fathers of sons born in the past year, the *koureion* offered when the boy attained military age and became eligible for membership. It is also important in this inscription that the group called the household of the Deceleans forms the hereditary priesthood of the phratry.

In the Demotionidae phratry the subgroups are *thiasoi*. A *thiasos* did not necessarily involve kinship. It was in general a private corporation dedicated to a cult not provided for in the state religion. Our evidence is mostly epigraphic. From the early fifth century we have the *thiasos* of the Etionidae, and it was certainly involved in cult. The name looks like a patronymic, implying a kinship group, but it may rather be geographical and linked to Eetioneia. Otherwise our evidence comes from the first half of the fourth century. The groups there identified seem well established, but not of great antiquity; they took their names from their current president, Hagnotheus, Antiphanes, or Diogenes (*IG* II $^2$1237). Another inscription which does not mention the word *thiasos* has a list of only twenty names, too few for a phratry, and was probably in fact a *thiasos*; it is interesting that they honour 'the gods of the phratry' (*IG* II $^2$2344). It looks then as if the *thiasos* may have been introduced in the fifth century as a subgroup of the phratry, fallen into disuse, and been revived with a more general connotation as a religious group.

Members of a *thiasos* are sometimes called *orgeones* (*CIA* IV 2, 620b). *Orgeones*, whatever they were precisely, can be seen on epigraphic evidence to constitute a small upper-class minority, probably depending for their power on wealth rather than birth. This is not the usual view, which is that they formed the mass of the commoners, but the only evidence is that they are opposed to the *gennetai*, the aristocracy of birth. Groups identified seem to be small in number, well-off, well established, and each responsible for a shrine of a hero where they would meet once a year.[2] It is false to suppose, however, that *thiasoi* were composed exclusively of *orgeones*. The nobly born are found alongside the others: Stratophon and Demon of Agryle are members of a *thiasos* (*IG* II $^2$2345) and of a *genos* (*Hesp.* 7 (1938) 3–5).

The *orgeones* then were a religious association devoted to a cult of a particular god or hero. An especially interesting inscription relates to the *orgeones* of a hero named Egretes. They agreed to rent the sanctuary to one Diognetus for ten years at 200 drachmas a year. He agreed to maintain the sanctuary as a sanctuary, to keep the buildings in good order, to whitewash the walls and to look after the trees, and replace any which died. He was to open the shrine and the other buildings, which included two dining-rooms, to the *orgeones* for the annual sacrifice. At the end of his tenancy he would be entitled to remove the woodwork, roof-tiles, doors, and posts (a somewhat strange provision) but nothing else; in the event of arrears of rent or other offence against the terms of the lease he would forfeit this entitlement. He was also required to make the record of the lease at his own expense. The interest of the document is threefold. First, the *orgeones* are not directly interested in the shrine except once a year, and then the religious obligation is an opportunity for dining together and good fellowship. Secondly, they act responsibly in relation to the finances of the shrine in securing a good deal from the lease. Thirdly, Diognetus, unless he is an altruist or a religious enthusiast, presumably thinks that he is going to gain by the transaction, which means that some steady income is ensured from the sanctuary, perhaps through private devotion (*SIG* $^3$1097).

In 333 BC the merchants of Cition resident in Athens as metics requested the Council for permission to occupy a site in order to build a temple to Aphrodite (presumably their own Astarte). They would form the associated *thiasos* (*CIA* II i 168). This shows clearly enough the changed meaning of the word. Similarly in the second century BC the merchants of Tyre resident in Delos requested the Athenian people for permission to found a temple to Baal Margod on the island (*CIG* 2271); they would provide the *thiasos*.

In an inscription from Thera a woman named Epicteta made some religious provisions of great interest and importance (*CIG* 2448). Her husband Phoenix had dedicated a temple to the Muses in memory of a dead son. On her husband's death Epicteta made a further endowment. She put up statues and shrines appropriate to heroes or demigods in close association with the temple, bequeathing 3,000 drachmas for sacred purposes. She bequeathed the property itself to her daughter Epiteleia, on condition that she paid 210 drachmas a year to the trustees, who are called the Society of Kinsfolk. Their primary duties were to take care of the sanctuary, to ensure that it was not sold or mortgaged, that no building was added except a portico, and that it was never used for any extraneous purpose except Epiteleia's wedding. The priesthood of the Muses and Heroes was vested in Epiteleia's son, and the succeeding eldest males. The Society had to appoint three of its members to supervise the sacrifices on due days to the Muses and Heroes, and the accompanying banquet; precise and detailed rules were laid down for the Society and its conduct of its responsibilities. This is an exceptional and individual instance, but it fits the general pattern.

Another form of cult-society was the *eranos*. In the second century AD a Lycian slave named Xanthus was working in the silver mines of Laurium. He founded a sanctuary in honour of the Lycian god Men Tyrannus. He could not afford to build a shrine himself but took over a disused *heroon*. He laid out the circumstances of pollution which precluded entry into the sanctuary, and invited other interested people to join him in forming an *eranos* (*CIA* III i 73–4). The word *eranos* has many connotations. Sometimes it seems little more than a dining club; sometimes it is a friendly society or charitable institution. But at other times it is certainly a religious guild, and, according to a passage in Athenaeus, meant the same as *thiasos* (Ath. 8, 362E). We can trace such a religious *eranos* on Rhodes in the second century BC (*IG* XII 1, 155, 12) or in Athens in the second century AD (*IG* II$^2$ 1369). Unfortunately we have little indication of details of the life of an *eranos*.[3]

Another private religious corporation was the *dendrophoroi* or tree-bearers, a guild involved in the cult of Cybele, prominent during the Roman imperial period, and found as far away as Tomis (*IGRR* 1, 614) in the third century AD. They seem to have enjoyed fraternal relations with the guilds of woodcarvers. The *dendrophoroi* are especially interesting for two reasons. On the one hand they were the inheritors of religious practices more immediately associated with the Greeks, especially the worship of Demeter and Dionysus, deities of vegetation. On the other the corporation itself had a strong appeal to the Romans, who adapted the word into their own tongue.

# 12

# MAGIC

Martin Nilsson makes the interesting observation that 'the belief in magic vanishes from the Greek religion, although the rites upon which it was created remain'. He notes too that magicians are conspicuously absent in classical Greece.[1] The magical rites become sacral rites. As examples he cites the sacred bough, *eiresione* or *corythale*, an olive branch hung about with fruits and used to promote fertility, carried in procession at the Thargelia and Pyanopsia, and hung up before the house and before Apollo's temple; at the Oschophoria a vine branch with a cluster of grapes; in acts of supplication carried with woollen fillets by the suppliant; prominent at *rites de passage*, such as the entry of an ephebe into manhood, or a wedding ceremony. Another example is rain magic. On Mt Lycaeon in Arcadia there was a sacred well. In drought the priest would offer sacrifice to Zeus and dip a twig stirring up the waters and summoning the mist and rainclouds. Here simple rain magic has become religious ritual. At Crannon rain magic was carried out by a cart carrying an amphora. The cart was pushed about so that the water splashed, and the rattle of the cart would be a similar sympathetic magic for thunder. The cart appears on coins of the city (*BMC Thessaly* 16). Yet another example is the scapegoat, *pharmakos* (medicine), *katharma* (offscourings), *peripsema* (that which is wiped off). This was prominent in the Thargelia. But some acts of sacrifice seem to be placing impurities upon the animal sacrificed: so with the pig sacrifice to clear a homicide of the taint on him, to render initiates at Eleusis pure, to cleanse the assembly place in Athens. Sometimes a dog was used, as to purify the Macedonian army which marched between the two parts of the sacrifice, laying their impurities on the bleeding animal. Another is the magic circle. At Methana when the vine harvest was threatened by an adverse wind, a cock was sacrificed and cut in two. Two men walked round the vineyards in opposite directions, and buried the two parts where they met, when the circle was complete. There is a notable example of the magic circle in one of the early encounters of Rome and Greece. C. Popillius Laenas was the Roman envoy to Antiochus of Syria when the latter was campaigning against Egypt. Popillius handed him an ultimatum from the senate, drew a circle round him with a cane in the sand, and forbade him to leave the circle before giving a clear answer (Liv. 45, 12).

Various fertility rites bear signs of magical origins. The *panspermia* was a mixture of the first fruits baked into a cake and consumed. The very name is significant; it is 'all the seeds'. The harvest of one year, in its rich blessing, is passing on its fertility to the household and to the following year. In the rite of the Bucoliastae in Sicily a company went round the houses, strewing the doorway with lentils and offering a draught of wine, singing 'Take the good fortune, take the blessing we bring from the goddess who commanded this.' The ritual certainly antedates its association with Artemis. On Samos the sacred bough was carried round, on Rhodes an image of a swallow, bird of spring, at Colophon a crow, harbinger of rain.[2] Pinecones and phalluses were other fertility emblems, sometimes buried in underground chambers to help the power of Earth.

Magic and superstition in fact abounded in classical Greece, though the Athenians thought witchcraft alien and Thessalian (Ar. *Cl.* 749). The comic writers refer to rings worn as charms (Ar. *Plut.* 884; Antiphanes fr. 18K) and to written charms worn round the neck in a small bag and called 'Ephesian writings' (Anaxilas fr. 181). Unfortunately very little has survived. It seems that protective rings may have been worn by the poorer people, in which case they will have been of cheap metal and perishable. But sealstones which bear no obvious magical symbols may have been regarded as endowed with power. The god on the ring may be there for protection or inspiration; we should not forget that one title of Heracles was Averter of Evil, Alexikakos. Animals portrayed may have served a similar function. The different stones themselves were believed to be endowed with power. One charm has survived in the form of Ephesian writings. It dates from the fourth century BC, is made of lead, a heavy substance, powerful to fix a spell, and was found in Crete.[3]

Much of the evidence from the classical period is literary, such as Theophrastus's characterization of the Superstitious Man (*Char.* 16), or scenes from Sophron (Page no. 73) or Theocritus (2). But much magic is 'sympathetic', that is to say that there is a binding parallel between an act performed and a result desired; mathematically A:B::C:D. So the Curetes leap for tall crops and herds. So the sexual union between male and female will ensure the fertility of the land and all living creatures. It is probable that the myth of Pasiphae and the bull records an ancient tradition of union between a priest and priestess. At Athens the *basilinna*, the wife of the Archon Basileus, in the course of the Anthesteria, a spring fertility festival of Dionysus, was wedded to the god and united with him for the blessing on the year. We cannot be certain, but there is a reasonable probability that the Archon Basileus took on the role of the god. This ritual was unique at Athens and comparatively rare in the Greek world.[4] Sacred prostitution was found, especially in cults with eastern associations. At Corinth Aphrodite is said to have had a thousand temple prostitutes; they were called *hieroduli* ('servants of the sacred'). There was ritual prostitution associated with the worship of Aphrodite on Cyprus, and in Syria where its abolition by Constantine occasioned a violent reaction from the people (Eus. *V. Const.* 3, 58; Sozom. *HE* 5, 10). The magic practised by Simaetha in Theocritus is largely sympathetic. She burns barley to burn her lover's bones; she burns laurel to burn his flesh; she melts wax to melt his heart; she whirls the bull-roarer to make him turn about her door (Theocr. *Id.* 2). Ceremonial lustration or baptism is a form of sympathetic magic; spiritual impurities are washed away.

Another great section of magic is 'contagious', that is to say that by acting upon an object which has been in contact with a person or thing it is believed to be possible to affect the person or thing itself. We have a record of a number of ancient taboos practised by the Pythagoreans (Diog. Laert. 8, 17). They include such injunctions as 'Always roll your bedclothes up' and 'Don't leave the imprint of your pan on the ashes'. The imprint of a body could be used for black magic against the body itself; even the imprint of a pan could be used for black magic against the pan's owner. Nail-parings and hair-clippings were peculiarly dangerous. The Pythagorean taboos warn against standing on them or urinating on them; this would be to damage the self.

Objects or gestures may have 'apotropaic' power, that is the power to turn away evil. The laurel or bay is one such, perhaps because of its odour. Wool is another. The colour crimson has apotropaic power. Magicians wear fillets of crimson wool (*Pap. Gr. Mag.* 2, 70) as do others engaged in religious practices. Objects used for magical purposes are wrapped in crimson (*Pap. Gr. Mag.* 4, 2703). Spitting is an apotropaic action. The thought here is perhaps complex. It may be in part a projection of part of one's inner being in the direction of an evil influence. So in Theocritus the old hag spits as a precaution against evils (*Id.* 7, 127). But sometimes the power is achieved by spitting into one's own lap. Here perhaps the emphasis is on getting rid of some internal danger, but as spittle is a part of one's being and could be used through contagious magic against the spitter, the spittle is guarded by the owner (Theocr. *Id.* 6, 39; 20, 11; Theophr. *Char.* 16, 15 and often). The clashing of metal is another apotropaic action. It was used at eclipses to drive off the evil powers attacking the heavenly body (Plut. *Mor.* 944 B; Lucian *Philops.* 15; Alex. Aphr. *Prob.* 2, 46). There is a fascinating example in a magical papyrus, where the spell is given 'I use the *rhombus* and refrain from cymbals' (*Pap. Gr. Mag.* 4, 2296); that is to say, use attractive and avoid apotropaic magic. The phallus, as well as a symbol of fertility, was apotropaic, perhaps as a symbol of male aggressiveness, perhaps as the instrument of projecting part of the self. Apotropaic magic is an important part of almost all practices, since the magician is in the business of unleashing dark forces which may endanger himself unless he takes precautions (*Pap. Gr. Mag.* 4, 2110; 2507; 2877; 2897; 3094 etc.). Monsters can perform apotropaic functions, the Gorgon's head, which in myth turns everything to stone, or the Sphinx, a strange devouring monster. In certain circumstances letters of the alphabet were regarded as having apotropaic power, and it is thought that this was the purpose of the discrete letters which appear on the fourth-century Niinion tablet from Eleusis. A maze symbol might be used to keep evil spirits away; the simple principle was that they would be stuck in the maze.

Superstition is not logical, and spells and prayers go hand in hand. Prayers are often formulaic, and (for example) in love-magic may refer indefinitely to the one who has ousted the petitioner.

> Lady three times I pour libation, three times I pray,
> be it a woman, be it a man, who sleeps at his side,
> be they forgotten, as Theseus of old on Dia
> forgot Ariadne of the lovely hair.
> (Theocr. *Id* 2, 43–6)

Similarly indefinite formulae are found in curses (Audollent *Defixionum Tabellae* 38; 68; 198) and in magical papyri (*Pap. Gr. Mag.* 4,

1511; 2740; 2757; 2960). Even the mythological allusion is not a literary conceit, but can be paralleled (ibid., 4, 2905).

Metal has magical power. Many magical rituals go back to before the use of iron and insist on bronze instruments for efficacy. Bronze nails used for magical purposes can be seen in the British Museum. Iron creates a new power, and iron nails can be used to fix curses. A curse affixed to the wall of the temple of Demeter in Cnidos, now in the British Museum, still has its iron nail. Lead was a dark heavy metal, much used for curses which it would make heavy with power and carry downwards to Hecate and the underworld deities concerned with magic. Gold by reason of its brilliance is associated with the upper world, with light and life.

Numbers have magical power, especially the number three; divinity delights in odd numbers (Verg. *Ecl.* 8, 75 cf. *Ciris* 373). This is particularly appropriate to Hecate with her magical associations, her three forms (Selene in the sky, Artemis on earth, and Hecate in the underworld), and her association with the places where three roads meet. In a magical papyrus the threefold goddess is invoked as Selene under a wide variety of triple titles, 'thrice-resounding, three-voiced, three-headed, threefold, three-faced, three-necked, worshipped at the three roads, who holds the unquenched flame of fire in three baskets, who haunts the meeting of three ways, who rules the threes and tens, with three forms, flames and hounds' (*Pap. Gr. Mag.* 4, 2524). Theocritus, who is accurate in his magical references, makes good use of the number. Simaetha's spell is in nine quatrains (*Id.* 2); on more than one occasion a character spits three times (*Id.* 6, 39; 20, 11); the cities of Egypt are enumerated as $3 \times 100 + 3 \times 1000 + 3 \times 10{,}000 + 2 \times 3 + 3 \times 9$, making 33,333 (*Id.* 17, 82).

The erect phallus was a fertility symbol. A late religious thinker says that it was symbolic of the generative energy of the world, and that for this reason the phallus was consecrated in the spring (Iambl. *De Myst.* i, 11).

It stood for good luck. At the same time it had a strong assertive aggressive masculine apotropaic function. The herms which in the fifth century guarded the entrances in Athens were ithyphallic. They were protective of those entrances. At the same time it was good luck to touch the phallus as you passed. It was an appalling act of irreligion when shortly before the Athenian expedition sailed against Sicily in 415 BC the herms were mutilated by having their phalluses broken off. Houses often had a phallus in relief on the outside. On one in Thera it is accompanied by the inscription 'Good luck to my friends.' Some houses on Delos have them incised. Moulded vases in the shape of a phallus were found from the sixth century BC; there is an excellent example from Cameiros in the British Museum. They were undoubtedly good luck symbols. It is hard to know how they were used. They are dedicated in sanctuaries and interred in tombs, but there is no special reason to suppose that they were not used in everyday life. Priapus, a fertility god associated with gardens, ithyphallic, sometimes appears as a power of blessing, his penis supporting an array of fruits or even children. But he stood apotropaically in gardens to scare away thieves. Sometimes the phallus becomes a phallus-bird, a bird with a phallus in place of its head; one such is to be seen in low relief in the temenos of Dionysus on Delos among the colossal monumental phalluses there. A curious little bronze now in Boston shows a phallus with human legs, and its own little phallus. This must have been for good luck or apotropaic purposes. Similarly a small bronze in Copenhagen shows a youth with cape and hood. The top part is detachable and reveals a two-legged phallus beneath. The provenance is not known; a similar statuette of a bearded man was found in a grave near Amiens, so these last two may have no Greek connections.[5] In the uncertainties of the Hellenistic age such emblems appear more frequently.

Curses, though a very small number have been found on gold or silver, were usually inscribed on lead tablets, a dark, heavy metal, fixing them firmly, weighing them down and carrying them below to the powers of the underworld; they were then usually buried in the ground. There are many examples on many topics. Here is one from the temple of Demeter at Cnidos:

> I consign to damnation, in the name of Artemis, Demeter, Kore and all the gods with Demeter, the person who at my demand does not return to me the cloaks, clothes and tunic which I left behind. Let him pay the penalty before Demeter, and if anyone else has any possessions of mine, let him be in torment till he confesses. And grant me purity and freedom, fellowship in drink, and food and house. I have been wronged, Lady Demeter. (*SIG*$^3$1179)

Another from the same source is an example of self-cursing. Antigone has been charged with an attempt to poison Asclepiades, and invokes the curse on herself if the charge is true. In the temple at Cnidos the tablets were not buried, but fastened to the wall with iron nails. Some curses are public and conditional, for example, a call to Pluto, Demeter, Persephone, and the Furies to protect a shrine, combined with a curse on any who shall desecrate it (*CIA* III 1423; app. ix). Others are personal and unconditional, such as one found in Attica consigning Meno, Philocydes, Philostratus, Cephisodorus, and their confrères to Hermes to deal with; they seem to have been the curser's opponents in a lawsuit (Aud. *Def. Tab.* 67). Many of the curses date from the Roman imperial period; many are in Latin. But it is the general view of scholars in this field that they are essentially a Greek phenomenon which spread to the Romans, and Greek examples can be found from a fairly early stage. Those from Styra on Euboea, for example, are dated to the fifth century BC (Aud. *Def. Tab.* 80); a fragmentary example from Melos to the fourth (Aud. *Def. Tab.* 39); so with a number from Attica (e.g. Aud. *Def. Tab.* 50).

The curses are naturally formulaic, but there is a lot of freedom and variation in the formulae. The deities addressed include Demeter (also the Lady), Kore (Persephone, Phersephone, Pherephatte, etc.), Pluto (also called Pasianax, Lord of All), Hermes, Hecate, Selene, Hades, Ananke (Necessity), Cronos, the Furies, Earth, Iacchus, Osiris, the Mother of the Gods. One fragmentary tablet may call on Zeus, but it is too uncertain to build anything on this. Occasionally there are vaguer invocations, to the underworld deities, or the gods at Demeter's side. In the later period other spiritual beings are invoked. Some show the influence of Judaism, Adonai (ibid. 27), or Iao (ibid. 22, where he is twice invoked, in heaven, and beneath the earth). Or there is, from Cyprus, Achalemorpoth 'the only god on earth' (ibid. 22 etc.), or, from Rome, Eulamo (ibid. 140 etc.). From Carthage, from a late period, comes a fascinating mixture of Greek and Latin, invoking 'Bachachych, who is a great demon in Egypt, to hold him and hold him fast; Iecri, to take sleep from him; Parpaxin, almighty god, to take him to the halls of the underworld', and so on (ibid. 250). A curse from Hadrumetum invokes in Greek Abar Barbarie Eloe Sabaoth Pachnuphy Pythipemi as a single spirit (ibid. 270). Sometimes the spiritual powers are invoked in general language. The curse may be in the present indicative ('I hand over'), the perfect indicative ('I have handed over': the examples are all Latin), the future indicative ('They will do it' expressing a certainty or hoped for certainty of outcome), the subjunctive or optative (a wish or prayer), the imperative (a command), and even the infinitive (in place of the imperative). There are many different words for consigning to the spiritual powers, but their purport is essentially the same, and for the action required of the spiritual powers, but they are all unpleasant in effect. Sometimes the curse is fixed by magic letters.

We have a great deal of evidence from the Roman imperial period. Much of it comes from Egypt, which was a peculiar area religiously. In Ptolemaic Egypt Greek sealstones came to be substituted for the Egyptian scarab, because they were more varied and less easy to falsify.[6] As a result the scarab fell into disuse whether as sealstone or amulet. The later amulets are Greek. They take on Greek art-forms as ringstones or pendants. They were generally inscribed in Greek. But they belong to the Hellenistic–Roman cosmopolis. The symbols, demonic figures, and words are not necessarily Greek in origin, but they have been Hellenized.

C. Bonner in his magisterial *Studies in Magical Amulets* (Ann Arbor, Mich., 1950) has examined these in all their aspects. The inscription they bear may be a prayer 'Protect', 'Protect from evil', 'Help', 'Grant me favour', 'Stand by me' and the like. Sometimes a god is addressed: 'One Zeus Sarapis [be] gracious to the wearer'; 'Apollo Horus Harpocrates [be] propitious to the wearer'; 'Iao Sabaoth Abrasax He-that-is-Lord, stand by me'. Sometimes there is no prayer but a religious affirmation – 'One God', 'One Zeus Sarapis', 'Isis is victorious', 'Great [is] the name of Sarapis', 'The god who hears prayers is victorious', 'Power'. Sometimes we encounter more elaborate liturgical formulae: 'Water for thirst, bread for hunger, fire for cold' runs one. The most elaborate is in the Brooklyn Museum, a red jasper veined with black showing a lion-headed god. The inscription reads:

> Hear me, thou who hast for thy portion the dwelling in Leontopolis, who art established in the holy enclosure, who sendest lightning and thunder, and art lord of darkness and winds, who hast as thy province the celestial force that drives eternal nature. Thou art the god who worketh swiftly, that giveth ear to prayer, he of great glory, who is in the form of a lion. Thy name is Mios, Miosi, Harmios, Ousirmios, Phre, Simiephe, Phnouto, Light, Fire, Flame. Be gracious to Ammonius.

Mios, as Bonner explains, is 'the lion that casts a spell' by his eyes, Harmios is Horus-lion, and Ousirmios Osiris-lion. Phre is the sun. Simiephe and Phnouto are uncertain.

Other inscriptions on amulets are far more cryptic. Some are secret names of gods, as the accompanying pictures reveal – Aththa Baththa rather charmingly for Isis and baby Horus, Aroriphrasis for Aphrodite-Hathor, Daryngo for Hermes-Thoth, Ereschigal (the Babylonian goddess of the Underworld Ereshkigal) for Hecate. Some names, Damnameneus and Nicharoplex for instance, are associated with the power of the sun. Abrasax appears on a great many amulets accompanied by the image of a cock-headed monster with snake legs. This is a strange and puzzling image. In Persian tradition the cock is on the side of light. In one passage it is said 'The cock is created in opposition to demons and wizards' (*Bundalish* 19, 33), and in another Ahura Mazda, the great god of order and light, cries 'That bird lifts up his voice at the great break of day crying "Arise, men, give praise to Best Righteousness, spurn the demons"' (*Vendidad* 18, 2, 14). But the snake-legs imply a power of the earth. An ingenious attempt has been made to link the image with the Jewish text about the Sun: 'He shall rejoice as a giant to run his course' (Ps. 18:6), the giant being a power of earth. This is far-fetched. Abrasax is perhaps an invented figure – clearly a being, despite Augustine who thought it just a word with power (*De haer.* 4) because of its numerical equivalent to 365 – who brings together the power of light and the power of darkness; it is characteristic of magic to back both horses.

Other words or phrases are simply regarded as having power in themselves. Abrasax was undoubtedly coined for its equivalence to 365. On several Harpocrates amulets we have 'chabrach phneschēr phichro phurō phōchō bōch' which adds up to 9,999. Two gems show Harpocrates on his lotus in a papyrus boat with the word *abimiōchōssōs*. This is otherwise unknown, but its numerical equivalent is 3,663, the same as the commoner but equally mysterious *bainchōōōch* or its anagram *abōchōniōch*. Palindromes are regarded as endowed with power. There are palindromic Greek words, such as *erre* or *iatai*, but no use is made of these, and it is a mistake to look for meaning in the magical palindromes which take their power from their palindromic quality. The commonest is *ablanathanalba* (where *th* is of course a single letter). Some nonsense words seem to take their power from heavy and strongly aspirated combinations of consonants, such as *ōmephtharchenthechtha*.

From Palestine and Syria we have preserved quantities of bronze amulet pendants, distinctively shaped like a spade or leaf with a loop at the top, cast with the piece, at right angles to the whole. Several of these show on the obverse a rider with a nimbus, or halo, charging from left to right to spear a female figure lying on the ground, sometimes with hands tied. The usual inscription is 'One God who overcomes evil'. On some there is a lion below the scene. One, uniquely, has an upper and lower register. The normal scene is in the lower portion. Above a figure with human body and donkey's head leans with right hand raised across a low pillar with a crossbar towards a lion. The meaning is uncertain: is the ass-headed figure threatening or honouring the lion?

The design on the other side is more varied. The commonest shows the 'much-suffering eye' (as it is called in *The Testament of Solomon*) assailed by trident, spear or nail, and animals. This is the answer to the power of the evil eye. The inscription runs 'IAO SABAOTH MICHAEL help'. This places it within the area influenced by Judaism. Another design on the reverse shows a long-legged bird, ostrich, stork, or crane attacking a snake. In one version the inscription runs *pino*, possibly 'I am hungry', but more likely 'I drink'. Sometimes the reverse simply bears an inscription. One runs 'I am noskamardotenan'. The last word is unparalleled. Another has a formula which appears with slight variants elsewhere: 'Horse Mule Ibis Erect-phallus-of-a-man Ostrich Apollo'.[7] One bronze stamp from Syria bears the inscription 'Joy'; the same word has been found on houses and tombs, though always late. A magical amulet from Byblos invokes the unknown Ortineus: 'Lord of land and sea, who shakest the world, Ortineus of the Nine Forms, cloud-wrapped, cleaving the ether, put an end to every disease and to plotting by every man.' Ortineus is perhaps the sun-god.

A particularly complex example of magical symbolism from the Greek world under Roman sway takes the form of a bronze hand. A number of these are to be seen in the British Museum. The thumb and first two fingers are extended, the other two fingers doubled up in a ritual gesture. The surface of the hand is covered with magical symbols. On one, for example, the thumb terminates in a pinecone, and a snake with cockscomb is clambering over the first of the doubled-up fingers. On the back of the hand are a winged caduceus, a frog, a tortoise, and a variety of magical implements. One of these hands is inscribed by a man named Aristocles in honour of Zeus Sabazius. Another declares 'Zugaras dedicated me to Sabazius in fulfilment of a vow.' Sabazius was a deity found in Phrygia and Thrace, identified with Zeus, and yet, because of his alien nature, endowed with mysterious power.

Papyri give us further insights into magical practices. Again they date from the Roman imperial period, some as early as the early second century AD. There is a reasonable but not unchallenged assumption that the formulae in part go back to Hellenistic times. Certainly they refer to 'kings', and can be paralleled with earlier literary references to magic. But here, as with the gems, there is evidence that there was an intensification of magical practice in the first century AD. They vary in length from the Paris book with its 3,274 lines to single recipes. They are mostly in Greek, and some show signs of educated composition, such as hexameter hymns incorporating magical words accurately, where others make unmetrical insertions into such passages, destroying the incantation effect, use ungrammatical forms, and confuse one vowel with another. Greek magic, formerly concentrated on Hecate, now becomes all-embracing. Greek names jostle with Egyptian, Coptic, Jewish, Mesopotamian, Iranian names. The Sun is a great magical power here too. He is invoked, holy, king, god of gods. But the practitioner binds him by describing his twelve shapes, binds him by necessity to do the practitioner's will 'lest I shake the heavens' – and then invites him to come freely, since magic is not afraid of self-contradiction of such a kind. There follow prayers of thanksgiving. One document of prayer to Hermes-Thoth (*PGM* viii = *P. Lond.* 122) involves the identification of the magician with the god he invokes, in language where crude magic comes close to sublime mysticism: 'Give me grace and victory and success and riches: for thou art I and I am thou. Thy name is mine, my name is thine: for I am thy image.' Possession of the name is an important part of magical power. Sometimes, the address is to a power of darkness, such as Set, not a power of light. Sometimes, as with the amulets, the power of an incantation lies in its incomprehensibility, and in the power of vowels without consonants. In one papyrus the formula to be uttered is A O I A Ō E O Ē Y: 'the A with mouth open, billowingly; the O in a clipped manner, to frighten off spirits; the I A Ō directed to earth, air and sky; the E like a dog-faced baboon, the O as before, the Ē with lingering enjoyment; the Y like a shepherd, extending it' (*PGM* IV 578ff.).

There seems to have been a common stock of such instructions in magic, recipes, and formulae. Some of them recur in several papyri. We have evidence that they were transcribed for enquirers. Sometimes discrepancies arose, and it is not always easy to tell whether we have to do with a miscopying or with actual alternatives prescribed by the expert consulted. In the Oslo papyrus (*P. Osl.* 1, 38) there are internal contradictions between text and diagram. One hymn to Apollo appears with variants at least five times (*PGM* I 300; III 211; IV 442; IV 1963; VIII 74 cf. also II 81; VI; XII 3, 6–15). Sometimes, however, the text records the compiler's own experience. 'I often used this method and was very impressed by it. But the god said to me "Do not use this ointment any more. Throw it into the river and go on to seek oracles by wearing the great mystery of the scarab brought to life again through the twenty-five birds. Do so, not just three times a year, but every month at full moon"' (*PGM* IV 790).

One of the most important magical documents is the so-called *Mithrasliturgy*.[8] It is a curious hotch-potch, with a mass of occult paraphernalia surrounding the aspiration to immortality. Mithras, whose name, as MEITHRAS, has the numerical equivalent of 365, is invoked 'in a white tunic and a scarlet cloak, with a crown of fire', 'almighty with a shining countenance, young with golden hair, with a white tunic, trousers and a crown of gold, holding in his right hand a calf's shoulder of gold which is the Great Bear.' It consists mostly of a long series of invocations. There is prayer rather than magical binding, though, as we have seen, the two are not to be rigidly separated: the phrase 'if it be thy will' recurs. The first prayer is for initiation and rebirth; the practitioner seeks 'that I alone may enter heaven and see everything'. Throughout there is a contrast between physical birth and spiritual rebirth. Later he claims to have been granted his prayer, and, out of many myriads, to have been made immortal in accordance with the god's will. The closing words show a high exaltation of spirit: 'O Lord! I have been born again and pass away in exaltation. In exaltation I die. Birth that produces life brings me into being and frees me from death. I go my way as thou hast ordered, as thou hast established the law and ordained the sacrament.'

# 13
# POLITICS AND RELIGION

In any society which has not learned either individualism or scepticism, religion embraces the whole of life, and that of course includes corporate political life. We can see this clearly enough at Athens. Athene in some sense is Athens. So too Hera is Argos – or Samos. It is harder now to disentangle the emotional attitudes which might arise if Argos found itself in conflict with Samos. But when Athens and Samos came to agreement the stone recording the treaty showed Athene and Hera exchanging greetings.

The power of the gods was regarded as real and their blessings essential. This is why it is not easy to evaluate the rights and wrongs of the Athenian use of the moneys, contributed by the allies towards the defence against the Persians, for the development of building schemes on the Acropolis at Athens. Athens was the leader of the League. Athene, a soldier-goddess, was thus the divine leader of the struggle against the Persians. Her favour was essential to the enterprise, and there could be no better way of ensuring that favour than giving her for her divine house the finest temple in the world.

Deities as city protectors could be of vital importance. At Thasos the gates were all guarded by the gods. On one we see ithyphallic Silenus; another had Dionysus on one side and Heracles as an archer on the other: Heracles also appears on the coinage. An inscription at this last gate declares that Zeus, Semele, and Alcmene set up their children as guardians of the city (*IG* XII 8). Another gate was protected by Zeus and Hera together with their messengers Hermes and Iris. Apart from the gates Athene was honoured with her own temple as Poliouchos, Protectress of the city, as we know from fragments of vases discovered on the site. This – or something like it –

is in fact a common cult-title of Zeus or Athene throughout the Greek world.

In 308 BC the Macedonians left the town of Eretria. A fragmentary inscription celebrates the event in religious terms. The day of withdrawal was the festival of Dionysus. The liberation was ascribed to the power of the god. A decree was jointly moved by the priest of Dionysus and the military commanders, and voted by the council and people, that in commemoration of the liberating act all the citizens and inhabitants of Eretria should, at public expense, wear a garland of ivy at the festival of Dionysus. The dances would be in honour of Dionysus, and wine would flow (*SIG*³373).

At Lindos we have seen how Athene acted as protectress of the city during the siege by Datis in 490 BC and again during the assault by Demetrius Poliorcetes in 305–304 BC; on each occasion there was a divine epiphany (*Lindos: Fouilles et Recherches* 1902–14 II Inscriptions no. 2).

Sometime about 100 BC the people of Lagina in Caria dedicated a temple to Hecate. The frieze, now in the archaeological museum in Istanbul, has different subjects on each of its four sides. On the east are episodes from the lives of Zeus and Hecate, with the birth of Zeus clearly depicted as being in Caria. On the south is an assembly of the local gods of Caria. On the west is the battle of gods and giants, as usual combining the themes of the triumph of religion over irreligion and of Greek civilization over barbarism. And the north shows Rome entering into an alliance with Stratonicea and her dependents. Religion, culture, and politics are all intertwined.

The city of Stratonicea itself set up a decree in the second century AD. The preamble acknowledges the way the tutelary deities of the city, Zeus Panamerius and Hecate, have protected and blessed it. The city expresses its gratitude by providing for the training of thirty young choristers to sing the daily praises of the guardian deities (*CIG* 2715).

This need for divine protection permeated all ancient city-life. The ephebe was a young man of military age, essential to the military defence of his country. The solidity of that defence had to be reinforced by religious sanctions. So the ephebe at Athens had to swear an oath:

>I will not disgrace these sacred arms, and
>I will not desert the comrade beside me wherever I shall be stationed in a battle-line.

I will defend our sacred and public institutions, and

I will not hand on the fatherland smaller, but, so far as I am able, by myself or with the help of all, greater and better.

I will obey those who for the time being exercise authority reasonably and the established laws and those which they will establish reasonably in the future.

I will not allow anyone who tries to destroy them, so far as I am able, by myself or with the help of all.

I will honour the traditional sacred institutions.

Witnesses are the gods Aglauros, Hestia, Enyo, Enyalios, Ares, Athene Areia, Zeus, Thallo, Auxo, Hegemone, Heracles, and the boundaries of the fatherland, wheat, barley, vines, olive-trees, fig-trees.[1]

Here military security and religion twine in and out of one another. We must not think of religion being introduced by a cynical establishment to enforce their will on the impressionable. This has undoubtedly happened from time to time in history, and Polybius praised the Romans for it (6, 56 cf. Aug. *CD* 4, 32). Here religion is part of the fabric of society.

Not only was political business religious business. Religious business was political business. It was handled by the political institutions, and it took priority over other state matters (*IG* II [2]107; 212). Priesthoods were state offices. Religious offences were serious matters of state, as the episodes of the Mutilation of the Hermae and the Profanation of the Mysteries at Athens may remind us.

The oracles had an important political role to play, the Delphic oracle above all. It is essential to recognize that these were religious consultations, that there was a genuine desire to elucidate the will of the gods. The political influence of Delphi in a narrow secular sense of the word has been exaggerated by some authorities. The very ambiguity of some of the responses does not suggest a strong central political directive. But influence there was. The oracle patently enjoyed an excellent information service, and it was rare to undertake a colonial enterprise without consulting Delphi.[2] We have inscriptional evidence of a particularly close relationship with Delphi on the part of Magnesia-on-the-Maeander, for example (*I Magn.* 17; 20), or Cyzicus (*SIG*[3]1158; Collitz 2970; *BCH* 4, 471; 59, 93). Delphi had to be accessible even in time of war, and a study of the epigraphical evidence shows that in the Archidamian war of 431–421 BC the relationship of Athens to Delphi was not essentially changed.[3] The truce of 423 BC guaranteed access to the oracle by both sides (Thuc. 4, 119, 1). Other oracles also received political consultations, Dodona for example, or Ammon (Cic. *Div.* 1, 43, 95). The Athenian generals in 333 BC offered sacrifice to Ammon (*IG* II $^2$1496, 96–7), and we know that the Athenians had a sacred ship, the Ammoni(a)s, to send on consultations as early as about 363 BC (*IG* II $^2$1642; *BSA* 57 (1962) 8).[4]

In colonial enterprises it was not merely incumbent to check with Delphi beforehand. Religious provision for the colony had to be made. In 446–445 BC the Athenians colonized Brea in Thrace. The inscription relating to this is the only example of a contemporary record of such a foundation. In it it is clearly stated that the founders of the colony are to provide for sacrifices on behalf of the colony, that the consecrated precincts are to remain as at present with no fresh consecrations, and that they are to offer an ox and a full set of armour at the Great Panathenaea, and a phallus at the festival of Dionysus (*IG* I $^2$45).[5]

Equally interesting, because it deals with an ally not a colony, is a fragment of a decree of the Athenian Council and people in 372 BC referring to some unknown trouble on the island of Paros. The Parians are required to put things right not merely politically, but religiously as well, and 'in accordance with ancestral tradition, and to present at the Panathenaic festival an ox and a full set of armour, and at the festival of Dionysus an ox and a phallus' (*AJA* 40 (1936) 461ff.).

In diplomatic exchanges the person of a herald was sacrosanct. He carried a staff, which aligned him with the traditional work of Hermes. In Sparta and Athens there were families entrusted with the duty of the herald, in Sparta the Talthybii, in Athens the Kerykes (which simply means 'heralds'). In extreme bitterness a herald might be refused access, but he could not be maltreated without risking the wrath of the gods. It is a sign of the secularization of politics that heralds tended to be replaced by envoys, more in number. Sparta regularly used three, and Athens varied from two to ten. The fact that the regular numbers were three or ten suggests that there was a religious aura attaching to the right number. But they enjoyed no sacrosanctity, and the Athenians killed Spartan envoys in 430–429 (Thuc. 2, 67); the Spartans treated Athenian envoys in the same way in 396–395 (*Hell. Oxy.* 2, 1). The appointment of envoys was temporary and *ad hoc*. They were chosen as skilled negotiators rather than authoritative exponents of divine law. But heralds were retained for special purposes, such as the recovery of the dead after a defeat in battle.[6]

Treaties were sacred. The Greek word for treaty was *spondai*, literally the libation accompanying the agreement. The treaty was reinforced by an oath. Thus in the alliance between Athens and Corcyra in 375 BC both sides took the oath:

> I shall come to the aid of the people of (Corcyra) (Athens) with all my might and to the utmost of my ability accordingly as the (Corcyraeans) (Athenians) may request if anyone proceeds with hostile intent against the territory of (Corcyra) (Athens) either by land or by sea, and with respect to war and peace I shall act in accordance with the decisions of (Athens and) the majority of the allies, and in all other respects I shall act in accordance with the resolutions of (Athens and) the allies. I swear this by Zeus, Apollo and Demeter. May much good fortune attend me if I abide by the oath, may the opposite befall me if I fail. (*IG* II $^2$97)

The Greek states who were forced into the League of Corinth by Philip of Macedon in 338–337 BC took an even more solemn oath 'by Zeus, Ge, Helios, Poseidon, Athene, Ares and all the gods and goddesses' (*IG* II $^2$236). Penalties for infringement were paid not to the offended party but to a divinity. Thus in the treaty between Heraea and Elis, datable to about 500 BC, any infractor had to pay a talent of silver to Olympian Zeus to be used in his service (Meiggs–Lewis 17). A business arrangement between Athens and Phaselis carried with it a fine of 10,000 drachmas to Athene for infringement (Meiggs–Lewis 31). An agreement between Athens and Chalcis in 446–445 had to be sworn to by every adult citizen of Chalcis individually; any who refused would forfeit his political rights and have his goods confiscated and a tithe paid to Olympian Zeus (Meiggs–Lewis 52). We have many more examples of the use of oaths. In dealings between Athens and Erythrae in the 450s, the Council of Erythrae have to take an oath by Zeus, Apollo, and Demeter, laying a curse of annihilation upon those who swear falsely and upon their children, and have to offer sacrifice on pain of a fine of 1,000 drachmas (*IG* I $^2$10). In 362 the four cities on the island of Ceos asserted their independence of the Athenian League, with some bloodshed. The uprising was repressed and those responsible punished. The generals of the League then swore solemnly by Zeus, Athene, Poseidon, and Demeter that there would be no further reprisals and the cities of Ceos swore that there would be no further trouble, in the names of the same gods. Both parties used the formula 'May I be blessed in observing this oath, cursed in forswearing' (*SIG* ³173). In general political agreements invariably have a religious dimension.

Treaties were regularly placed in temples in the care of the gods. A sixth-century treaty between the Metapians and the Anaetoi was inscribed in bronze and deposited at Olympia (*I Ol*. 10). So was the treaty between Heraea and Elis (Meiggs–Lewis 17). The agreement between Athens and Chalcis in 446–445 was to be set up in the temple of Olympian Zeus in Chalcis (Meiggs–Lewis 52). The Peace of Nicias is said by Thucydides to have been placed on the Acropolis at Athens, in the temple of Amyclae at Sparta, and at Olympia, Delphi and Isthmia (5, 18, 10); the alliance in the following year was to be set up on the Acropolis at Athens, in the temple of Apollo at Argos, and in the temple of Zeus at Mantinea, and to be commemorated jointly in bronze at the Olympic Games (5, 47, 11). Nor was it only treaties. After the restoration of democracy at Athens at the end of the fifth century, five men from the island of Thasos are recorded as having the right of *proxenia* or official representation restored to them by decree of the Athenian assembly. The record was set up on the Acropolis at Athens at the expense of one of the Thasians (*IG* II ²6).

Religious observance might even cut across war. The sacred truce associated with the Olympic Games is an obvious example. The Spartans were notorious for their religious observances. At the time of Marathon they were waiting for the full moon (Hdt. 6, 106). At Thermopylae they were held up by the festival of the Carneia (Hdt. 7, 206). Before Plataea they were delayed by the Hyacinthia (Hdt. 9, 6–7). Sacrifices were offered by the Spartans before an army crossed a frontier (Thuc. 5, 54), and if they were unfavourable the army withdrew; they were known as *diabateria*.[7] It is strange that there is no record of its practice by other states. Sacrifices were offered before crossing rivers. River gods were awesome and dangerous beings, to be propitiated (Hes. *WD* 737–8; Xen. *Anab*. 4, 3, 18–9; 4, 7, 2 etc.). Sacrifices were naturally regular before battle. Before Salamis Themistocles was sacrificing when someone sneezed on the right, a favourable portent (Plut. *Them*. 13). At Plataea, despite the fact that the Greeks were hard-pressed, Pausanias would not give the battle order because the omens were unfavourable. Only when he fixed his gaze on Hera's temple and prayed to the goddess, and the omens changed, did he give the command (Hdt. 9, 72). Notoriously, Nicias failed to extricate the Athenian armies from Sicily because of an eclipse (Thuc. 7, 50, 4). After victory thanksgiving was made to the gods. After Plataea there was a four-yearly festival of Greek freedom, the Eleutheria. We have many inscriptional records of it from all over the Greek world, Athens (*IG* II $^2$3158; 3162), Epidaurus (*IG* IV $^2$629, 5), Sparta (*IG* V 1, 656–7), Megara (*IG* VII 49, 11), Plataea (*IG* VII 1711), Thespiae (*IG* VII 1856, 5), Rhodes (*IG* XII 1, 78), Halicarnassus (*SIG* $^3$1064, 11), Miletus (Moretti 59). This was an exceptionally great occasion. A smaller instance is the institution, by the comic dramatist Philippides, of a contest in honour of Demeter and Kore at Athens in honour of the liberation of the hill of the Muses from the Macedonians in 283 BC (*IG* II $^2$657 ll. 43–5). Sometimes the receipt of the good news of a victory might be celebrated (*BCH* 60 (1936) 184–7); we have a number of examples.[8]

The intertwining of politics and religion can be seen in the curious institution of the amphictionies. These were religious associations centring upon some temple and its cult. They had no overt political function, but they not infrequently became politically involved. The best known was associated with the temple of Apollo at Delphi, though in origin its centre was the temple of Demeter at Anthela near Thermopylae. The ancient association was preserved in a number of ways. The associated tribes – Thessalians, Boeotians, Dorians, Ionians, Perrhaebians, Dolopians, Magnetes, Locrians, Aenianes, Phthiotic Achaeans, Malians, and Phocians – lie to the north of Delphi and centre on Anthela. The meetings in spring and autumn began in Anthela and adjourned to Delphi. Nothing is known of the foundation, nor of the way the association with Delphi came about. The function of the amphictiony was to administer the temple of Apollo and its possessions and to organize the Pythian Games. They issued coins, however, which indicates a political and economic function. The oath required contracting parties not to destroy cities within the League or to cut off their water supply. The officials, called *hieromnemones*, or sacred recorders, could declare a sacred war against infractors. The League became something of a political plaything, not strong enough to assert its independence of a major power, but strong enough to be worth cultivating and manipulating, which Philip II of Macedon did to great effect. Several other amphictionies are known, though we know little enough about them. The Panionian amphictiony administered the Panionion, a temple of Apollo on the coast of Asia Minor. This was politically important as a gathering of the Ionians. So too was the Ionian amphictiony centring on Delos. A minor amphictiony was associated with the temple of Poseidon on the island of Calauria off the east coast of the Peloponnese.

An inscription from Magnesia-on-the-Maeander, already referred to, tells of a series of epiphanies of Apollo and Artemis in the late third century. They naturally enquired of the oracle, which apparently said that the Ionian cities were to honour Apollo Pythius and Artemis Leucophryene, to give golden wreaths to the people of Magnesia and declare their territory sacrosanct. It seems that the other cities were reluctant to do this, so fourteen years later the Magnesians tried again with a demonstrative exhibition of piety. This time the other states acceded 'both on account of the god's advice and of the ancient friendship and kinship between them and the people of Magnesia from the days of their forbears' (*SIG* $^3$557).

A particularly interesting example of the impact of politics on religion will be found on Delos. The sanctuary of the Dioscuri lies away from the main centre of population by the sea to the south. The Dioscuri were gods of particular blessing to mariners, and the appearance of St Elmo's fire on the rigging of a ship was associated with their presence. The sanctuary had a curious history. It originated in the seventh century and was in use throughout the sixth. In the fifth and fourth centuries it was neglected. It was restored at the end of the fourth century, and a new and larger temple was constructed. For a century and a half it prospered. Then suddenly, in about 166 BC it was again abandoned for over half a century, coming to brief life again at the beginning of the first century until the final disasters overtook the whole island. These were not periods of comparative popularity and comparative indifference. There is no trace of the use of the sanctuary during the interregna. F. Robert noticed that the periods of neglect attested by archaeology coincide almost precisely with the periods of Athenian domination over the island, and suggested that the Dioscuri represented the divine sanction for the naval and mercantile independence of Delos, which they suppressed when they had the power.

In the Hellenistic period Tyche (Fortune) became among other things a city goddess, associated with particular cities, and wearing a turreted crown as a distinguishing mark. For example, a stone on the road from Mytilene to Thermae on the island of Lesbos proclaims on one side 'Great Artemis Thermia' and on the other 'Great Tyche of Mytilene'. The stone seems to represent a demarcation of political territories. Coins from the island dating from the Roman Empire show the goddess with her turreted crown, enthroned, with a patera in her hand.

The most famous such representation is the Tyche of Antioch portrayed in sculpture by Eutychides, though we have only a later copy. The goddess sits on a rock representing a local mountain. She has her right knee raised to take the weight of her right elbow as she holds up the palmleaves of victory. Her left hand rests lightly on the rock, allowing the voluminous drapery of her dress to tumble round it. She wears the turreted crown. At her feet swims the young river god of the Orontes, arching his back so that he can gaze up admiringly at his glorious queen. She is oblivious, her eyes fixed on the distant future. The whole is technically superb. It scarcely moves our emotions today, but it may have had a considerable emotional impact in its own period. It is far superior to most political-religious art.

Coins of the Hellenistic age are particularly illuminating about fresh developments in political religion.[9]

We may start with Alexander the Great. On coins he can be seen wearing the lionskin of Heracles. The Macedonian royal house claimed descent from the demigod; at the same time it placed Alexander firmly among the divine heroes, son of Zeus. A posthumous representation by Ptolemy I of Egypt is more complex in its allusions. Alexander wears the elephant scalp of Dionysus, the ram's horn of Zeus Ammon, the aegis of Zeus, and carries the royal diadem of Persia. On the reverse of Alexander's coinage we find Zeus enthroned, with sceptre and eagle. This is an assertion of the religious unity of Greece under Alexander, but it has a wider potential, for Zeus was already being identified with Baal in Syria and beyond.

Once Alexander was established as the divine monarch it was natural for the Successors to follow suit, above all in Egypt where the Pharaohs were already regarded as divine. Ptolemy I established the norm of the Ptolemaic coinage. He himself was represented with the aegis of Zeus over his shoulders, and placed on the reverse the eagle and thunderbolt. Ptolemy III had himself portrayed with the aegis of Zeus, the trident of Poseidon, and the rays of Helios. No doubt there are political allusions here – to Greece, seapower, and Rhodes – but we are dealing with political religion. On the reverse a cornucopiae is crowned with the rays of Helios and bound with the royal diadem; the divine ruler works with the sun god for the fertility of the earth. Ptolemy III was concerned with this last. He placed a double cornucopiae on a coin which showed his mother Arsinoe II, who seems herself to have the horn of the cow goddess Hathor, and another, combined with caps symbolic of Castor and Pollux, on a coin showing his wife Berenice II.

Lysimachus, one of the immediate contenders for the succession, showed Alexander with the ram's horn of Zeus Ammon in allusion to his divine parentage, and with a touch of another son of Zeus, Dionysus, in his flowing locks. On the reverse is an important type showing Athene seated holding a figure of Nike, the goddess of victory. This last type was adopted for Seleucus I in Syria, and became the emblem and symbol of the Attalids of Pergamon; this was partly governed by gratitude to Lysimachus, partly to the patronage of culture by the Attalids, who saw Pergamon as the Athens of the East. Later, Eumenes II replaced Athene with Castor and Pollux. This was also a move of political religion; the type was used by the Romans who had been inspired by the Dioscuri at Lake Regillus.

Seleucus I showed himself with a helmet incorporating a bull's horn (a sign of superhuman strength), and covered with a panther's hide, another allusion to Dionysus. Where the Attalids gave their allegiance to Athene the Seleucids paid homage to Apollo, whose worship was established at Daphne outside Antioch. The god is usually examining his special weapon, the arrow; he is sometimes standing, sometimes seated on the omphalos, the navel of the world. Antiochus IV, however, preferred the type of Zeus holding Nike. It was he who resumed the building of the temple of Olympian Zeus in Athens. His coinage also bears the honorific appellation ΘΕΟΥ ΕΠΙΦΑΝΟΥΣ (God Manifest). Demetrius I also used the divine or semi-divine title ΣΩΤΗΡ (Saviour). He kept allegiance to Apollo by surrounding his head in a laurel wreath; the reverse bears the image of Tyche, with sceptre and cornucopiae. Luck as a divinity was becoming more prominent in the uncertainties of the time. Alexander Balas called himself ΘΕΟΠΑΤΩΡ (Divinely fathered) and returned to the type of Zeus seated. His young son Antiochus VI is ΕΠΙΦΑΝΗΣ ΔΙΟΝΥΣΟΣ (Dionysus Manifest); the rays emanating from his head may merely represent his manifest divinity. Tryphon reverted to the primacy of Zeus, portraying a curious helmet which incorporates the horn of Amalthea, the she-goat who suckled Zeus, and the thunderbolt. Cleopatra, wife of Demetrius II, appears as ΘΗΑΣ ΕΥΕΤΗΡΙΑΣ (goddess of fertility; the cornucopiae represents that fertility).

In Macedonia Demetrus Poliorcetes proclaimed himself son of Poseidon and put the god on his coins; he himself wears the diadem of Persia and a bull's horn. Antigonus Gonatas, who attributed his victory over the Gauls to the god Pan, showed Pan with his own features, and on the reverse Athene, warrior and goddess of Pella. She and Zeus are common on the Macedonian coinage.

In Bactria Heracles is used to represent achievement and service; Poseidon is more surprising in view of the inland nature of the kingdom. Zeus is also found, once with an image of Hecate. In India Menander used Athene to allude to his Macedonian roots. His own title is ΣΩΤΗΡ (Saviour). In Bithynia too Zeus represents the permanence of Greek power, but there are more exotic types, the Thracian goddess Bendis or (by allusion) the hero Perseus. Nicomedes II calls himself ΕΠΙΦΑΝΗΣ but this need mean no more than 'glorious'. In Pontus too Zeus appears, and the royal couple Mithradates IV and Laodice show the divine couple Zeus and Hera. Pharnaces I portrays a male deity with cornucopiae, caduceus, and vine, a pretty piece of syncretism.

One of the more remarkable expressions of ruler worship is recorded in a late literary source from the contemporary author Duris of Samos (Ath. 6, 253 D–F). Demetrius the Besieger came to Athens in 307 BC. They escorted him in a car with an image of Demeter, singing a hymn which proclaimed him child of Poseidon and Aphrodite and declared that the other gods were distant, deaf, non-existent, or indifferent, but him they could see face to face, in flesh and blood, real. They prayed him for the gift of peace. This is the product of an age of disillusion, an age which combined scepticism and credulity. Divinity meant power, and the power of the great rulers was plain to all. Athens, that is Athene, had lost her power. The Athenians actually gave Demetrius the Parthenon as his palace, and the titles Saviour and Benefactor, which were to become commonplace among the Hellenistic monarchs.

The Egyptian practice is recorded in 196 BC on the celebrated Rosetta stone (*OGIS* 90), a decree in honour of Ptolemy V Epiphanes. The royal titles are spelt out in eloquent fullness, and due deference is paid to his divine predecessors, 'Alexander, the Saviour Gods, the Brother Gods, the Benefactor Gods, the Parent-loving Gods', leading up to himself, 'the God Manifest and Gracious'. There follows the proclamation of the priests and religious officials, met in due assembly for his coronation. They declare him to be 'the ever-living, beloved by

Ptah, God Manifest and Gracious'; he was 'from the beginning a God born of a God and Goddess, like Horus, the son of Isis and Osiris, who came to the help of his Father Osiris'. For his benefactions to the temples they affirm that 'the gods have rewarded him with health, victory, power, and all other good things, his sovereignty to continue to him and his children for ever'. There is some ambiguity in Ptolemy's position. He is a god; he is also blessed by the gods. But there is no ambiguity about the integration of political and religious emotion.

One of the most interesting expressions of ruler worship comes from the little kingdom of Commagene, set among mountains in the east of the Greek world, during the first century BC. Antiochus I of Commagene was ruling between 69 and 38 BC, perhaps longer. He was of mixed blood, part Greek, part Persian; his kingdom was Hellenized but retained some Persian elements. High in the mountains stand figures of Greek and Persian deities, and nearby a long magniloquent inscription, in which he expresses his belief that religion is the great bulwark of his kingdom, and his consequent determination that his realm should be the common home of all the gods. He then goes on to speak of five images he has set up. Three are of syncretistic figures: Zeus-Ahuramazda, Apollo-Mithras-Helios-Hermes, and Artagnes-Heracles-Ares. The fourth is the personification of the motherland Commagene. The fifth is his own Person. He declares the consecration of four days for special offerings, of which one is his own birthday, and another the day of his accession, and proceeds to detailed regulations of the royal cult, ending with blessings on his successors if they preserve the cult, and curses if they do not. This is an exceptionally important expression of political religion. It is patently and elaborately sincere. In his understanding of the great gods he is protecting the Greek and Persian sides of his kingdom. He cannot believe that the Greek 'father of gods and men' and the Persian supreme god of order and light are different from one another. He expressly states that the great gods have been his guides for prosperous government and the authors of general good to the whole kingdom. But to these three great gods he adds Commagene herself and his own divine Person (*Rec. IG* 735).

The Roman rulers similarly received divine honours in the Greek world on a scale which was more circumscribed in the west. Not merely rulers – in 212 BC Marcellus was hailed as Saviour of Syracuse and a festival established in his honour (Cic. 2 *Verr.* 2, 51). In 195

Flamininus was given a priesthood in Chalcis, which certainly lasted three centuries, and a hymn sung with the words 'Hail, Paean Apollo, hail, Titus our Saviour' (Plut. *Flam.* 16). At Ephesus there was a shrine of Roma and P. Servilius Isauricus, proconsul in the mid-40s (*Forsch. in Eph.* 3, 148). M. Aquilius had a priest at Pergamon (*IGRR* 4, 297). The whole process was intensified with full imperial power. Julius Caesar had a statue at Carthaea as 'God, Imperator and Saviour of the World' (*CIG* 2369), and a decree at Ephesus inscribed on an aqueduct honoured him as 'sprung from Ares and Aphrodite, God Manifest and Universal Saviour of human society' – this in his lifetime too (*CIG* 2957). We have a long fragment of a letter from the proconsul to the cities of Asia from about 9 BC, followed by a decree of the provincial synod. The proconsul calls Augustus 'the most divine Caesar' and encourages the cities to observe his birthday; the decree calls the Emperor 'god', and resolves that 'time in human affairs should be reckoned from his birth' (*OGIS* 458). The megalomaniac Gaius ordered his own image to replace that of Zeus at Olympia. The eminently sane Claudius tried to stem the tide and refuse divine honours in Alexandria, but the governor in publishing the refusal called him 'Caesar our god' (*P. Lond.* 1912). Nero, another megalomaniac, identified himself with Zeus the Liberator. Hadrian was honoured as Zeus Olympius, and there was a festival Hadrianeia Olympia. The imperial cult flourished most vigorously in the Asiatic provinces, where the cities engaged in rivalry for the office of *neocorus*, temple attendant for the cult of its divine emperors. Under the Julio-Claudians the title was granted to Ephesus, Pergamon, Smyrna, Ancyra, and (probably) Tarsus. In the second century AD we find Cyzicus and Laodicea as well as Ephesus, Pergamon, Smyrna and Tarsus for the second time. The Severans add Perinthus, Sardis, and Mazaca-Caesarea, as well as Ephesus for the third time. We know of awards of unknown date at Tomis, Philippopolis, Thessalonica, Nicomedia, Amasia, Neocaesarea, Nicopolis, Synnada, Tralles, Anazarbus, Perge, Side, Tripolis and Laodicea-in-Syria, and of cults at Juliopolis, Hierapolis, Aegae, Neapolis, Teos, Aemonia, Nysa, and Abila-Leucas.

One of our most important pieces of information about ruler-cult in the Greek world under the Romans comes from an inscription (*SEG* 11, 923) from Gytheum, a little way from Sparta. At the festival in question the procession started from the Temple of Asclepius and Hygieia; this shows clearly enough that the celebration was designed to secure the emperor's health. The procession made its way to the Caesareum, where a bull was sacrificed. We know that there was a priest of Augustus at Gytheum, but he had no part in the ceremony, which was performed by the civic officials. We can be quite certain that the sacrifice was not made to the emperor but on behalf of the emperor. So at Aphrodisias we find a priestess offering sacrifice for the health of the Sebastoi (*MAMA* 8, 492b), and a high priest of the imperial cult sacrificing to the ancestral gods, and offering prayer for their health and safety and the eternal duration of their rule.[10]

# 14

# SOME ISLANDS AND THEIR CULTS

The island of Cos lies in the south-east Aegean off the coast of Asia Minor. Any real knowledge of the religious life of the island dates only from after the synoecism of the island communities in 366 BC. We catch glimpses of earlier cults. For example a sanctuary associated with a spring, going back at least to the sixth century, was dedicated to Demeter and Kore (*Arch. Anz.* (1901) 134ff.), and Apollo Pythius and Apollo Dalios, that is Apollo of Delphi and Delos, had an early place; an inscription to the former is datable to about 450 BC (*Koische Forschungen* 36).

We possess substantial fragments of a cult calendar, datable to 325–300 BC (*Inscr. Cos* 37–9 = *SIG*$^3$ 1025–7). The guardian deities of the community were Zeus Polieus and Athene Polias. These deities were also worshipped as patrons of technology under the titles Zeus Machaneus and Athene Machanis, as deliverers (especially from the Gauls in 279) under the titles of Zeus Soter and Athene Soteira (*Inscr. Cos* 34) with a festival and competitions, and as protectors of the sacred grove of cypresses above the Asclepieion with the titles Zeus Alseios and Athene Alseia (*Inscr. Cos* 55). Zeus had other titles too: the panhellenic title of Megistos (Greatest), the political title of Boulaios, the guarantor of property as Horios, and others as well (Sherwin-White 295–6). His political importance is seen in that civic oaths were taken in the names of Zeus, Hera, and Poseidon (*Riv. Fil.* NS 20 (1942) 5, no. 2).

Hera was important. The famous court doctor Xenophon was priest of Argeia Heleia Basileia, a cult-title of Hera (Maiuri 475, 10). We have evidence from a Roman Imperial inscription of a ceremony of tree-cutting in honour of Hera (*Par. del Pass.* 13 (1958) 418–19); we can speculate about the significance of the ritual, but it would be guesswork only. The third of the civic deities, Poseidon, was naturally found in a sea-surrounded island. He had his own festival (*Inscr. Cos* 43 = *SIG* ³1028), and the seagoing people of the island had special obligations towards him (*SIG* ³1000). He was worshipped as Gerastios, a name from Euboea, and in this form had a month named after him (*Inscr. Cos* 27 = *SIG* ³1012).

Asclepius was the greatest of the divinities on the island from the Hellenistic Age. He is discussed elsewhere as a healing god. His father Apollo, as we have noticed, was found from an early date, and though ousted at the great healing sanctuary retained his hold both civically and locally. As Oulios, a healing title, he had a sanctuary of his own, and there were rules about what was to be worn within the sacred precincts (*Par. del Pass.* 12 (1957) 443–4). Apollo was also a patron of the arts, and received dedications from successful musicians (*Inscr. Cos* 58–9). Artemis appears curiously rarely, but we have fragmentary rules associated with three or four sanctuaries (*Inscr. Cos* 372; *SEG* 14, 529; *Par. del Pass.* 27 (1972) 182–4; Herzog 8).

Demeter we have already noted as early: the story of Erysichthon, told whimsically by Callimachus, has associations with Cos, and Theocritus writes of her festival, the Thalysia. She was naturally well-loved in the countryside (*Clara Rhodos* 5, 158, 162, 169, 179, 186–9; 9, 24). An important inscription shows a number of women gathered to celebrate the Mysteries of Demeter, when they are suddenly overtaken by thunder and earthquake. One, Aeschron, makes haste to appease Demeter Soteira, and the terror is stilled (*Phil. Woch.* 1932 no. 52, 1011–7).

The worship of Aphrodite is spread all over the island at all periods; sex and fertility are the concerns of all people at all times. Hermes too has fertility as one of his functions. He appears in the countryside as a pastoral god; one of his titles Eumelius is borrowed from another pastoral power Eumelus (Maiuri 492). Hermes was also honoured by traders (ibid., 466). Dionysus, who is explicitly referred to as a god of vegetation and trees, appears frequently. The calendar prescribes three sacrifices to him under the title Scyllites in a single month (*Inscr. Cos.* 37 = *SIG* ³1025). We know of a procession (*Inscr. Cos* 43 = *SIG* ³ 1028) to an altar or temple (*Inscr. Cos* 10, 28–9); these have been cautiously identified among the excavated remains. Dionysiac friezes with satyrs and maenads survive. We know of at least two festivals to the god with dramatic and musical contests (*Inscr. Cos* 13, 16, 45). We also know of a private thiasos of votaries of Bacchus (Maiuri 492).

Heracles was popular enough to appear on coins of Cos before Asclepius pushed him out. His club was used as an emblem. A crab also appears apparently as his ally: this suggests some local legend which we have lost.

Hecate had her place in the civic cult (*Inscr. Cos* 401). As an underworld goddess she was feared, and participants in the cult of Hecate Megala were debarred from some other priesthoods (Herzog 5). She had other functions. Pontia shows her a sea-goddess (*Koische Forschungen* 217; cf. perhaps Maiuri 475, 12). Soteira and Stratia are military titles (*Inscr. Cos* 370; Maiuri 676).

The other important civic cult was that of Hestia, the power of the hearth. The focal point of her worship was the agora or city centre. We happen to have an important account of some of the ritual (*Inscr. Cos* 37). A complex procedure was followed for choosing sacrificial animals. Nine oxen were chosen, and put together. They came up in threes for selection. If they were unsuitable another nine were picked out. The first choice went to Zeus Polieus, the second to Hestia. The owner of the ox cried 'I offer the ox to the people of Cos; let the people of Cos pay the price to Hestia.' The ox was then sacrificed on the altar of Hestia by an official called the gift-bearer of the Kings; the title is unparalleled and was perhaps antique. Hestia had an ancient priority as of right.

The other ancient cults were of no more than limited importance in Cos. But new cults appeared in the Hellenistic Age. Cos herself was personified, as was Rhodos, the eponymous nymph of Rhodes, and the two were associated with Poseidon (*SIG*$^3$ 1000). Homonoia or Concord was first found as a goddess on a coin of Metapontum in the fifth century (*BMC Italy*, 244), but her great period was the Hellenistic Age. On Cos she appears in a cult calendar of the early third century (*Inscr. Cos* 401). We have other dedications from the Augustan period or thereabouts. It is never clear whether such dedications reflect a time of strife or a time of peace. Nike, Victory, was honoured, not least after the defeat of the Gauls in 279 BC (*SIG*$^3$ 398). She appears in the public cult, with her own priest, sanctuary, treasury, and festival. An inscription gives instructions about a colourful procession with musical accompaniment, and libations and sacrifice (*Inscr. Cos* 43 = *SIG*$^3$ 1028; Maiuri 441; Herzog 9). Adrasteia and Nemesis had a joint cult with regular sacrifices; they presided over public works and the manumission of slaves (*Koische Forschungen* 9, 10; *Inscr. Cos* 29). Other powers of Fate, the Moirai, were also honoured publicly and privately (*Inscr. Cos* 36 = *SIG* $^3$1108). The Theoi Patrooi or Ancestral Gods received a number of dedications in the form of small altars or altar plaques (*Inscr. Cos* 76–80; Maiuri 479–81); these are associated with a first-century dictator named Nicias, who evidently wanted to use religion to establish his traditionalism.

The Hellenistic Age was also the age of ruler-worship. As early as the mid-fourth century a coin of Cos depicts Mausolus in the guise of Heracles (*BMC Caria* 194–5); this seems to be the earliest representation of a monarch in the guise of a god. There is no evidence of ruler-cult, however, before Ptolemy II Philadelphus when a precinct was set up in honour of the goddess Arsinoa Philadelphus; this was freely given, for Cos was not an Egyptian dependency. From the end of the third century ruler-cult became common. With the rise of Pergamon there was a festival called the Attaleia (*Inscr. Cos* 43 = *SIG*$^3$ 1028; Herzog 26); rulers of Cappadocia and Bithynia were also honoured. All this aspect of religion was absorbed in the cult of the Roman emperors.

Private religion did not differ greatly in emphasis from public religion, except that there were important developments in family cult (*Arch. Dr. Or.* 1 (1937) 145–79; *ZPE* 24 (1977) 207–17). We do however know of numbers of thiasoi, or religious fellowships, perhaps organizations of slaves or metics. They are centred on Aphrodite, Athene, Apollo, Helios (the Sun-god), Zeus, Hermes, Dionysus (*Inscr. Cos* 155–8; Maiuri, 489–96); foreign gods include Isis, Osiris, Sarapis, and Astarte (*Inscr. Cos* 54; 371; Maiuri 493; 496). Eastern cults do not seem to have been prominent.[1]

Delos was Apollo's island. There was pre-Greek habitation and the name of the little hill Cynthus is pre-Greek. The hill itself was occupied in the third millennium BC, but there is a curious gap in evidence in the first half of the second millennium. The Mycenaean age saw the island in a new prominence. The main deity was a goddess, who survived on the island as Apollo's twin sister Artemis, as the evidence from the Artemision shows. From this period there seems to have been continuity of occupation and of some aspects of culture, though Delos decreased in population and importance in the Protogeometric period. But the Geometric period saw considerable developments, and it must have been in this period that Apollo was established on the island. During the seventh and early sixth century, as the archaeological remains show, Naxos was the dominant influence on the island. In the mid-sixth century Paros also became important. But from the second half of the sixth century Athens, now the leading Ionian state, took over effective control. Thucydides (3, 104) tells us that Pisistratus purified the island, removing all tombs at least from the sanctuary area. Samos under Polycrates also had a brief period of dominance. After the Persian wars in the fifth century Delos became the centre and treasury of the confederacy of liberated states, which turned gradually into an Athenian empire. There was a further purification in 426 (Thuc. 3, 104). All the remaining tombs, except for one or two of special sanctity, were removed. There were to be no births or deaths on the island, and inscriptions show the complex problem of dealing with bodies from shipwrecks. In the Hellenistic Age Delos had 150 years of independence and prosperity, followed by 100 years as a free port and major commercial centre under the political dominion of Athens. But in the first century BC Mithradates and his pirate allies sacked the island, which never recovered, though Hadrian characteristically tried to restore the religious life.

Apollo had two great sanctuaries, at Delphi and Delos, and this is part of the evidence that he is a composite god, with independent origins in the north and east. He came to Delos, we may presume, from Asia Minor, where the Hittites had a god Apulunas. He was perhaps in origin a sun god, as his title Phoebus, Shining One, suggests, though the Greeks did not so think of him. He was a power of healing and destruction. Delos was the scene of his legendary birth. Leto was loved by Zeus, and Hera in jealousy forbade any land to deliver her of Apollo and Artemis. But a floating island named Asterie or Starlet took pity on her, and because its nymph had rebuffed Zeus's advances, Hera stayed her hand, and Zeus in celebration rooted the island and gave it the name Delos, Clear or Famous. So much for myth.

In one sense the whole island was a sanctuary. In the narrower sense there was a limited sanctuary, irregular in plan, with a Hellenistic ceremonial entrance in the south-west leading to a paved courtyard. A tiny temple, 7.95 × 3.55 m, orientated north–south, may perhaps go back to the Mycenaean Age, but there are puzzling features. The oldest discernible classical temple belongs to the seventh century, replaced in the sixth, and was built by the people of Naxos. They also dedicated a colossal statue of Apollo, freestanding, for the whole sanctuary and the whole island were his: a few shattered pieces testify to its size. A sixth-century temple facing west may be associated with Pisistratus. Near it a peripteral temple to the god was begun in the fifth century. It was of no great size, 28.53 × 12.47 m, and shows curious features; for example, it seems to have been Ionic in conception and Doric in execution. It was never in fact completed. Later in the century the Athenians built a new temple hexastyle, but without side porticoes, which the limitations of the site did not permit. This too has curious features, a pronaos of unusual form, and a semicircular plinth for seven statues, taken from the oldest temple, in the cella. Monuments of all periods surrounded the temple. Notable was the bronze palm-tree dedicated by the Athenian Nicias recalling the tree which supported Leto as she gave birth to the god.

To the west and slightly to the north of these lie some important sacred structures. These include: a small innominate temple on the site of a Mycenaean megaron, presumably also sacred; the almost indiscernible remains of an *abaton* going back to Mycenaean times, and which has been identified with the Tomb of Hyperborean Maidens, Laodice and Hyperoche, who play some part in the mythical traditions, coming from an ideal land in the far north visited by Apollo (Hdt. 4, 34); a large rectangular fourth-century building with a frieze of episodes in the life of Theseus, called in an inscription 'the temple', but thought to be the Keraton, or altar of horns. Most important is the Artemision. A small building of the Mycenaean period, long and narrow, with a cache of gold and ivory offerings, lay under the later temples. Next came a simple but sizable temple of the early seventh century with a cella no smaller than 9.6 × 8.6 m. Here were found some excellent statues of korai, one of which is now in Athens. This was replaced in the Hellenistic Age by a new hexastyle temple. This may be considered the oldest sacred spot on the island.

The north side of the sanctuary was closed in the Hellenistic Age by a great stoa. Outside is a sacred well and a small semicircular *abaton*, and, at the east end, a sanctuary of Dionysus, marked by phalluses of stone, and reliefs with Dionysiac scenes. Within the sanctuary in the north-west corner a building has been somewhat precariously identified as the sanctuary of Demeter and Kore, or Thesmophorion, mentioned in inscriptions. To the south of the stoa are five rectangular buildings identified, no doubt rightly, as treasuries. Closer to the stoa is another *abaton* associated with two more Hyperborean maidens, Opis and Arge.

Towards the west is a puzzling monument, a long narrow structure, about 70 × 12 m, known popularly as the Monument of the Bulls, but perhaps the Neorion of the inscriptions. It had a Victory above it; there were marine figures along the walls, and a frieze showing a battle. It has therefore been supposed that it commemorates a naval victory, that the long central gallery housed a warship dedicated in thanks, and that this accounts for the shape of the building. Around this is a series of altars, some of which go back to the sixth century. Some are innominate, but we can identify an archaic altar to Zeus Polieus, a classical altar to Athene and Apollo Paeon and a Hellenistic altar to Zeus Soter and Polieus.

As we emerge from the sanctuary to the north there is a huge Hellenistic agora over on the right. The most important religious monuments are closer at hand. One is the sanctuary of the Twelve Gods (*Explor. arch. de Délos* XXII). Some archaic statues belong to the early stages of the sanctuary, and there were several altars within the precincts. In the early third century a temple was added with its own altar. The twelve gods were worshipped as a group in various quarters of the Greek world, including Athens, but the composition of the group was unstable. We have already noted the evidence from Delos. One altar was dedicated to Zeus, Athene, and Hera, and we can reasonably assume one to Apollo, Artemis and Leto. The other triads are more speculative – perhaps Demeter, Kore, and Zeus Eubuleus (as an equivalent to Pluto) and Poseidon, Aphrodite, and Hermes, but we cannot be certain. Across the way from this sanctuary lies the temple of Leto, datable from architectural style and pottery to about 540 BC. There are indications that this sanctuary extended further east in the form of a garden referred to in an inscription, and that the later Agora of the Italians encroached upon this.

Further north the sacred wheel-shaped lake lies to the east, and the terrace of the lions to the west. These seventh-century wild animals in marble from Naxos are without parallel. They are plainly guardians of the Sacred Way, leading to the sanctuaries of Leto, Artemis, and Apollo, and their presence makes it highly probable that the earliest landing-place was the bay to the north.

There were other sanctuaries. The holy mountain was sacred to Zeus Cynthius and Athene Cynthia, as a mosaic inscription found on the summit declares. A spur of the peak was dedicated to Zeus Hypsistos. There are various sanctuaries on the slopes. The most puzzling is the cave, a natural cleft in the rock, turned into an elaborate sanctuary in the Hellenistic Age when it was dedicated to Heracles, presumably by Ptolemy II. The puzzle is that there are no remains before the Hellenistic Age, but it is hard to believe that such a cave would not have been regarded as holy. Nearby is a Hellenistic sanctuary. It seems to have been the Philadelpheion, dedicated to the divine monarchs Ptolemy II Philadelphus and his sister and wife Arsinoe Philadelphus. Arsinoe was often depicted with a cornucopiae as Agathe Tyche (Good Fortune), and this was also the sanctuary of Agathe Tyche found in inscriptions. On the northern slopes are some unidentified sanctuaries, seemingly to Semitic gods (Sin of Alam and the First Gods are mentioned in inscriptions). There were ritual banquets here. To the east lay the Rock of Leto with an inscription 'Boundary of Leto', another Semitic sanctuary to the gods of Ascalon, identified with Aphrodite and Poseidon, and the precinct of Artemis Lochia.

Another important block of sanctuaries lies on the lower slopes to the north-west of the holy mountain. Here were set places sacred to gods who did not belong to the early Greek pantheon. There was a Sarapieion where Sarapis, that strange universal god successfully invented by the Ptolemaic dynasty, was accompanied by Isis and Anubis, and, later, Harpocrates, the Greek form of Horus. According to an inscription, an Egyptian priest brought the cult from Egypt at the outset of the third century BC. His son succeeded him, and his grandson built the first sanctuary on instructions received in a dream by the god himself, who chose an area of particular filth to his own greater glory. The sanctuary was entered by a flight of steps leading to a paved courtyard of irregular shape, with a room for ritual banquets to the west, and colonnades to north and south, with niches for lamps in the former. In the court in addition to a chapel were three altars and a place for offerings. There were actually two more sanctuaries of Sarapis and the Egyptian gods in the area, of which the largest is impressively situated on a terrace. It was entered from the south through a portico with six columns. This led to a long trapezoidal approach, some 90 m in length, incorporating a small shrine. Within the main sanctuary stood a small temple to Sarapis facing south, a temple of unknown dedication facing west, and next to it the pleasant façade of the temple of Isis, with a fine statue of the goddess. There was a bust of some divinity in the pediment, and a Victory or similar figure above. An altar stands in front. This was the official Sarapieion and numerous inscriptions attest its prosperity. It lies above the basins of the river Inopus, and some scholars think that these had some part in the Egyptian cult, perhaps by housing sacred crocodiles.

Other sanctuaries in the same general area include the sanctuary of the Syrian gods; the approach was dedicated by one Diophantus to Atargatis (identified by the Greeks with Aphrodite) and her consort Hadad (identified by the Greeks with Zeus). To the south a square courtyard incorporates a small temple, whose mosaic pavement declares its dedication to the minor deity Hadran. Towards the north extends a long terrace, whose east side is occupied by a theatre for sacred drama, holding 400 or 500 spectators, and enclosed in a portico with ritual basins and special rooms. Towards the northern end of the terrace is a kind of baptistery for the ritual 'Descent into the Lake' known from other sources (Lucian *DD Syr.* 47–9), rooms, holy places, and another entrance. Another sanctuary in the area belongs to the divinities of Samothrace. To judge from the inscriptions, if it did not incorporate a shrine to Heracles, there was one nearby. A little below again lay the sanctuary of Aphrodite, with a south-facing marble temple consecrated by Stesileius who was archon in 302. An inscription tells us that the cult-statue was of marble showing Aphrodite wearing gold earrings, and carrying a cup of gilded wood in her hand. Just to the east of the largest Sarapieion is the sanctuary of Hera. To judge from the votives the original temple (perhaps with a wooden colonnade) was of the early seventh century and was replaced at the end of the sixth. The sanctuary had a vast sustaining terrace, a surrounding wall, and an independent altar.

Visitors tend to neglect the southern part of the island, but there are remains of interest there. The sanctuary of the Dioscuri, protectors of shipping, goes back to the seventh century. Relics of the original temple can be seen together with two altars, one small, associated with the temple, one the main sanctuary altar. The sanctuary fell into disuse in the fifth and fourth centuries, but it was restored in the early Hellenistic age. A larger temple was built aligned north–south (at right angles to the archaic shrine) with its own altar. The sanctuary had a chequered history, since it seems to have been abandoned from 166 to 100 BC, and then briefly restored. F. Robert has suggested that the periods of abandonment coincided with those of Athenian domination. The Dioscuri were the symbols of Delian maritime independence (*Explor. arch. de Délos*, XX). Further along on a promontory by the bay of Fourni was the Asclepieion in a marvellous isolated situation. It is possible to make out the propylaea, the temple, the building for 'incubation', and a room for storing votives. Two other seaside sanctuaries cannot be identified with certainty, but one may pertain to the sea-goddess Leucothea; she is known from inscriptions to have had a shrine.²

Thera is in many ways the most fascinating of the Aegean islands because of the colossal eruption which caused the centre of the island to vanish in the middle of the second millennium BC, the possible relation of this cataclysm to some of the stories of flood preserved in legend, to the eventual destruction of Minoan Crete, and indeed to the account of Atlantis in Plato. Neither this nor the breathtaking discoveries of the town at Akrotiri beneath the pumice are directly relevant to the classical city, which was set on a mountain ridge enhanced by massive terraces. Occupation perhaps went back to the tenth century BC on the evidence of the tombs, but the remains are mostly Hellenistic. The main sanctuary area is somewhat apart from the town to the south and below. To the extreme south is a gymnasium with nearby a grotto sacred to Hermes and Heracles, patron deities of the ephebes who used the gymnasium. Next comes the so-called Terrace of the Festivals, which goes back to the sixth century BC, and was the religious centre of the cults of the Dorians who occupied the island. At the north end is the temple of Apollo Carneius, the Dorian god, dating from the sixth century, occupying an area of about $32 \times 10$ m, and the Heroon of the eponymous founder Theras. Along the terrace was celebrated the Gymnopaediae, a festival of dances by nude boys in honour of the god. Graffiti round about express the glory of Apollo and other deities – and the attractive beauty of some of the boys. A Sacred Way connects the sanctuary with the main city, passing a column dedicated to Artemis, and a small temple in honour of the divine monarch Ptolemy III. As we enter the main city high to the left is the sanctuary of the Egyptian gods and the Temple of Pythian Apollo, later replaced by a Byzantine church. The agora is in two sections. Adjacent to one is a Mithraeum of the Roman period, to the other a temple of Dionysus and an altar to Ptolemy Philometor. Other sacred sites meriting special mention are a large cave with a rock-carved throne and votive niche to Demeter and Kore at the entrance, and the sanctuary of Admiral Artemidorus, with an altar of Concord and a multiplicity of religious reliefs including the eagle of Zeus, the dolphin of Poseidon, and the lion of Apollo.

Lesbos is the largest of the islands lying off the Asia Minor coast. There was an important Bronze Age settlement at Thermi. The Greek occupation was Aeolian and led to the establishment of five city-states on the island, Mytilene, Methymna, Eresus, Antissa, and Pyrrha.

Zeus, Hera, Apollo, Artemis, Athene, Hermes, Poseidon, Demeter, Hephaestus, and Dionysus appear on coins from the island; so does Asclepius. Ares and Aphrodite have been tentatively but not certainly identified on coins. One of the most interesting coins comes from Mytilene and shows Zeus, Pluto, and Poseidon with the inscription 'High gods of Mytilene'. An inscription of thanksgiving for deliverance is offered by one Zosime to the same three (*Ath. Mitt.* 24 (1889) 358). It is hard to know whether these are united as the gods of storm, death, and sea by Zosime; whether they cover sky, sea, and underworld; or whether they happen to have been linked as 'high' gods (*akraioi*) on the acropolis.

Zeus is well represented in inscriptions with a variety of cult-titles. The most interesting is Maenolius (*IG* XII ii 484), which is not applied to him elsewhere, though it has links with the cult of Dionysus. But in popularity Zeus was outstripped by Apollo, Artemis, and Dionysus, especially in the later period. On an out-of-the-way site about 27 miles from Mytilene stood an archaic temple of Apollo Napaeus, which yielded Aeolian capitals of the sixth century BC. Thucydides tells us of a festival of Apollo Maloeis held outside the city of Mytilene (3,3), and the scholiast adds an aetiological myth about the prophetess Manto losing a golden apple from her necklace and promising to found a temple to Apollo if she recovered it. The festival still existed in the first century AD (*IG* XII ii 484). At Eresus there were cults of Apollo Eresius (Hesych. s.v.) and Apollo Lyceius (*IG* XII ii 526b). At Methymna there was a cult of Apollo Smintheus (*IG* XII ii 519). Lesbos as a whole seems to have been in special relationship with Apollo's island of Delos (*IG* XI ii 105; 108; XI iv 590; 594; 623; *BCH* 29, 210–11; *CIG* add. 2265b). Artemis was naturally found where Apollo was established, naturally too near to the coast of Asia Minor. She enjoyed a state cult as Artemis Thermia, presiding over the hot springs at Thermae (*IG* XII, ii, 101; 103; 105; 106). An important stone found on the road from Mytilene to Thermae bears the inscription on one side 'Great Artemis Thermia' and on the other 'Great Fortune of Mytilene (*IG* XII ii 270). Interpretation is uncertain; probably it was a boundary stone between the territory of Mytilene and the domain of Artemis Thermia. Artemis appears with other cult-titles too, as Aethiopia at Mytilene (*IG* XII ii 92) and Dreneia at Eresus (*Arch. Eph.* (1913) 227). One of the finest statues of Artemis was found on Lesbos; it is now in the archaeological museum in Istanbul. Dionysus had one of his numerous birthplaces at Brisa, with a temple there (Steph. Byz. s.v.), and had another sanctuary near the supposed grave of Orpheus at Antissa. At Methymna he had a festival, the Dionysia, when a very ancient image of the god was carried round (*IG* XII ii 499; 503). There seems to have been a parallel ritual at Eresus (*IG* XII ii 527 l. 28). The Dionysia was a major festival at Mytilene (*IG* XII ii 5, l. 9; 15 l. 29; 18 l. 9; 49 l. 4; 64 etc.). So was the Theodaisia in honour of Dionysus and the Nymphs (*IG* XII ii 68–70); in one inscription the god is called Zonnysus, perhaps a phonetic transcription of a local pronunciation.

An Ionic temple, probably to Aphrodite, has been found at Mesa about 19 miles from Mytilene, not far from ancient Pyrrha. It is of the Ionic order, and pseudo-dipteral with 8 × 14 columns. It has often been supposed that the poetess Sappho was involved in the cult of Aphrodite, but the evidence associating the goddess with the island is curiously meagre. We have an inscription regulating the offerings at an altar of Aphrodite Peitho and Hermes; any bird may be offered and any animal except the pig (*IG* XII ii 73). One dedication from Mytilene associates the goddess with Athene (*IG* XII ii 476). Another from Kato-Pyrgi is an offering by a guild of tanners and suggests a sanctuary in the vicinity (*IG* XII ii 109). Hermes himself appears on the coins of Eresus and his staff on the coins of Mytilene. A relief shows him as cupbearer to the Mother of the Gods. A most interesting inscription of the Roman period invokes him as the god of fruitfulness (*IG* XII ii 476). In Roman times also there was a guild of merchants called Hermaistai (*IG* XII ii 22).

Athene first appears indirectly through her attribute the *gorgoneion* on a sixth-century coin. She had two unique cult-titles on Lesbos, Hyperdexia (Steph. Byz. s.v. *hyperdexion*) and Idena (*IG* XII ii 476). She is especially prominent on coins of Methymna, as well as inscriptions there (*IG* XII ii 505). There was a temple of Athene Polias at Eresus, where decrees were placed (*IG* XII ii 529; P. N. Papageorgiu *Rhodos kai Lesbos* 1913). At Mytilene she was Athene Soteira, and her temple was probably on the acropolis to judge from inscriptions found there (*IG* XII ii 5; 12; 111; 121). A pleasant smiling head of the goddess wearing a Corinthian helmet was found on the island.

Poseidon was naturally prominent, and there is evidence of cult at Methymna, Eresus, and Mytilene; he seems to have had a month named after him (*CIG* 4, 6850). Demeter's name does not appear on inscriptions, but we have references to Kore (*IG* XII ii 112) and Persephone (*IG* XII ii 466). Nor does Hera appear in inscriptions though we know of a beauty-contest at her sanctuary (Schol. Hom. *Il.* 9, 129).

Asclepius had an important healing sanctuary at Mytilene. Eumenes of Pergamum placed his promises to his army there (*OGIS* 266), and international decrees generally were presented there (*AJA* 6, 1890, 355). An architrave block from the temple was built into the Turkish fortress on the Acropolis (*IG* XII ii 116). This does not mean that the temple was on the height, but it is unlikely to have been far away. We know also of a hereditary priesthood (*IG* XII ii 102).

A few other divine beings are recorded. Caistris appears to be a local nymph (*IG* XII ii 120); so perhaps Eriboea (*IG* XII ii 130).[3]

Thasos is the most northerly of the Aegean islands, lying close to the coast of Thrace. It is a little less than 400 square kilometres in size. There are some puzzles about the early occupation of the island. Our real knowledge dates from Greek colonization from the island of Paros in about 680BC. In the fifth century Thasos was a member of the Confederacy of Delos and the Athenian empire, only to suffer at the hands of the Spartan Lysander. The island succeeded in retaining a good deal of economic and political independence in the Hellenistic Age.

The religious life of Thasos is displayed before us in an inscription of the late fourth century BC giving the principal festivals (*BCH* (1958) 193ff.):

| | | |
|---|---|---|
| Apaturia (Oct–Nov) | Apaturia | Zeus Patroos Athene Patroa |
| | Festival of All the Gods | |
| Maimakterion (Nov–Dec) | Maimakteria | Zeus |
| Poseidon (Dec–Jan) | Poseideia | Poseidon |
| ——(Jan–Feb) | None | |
| Anthesterion (Feb–Mar) | Anthesteria | Dionysus |
| | Soteria | Heracles Soter |
| Galaxion (Mar–Apr) | Dionysia | Dionysus |
| Artemision (Apr–May) | Diasia | Zeus |
| Thargelion (May–Jun) | Great Heracleia | Heracles |
| | Choreia | Dionysus |
| Plyntherion (Jun–July) | Duodecathea | The Twelve Olympians |
| Hecatombaion (Jul–Aug) | Alexandreia | Alexander the Great |
| | Thesmophoria | Demeter and Kore |
| ——(Aug–Sept) | Great Asclepieia | Asclepius |
| ——(Sept–Oct) | Demetrieia | Demeter |
| | Heroxeinia | The Heroes |
| | Dioscuria | Dioscuri |
| | Great Romaia | Apollo Romaios |

It will be noticed that we do not know all the local month names – and that there was no festival in the bitter weather of January and February.

The circuit of the walls is punctuated by gates, some of which are known by the names of divinities from relief sculptures found there. Such are the Gate of Hermes and the Graces, the Gate of Zeus and Hera, the Gate of Heracles, and the Gate of Silenus. Another is known as the Gate of the Goddess in the chariot, probably Artemis escorted by Hermes.

Zeus was naturally of high importance. On the gate of Zeus and Hera he is seated on a throne adorned with a sphinx, facing outside the city, guarding against invaders. He has Hermes with him. His main sanctuary yet discovered is in the north-west corner of the agora where he was worshipped as Zeus Agoraeos Thasios (*IG* XII 8, 361). On the rocky headland which extends at the north-east corner of the town of Thasos an early Christian church was built on the site of an older sanctuary. We do not know the dedication of this sanctuary, but numerous votive terracottas have been found, and inscriptions honour Zeus Alastoros, Zeus Ctesios, and Zeus Patroos, as well as Athene, Artemis, Kore, and the Nymphs. We know also that in the first century BC there was a priestess of Zeus Eubuleus.

Priests are attested from the fifth or fourth century for Heracles, Dionysus, Aphrodite, and Asclepius, and there was probably a priestess of Demeter. Later we know also of priests of Poseidon (a life appointment, as was that of Heracles), and of Helios-Sarapis, and priestesses of Athene and Artemis. In Roman times the office of priest of the imperial cult was a major honour.

A number of other temples and sanctuaries have been identified. Poseidon was naturally important on an island surrounded by his domain. His sanctuary, dating from the fourth century and dedicated by one Xenophanes (*IG* XII suppl. 452) is a strange shape, an irregular quadrilateral about 48.5 × 33 m – but the opposite sides are not parallel. There was a monumental propylaea to the west, and a stoa along the north side. In the courtyard were two altars, one circular and one formed like the letter pi, and a small chapel. A statue, probably of his consort Amphitrite, riding on a dolphin, was found in the sanctuary. Just outside the propylaea was found an altar with an inscription forbidding the sacrifice of a goat to Hera Epilimenia.

Dionysiac cult was prominent on the island of Thasos. We do not know how or when it was introduced, but a date of about 680 BC is reasonable. The main sanctuary of the god contains two altars: one goes back to the sixth century, the other to the fifth or fourth. An inscription honours Agathos Daemon (Good Spirit) and bans the invocation of Agathe Tyche (Good Luck). The sanctuary is mentioned in the Hippocratic corpus. The head of the main cult statue has been discovered: it is an impressive work of the Praxitelean school, with fine, sensitive, somewhat effeminate features. Within the sanctuary is a curving base for statues of the god with to his left Tragedy, Comedy, Dithyramb and Nocturnal Serenade; corresponding figures to his right can only be guessed at. This was an early Hellenistic dedication. A flight of wide marble steps connected this sanctuary with the theatre, whose proscenium was dedicated to the god by one Lysistratus (*IG* XII supp. 399). This, with part of the later frieze of Dionysus and his panther, is in Istanbul.

Three festivals of Dionysus are known to have been celebrated on the island: the Anthesteria in January–February, the Dionysia in March–April, and the evocatively named Choreia in May–June. The last two centred on the theatre.

The worship of the god continued prominently through the Hellenistic and Roman periods, and there were numerous Dionysiac associations on the island, some of them close-knit family affairs, meeting for ceremonial banquets. It was for one of these that in the first century AD Timocleides, a doctor by profession, dedicated, with a charming inscription, a sanctuary open to the sky enclosing an altar, and an arbour of vine branches, and a small building for initiates, and a stream.

The importance of the god at Thasos can be seen in that he appeared with his rout as a guardian of the gates (the block with this relief was unfortunately lost between Thasos and Istanbul), and the coin-type of Maenad and Satyr. Another gate is guarded by an ithyphallic Silenus.[4]

Artemis had a major sanctuary elevated on a terrace. Its present form is largely Hellenistic, but the sanctuary goes back at least to the fifth century BC. The monumental propylaea we know from an inscription, dating from the first century BC (*BCH* (1959) 363), and honouring her as Artemis Eilithyia, goddess of childbirth. The sanctuary is a square enclosure 33 m wide. It contained honorific statues of notable Thasians. A votive relief shows the goddess. The sanctuary has recently been re-explored (*BSA Arch. Rep.* 1980–1, 38).

The walls climb high on to the acropolis, and here there are other sanctuaries. A medieval fortress covers the sanctuary of Pythian Apollo, which was impressively situated on a platform 85 × 35 m oriented north–south. Beyond is the temple of Athene, a fifth-century structure replacing one of a century earlier, approached through a ceremonial entrance, and having its altar to the west. This too is a magnificent situation. Athene was honoured as Poliuchus, Guardian of the City. We also have an inscription from the early fifth century regulating the cult of Athene Patroa involving full participation of women (*BCH* (1965) 447). To the south-west of this again is the sanctuary of Pan, a simple niche in the rock with carved figures. On the height also was a sanctuary of the family gods, the Theoi Patrooi, recently excavated. Here a retaining wall of the sixth century was raised in the fifth. A stoa in the south-east corner had a bench along the walls; this probably dates from the third century (*BSA Arch. Rep.* 1980–1, 38–41).

Heracles was especially prominent on the island of Thasos. He appears on the coins, and has the title 'Protector of the City'. An unfinished sculpture of him leaning on a shaft was recently found in the quarries (*BSA Arch. Rep.* 1980–1, 40–1). His sanctuary is of particular interest in the history of hero-cults, for it reflects the ambiguity of heroic status. This is a god's sanctuary, but it seems probable that it was originally organized so that sacrifice could be made not on a raised altar to the upper world, but down into a pit and the world of the dead. There are foundations of the altar, 10 × 5.7 m, but no more.

The early sanctuary was of the simplest with a rough-hewn altar, and pits. There was no temple. In the sixth century a small rectangular building was constructed within the sanctuary. It is 6.3 m in width, and Birgitta Bergquist, noting that this approximates to the dimensions of a normal dining enclave, suggested that this might be the function in this case. The temple itself is squarer than most, 23.4 × 20.1 m. It is of simple design, a rectangular naos without pronaos or opisthodomus, surrounded by an Ionic portico of twenty-four columns (six rows of eight). The sanctuary was gradually improved, and given a ceremonial entrance. There was a long gallery to the east, and a set of five rooms to the south with a triangular courtyard behind. We have an inscription relating to the cult (*IG* XII, suppl. 414). Women are excluded, and the sacrifice is not to be goat or pig.

Near this was an obviously important monument, a square marble building with a Doric portico, but with Ionic elements elsewhere. It dates from the late fourth century, and was dedicated by one Thersilochus, but we do not know its purpose.

A few pieces of sculpture extend the picture slightly – a statue of Hermes from the agora; twin statues of Nemesis from the Roman period; from the same period an altar front to Cybele, a votive relief to the Dioscuri.

Of the rest of the island we know little, but an important sanctuary has been found on the neck of the peninsula of Aliki, which goes right back to the original coming of the Parians in the seventh century BC. There are two very similar buildings, going back to about 500 BC. A statue of a kouros was found there, and some later graffiti, which make it probable that the sanctuary was dedicated to the Dioscuri as protectors of shipping.[5]

# 15
# THE RELIGIOUS LIFE OF ATHENS AND ATTICA

Athens is inevitably of special interest to us because of its cultural achievements in antiquity, even though the modern capital city spreads its ugly tentacles across the plain and implants a pall of smog on the atmosphere. This is enhanced by the magnificence of the Acropolis, threatened by the tramp of tourists as well as by the corrosion of chemicals in the air, and by the superb American excavations in the agora. Despite the modern city, a great deal of the ancient city is visible today.[1]

The Acropolis is often thought of as a citadel. That it was, but it was also the part of the city which was nearest to the heavens, the meeting point of heaven and earth, the dwelling-place of the gods, and under their special protection.

The Persian invasion of 480 BC sacked and burned the buildings on the Acropolis. Before that date there had been two main temples, one to the north close to the later Erechtheum, the other to the south underlying the Parthenon. Both were dedicated to Athene. The second was an incomplete replacement in marble of a large sixth-century temple. But already by the sixth century the rock was filled with smaller buildings and statues, as a visit to the museum will instantly make clear. A large number of dedications of statue bases of *korai* (statues of girls) or other offerings have survived. They come from people of many occupations, from a fuller (*IG* I $^2$436), a bread-seller (444), a washerwoman (473), a potter (485), a fisherman (706). They come in gratitude for favours received (658) or in the hope of favours to come (631). They come from first fruits (408; 499; 706) or as a tithe (422; 684). One victorious athlete celebrates victories in the pancratium: once at Olympia, twice at Delphi, five times at Isthmia, four times at Nemea, once at the Great Panathenaea (606).[2]

The fifth-century acropolis was largely due to Pericles, as we know from various sources. The approach, used by the Panathenaic procession, was by a zigzag path. This led to the ceremonial entrance or Propylaea, a double six-columned porch with side-wings, built of white marble. The effect today is somewhat marred by a towering base for a bronze chariot added in 174 BC. On a projecting bastion to the right stands the exquisite little temple of Athene Nike, built just after the Propylaea to complement the design. The Ionic volutes are large. A parapet went round with figures of the goddess Nike or Victory; one of the most famous shows her unfastening her sandal. There was a large altar in front of the temple.

Those who passed through the Propylaea had on the right the sanctuary of Artemis of Brauron with a long Doric stoa, and beyond that the Chalkotheke, where sacred bronze objects were stored. To the left lay a stairway of great antiquity and religious significance, and the small house of the Arrephoroi, young assistant-priestesses who, we are told, used the stairway for ritual purposes. No major building lay straight ahead, and Le Corbusier was deeply impressed by the use of space, the view sweeping between the Erechtheum and the Parthenon. Directly opposite, however, about 36 metres in front, stood the now lost statue of Athene Promachos by Pheidias, some 30 feet in height. Many feel that this might have proved more impressive than his cult statue in the Parthenon. There were many other statues scattered over the surface, and we can trace the cuttings for them in the rock.

The Erechtheum lies to the left or north. It was built over some fifteen years during war towards the end of the fifth century. It is a curious, irregular building, whose shape is perhaps governed by the variety of sacred places it enshrined. It was sacred to Athene Polias, guardian of the city, and her sacred olive tree lay just below the west façade. Other parts of the building were dedicated to the mythical king Erechtheus and other semi-divine figures. A hole in the roof and in the pavement indicate spots which Zeus struck with his thunderbolt. The style is Ionic, and the architect has brilliantly manipulated a diversity of levels. Puzzles remain, and the celebrated Caryatid porch makes little sense religiously or architecturally.[3]

The architectural glory of the Acropolis is the Parthenon, built over nine years from 447 BC. The architects are known to have been Ictinus (who was responsible for Bassae) and Callicrates, and Pheidias was in charge of the sculpture, and particularly the great chryselephantine statue of the goddess. The temple is of the Doric order, and a miracle of balance and organization. The sculptural decoration was all religiously relevant. The pediments showed the birth of Athene, and the contest between Athene and Poseidon for the possession of Athens. The metopes represented in different forms the triumph of civilization (for which Athens and her goddess claimed to stand) over barbarism, the battles of Gods against Giants, Lapiths against Centaurs, Greeks against Trojans, Greeks against Amazons. The great frieze portrayed the Panathenaic procession. Some have seen in this a spirit of narcissistic self-contemplation, but John Boardman in counting the figures as 192 suggested that they are the heroic Athenian dead at Marathon.[4]

There is one particularly interesting feature of the Parthenon. Scientific tests have shown that we are capable of taking six units simultaneously without counting, seven at a pinch, eight seldom. The Parthenon is fronted by eight columns, too many to take in at a glance. Martiennsen criticized the temple on these grounds. Perhaps we should rather commend the architects. Athene was for the citizen of Athens always a little larger than life, not to be taken in at a glance, pigeonholed, and dismissed.

Athene was the daughter of Zeus, born from his head without a mother's womb. She is thus a very masculine goddess: another way in which the earthmother asserted her independence of all males but Zeus. Something of this is reflected in the architecture of the Parthenon. Vincent Scully puts it well:

> The Parthenon, therefore, is itself the fullest balance between and synthesis of the two opposed kinds of architecture which we have considered: that in which the building is a hollow, female shell, associated with enclosure by the goddess and by the earth, and that in which the building is an exterior, impenetrable presence, associated with the active force of the male standing out against the sky. All peripteral Doric temples had combined these qualities; the Parthenon pushes each almost to its limit and makes them one. Down to its smallest details, where Doric and Ionic elements are juxtaposed, it embodies the act of reconciliation, and therefore wholly embodies Athena, who was herself both female gentleness and male force, both earth goddess and intellectual will.[5]

At the east end of the Acropolis lay the sanctuary of Zeus Polieus, guardian of the city, where the strange ritual of the Bouphonia was perhaps practised, and that of Pandion, but scarcely the foundations remain.[6]

The north slope of the Acropolis was riddled with sacred places, caves, niches, shrines, and rock-cut inscriptions. Many of them defy identification. One, which is certain from inscriptions in the rock and dedications including phalluses, is a shrine of Aphrodite and Eros, and we know that she had two other sanctuaries not far away. The virgin might prevail on the heights, but once we reach ground level the power of sex takes over. One cave on the north face was probably the shrine of Aglauros, daughter of Cecrops. On the west slope also there are many caves, but only one can be surely named. Many dedications show it to have been sacred to Apollo, and this therefore is the cave of Euripides' *Ion*, where in myth Apollo met Creusa and fathered Ion, the ancestor of the Ionians, on her. A little further along Pan was worshipped and there was a spring sacred to a nymph named Empedo. T. L. Shear has published a fourth-century relief which he relates (though other scholars demur) to the western slopes. Zeus sits above the scene, perhaps in his sanctuary on top, though the whole is within a cave. Pan and the Nymphs can be seen, and Apollo, Artemis, and Demeter (*Hesp.* 42 (1973) 168–70).

The south side of the Acropolis has the Theatre of Dionysus, a place so emotive for lovers of literature that it is sometimes forgotten that it was a sacred place. Two temples and an altar to the god lie below the theatre. An inscription gives a vivid picture of the sacred place, when it records how the youths accompanied Dionysus from the hearth to the theatre with torches and sent to the Dionysia a bull for sacrifice (*IG* II $^2$1006). Close by is another sacred precinct, dedicated to Asclepius, the god of healing, as we have noted. Nearby is a sacred spring, and a temple of uncertain dedication, perhaps a temple of Themis. A bronze-casting pit is of technological importance, and of religious too since it must have been used for a major cult-statue, but we do not know which. The other remains at the south-west corner are indeterminate, though material appropriate to a cult of Aphrodite was found here too.

West of the Acropolis lies the small hill dedicated to Ares, which gave its name to the sacred council of the Areopagus, once the aristocratic governing body of the city, till the democrats shore it of its power and made it a court for homicide. There is little to see now except cuttings in the bare rock. Athene Areia was worshipped here, as were the Semnai, the Awesome Goddesses, the Furies. Curiously, it is doubtful whether Ares himself had a shrine.

The view from the Areopagus extends diagonally across the agora to the north-west, where lies the temple of Hephaestus, god of fire, in an area where smiths worked. It is Doric, and relatively complete, but conspicously lacks the genius which shaped the Parthenon. Inside stood cult-statues of Hephaestus and Athene. The metopes showed the labours of Heracles and the exploits of Theseus, the eastern pediment the apotheosis of Heracles. This was a popular temple with popular appeal.

From north of the Hephaesteion the Sacred Way led to (or from) the sacred gate. At this end was a sanctuary of Aphrodite Urania, and a sanctuary of Aphrodite Hegemone, Demos, and the Graces. This last is oddly not mentioned by Pausanias, but an inscribed altar and numerous other inscriptions identify it. A little further along on the other side stood a monument devised by a Hellenistic sculptor named Eubulides. According to Pausanias there were statues of Athene Paeonia, Zeus, Mnemosyne, and the Muses. A dedicatory inscription was found, a large head of Athene, and some other fragments of huge statuary which may belong to the monument. Near the gate was the sanctuary of Demeter, Kore, and Iacchus. A fourth-century inscription probably referring to this was found on a reused block of marble. By the sacred gate towards the Dipylon Gate stood the Pompeion, from which sacred processions would set out, and where the sacred equipment was stored.

The Acropolis, Areopagus, and Temple of Hephaestus sweep round two sides of the Agora or city centre. It was in early times a cemetery, then a residential area, but it gradually became the administrative and commercial centre, with public offices and shops. No doubt all the main public buildings were believed to be under divine protection. Those currently in office as members of council met in the Tholos, a round building. The archives were kept in the Metroon, under the guard of the Mother of the Gods. In front, to the east are a set of monument bases, in front of these the shrine of the eponymous heroes, and, in front again, the altar of Zeus Agoraeus. To the north of the Metroon lie the Temple of Apollo Patroos and the tiny temple of Zeus Phatrius and Athene Phatria, and, beyond, the Stoa of Zeus crowned with figures of Victories, with an altar in front. Nearby was the Altar of the Twelve Gods, clearly identified by an inscription. It is thought that this is the same as that called by later writers the Altar of

Pity. When it was proposed to introduce gladiatorial shows at Athens Demonax said, 'First you must abolish the Altar of Pity'.

The north side of the agora was closed by the famous Painted Stoa, recently excavated. In the north-east corner in the fifth century there stood a courtyard with rooms off it. As bronze ballots used in lawcourts were found there, some legal procedures may have been practised, perhaps to do with commercial transactions. This was rebuilt in the fourth century, but in the second the whole was replaced, and the east side closed, by the Stoa of Attalus, now brilliantly reconstructed as a museum.

In the centre, south of the Altar of the Twelve Gods, stood the Temple of Ares with its altar in front of it. This was a fifth-century structure, and it has been argued from the fragmentary remains that it was a twin of the Temple of Hephaestus, designed by the same architect. The altar had a finely sculptured frieze. Nearby one of the marble blocks held an iron ring, no doubt for tethering sacrificial animals. South of the altar stood in later times the statues of Harmodius and Aristogeiton, heroized as 'tyrannicides', though their assassination of Hipparchus was due to personal reasons rather than political protest. These had been in the orchestra or dancing floor further to the south; over this in Roman times was built an odeon or concert-hall, and much later a large gymnasium. The buildings to the south of the agora call for little comment religiously. This side was closed in the Hellenistic period by two parallel stoas. There were various administrative buildings, including probably the lawcourts and the mint. The one doubtful area is the south-east corner. Here stands the eleventh-century Church of the Holy Apostles, and in view of the continuity of religious sites in Greece it seems likely that this was a sanctified place. The only building traced on the site was a nymphaeum or fountain-house, sacred to the Nymphs, and equipped with statues of divinities. Outside the agora to the south-east the Sacred Way passed the Eleusinion, the sanctuary of Demeter and Kore. It has not been fully excavated, but inscriptions, votive pots, and marble plaques with Eleusinian themes make the identification certain; of historical interest is a fragmentary record of the sale of the property of Alcibiades and the others convicted of mutilating the Hermae and profaning the Mysteries.[7]

Even in its ruinous state, the sanctuary of Olympian Zeus remains one of the most impressive of the sacred monuments of Athens. It was begun in the sixth century BC and abandoned, although presumably the precinct remained holy, restarted by Antiochus IV of Syria in about 170 BC, and finally completed by Hadrian in about AD 130. The platform measured 107.79 × 41.1 m, and the cella was actually 75 × 19 m; it is not clear whether it was roofed. The temple was dipteral with an additional row of columns at front and rear. The statue was chryselephantine. The whole was set within a huge courtyard. In its final erection we should not forget that Hadrian was identified with Zeus Olympius: Wycherley remarks wryly in *The Stones of Athens* that the old title 'The Palace of Hadrian' was not a complete misnomer.[8]

Nearby are a number of other sacred places, not far from the river Ilissus – temples which may tentatively be identified as a sanctuary of Apollo Delphinius, which was also a lawcourt, in use from the Mycenaean period, and incorporating a fifth-century Doric temple: a Roman temple to Zeus Panhellenius. Not far away must have been the shrine of Apollo Pythius whose altar was found, perhaps displaced. There was a large precinct to the legendary king Codrus, marked by a boundary stone, and a stoa perhaps pertaining to yet another lawcourt sacred to Athene and Zeus. On the south bank we can identify a shrine of Pan from a worn rock-cut relief, and the site of Cynosarges, a gymnasium sacred to Heracles. We know from other sources of an altar to the Muses of Ilissus, and an altar of Boreas hereabouts, but cannot locate them precisely, any more than we can precisely find two major sanctuaries, of Aphrodite in the Gardens (Paus. 1, 19, 2) or Dionysus in the Marshes (Thuc. 2, 15, 4). Further up the river near the stadium a relief was found (*IG* II $^2$2934) dedicated by some cleaners to the Nymphs and all the gods with pictures of Achelous, Hermes, three Nymphs, and Pan above, and a man leading a horse, an altar, Demeter, and Persephone below. A little further on is a strange shrine dedicated to Pancrates ('Almighty'), a chthonic and healing deity. There was probably a temple with a statue of Heracles in one pediment.

Other sacred places must be passed over more cursorily. We should note the Hill of the Nymphs, attested by an inscription near the summit. Lower down the hill a sixth-century rock-cut inscription marks the boundary of a precinct of Zeus. A fourth-century boundary-stone lower still marks a sanctuary of Zeus Exopsius ('Looking out') or Exousius. On the other side of the hill dedications to Zeus Meilichios have been found. At the northern foot of the hill is a small temple of Artemis with an altar in front not aligned with it. The site was in use from the eighth century, but there are no clear signs of religious usage before the fifth. There was however a surrounding precinct, and it looks probable on the evidence that the altar site antedates the temple site. The temple was controlled by the deme of Melite according to an inscription. This means that it may be the one founded by Themistocles of that deme, giving the goddess the cult-title Aristobule ('excellent in counsel') (Plut. *Them.* 22, 1).

The Pnyx was the place of political assembly. Religiously the most interesting feature is a holy place of Zeus Hypsistos as a god of healing, with a niche for a cult-statue, and fifty-seven others for votives of replicas of parts of the body. The old view that the Thesmophoria was celebrated on the Pnyx has not very much to commend it; more likely it was in the Eleusinion (*Hesp.* 11, 250–74). East of the Pnyx and south of the Areopagus were some interesting holy places, a triangular precinct without entrance, an inaccessible *abaton*, with a boundary-stone proclaiming it 'the sacred place' without further definition. It was perhaps associated with some hero. Another triangular sanctuary with a small temple was perhaps sacred to Dionysus. Opposite is a miniature temple (2.5 × 2 m) with a circular altar-base. Another important shrine in these parts is identified by inscriptions as belonging to a semi-divine healer named Amynus (*IG* II $^2$1252–3; 4365; 4385–7; 4422; 4424; 4435; 4457). It is an irregular, messily designed quadrilateral, with water supply laid on. An offering table with carved snakes was found, and dedications including representations of parts of the body healed or in need of healing. This shrine was in the care of *orgeones*. Further along towards the Acropolis but a little aloof from it is a small shrine to a divinity called Nymphe ('Bride'). Early votive pottery was found here, a fragment of a fine female statue, no doubt Nymphe, and an altar.

Jon D. Mikalson's study, *The Sacred and Civil Calendar of the Athenian Year* enables us, mainly on archaeological and epigraphical evidence, to see the pattern of public celebration throughout the year in Athens and Attica.

We must first recognize that some days were the occasion of monthly festivals. These were:

1 Noumenia or New-Moon Day, so recognized throughout the Greek world. It was so holy that at Athens no other festival ever fell on that day. We know from various sources that there was a public act on the acropolis (e.g. Dem. 25, 99), and that there was a private offering of frankincense at the statues of gods (Schol. ad Ar. *W.* 94–6).

2 Sacred to the *agathos daimon*.
3 Birthday of Athene; perhaps also sacred to the Graces.
4 Birthday of Heracles, Hermes and Aphrodite, and also naturally sacred to Eros and the Hermaphrodites. On Munichion 4 we have a record of a perhaps private feast for Eros in mid-fifth century (*Hesp.* (1932) 43–4) and sacrifice to the Children of Heracles by the deme Erchia; on Thargelion 4 Hermes receives honour (Col. E 47–58).
5 Birthday of Artemis, so recognized throughout Hellas. On Boedromion 6 there was a festival of Artemis Agrotera at Athens, associated also with the victory at Marathon, and on Munichion 6 a procession to the Delphinion (Plut. *Thes.* 18, 1) by young girls, no doubt in honour of Artemis, and a meeting of the Soteriastai in 37–36 BC in honour of Artemis Soteira (*IG* II $^2$1343, 6–7).
7 Birthday of Apollo (Hes. *WD* 770), with many festivals through the Greek world. At Athens no other festival fell on the day. Many months had Apollo festivals. On Hecatombaion 7 there was a sacrifice to Apollo Hecatombaios on Myconos (*SIG* $^3$1024, 29–30), and it is a reasonable deduction that the Hecatombaia at Athens fell on that date. There is also record of sacrifice to Apollo Apotropaios, probably on that date (*IG* II $^2$1358 col. 1, 24–6). On Metageitnion 7 the Salaminioi sacrificed to Apollo Patroos, Leto, Artemis and Athene (*Hesp.* (1938) 3–5, ll. 89–90). We can reasonably place the Boedromia on Boedromion 7. On Pyanopsion 7 the Pyanopsia is recorded in the sacred calendar of Eleusis (*IG* II $^2$ 1363, ll. 8–19) as well as in literary sources (Harpocration s.v.; *Suda* s.v.; Plut. *Thes.* 22, 4), and we also know of private sacrifice on the date (*IG* II $^2$1367, ll. 9–11). The festival involved the offering of a vegetable stew, and the use of olive boughs wreathed with wool (*eiresione*) as symbols of good luck. On Gamelion 7 the sacrificial calendar of the deme Erchia (*BCH* 87 (1903) 603–38) calls for sacrifice to Kourotrophos, Apollo Delphinios, and also Apollo Lyceios (col. A, 23–30; E, 31–8). The Thargelia took place on Thargelion 7 (Plut. *Mor.* 717 B–D).
8 Sacred to Poseidon (*IG* II $^2$1367, ll. 16–18; Procl. ad Hes. *WD* 790; Plut. *Thes.* 36). His special day was no doubt Poseidon 8. At Athens it was a day of special honour for Theseus, Poseidon's son. The special Theseia was on Pyanopsion 8, and then, or about then, the sacrifice to the Amazons and the Oschophoria, a procession from a shrine of Dionysus to one of Athene recalling events in the hero's life. But they did not claim exclusive rights: the Iobacchoi met on

Elaphebolion 8 (*IG* II²1368 ll. 2–3), and the initiates of Bendis on Hecatombaion 8 (*IG* II²1283, ll. 2–3) and Scirophorion 8 (*IG* II² 1284, ll. 19–21).

Mikalson shows that in all 120 monthly and annual festival days are attested by evidence, that to these must be added twenty-four for which dates may be reasonably fixed, and a number, including the Apaturia and the Mysteries at Agrae, whose precise dates are unknown. The total number of festivals thus covers almost half the year. But the Council was in session on all except the annual festivals; the Assembly did not meet on the monthly festivals. The ordinary citizen must have been at work on many festival days.

We must next look at the major festivals.

## PANATHENAEA

This seems to have taken place on a varying number of days between Hecatombaion 23–30; the major activity fell on Hecatombaion 28. The primary object of the celebration was the presentation of a new robe to the goddess Athene. This was set on the mast of a ship-cart, and borne with holy implements and sacrificial animals to her home on the acropolis. The Parthenon frieze is an idealized record of this procession, perhaps (as John Boardman has argued) being performed by the dead heroes of Marathon; it is curious that the frieze does not portray the ship-cart, though there seems to be a representation of acolytes folding the robe. Extensive sacrifice was offered, the altar being lit by the winner in a torch-race from the altar of Eros outside the walls. The sacrifices were liberal and subject to complex regulations, which we have recorded from the fourth century BC (*SIG*³ 271); the meat was distributed in the Ceramicus to the people. Celebrations involved an all-night service: it is not clear whether this came the night before or the night after. Every four years there was an athletics festival, including horse-racing and chariot-racing, and a famous regatta.

## ELEUSINIA

Four days in the period Metageitnion 13–20, most probably 15–18. It was the next great festival (*IG* II²1496, ll. 129–33). There is a record of private offering to the goddesses on the 15th (*IG* II²1367, ll. 1–3). The festival is discussed in the chapter on Mysteries.

## STENIA

Women's festival in honour of Demeter and Persephone, marked by ritual backbiting, with public sacrifice (Hesych. s.v.; Phot. s.v.; Schol. ad Ar. *Thesm.* 834). Overshadowed by Thesmophoria.

## THESMOPHORIA

Women's festival on Pyanopsion 11–13. The first day was the day of assembly, the second a day of fasting, the third, Calligeneia, the day of Fair Offspring. It was a fertility festival, with fertility magic, but there is much that we do not know about it, and the parody by Aristophanes does not help.

## APATURIA

A three-day festival, either Pyanopsion 19–21 or 26–8. A festival of the Phratriai or Brotherhoods. The three days with Dorpia (the Supper), Anarrhysis (the Sacrifice) and Cureotis (the Day of Youths) (Schol. ad Ar. *Ach.* 146). Offerings were made to Zeus Phratrios and Athene Phratria; the name of the festival perhaps means 'The Festival of Common Fatherhood'.

## CHALCEIA

Festival on Pyanopsion 30 honouring Hephaestus, god of the smiths, and Athene as the mistress of technology. On this day the loom for weaving the robe of the Panathenaea was set up (*Suda* s.v.; *Harpocrat.* s.v.).

## POMPAIA

Festival in Maimacterion, of uncertain date. A sheepskin of a victim offered to Zeus was carried round in ceremonial procession together with the staff of Hermes. The month is named after Zeus the Blusterer, and represents the onset of winter. The ceremony seems designed to avert evil.

## RURAL DIONYSIA

Celebrated at different dates in different places. There was a procession with fruit in a basket, a ceremonial phallus, the sacrifice of a goat, and dramatic performances (Ar. *Ach.* 247ff.; Plut. *Mor.* 527D; Dem. 18, 180; 18, 262; *IG* II ²456, l. 32).

## HALOA

Fertility festival in honour of Demeter and Dionysus on Poseideon 26 (*IG* II ²1672, l. 124).

## LENAEA

Festival of Dionysus including a procession and drama and lasting at least four days. On the frieze from the church of Ayios Eleutherios representing a pictorial calendar, Gamelion shows Dionysus on a ram. At Myconos Lenaeon 12 (= Gamelion 12) was the day of festival to Dionysus Lenaeus (*SIG* ³1024, l. 24). There is not much evidence from Athens, except that the Council did not meet before the 22nd. We have a record from the Roman imperial period of private wreathing of the god's statues with ivy on Gamelion 19 (*IG* II ²1367, l. 21).

## ANTHESTERIA

Festival of Dionysus, a spring festival involving flowers, wine, and the spirits of the dead. The dates were Anthesteria 11–13 (Schol. ad Thuc. 2, 15, 4). The first day was the Pithoigia, the Opening of the Jars. New wine was brought to the shrine of the god. The second was the Choes or Wine-Jars. There was a procession, and black-figure vases of the sixth century show us the god arriving in a ship-cart. The wife of the Archon Basileus was then united in sacred marriage to the god; the scene of the wedding procession is delightfully re-enacted by small children on a *chous* in the Metropolitan Museum, New York. The third day was the Chytrai or Pots, pots holding a vegetable stew for the dead, who were believed to come to life. The sanctuaries were closed against them, and the day ended with the cry 'Away, dread spirits; Anthesteria is over!'

## LESSER MYSTERIES

The Mysteries at Agrae were a preparation for the Eleusinian festival, held in the suburb of Agrai. They must have lasted for some days, and as there are no meetings recorded for Anthesterion 20–6, the festival will have been in this period. Anthesterion 23 is the date of the Diasia or festival of Zeus Meilichios as we know from the record of the deme Erchia (Col. A. 37–43; Schol. ad Ar. *Cl.* 408). Zeus Meilichios, the gentle protector of those who propitiate him, is familiar through the Greek world (*IG* I $^2$866; III 3169 etc.) and has associations with the Mysteries (*BCH* 89 (1965) 159–72), so that this may be one of the days.

## CITY DIONYSIA

Although the month of Elaphebolion was named after Artemis as Shooter of Deer it was dominated by the new festival of Dionysus, involving the performances of drama. It is possible that the masquerade often associated with the return of the dead was transferred here from the Anthesteria. It can be taken as certain that the festival did not begin before the 10th; on that day we have a record of a sacrifice to the god by the Iobacchoi (*IG* II $^2$1368, ll. 117–21). They lasted for at least four days, but there are records of meetings of the assembly during this period (*Hesp.* (1936) 419–29, no. 15, ll. 1–4; (1938) 476–9, no. 31, ll. 1–7), which suggests some flexibility. The deme Erchia sacrificed to Dionysus and Semele on the 16th (Col. A 44–51; D 33–40), which perhaps was the end of the festival. In that case the Pandia, a festival of Zeus, of which we know surprisingly little, except that it was used for a *post mortem* on the Dionysia, will have been held on the 17th, and this would accord with meetings of the Assembly held on the 18th straight after the Dionysia (Aeschin. 261; 3, 68).

Omitting those already mentioned, we can offer a selective conspectus of some of the festivals.

## HECATOMBEION

| | |
|---|---|
| 12 | Festival of Cronos (Dem. 24, 26). |
| 15 | Biennial sacrifice, no doubt preparatory to Synoecia (*Hesp.* (1935) no. 2, 21, ll. 30–43). |
| 16 | Synoecia (Thuc. 2, 15), an annual festival, with no public meetings. Biennial sacrifice is recorded (*Hesp.* (1935) no. 2, 21, ll. 44–58), but it is clear that there was annual sacrifice (*IG* II $^2$ 1496). This was a religious celebration of the coming together of the peoples of Attica. |

17–18 Private celebration of Orgeones, a religious association, recorded (*Hesp.* (1942) no. 55, 282–7, ll. 12–16).
21 Deme Erchia sacrifice to Kourotrophos and Artemis (cols C, 1–12; D, 1–12).
23 Meeting of a private religious society recorded (*IG* II²1282, ll. 2–3).


## METAGEITNION

14–5 In the second century BC a senior official of Dionysus made an offering for King Ariarathes V (*IG* II²1330, ll. 30–4) and Queen Nysa on their birthdays.
16 The deme Erchia sacrifice to Kourotrophos and Artemis Hecate (Col. B 6–13).
19 The deme Erchia sacrifice to the Heroines (Col. E 1–8).
20 The deme Erchia sacrifice to Hera Thelchinia (Col. A 6–11).
25 The deme Erchia sacrifice to Zeus Epoptes (Col. C 19–25).


## BOEDROMION

4 The deme Erchia sacrifice to Basile (Col. B 14–20), a divine figure associated with the legendary king Codrus and his ancester Neleus (*IG* I²94).
5 Genesia, a public festival for the dead (Philochorus in *F. Gr. Hist.* 328 F 168; *IG* II²1357a, ll. 3–22). The deme Erchia sacrifice to Epops a holocaust without wine (Col. D 18–23; E 9–15); there is probably some connection.
12 Probable date of Democratia (*IG* II²1496, ll. 131–2), a festival in honour of Democracy after the return from Phyle in 403 BC (Plut. *Mor.* 349F).
17 or 18 Epidauria or festival of the healing god Asclepius. There is also record of a private sacrifice on both days (*IG* II²1367, ll. 6–8).
27 The deme Erchia sacrifice to the Nymphs, Achelous, Alochus, Hermes, and Ge (Col. A 1–16; B 21–5; C 26–30; D 24–7; E 16–21). The deme Teithras sacrifice to Athene (*Hesp.* (1961) 293–8).

## PYANOPSION

5  Advance proclamation from Eleusis of Proerosia (*IG* II ²1363). Meeting of religious confraternity of Thiasotae in 300–299 BC (*IG* II ²1263, ll. 1–3).
6  Possible date for Proerosia 'the Preliminary to the Ploughing', an agricultural festival involving the offering of first-fruits in gratitude for deliverance from a legendary plague. But as a meeting of the Council is attested for this date it was perhaps not an official festival of the Athenian state, and it is nowhere mentioned in comedy.
14 The deme Erchia sacrifice to the Heroines (Col. A 17–22).

## MAIMACTERION

It is strange that no religious observance is recorded apart from the Pompaia.

## POSEIDEON

5  Local celebration of Plerosia by the deme Myrrhinus (*IG* II ²1183, ll. 32–7).
16 The deme Erchia sacrifice to Zeus Horios, Zeus of the Boundary (Col. E 22–30); interestingly, we have record of the arbitration of a boundary dispute starting on this day (*IG* II ²204, ll. 10–12).
19 Private sacrificial offering to the Winds (*IG* II ²1367, ll. 18–20). The deme Myrrhinus meet on matters concerned with Dionysus (*IG* II ²1183, ll. 36–7).

## GAMELION

8  The deme Erchia sacrifice to Apollo Apotropaeus, Apollo Nymphegetes and the Nymphs (Col. A 31–6; C 31–7; E 39–46).
9  The deme Erchia sacrifice to Athene (Col. B 26–31).
27 The deme Erchia sacrifice to Kourotrophos, Hera, Zeus Teleios and Poseidon (Col. C 38–41; D 28–32; B 32–9). This suggests that the Theogamia should be set on this date (*BCH* 88 (1964) 647–9), especially as the month was sacred to Hera. This festival celebrating the sacred marriage between Hera and Zeus, Earth and Sky, was seemingly also called the Gamelia.

## ANTHESTERION

2 The deme Erchia sacrifice to Dionysus (Col. C 42–7).
3 In 244–3 BC the initiates of the Thracian goddess Bendis met on Salamis (*SEG* 2 no. 9, ll. 1–2).

## ELAPHEBOLION

8 Meeting of the Iobacchoi (*IG* II $^2$1368, ll. 2–3).
10 The Marathonian tetrapolis sacrifice, almost certainly to Ge, Earth, as no other divinity will fit the space in the inscription (*IG* II $^2$1358, Col. 2, ll. 17–18).
15 Private sacrifice to Cronos (*IG* II $^2$1367, ll. 23–6).

## MUNICHION

16 Munichia, a festival in honour of Artemis, involving the sacrifice of a she-goat dressed as a girl (a substitutionary human sacrifice), and special cakes stuck with candles and said to be moon-symbols.
17 The religious association of the Thiasotai are recorded as meeting on this day (*IC* II $^2$1277, ll. 1–2).
18 The religious association of the Eranistai are recorded as meeting (*IG* II $^2$1369, ll. 24ff.). The sacrificial calendar of the island of Salamis calls for an offering to their legendary king Eurysaces (*Hesp.* (1938) 3–5, l. 88).
19 Olympieia, a festival of Olympian Zeus, instituted by Pisistratus, and associated with his inauguration of the great but long unfinished temple. There was a procession of the cavalry (*IG* II $^2$ 1496, ll. 80–6; II $^2$3079; Plut. *Phoc.* 37, 1).
20 The deme Erchia sacrifice to Leucaspis, the deity of the White Shield (Col. C 48–53).
21 The deme Erchia sacrifice to the Tritopatores or the Ancestors (though some ancient authorities identify them with Wind-gods).

## THARGELION

4 The deme Erchia sacrifice to Leto (Col. A 52–6), Pythian Apollo (B 45–54), Zeus (C 54–8), Hermes (E 47–58) and the Dioscuri (D 47–51).
16 The deme Erchia sacrifice to Zeus Epacrios (Col. E 59–64), Zeus of the heights.

19  The festival of the Thracian goddess Bendis (Schol. ad Plat. *Rep.* 327A; Procl. in *Tim.* 9B, 27A). There was a torch-race on horseback and an all-night festival. The deme Erchia sacrifice to Menedeius, the One who Stands his Ground (Col. D 52–5): the two may be connected (*BCH* 89 (1965) 158–9).

24  Most probable date for Callynteria, the spring-cleaning of Athene's temple, and, no doubt, refilling of the ever-burning lamp.

25  Plynteria, the Festival of Washing, when the image of Athene (and perhaps her robe) were ceremonially bathed. It was a dangerous day, because the goddess's attention was preoccupied.

## SCIROPHORION

2  The initiates of Bendis on Salamis hold a regular meeting (*IG* II, 1317 l. 1; 1317b add. ll. 2–3; *SEG* 2 no. 10. ll. 2–3).

3  The deme Erchia sacrifice to Kourotrophos, Athene Polias, Aglauros, Zeus Polieus, Poseidon, and perhaps Pandrosus (Col. A 57–65; B 55–9; C 59–64; D 56–60; E 65–70).

8  The celebrants of Bendis are recorded as meeting (*IG* II $^2$1284, ll. 19–21).

12  Scira. A mysterious, predominantly but not exclusively women's festival. There was a procession of the priestess of Athene, the priest of Poseidon, and the priest of Apollo (?) under a large parasol (Harpocrat. s.v. skiron). There was also women's fertility ritual in honour of Demeter, involving the immolation of piglets. But much remains unsolved.

14  Dipolieia. A festival of Zeus, guardian of the city. It was the occasion of a strange ritual. Barley and wheat were placed on the altar. The sacrificial bull moves to eat them. One of the priests kills it, throws down the pole-axe and escapes. The inanimate weapon is then tried for murder. (Paus. 1, 24, 4; 1, 28, 10; Porphyr. *Abstin.* 2, 28). Many explanations have been given and parallels adduced. Perhaps it is best simply to say that this is a very ancient ritual, and there was a felt need to justify the sacrifice by the action of the beast, and subsequently to atone for it. Also called Bouphonia.

Every fourth year the Panathenaic festival was celebrated on a larger scale.[9] There are of course literary references to the Festival, but it is not too much to say that the three main sources of our knowledge are due to archaeology. An inscription (unfortunately incomplete), datable to the early fourth century BC, gives us details of the various competitions and prizes associated with the festival. First come the musical events, for rhapsodes, singers to the lyre, flute players and lyre players. The singer received as first prize a gold-leaf crown worth 1000 drachmas and 500 silver drachmas, and even the fifth prize was as much as the first prize for the flute; these were evidently highly rewarded professionals. Next come the athletic events, foot-race, pentathlon, wrestling, boxing, and pancratium, each organized by age groups. The prizes were jars of oil. Then follow the equestrian events, including javelin-throwing from horseback. Next we have team events, an armoured dance, a test of physical fitness, and a torch race from the altar of Eros in the Academy outside the walls, close to the altar of Prometheus, a fire god, over two miles ending with the sharp climb to the altar of Athene on the Acropolis: this was part of the sacrificial ritual. Finally there is the regatta, which must have taken place at the Piraeus ($SIG^2$ 1055).

Secondly, we have the Parthenon frieze portraying in some sense the Panathenaic procession.[10] The frieze, we can be sure, does not purport to be an actual record of a datable Panathenaic procession. It is selective, and aspects recorded in our literary sources do not appear. For example a robe for the goddess was woven afresh each year on a colossal scale. It was mounted in the form of a sail on a ship-cart, a concept borrowed from Dionysus but wholly appropriate to the naval power of Athens.[11] The ship-cart does not appear on the frieze, and the robe only folded and on a small scale; it would no doubt have been artistically disproportionate. Further, John Boardman has brilliantly suggested that the 192 figures in the procession may represent the 192 Athenian dead at Marathon; in the frieze the heroic ancestors are joining in the celebration with their descendents. But we can still see the women who wove the cloak, and others bearing the accoutrements of sacrifice, the religious officials, the military represented by cavalry and chariots, the handsome old men. We can also trace the procession on the ground as it were, from the Pompeion, or Place of the Procession, a large open court, 140 × 50 ft, dating from the early fourth century, and set between the sacred gate and the Dipylon Gate, through the Agora, and up the zigzag approach to the Acropolis, though the Propylaea to the Temple of the Goddess.

Our third piece of evidence is a decree dating to about 335 BC at a time of reorganization by the great statesman Lycurgus ($IG$ II $^2$334 =

*SIG* ³271). These are regulations controlling the sacrifices at the annual festival 'in order that the procession may be equipped and marshalled as efficiently as possible each year for Athene on behalf of the people of Athens'. There are to be two special sacrifices, one to Athene Hygieia (that is Athene identified with the goddess of health) and the other at the old temple. Portions are allocated to various officials and to those who took part in the procession. The meat from the other sacrifices is to be distributed among the citizens. There are instructions about the purchase of the sacrificial animals from the rent of the sacred land, and the sacrifice on the great altar of Athene, with a special offering on the altar of Nike. Fifty drachmas are voted for incidental expenses.

The calendar of sacrifices to be held by the deme of Marathon gives a picture of the religious year (*IG* II ²1358; *AJA* 10 (1895) 209–26). It can be dated to their early fourth century.

> The chairman of the deme of Marathon is to make the following sacrifices in the first quarter . . . within ten days. To the Hero, a pig, 3 drachmas. To the Heroine, a pig, 3 drachmas. A table of offerings for the Hero and Heroine, 1 drachma. In the month Boedromion, before the Mysteries . . . an ox, 90 drachmas; a sheep, 12 drachmas. To Kourotrophos. . . .
>
> In the second quarter. In the month of Posideon . . . an ox, 150 drachmas; a sheep, 12 drachmas. To the Heroine, a sheep, 11 drachmas, portion for the priest, 7 drachmas. To Ge in the Meadows; a pregnant cow, 70 drachmas, portion for the priest. . . . To Telete, *epylia*, 40 drachmas.
>
> In the third quarter. In the month Gamelion. To Daira, a pregnant ewe, 16 drachmas, portion for the priest, 1 drachma. To Ge at the Oracle, a sheep, 11 drachmas. To Zeus Hypatos . . . drachmas. To Ioleus, a sheep, 12 drachmas. To Kourotrophos, a pig, 3 drachmas, a table of offerings, 1 drachma, portion for the priest, 2 drachmas 1½ obols. To the Hero Pheraeus, a sheep, 12 drachmas. To the Heroine, a sheep, 11 drachmas, portion for the priest, 3 drachmas. In the month Elaphebolion. On the 10th, to Ge at the Oracle, a totally black goat, 15 drachmas, portion for the priest, 1 drachma.
>
> In the fourth quarter. In the month Munichion. To Ar . . . Nechos, an ox, 90 drachmas; a sheep, 12 drachmas. To the Heroine, a sheep, 11 drachmas; portion for the priest, 7 drachmas.

To Neanias, an ox, 90 drachmas; a sheep, 12 drachmas; a pig, 3 drachmas. To the Heroine, a sheep, 11 drachmas, portion for the priest, 7 drachmas 1½ obols.

The chairman of the deme of Marathon is to make the following sacrifices. To the Hero in . . . rasileia, a sheep, 12 drachmas; a table of offerings, 1 drachma. To the Heroine, a sheep, 11 drachmas. To the Hero by the Hellotion, a sheep, 12 drachmas, a table of offerings, 1 drachma. To the Heroine, a sheep, 6 drachmas. In the month Thargelion. To Achaia, a ram, 12 drachmas; a ewe, 11 drachmas; portion for the priest, 3 drachmas. To the Moirae a pig, 3 drachmas; portion for the priest 1½ obols. In the month Scirophorion, before the Scira. To Hyttenios, fruits in season; a sheep, 12 drachmas. To Kourotrophos, a pig, 3 drachmas, portion for the priest, 2 drachmas 1 obol. To the Tritopateres, a sheep; portion for the priest, 2 drachmas. To the Acamantes, a sheep, 12 drachmas; priestly portion 2 drachmas.

The following in alternate years. First group. In Hecatombaion, to Athene Hellotis, an ox, 90 drachmas; 3 sheep, 33 drachmas; a pig, 3 drachmas; portion for the priest 6 . . . drachmas. To Kourotrophos, a sheep, 11 drachmas; a pig, 3 drachmas; portion for the priest, 4 . . . drachmas . . . boughs of laurel, 7 drachmas.

The following sacrifices are to be offered in alternate years, beginning in the Tetrapolis in the archonship of Eubulus. Second group. In Hecatombaion, to Athene Hellotis, a sheep, 11 drachmas. To Kourotrophos, a pig, 3 drachmas; portion for the priest 1 drachma 1½ obols. In Metageitnion. To the goddess of Eleusis, an ox, 90 drachmas; to Kore, a ram, 12 drachmas; 3 pigs, 9 drachmas; portion for the priest 6 drachmas 4½ obols; 8½ litres of barley, 4 obols; 3 litres of wine. . . . To Kourotrophos, a sheep, 11 drachmas; portion for the priest, 1 drachma. To Zeus Anthaleus, a sheep, 12 drachmas; portion for the priest 2 drachmas. In Anthesterion, to the goddess of Eleusis, a pregnant sow, 20 drachmas; portion for the priest, 1 drachma 1 obol. To Chloe beside Medylus's place, a pregnant sow, 20 drachmas, portion for the priest, 1 drachma; 8½ litres of barley, 4 obols; 3 litres of wine. . . . In Scirophorion, before the Scira, to Galios, a ram, 12 drachmas, portion for the priest, 2 drachmas; . . . 6 drachmas. To the Tritopateres, a table of offerings, 1 drachma. (Note: There are a number of uncertainties about the text. Some gaps have been filled in fairly securely. Some of the references are clear, others less so. Some of the divinities are local and minor. I take the Hero and Heroine to be the eponymous ancestors of the tribe. Kourotrophos, or Nurse, is applied to many divinities, Artemis and Hecate and Aphrodite, but is seemingly here some lesser power. Ge is the Earth-goddess, and Telete the spirit of the Mysteries. *Epylia* are unknown. Ioleus is perhaps Iolaus, semi-divine associate of Heracles. Neanias simply means 'the young man'. Achaia is a title of Demeter, as is Chloe, and Daira of Persephone-Kore. The Tritopateres are the divine ancestors. The Acamantes are 'the untiring ones'; the title is applied to natural phenomena such as the winds. Galios may be Galeos, a son of Apollo.)

At Erchia (*BCH* 87 (1963) 603–38) there are prescribed fifty-seven sacrifices unevenly distributed through the year (one in Pyanopsion and twelve in Gamelion, for example). They are to a variety of divine powers. Zeus appears on his own or with the cult titles Polieus, Meilichios, Epopetes (confirming a text in Hesychius), Horios (attested in Marathon: *IG* II $^2$1358, l. 11), Teleios and the fairly rare Epacrios (cf. *IG* II $^2$1294). Athene appears on her own and as Polias. She is not as prominent as one might expect. Apollo appears as Lyeios, Delphinios, Apotropaeus, Nymphegetes, Pythius, and Paeon. Artemis appears without cult-title or as Artemis Hecate. Hera similarly appears simply or as Thelchinia, again confirming but correcting the spelling of Hesychius. Other deities, more or less expected, are Demeter, Hermes, Dionysus, Poseidon, and Ge. Other semi-divine beings or spiritual powers include Kourotrophos (possibly the same as Ge), the Heroines, Basile (rarely found but cf. *IG* I $^2$ 94), Epops (the hoopoe: without parallel), the Nymphs, Achelous (a river god), Alochus (the Virgin, here for the first time), Semele, the Heraclidae, Leucaspis ('of the white shield': unparalleled), the Tritopatores or Ancestors, Leto, the Anakes or Dioscuri, Menedeius (unparalleled), Aglauros with a familiar cult at Athens.[12] The places of sacrifice vary between Erchia and Athens; sometimes it is made more precise – the sanctuary of a particular deity, the Acropolis (whether in Erchia or Athens), the Agora, and (for Zeus Epacrius) Mt Hymettus. The victims to be offered are sheep (on twenty-nine occasions), goat (eleven), pig (ten), lamb (two), ewe lamb (two), kid (one), ram (one). The rites are sometimes specified. There are four 'holocausts', and a number of occasions when the sacrifice is to be without wine. The phrase *ou phora* appears nineteen times, and probably means that nothing is to be removed. In five instances the offerings are reserved either for women, or with sacrifices to Apollo for Pythaists, that is those who have been on sacred missions to Delphi.

Another aspect of the religious life of Attica is revealed by a lengthy inscription found in the Agora at Athens (*Hesp.* 7 (1938) 1–75). This relates to one of the clans, the Salaminians. They came originally, as their name implies, from the island of Salamis, but somewhere around 600 BC were resettled in two groups, one near Sunion and the other near Phaleron. At home they had worshipped a fertility goddess named Sciras. Now they identified their goddess with the patron goddess of Athens under the cult-title Athene Sciras. Unfortunately the two groups fell out over the control of the goddess's sanctuary. In 363–2 BC the matter was put to arbitration, and it was agreed that all priesthoods should be held jointly; these included not just Athene Sciras, but also Heracles at Porthmos, Eurysaces, Aglauros and Pandrosos, and Korotrophos. This meant that the priests, when vacancies occurred, were chosen by lot from a joint meeting of both parts of the tribe. The Salaminians were evidently responsible for the *deipnophoria*, a solemn procession with meat offerings for the last three divinities, and the *oschophoria*, in which two young men, clothed as women, carried vineshoots with clusters of grapes from the sanctuary of Dionysus to the sanctuary of Athene Sciras; this was recognized as part of the public cult, and regulated accordingly. The healing of the breach however was only temporary, and a further inscription a century later makes another attempt at reconciliation.

Brauron is surely one of the most attractive religious sites in Greece. It lies on the east coast of Attica, sacred to Artemis, Our Lady of the Animals, and associated with the legendary Iphigeneia, daughter of Agamemnon, sacrificed by her father to secure a favourable wind to Troy, rescued by Artemis through the substitution of an animal, priestess of the goddess among the Tauri, escaping with her brother Orestes and an ancient image of the goddess, to settle and die at Brauron.

So the stories went, and at Brauron they claimed that it was here not at Aulis that the sacrifice took place, and the substituted animal not a deer but a bear.

Excavation has revealed a fifth-century Doric temple (66 × 33 ft), itself on the site of an older building, lying just under a rocky outcrop on which the altar stood (under the present chapel of St George), not aligned with the temple, nor at one end of it. The temple had no colonnade. In the same rocky outcrop a stairway is cut; Euripides in *Iphigeneia Among the Taurians* mentions the Sacred Steps (1462), and further along a sacred cave and the so-called Tomb of Iphigeneia. Within the temple were discovered votive offerings of jewellery, bronze mirrors, and coloured terracotta reliefs.

What makes Brauron especially fascinating is that adjoining the temple is a courtyard with square pillars bearing the names of girls, surrounded with colonnades of the Doric order, and on the north side six rooms each with seven built-in dining-tables of stones, and with bronze clamps to hold eleven couches for dining and sleeping. Behind is a blind stoa with slots for wooden boards; it has been argued on the basis of Euripides that these were for the dedicated robes of women who died in childbirth (Eur. *IT* 1463–6).

The unique establishment has been shown from its contents to be an institution where little girls of good families lived from the ages of 7 to 11 under the goddess's care; it is slightly odd that there were boys among them. They were called 'bears' (cf. Ar. *Lys.* 645). Many of them are commemorated in utterly charming statues now to be seen in the museum.

In a sacred spring nearby were found a number of wooden objects preserved by the mud, including a unique wooden statue from the fifth century, olive-wood vases, and a pipe of polished bone.

The combination of Artemis, the virgin-huntress, and at the same time the protectress of childbirth, and the motif of the bear, is realized mythically in the story of Callisto.

The river Erasinos, which is crossed by a remarkable stone bridge of the same period, tends to silt up, and within a century the site had to be abandoned because of flooding. It remains a unique record of a particular kind of religious dedication.

Brauron is of exceptional interest. But there are other sacred sites throughout Attica. We have treated Eleusis elsewhere, and the Sanctuary of Zeus on Mt Hymettus, and the Cave of Pan and the Nymphs. On the outskirts of modern Athens we should note the sanctuary of Aphrodite with its sacred spring, where the monastery of Kaisariani now stands, the sanctuary of Apollo now occupied by the monastery of Daphni with its awesome mosaics, and the sanctuary of Dionysus at Ikaria. At Cape Sunion is a spot beloved by tourists at sunset in summer, the spectacularly situated Temple of Poseidon, which Byron celebrated and vandalized, the sign of home for Athenians sailing across the Aegean. Two colossal statues of *kouroi* were found here and are now in the National Museum: the more complete stands 3.05 m high, the left foot advanced, the torso muscular, the face stylized, impassive, hieratic. The frieze of the temple is deeply worn; it perhaps shows the heroic exploits of Theseus, the battle of Gods and Giants and the battle of Lapiths and Centaurs. Hard by, generally ignored by sightseers, but religiously important, are the foundations of a small, unusual, and irregular temple of Athene adorned on two sides with an Ionic colonnade. A few miles to the north lies Thorikos. Here there was Mycenaean occupation, and two beehive tombs have been found. The main visual remains of classical times are a very odd theatre with a small temple of Dionysus and a large altar. An unusual temple of Demeter and Kore, Doric, and peripteral (seven rows of fourteen columns) was excavated nearby. Another important religious site, considerably further up the east coast of Attica, is Rhamnus. Here the worship of Nemesis, the power of distribution and retribution, went back at least to the sixth century BC. The surviving temple was seemingly founded on 30 September (Boedromion 5, the Festival of Nemesis), 436 BC. Fragments associated with the cult-statue of Nemesis by Agoracritus are in the British Museum. An amusing pendant to the history of the temple is that under the Romans it was rededicated to the Empress Livia. Nearby is a somewhat earlier temple of Themis, the goddess of justice, a small Doric building only 10.6 × 6.3 m. A statue of the goddess by Chaerestratus from the early third century BC is in the national museum. She appears frontally formal, and her gaze is distant and inflexible, though the face is Praxitelean and the draped body full of life. Many more sacred sites could be mentioned. Attica displays the rich variety of religious activity in the ancient world.

# NOTES

## 1 THE RELIGION OF ANCIENT CRETE

1. M. Ventris and J. Chadwick, *Documents in Mycenaean Greek* (Cambridge, ³1973), 509.
2. R. F. Willetts, *Cretan Cults and Festivals* (London, 1962), 75.
3. M. P. Nilsson, *The Minoan–Mycenaean Religion* (Lund, ²1950), 527–8.
4. A. B. Cook, *Zeus* (Cambridge, 1914–40), I: 521ff.; J. G. Frazer, *The Golden Bough* (London, 1923–7), III, 71.
5. Nilsson, op. cit., 516.
6. Sir A. Evans, *The Palace of Minos* (London, 1921–35), III, 468.
7. Willetts, op. cit., 199.
8. W. K. C. Guthrie, *Orpheus and Greek Religion* (London, ²1952), 112–13.
9. A. Evans, 'Mycenaean Tree and Pillar Cult', *JHS* 21 (1962); Nilsson, op. cit., ch. vii.
10. Willetts, op. cit., 73.
11. Against: Nilsson, op. cit., 291. For: G. Thomson, *Studies in Ancient Greek Society: The Prehistoric Aegean* (London, ²1954), 114.
12. In general see Nilsson, op. cit., 194ff.
13. I am grateful to Dr Miranda Green for her comments on these paragraphs.
14. Willetts, op. cit., 85–6.
15. Nilsson, op. cit., 486; Evans, *Palace of Minos*, *passim*.

## 2 GODS AND GODDESSES

1. K. Schefold, *Myth and Legend in Early Greek Art* (New York, n.d.), fig. 5.
2. A. B. Cook, *Zeus* (Cambridge 1914–40), II, 23–9, 731–3.
3. ibid., I, 84–6; II, 740–51, 1222–3.
4. ibid., I, 68–70.
5. ibid., I, 93.
6. A. D. Nock *et al.*, 'The gild of Zeus Hypsistos', *HTR* 29 (1936), 39–88.
7. Schefold, op. cit., pl. 39.
8. G. Grigson, *The Goddess of Love* (London, 1976) is an attractive, well-illustrated, discursive book on the goddess.

9  G. E. Bean, *Lycian Turkey* (London, 1978).
10 P. Bruneau and J. Ducat, *Guide de Délos* (Paris, 1966), 107.
11 Throughout this chapter L. R. Farnell, *Cults of the Greek States* (Oxford, 1896–1909) has been valuable.

## 3  SANCTUARIES, TEMPLES, AND ALTARS

1  V. R. d'A. Desborough, *The Greek Dark Ages* (London, 1972).
2  *BSA Arch. Rep.* 15 (1968–9), 38. In general see R. F. Willetts, *Cretan Cults and Festivals* (London, 1962).
3  For Zeus on the mountains see the full treatment by A. B. Cook, *Zeus* (Cambridge, 1914–40), I, 117–86; II, 868–987.
4  M. K. Langdon, *A Sanctuary of Zeus on Mount Hymettos* (*Hesp.* Suppl. XVI) Princeton, 1976.
5  C. G. Yavis, *Greek Altars: Origins and Typology* (St Louis, Miss., 1949).
6  See A. D. Nock, 'The cult of heroes', *HTR* 37 (1944), 141–74.
7  J. N. Coldstream, *Geometric Greece* (London, 1977), 317–27.
8  ibid., 279–80.
9  H. Payne, *Perachora* (Oxford, 1940).
10 C. Waldstein et al., *The Argive Heraeum* (Boston and New York, 1902–5); H. Kähler, *Der griechische Tempel* (Berlin, 1964), 8–9.
11 W. B. Dinsmoor and H. Searls, 'The date of the Olympia Heraeum', *AJA* 49 (1945), 62–80.
12 P. C. Sestieri, 'Antiquities of Paestum', *Archaeology* 7 (1954), 206–13.
13 T. Wiegand, 'Der angebliche Urtempel auf der Ocha', *Ath. Mitt.* 21 (1896), 11–17.
14 P. Gardner, *Samos and Samian Coins* 18ff.
15 J. M. Cook, *The Greeks in Ionia and the East* (London, 1962), 101–2.
16 For the Samos Heraeum see E. Buschor in *Ath. Mitt.* 55 (1930), 1–99; O. Reuther, *Der Hera Tempel von Samos* (Berlin, 1957).
17 J. T. Wood, *Discoveries at Ephesus* (London, 1877).
18 For the architecture see W. B. Dinsmoor, *The Architecture of Ancient Greece* (London, 1950); D. S. Robertson, *A Handbook of Greek and Roman Architecture* (Cambridge, ²1943); A. W. Lawrence, *Greek Architecture* (Harmondsworth, 1967).
19 G. E. Bean, *Lycian Turkey* (London, 1978), 114.
20 W. B. Dinsmoor, 'Archaeology and astronomy', *Proc. Am. Phil. Soc.* 80 (1939), 95–123.

## 4  PRIESTHOOD

1  *SEG* 21 (1965), 193–8, no. 527. See W. S. Ferguson in *Hesp.* 7 (1938), 24; D. D. Feaver in *YCS* 15 (1957), 123–58; P. MacKendrick, *The Athenian Aristocracy 399 to 31 BC* (Cambridge, Mass., 1969), 13–15.
2  P. Girard, *L'Asclépieion d'Athènes* (Paris, 1881), 22–34.
3  M. P. Nilsson, *Dionysiac Mysteries of the Hellenistic Age* (Lund, 1957), 99–106.

## 5 GAMES AND FESTIVALS

1. For the remains see E. N. Gardiner, *Olympia: Its History and Remains* (Oxford, 1925); W. Dörpfeld, *Alt-Olympia* (Berlin, 1935); *Olympische Forschungen* (Berlin, 1944–66); and the convenient N. Yalouris, *Olympia* (Munich and Athens, 1972).
2. For the Games see E. N. Gardiner, *Athletics in the Ancient World* (Oxford, 1930); M. I. Finley and H. W. Pleket, *The Olympic Games* (London, 1976); J. Swaddling, *The Ancient Olympic Games* (London, 1980).
3. J. G. Frazer, *Pausanias* (London, 1898), V, 394.

## 6 ORACLES

1. For the excavation reports see C. Carapanos, *Dodone et ses Ruines* (Paris, 1878) and S. I. Dakaris in *Arch. Eph. 1959* (1964): for the oracle H. W. Parke, *The Oracles of Zeus* (Oxford, 1967).
2. For all this see H. W. Parke and D. E. W. Wormell, *The Delphic Oracle* (Oxford, $^2$1956).
3. For Delphi see *Fouilles de Delphes* (Paris, 1906–70); E. Bourguet, *Les Ruines de Delphes* (Paris, 1914); F. Poulsen, *Delphi* (London, 1920); P. de la Coste-Messelière, *Au musée de Delphes* (Paris, 1936); B. Petrakos, *Delphi* (Athens, 1977).
4. E. Philippson in *Symb. Osl.* fasc. suppl. IX 11ff.
5. S. I. Dakaris in *Ergon* (1958, 1963, 1964); S. I. Dakaris, *Antiquités de l'Empire* (Athens, n.d.); N. G. L. Hammond, *Epirus* (Oxford, 1967); J. Dalègre in *Archéologia* (August 1977), 58–65; E. Melas, *Temples and Sanctuaries of Ancient Greece* (London, ET 1973), 151–63.
6. Thebes: A. D. Keramopoulos *Arch. Delt.* 3 (1917).
7. Corinth: C. H. Morgan in *AJA* 41 (1937), 539–62; 43 (1939), 255–67.
8. R. Haussoulier in *Rev. phil.* 44 (1920), 268–71.
9. *Milet* 1 (1906), 178.
10. *Milet* 1, 3, 132.
11. *Didyma Inschr.* 504, 15–16; 29–31.
12. Iambl. *De Myst.* 3, 11.
13. See *AJA* 63 (1959), 83–4; 64 (1966), 66; *Ann. du Coll. de France* 1957–9; C. Delvoye and G. Roux, *La civilisation grecque* (Brussells, 1966).
14. G. E. Bean, *Lycian Turkey* (London, 1978), 130–3.
15. G. E. Bean, *Turkey's Southern Shore* (London, 1968), 172–3.
16. For Zeus Ammon, see A. B. Cook *Zeus* (Cambridge, 1914–40), I, 346–90; for the oracle, Parke, op. cit.; G. Steindorff *et al.* in *Zeitschrift für ägyptische Sprache und Altertumskundke* 69 (1933), 1–24; for the site Ahmed Fakry, *Siwa Oasis* (n.p., 1944).

## 7 HEALING SANCTUARIES

1. See C. Roebuck, *Corinth*, XIV (Princeton, NJ, 1951); M. Lang, *Cure and Cult in Ancient Corinth* (Princeton, NJ, 1977).
2. For Cos see: L. Cohn-Haft, *The Public Physicians of Ancient Greece* (Northampton, Mass., 1956); L. and J. Edelstein, *Asclepius*, 2 vols (Baltimore, 1945); D. Hadjiamullos, *Cos, History and Monuments*

(Athens, 1958); R. Herzog, *Heilige Gesetze von Kos* (Berlin 1928); *Koische Forschungen und Funde* (Leipzig 1899); W. R. Paton and E. L. Hicks, *The Inscriptions of Cos* (Oxford, 1891); E. D. Phillips, *Greek Medicine* (London, 1973); S. M. Sherwin-White, *Ancient Cos* (Göttingen, 1978).
3   O. Deubner, *Das Asklepieion von Pergamon* (Berlin, 1938).
4   *Explor. arch. de Délos* XX.
5   R. F. Hoddinott, *Bulgaria in Antiquity* (London, 1975); D. Zoutchew, *Le sanctuaire thrace près du village de Batkoun* (Sofia, 1941).
6   C. Vatin in *Gallia* 27 (1969), 320–30; *RA* (1969), 103–14; *Antiquity* 46 (1972), 39–42.

## 8   THE MYSTERIES

1   A. Skias, *Eph. Arch.* (1901), 1–39; J. Svoronos, *J. Int. Arch. Num.* 4 (1901), 268–9.
2   For Eleusis I have, apart from my own examination of the site, followed G. E. Mylonas, *Eleusis and the Eleusinian Mysteries* (Princeton, NJ, 1961). See also P. Foucart, *Les Mystères d'Eleusis* (Paris, 1914); O. Kern, *Die griechischen Mysterien der classischen Zeit* (Berlin, 1927); and the idiosyncratic and well-illustrated C. Kerenyi, *Eleusis* (London, ET 1967).
3   S. Accame in *Ann. sc. arch. Atene* 3–5 (1941–3) 76, 82, 87, 89ff.; J.-L. Robert in *REG* 57 (1944), 221.
4   S. G. Cole, *The Samothracian Mysteries* (Ann Arbor, Mich., and High Wycombe, 1975), 8–9.
5   For Samothrace, K. and P. W. Lehmann, *Samothrace* (Princeton, NJ, 1958–   ); K. Lehmann, *Samothrace* (New York, 1975); B. Hemberg, *Die Kabiren* (Uppsala, 1950); S. G. Cole, *The Samothracian Mysteries* (Ann Arbor, Mich., and High Wycombe, 1975).
6   W. Sauppe, *Die Mysterien-inschrift von Andania* (Göttingen, 1860); *SIG*$^2$ 653.
7   For a rather controversial treatment see C. Kerenyi in J. Campbell (ed.), *The Mysteries* (Princeton, NJ, 1955), 32–59.
8   For Orpheus see I. M. Linforth, *The Arts of Orpheus* (Berkeley, 1941); W. K. C. Guthrie, *Orpheus and Greek Religion* (London, $^2$1952); H. Liesegang in Campbell, op. cit., 194–260.
9   E. Ohlemutz, *Die Kulte und Götter in Pergamon* (Giessen, 1940).
10  M. P. Nilsson, *Dionysiac Mysteries of the Hellenistic and Roman Age* (Lund, 1957), 51–61, to which I am in general indebted.
11  For the sequence, with a variety of different interpretations, see P. D. Mudie-Cooke in *JRS* 3 (1913), 157–74; A. Maiuri, *La Villa dei Misteri* (Rome, 1931); V. Macchioro, *The Villa of the Mysteries in Pompei* (Naples, n.d.); M. P. Nilsson, op. cit.; G. Zuntz in *PBA* (1963), 177ff.; O. Brandel in *Jahrb. d. deutschen arch. Inst.* 81 (1966), 205ff.; A. M. G. Little, *A Roman Bridal Drama at the Villa of the Mysteries* (Wheaton, 1972); T. Kraus and L. von Matt, *Pompeii and Herculaneum: Living Cities of the Dead* (ET New York, 1975); F. Coarelli, *Guida Archeologica di Pompei* (Verona, 1976), 340–6.

## 9 DEATH AND BURIAL

1. See conveniently Lord William Taylour, *The Mycenaeans* (London, 1964); for Pylos *AJA* (1954), 27ff.; for Mycenae, G. Karo, *Die Schachtgräber von Mykenai* (Munich, 1950). Also M. S. F. Hood in *Antiquity* (1960), 166ff.; G. E. Mylonas in *Studies Presented to D. M. Robinson* (St Louis, Miss., 1951–3).
2. V. R. d'A. Desborough, *The Greek Dark Ages* (London, 1972).
3. J. N. Coldstream, *Geometric Greece* (London, 1977).
4. For all this see D. C. Kuntz and J. Boardman, *Greek Burial Customs* (London, 1971).
5. E. Reiner, *Die rituelle Totenklage der Griechen* (Tübingen, 1938), 37–8; J. Boardman in *JRS* 50 (1955), 51–66.
6. E. Freistadt in *Liturgiegeschichtliche Quellen u. Forschungen* 24 (1928), 90–126.
7. G. E. Bean, *Lycian Turkey* (London, 1978).
8. R. Lattimore, *Themes in Greek and Latin Epitaphs* (Urbana, 1962) is a useful compendium.
9. Boswell, *Life of Johnson* (London, 1775).

## 10 VOTIVE OFFERINGS

1. L. R. Palmer, *The Interpretation of Mycenaean Greek Texts* (Oxford, 1963), 235–68.
2. T. B. L. Webster, *Greek Terracottas* (Harmondsworth, 1951), pls 12, 13, 18.
3. See V. Tatton-Brown, *Cyprus BC* (London, 1979); and for more detailed ·studies the books and articles (mainly in *BCH* in the 1960s and 1970s) of V. Karageorghis.
4. W. H. D. Rouse, *Greek Votive Offerings* (Cambridge, 1902), 19.
5. B. Schweitzer, *Die geometrische Kunst Griechenlands* (Cologne, 1969), ch. 7.
6. Rouse, op. cit., 102 with refs.
7. Rouse, op. cit., 208.

## 11 PRIVATE CULTS

1. Evidence about the Athenian phratries was collected by W. S. Ferguson in *Cl. Ph.* 5 (1910), 257–84.
2. The evidence is in W. S. Ferguson in *HTR* 37 (1944), 61–140.
3. For the different meanings of *eranos* see H. Bolkestein, *Wohltätigkeit und Armenpflüge in vorchristlichen Altertum* (Utrecht, 1939), 240.

## 12 MAGIC

1. M. P. Nilsson, *A History of Greek Religion* (ET Oxford, $^2$1949), 97–8.
2. Nilsson, op. cit., 92–3.
3. *TAPA* 54 (1923) 128–40.
4. H. W. Parke, *Festivals of the Athenians* (London, 1977), 109–20.

5 A. B. Cook, *Zeus* (Cambridge, 1914–40), II, 1,089–90.
6 M. Pieper in *Aegyptus* 14 (1934), 245–52.
7 C. Bonner, *Studies in Magical Amulets* (Ann Arbor, Mich., 1950), nos 298–319.
8 A. Dieterich, *Eine Mithrasliturgie* (Leipzig, 1910); *Zeitschr. neut. Wiss.* 13, 13.

## 13 POLITICS AND RELIGION

1 See *JHS* 97 (1977), 102–12.
2 A. S. Pease in *Cl. Phil.* 7 (1912), 1ff.
3 *Athenian Studies Presented to W. S. Ferguson* (Cambridge, Mass., 1940), 46–8.
4 M. P. Nilsson, *Cults, Myths, Oracles and Politics in Ancient Greece* (Lund, 1951) is useful in this whole area.
5 H. B. Mattingly in *CQ* 16 (1966), 172–86 is a useful commentary.
6 F. E. Adcock and D. J. Mosley, *Diplomacy in Ancient Greece* (London, 1975), 152–61.
7 H. Popp, *Die Einwirkung von Vorzeichen, Opfern und Festen auf die Kriesführung der Griechen im 5. und 4. Jahrhundert v. Chr.* (Erlangen, 1957), 42–6.
8 For the whole subject see W. K. Pritchett, *The Greek State at War* pt III (1979), an excellent book, though perhaps inevitably using mainly literary evidence.
9 See N. Davis and C. M. Kraay, *The Hellenistic Kingdoms* (London, 1973).
10 See further M. I. Rostovtzeff in *Rev. Hist.* 163 (1930), 1; S. Eitrem in *Symb. Osl.* 101 (1932), 43–8; S. R. F. Price in *JRS* 70 (1980), 31–3.

## 14 SOME ISLANDS AND THEIR CULTS

1 R. Herzog, *Heilige Geschichte von Kos* (Berlin, 1928); A. Maiuri, *Nuova Silloge Epigrafica di Rodi e Cos* (Florence, 1925); S. M. Sherwin-White, *Ancient Cos* (Göttingen, 1978).
2 *Explor. arch. de Délos* has appeared in 26 vols (Paris, 1909–65); P. Bruneau and J. Ducat, *Guide de Délos* (Paris, 1966) is a convenient digest. P. Roussel, *Les cultes égyptiens à Délos* (Paris, 1915–16) is excellent on its subject. I have not covered the domestic cults of the Italian settlers.
3 In general see Emily L. Shields, *The Cults of Lesbos* (Menasha, 1917).
4 M. Nilsson, *Dionysiac Mysteries of the Hellenistic and Roman Age* (Lund, 1937); R. L. J. Wynne-Thomas, *Legacy of Thasos* (London, 1929).
5 For Thasos in general see G. Daux, *Guide de Thasos* (Paris, 1968), with bibliography.

## 15 THE RELIGIOUS LIFE OF ATHENS AND ATTICA

1 For a lucid treatment see R. E. Wycherley, *The Stones of Athens* Princeton, NJ, 1978); the more prosaic but still useful Ida Thallon Hill,

*The Ancient City of Athens* (London, 1953); and the older, full, scholarly, and stimulating Jane E. Harrison, *Mythology and Monuments of Ancient Athens* (London, 1890).

2  In general see A. E. Raubitschek, *Dedications from the Athenian Akropolis* (Cambridge, 1949).

3  The standard works are G. P. Stevens and J. M. Paton, *The Erechtheum* (Cambridge, 1927); J. Dell, *Das Erechtheion in Athen* (Brunn, 1934); W. Dörpfeld and H. Schleif, *Erechtheion* (Oslabruck, 1942).

4  For the sculpture see P. Corbett, *The Sculpture of the Parthenon* (Harmondsworth, 1959); M. Robertson and A. Frantz, *The Parthenon Frieze* (London, 1975). The metopes and pediments are the subjects of F. Brommer, *Die Skulpturen der Parthenon-Giebel* (Mainz, 1963) and *Die Metopen des Parthenon* (Mainz, 1967).

5  V. Scully, *The Earth, the Temple and the Gods* (New Haven, Conn., and London, 1962), 176. Rhys Carpenter's controversial thesis in *The Architects of the Parthenon* (Harmondsworth, 1970) has not won acceptance.

6  For the Acropolis generally see R. J. Hopper, *The Acropolis* (London, 1971).

7  See the many volumes of the American excavations, *The Athenian Agora* (Princeton, NJ); also the convenient handbook H. A. Thompson *et al.*, *The Athenian Agora* (Athens, $^3$1976).

8  See G. Welter in *Ath. Mitt.* 47 (1922), 61–71; 48 (1923), 182–201; R. E. Wycherley in *GRBS* 5 (1964), 161–79.

9  J. A. Davison in *JHS* 78 (1958), 23–42; 82 (1967), 141–2; H. A. Thompson in *Arch. Anz.* (1961), 224–31; H. W. Parke, *Festivals of the Athenians* (London, 1977), 35–50.

10  A. Michaelis, *Der Parthenon* (Leipzig, 1871); A. H. Smith, *The Sculptures of the Parthenon* (London, 1910); P. E. Corbett, *The Sculptures of the Parthenon* (Harmondsworth, 1959).

11  Schol. ad Ar. *Birds* 827; *Suda* s.v. *Chalceia*; Phot. s.v. *histos*; Paus. 1, 29, 1; Harpocr. s.v. *topeion*; Hesych. s.v. *Ergastinai*; Eur. *Hec.* 468; *SIG* $^3$718.

12  M. Ervin, 'The Sanctuary of Aglauros', *Archeion Pontou* 22 (1958), 129–66.

# GLOSSARY

| | |
|---|---|
| *abaton* | a place not to be trodden, a sanctuary |
| *adyton* | a place not to be entered, a sanctuary |
| amphictiony | religious association centring on a temple |
| amphora | large two-handled jar |
| aneconic | not in human form |
| apotropaic | designed to ward off evil |
| apsidal | with a semicircular recess at the end |
| arula | small altar |
| aryballos | small, globular oil flask |
| Baal (pl. Baalim) | 'The Lord', one of the high gods of Syria and Palestine |
| baldachin | canopy |
| *bouleuterion* | council chamber |
| bucrania | bulls' heads |
| cella | inner chamber of temple |
| centaur | mythical being, part human, part horse |
| chryselephantine | of gold and ivory |
| cist grave | tomb consisting of stone chest with stone covering |
| cornucopiae | horn of plenty |
| deme | commune, political division of Attica |
| dipteral | with two rows of columns |
| drachma | silver coin worth six obols |
| entablature | part of a building resting on the columns |
| entasis | swelling in outline of column |
| erotes | cupids |
| exedra | raised bench or seat, often in the open |
| frieze | band of sculpture |

| | |
|---|---|
| Geometric | period of Greek history, named after a pottery style *c.* 900–720 BC |
| graffito | an unofficial scrawl |
| gymnasium | place for physical exercise |
| hekatompedon | 100-ft-long building |
| herm | vertical stone, carved with male head and sex organ, named from the god Hermes |
| hero | demigod, offspring of a union between a divinity and a mortal |
| heroon | shrine for a 'hero' |
| hexastyle | with six columns in a row at front and rear |
| hieroglyphics | sacred signs or writing |
| hippodrome | course for chariot-racing |
| holocaust | burnt offering in which everything is consumed and nothing left for the worshippers |
| hydria | large vase for water |
| Hyperboreans | idealized mythical tribe in far north associated with Apollo |
| incubator | technical term for sleeping in a healing sanctuary |
| ithyphallic | with male sex organ erect |
| kouros | standing male figure in archaic Greek sculpture |
| Lapith | member of a Thessalian people who fought with the Centaurs |
| libation | liquid offering, often poured out |
| lustral | to do with purification |
| megaron | rectangular hall |
| metope | space for a rectangular sculptured slab in frieze of a Doric column |
| Minotaur | legendary being from Crete, part human, part bull |
| monolithic | built from a single block of stone |
| mountain-Baal | Baal (q.v.) associated with a mountain |
| *naiskos* | small shrine |
| *naos* | inner chamber of temple |
| narthex | front porch |
| neopalatial | period of new large palaces in Crete *c.* 1700–1400 BC |

# GLOSSARY

| | |
|---|---|
| obol | coin of low value, six of which made up a drachma |
| octastyle | with eight columns in a row at front and rear |
| omphalos | a navel, a conical stone at Delphi marking the earth's centre |
| *opisthodomus* | rear porch |
| palaestra | open space for wrestling, often surrounded with colonnades |
| pancratium | contest in all-in fighting, combining boxing and wrestling |
| panhellenic | shared in by all Greeks |
| pentathlon | athletic contest involving five events, jumping, running, discus, javelin, wrestling |
| phratry | kinship group |
| polychrome | multi-coloured |
| pronaos | front porch |
| proto-Geometric | period of Greek history named after a pottery style *c.* 1150–900 BC |
| proto-palatial | period of first large palaces in Crete *c.* 1900–1700 BC |
| putto | young boy in art, often winged |
| sarcophagus | a stone coffin |
| sherd | broken piece of pottery |
| stadium | track for footraces |
| stele | upright stone slab |
| stoa | portico or colonnade |
| strigil | metal implement used to scrape the body for cleansing |
| tholos | round building |
| thyrsus | staff wreathed with ivy, used by worshippers of Dionysus |
| tripod | anything with three legs |
| *xystus* | covered walk or track |
| zebu | humped cattle |

# INDEX

Abar Barbarie Eloe Sabaoth Pachnuphy Pythipemi 153
*abaton* 89, 90, 92, 94, 97, 178, 197
Abila-Leucas 171
*ablanathanalba* 155
Abrasax 155
acanthus column 75
Achalemorpoth 153
Achelous 196, 203, 210
Acheron 134
Achilles 20
Acmatidas 57
Acragas 35, 46, 80, 110
Acrocorinth 16, 18, 44, 109
Actaeon 23
Actia 66
Actium 66
Adonai 153
Adrasteia 175
Adrastus 61
*adyton* 62, 81, 84
Aegae 48, 49, 171
Aegeira 72
Aegina 2, 11, 30, 45, 62, 91, 138, 140
aegis: of Athene 13–14; of Zeus 167
Aelius Aristides 52, 96
Aeolian 111, 182
*aer* 132
Aeschines 202
Aeschron 174
Aeschylus 12, 105; *Agamemnon* 37; *Eumenides* 70; of Argos 141

aetiological myth 32, 104, 183
Aetion 112
Aetolia 43
Africa, North 84, 88
Agamedes 78
Agathe Tyche 24, 180, 187
Agathos Daemon 187, 198
age for priesthood 49–50
Aglaurus 51, 193, 206, 210, 211
*agon* 6, 58
agora 175, 179, 182, 186, 189
Agoracritus 213
Agrae 108, 199, 201
agricultural festival 204
agriculture 29
Ahura Mazda 155, 170
Aidoneus 79, 103
*akraioi* 183
Alcibiades 105, 195
Alciphron: *Epistulae* 30
Alcmaeon 76
Alcmene 159
Alcyoneus 35
Alectrona, temple of 32
Alexander IV 114
Alexander of Aphrodisias: *Problemata* 150
Alexander the Great 42, 77, 80, 87, 111, 130, 167
Alexandra, priestess 82
Alexandreia 185

Alexandria 83, 132
Alexiou, Margaret: *The Ritual Lament in Greek Tradition* 128
Alochus 203, 210
altar ch. 3 *passim*; carving 6, 38; circular 186; dedications 22, 28, 84, 94, 99; depictions of 8, 22, 53; earth 56; for offerings 92; in courtyard 180; of horns 178; painted 65; siting of 32, 33, 37, 62, 72, 75, 82; stone 31, 33; to Aphrodite 18, 184, 194; to Apollo 80; to Asclepius 88; to Athene 207; to Cybele 189; to Hecate 113; to Hera 181; to Hestia 21, 55; to Muses 196; to Theos Hypsistos 13; to Twelve Gods 179, 196; to Zeus 54, 62; well 35
Altis 54, 57
Amasia 171
Amazons 23, 42, 44, 58, 130, 192, 198
Amen-Ra 86
*American Journal of Archaeology* 162, 208
American School of Classical Studies of Athens: *Corinth* 132
Amiens 152
Ammon, oracle of 86–7, 162

225

# INDEX

Amorgos 32, 48, 133
Amphiaraa 65
Amphiaraon 50, 140
Amphiaraus 100, 126
amphictiones 165–6
Amphidamas 126
Amphitrite 60, 136
amulets 154–6
Amyclae 25–6, 125, 139, 164
Amyntas 129
Amynus 197
Anactoron 113
Anaetoi 164
Anakes 210
Ananke 153
Anarrhysis 200
Anaxapolis 14
Anaxilas 148
Anazarbus 171
Ancestor, Clan 137
ancestors 79, 85, 122, 205, 207, 210
ancestral gods 172, 176
Anchesmos, Mt 31
Anchises 18
Ancyra 171
Andania 52, 115
Andocides 105
Anemospilia 8
animal: figurines 25, 27, 138–9; handles 140; remains 30; sacrifice 6, 8, 27, 28, 32, 50, 57, 64, 72, 78–9, 96, 99, 107, 115, 141, 147, 186, 195, 200–1, 205–9
animals: and magic 147–8; as offerings 162; as symbols 1, 5–6, 43; god of wild 21; on artefacts 16, 22; our lady of the 1, 15, 211; regulation of 32
Anios 65
*Annuario della Scuola Archaeologica di Atene* 30–1
Antalya museum 53
Anthela 165
Anthesteria 149, 185, 187, 201, 202
Anthesterion 185, 205, 209.

*Anthologia Palatina* 142
Antigonus Gonatas 169
Antiochus I of Commagene 170; III of Syria 82; IV 168, 196; VI 168
Antiphanes 148
Antissa 36, 182, 184
Antoninus Liberalis 2
Antoria 33
Anubis 180
anxiety 77
Apaturia 143, 185, 199, 200
Apelles 18
Apesas, Mt 31
Aphaea 2, 45, 138
Aphrodisias 46, 51, 172
Aphrodite: and Eros 193; and magic 149; and politics 169; cult titles: Atargatis 181, Epitragia 19, Hegemone 194, Kallipygos 19, Peitho 184, Urania 194, Zerynthia 111; -Hathor 155; in Attica 198, 210; in Pantheon 18–20, 22; in the gardens 196; island cults of 174, 176, 179, 180, 186; on coins 183; priests of 49, 53; shrines and sanctuaries of 42, 44, 46, 68, 91, 181, 193, 194; temple of 145, 184
Apollo: and Crete 3, 5; and healing sanctuaries 88, 91, 98, 99; and magic 156; and politics 168, 170; cult titles: Apotropaios 198, 204, 210, Carneios 115, 182, Cyparissius 94, 96, Dalios 173, Daphnephorus 36, Delphinius 36, 37, 196, 198, 210, Epicurius 44, Eresius 183, Erisathaus 32, Hecatombaios 198, Hersus 28, Horus Harpocrates 154, Laphrius 44, Lyceius 183, 198, 210, Maleatas

28, Maloeis 183, Napaeus 183, Nymphegetes 204, 210, of Boza 33, of the Springs 100, Oulios 101, 174, Paeon 179, 210, Panionian 43, Patroos 194, 198, Pythius 17, 166, 173, 182, 188, 196, 205, 210, Romaios 186, Smintheus 183, Surius 84, Vindonnus 100; epiphanies of 166; hymn to 74, 158, 171; in Attica 193, 211; in Pantheon 11, 15–16, 17, 22, 23; island cults of 174, 176; oath to 163; on coins 183; oracles of 63, 70–3, 76–7, 80–5; sanctuaries of 25, 42, 64, 70, 88, 138; temples of 25, 34, 37, 43–4, 64, 75–6, 139, 164, 165, 178, 182, 183; votives 142
Apollonia 141
apse 36–7, 46, 55, 56
Aptera 97
Apulunas 177
Aquilius, M. 171
Arachnaion, Mt 31
arbitration 211
Arcadia 12, 30, 49, 97, 147
Arcadians 73; Cretan 97
archaic period; death and burial in 122, 127; games and festivals in 60, 65; healing in 83, 94; island cults in 179, 181, 183; Mysteries in 116; oracles in 74, 83; Pantheon in 13, 15, 17, 23; sanctuaries and temples in 35, 39, 41, 45; votive offerings in 138, 139
*Archaiologike Ephemeris* 183
*Archaiologion Deltion* 12, 68
*Archäologische Zeitung* 33
*Archäologischer Anzeiger* 34, 83, 94, 95, 173

226

# INDEX

Archegesion 65
Archegetes 36
Archelaus 29
Archidamian war 161
*Archives d'histoire du droit oriental et revue internationale des droits de l'antiquité* 176
Archon Basileus 149, 201
Ares 18, 19, 163, 170, 183, 193-4
Argeia Heleia Basileia 173
Argolid 27, 31, 34, 124-5, 138; coin of 13; *see also* Argos, Epidaurus, Heraeum, Mycenae
Argos 12, 13, 30, 33, 38, 61, 62-3, 71, 74, 141, 164; coin of 62; Hera is 159
Ariadne (Ariagne) 2, 9, 21-2, 118-20
Ariarathes V 203
Ariste (best) 131
Aristion 131
Aristocles 156
Aristodicus 81
Aristogeiton 195
Aristonous 11
Aristophanes: *Acharnians* 200, 201; *Clouds* 148, 202; *Lysistrata* 212; *Peace* 39; *Plutus* 148; *Thesmophoriazusae* 200; *Wasps* 197
Aristotle x, 86; *Politics* 48
Arkalokhori 1, 6, 26
arm gestures 7, 41, 123, 127-8
Aroriphrasis 155
Arrephoroi 191
*arrephorus* 52
Arsinoe Philadelphus 176, 180
arson 42
Artagnes 170
Artemidorus 85, 182
Artemis: and Crete 2, 3; and festivals 64; and healing 99; and magic 148, 151, 152; and oracles 83-4; column to 182; cult titles: Aethiopia 183, Aristobule 197, Boulephorus Sciris 82, Claria 84, Dreneia 183, Eilithyia 187, Ephesia 84, 140, Hecate 203, 210, Hymnia 49, Laphria 44, Leucophryene 17, 43, 46, 166, Lochia 180, Lye 101, of Brauron 191, of Comba 22, Orthia 26, Oulia 101, Pergaea 48, 50, Prosoea 37, Soteira 131, 198, Thermia 166, 183; epiphanies of 166; in Attica 193, 198, 202, 210, 211-12; in Pantheon 15-17, 22; island cults 186; on coins 183; priests of 53; sacrifice to 203; sanctuaries of 34, 37, 40, 42, 91, 174, 187, 191; temples of 11, 25, 34, 43-4, 45, 52, 64, 104, 196; votives 138
Artemision: Cape 16; at Delos 176, 178; month 185; Mt 16
Artemisium 12
arulae 34, 35
Ascalon 180
Asclepiadai 94
Asclepieia, Great 96, 97, 106, 185; on coins 183
Asclepieion; at Athens 52, 92-3, 140, 193; at Cos 94-5, 173; at Pergamon 96-7; on Delos 97, 181; on Lebera 97; on Pantolia 98
Asclepius: and healing 81, 91, 95-7, 98-9; Festival of 91, 185, 203; island cults 174-5, 186; offerings to 99; priesthood and 48, 49, 51; sanctuaries of 88, 91, 93, 97, 98, 185; temples of 171; the Saviour 142; votives 142
Ashmolean Museum 19
Asia (Minor) 2, 3, 24, 29, 40, 64, 66, 80, 88, 94, 124, 128, 165, 171, 177, 182-3; *see also* Antalya museum, Assos, Charonion, Didyma, Ephesus, Halicarnassus, Miletus, Mycale, Nysa, Panionia, Pergamon
Asine 34, 36
Assos 23
Astarte 18, 145, 176
Astypalaea 2, 133, 135
Atargatis 181
Athanasius: *De Incarnatione Verbi* 110
Athenaeus 146, 169
*Athenaion* 106
Athene: and Crete 3; and island cults 173, 179, 184, 186; and Mysteries 111; and oracles 76, 82; and politics 159, 168; and priesthood 49; and votives 138, 140; born from head of Zeus 13, 192; cult titles: Alseia 173, Areia 193, Cynthia 29, 179, Ergane 1, Hellotis 209, Hygieia 208, Hyperdexia 184, Idena 184, Lindia 14, Machanis 173, Nicephorus 32, Nike 34, 50, 191, Paeonia 194, Patroa 185, 187, Phatria 194, 200, Polias 46, 173, 184, 191, 206, 210, Poliouchos 159, 188, Promachos 191, Pronaia 25, 45, Sciras 51, 211, Soteria 173, 184; in Athens and Attica 190, 194, 199, 203, 204, 206; in

# INDEX

Athene – *cont.*
Pantheon 13–15, 16, 18, 22, 23; in Athens 159, 169; mistress of technology 200; oath to 163; on coins 168, 169, 183, 184; priestess of 206; sanctuaries of 45, 58, 71; temples of 26, 46, 159, 188, 206
Athens ch. 15 *passim*; Academy 207; acropolis 14, 18, 34, 63, 92, 94, 159, 164, 190–3, 197, 207, 210; agora 31, 194–5, 207, 210, 211; Areopagus 193; Asclepieion 52, 92–3, 140, 193; Athene is 159; Ceramicus 23, 123–4, 126, 131, 199; Dipylon Gate 106, 194, 207; festivals at 106–8, ch. 15 *passim*; Hephaesteion 45, 194; League 163–4; Metroon 194; museums 11, 12, 17, 140; odeon of Pericles 163; Parthenon 14, 44, 46, 55; Pnyx 197; Pompeion 207; priestly rules 48, 50–1, 149; Propylaea 191, 207; stadium 196; Stoa of Attalus 195, Painted 195; temple: of Aphrodite 145, of Ares 195, of Olympian Zeus 168, 195–6, 205, regulations 32; theatre of Dionysus 51, 193; Tholos 194; Treasury 23, 74
Athos, Mt 28
Aththa Baththa 154–5
Atlantis 182
Attaleia 176
Attalus 75
Attica 16, 26, 29–30, 31, 65, 100, 126–7, 128, 143, 153, 202, 212; *see also* Brauron, Daphni,

Deccleia, Eleusis, Hymettus, Ikaria, Kaisariani, Rhamnus, Sunion, Thorikos
Attic ware 27
Auberson, P. 36
Audollent, A.: *Defixionum Tabellae* 150, 153
Augustine: *De Civitate Dei* 160; *De haeresibus ad Quodvultdeum* 155
Augustonemetum 100
Augustus 66, 171
*auletes* 52
Aulis 16
Averter of Evil 148
axe, double 1, 5, 6–7, 8–9
Axieros 111–12
Axiocersa 111–12
Axiocersos 111–12
Ayia Irini (Ceos) 25; (Cyprus) 26, 139
Ayia Paraskevi 112
Ayia Triadha 5, 8, 9, 26
Ayios Elias, Mt 29, 78

Baal 12, 167; Margod 145
Baalbek 80
Bacchants 118–19
Bacchic companies 118
Bacchic votaries 174
Bachachych 153
Bactria 169
baldachin 46
banquets 13, 50–1, 112–13, 115, 145, 146; ceremonial 112–13, 142, 180
Bargoin, Musée 100
Basile 203, 210
*basilinna* 149, 201
basin, lustral 9
Bassae 37, 44, 45, 191
baths: and games 56–7, 58, 61, 62, 82; public 51, 91, 95; ritual 40, 97
Batkoun 98–9
'bears' 212
beetles 139
Bendis 169, 199, 205–6
Berbati 34
Berenice II 168
Bergquist, Birgitta 188

Berlin museum 14, 126, 128, 141
betyl image 18
birds: as symbols 1, 5, 7, 8–9, 15, 16, 148, 156; on artefacts 15, 16, 19, 116
birth, forbidden on Delos 177; *see also* childbirth, rebirth
Bithynia 76, 169, 176
blessedness 110
blessing, power of 6, 152
blessings 107, 112, 159, 164, 170
Blest, Isles of the 131
Blinkenberg, C., *et al.*: *Lindos: Fouilles et Recherches* 15, 160
Boardman, John 192, 199, 207
Boedromia 198
Boedromion 198, 203, 208, 213
Boeotia 16, 74, 99, 100, 123, 141
Boeotians 165
Boeotian ware 27
Bonner, C.: *Studies in Magical Amulets* 154
books, sacred 115
Boreas, altar of 196
Boston museum 12, 17, 18, 19–20, 21, 23
*bouleuterion* 55, 56, 75; *see also* council chamber
boundary: dispute 204; stones 183, 196, 197
Boundary, Zeus of the 204
Bouphonia 192, 206
boxing 57, 207
boys' events 62, 63, 182
Branchidae 141
Branchus 80
Brauron 16, 52, 211–12; Artemis of 191
Brea 162
breast symbolism 7, 9, 16, 43, 111
Brisa 184
Britain 84
British Museum 16, 18, 19, 20, 22, 23, 29, 42, 141, 151, 152, 156, 213

228

# INDEX

*British Museum Catalogue of Bronzes* 141
*British Museum Catalogue of Coins*: Caria 176; Galatia 29; Italy 175; Mysia 46; Thessaly 29, 147
*British School at Athens: Annual* of the 96, 162; *Archaeological Reports* 8, 41, 62, 63, 83, 120, 138, 140, 188
Britomartis (Britomarpis) 2
Broneer, Oscar 60
Bronze Age 64, 71, 182
bronze: amulets 155–6; and magic 151; artefacts 6, 11, 13, 23, 27, 30, 76, 100, 122, 139, 141, 178, 191, 212; ballots 195; caldrons 26, 40, 126, 140; -casting 193; coins 111; figurines 125; heads 65; phalluses 152; statues 12, 14, 23, 37, 73, 111; statuettes 14, 17, 23, 28, 139; treaty inscriptions 164; votive tablets 5, 7, 8, 54, 68; weapons 26, 27; workers 1
Brooklyn Museum 154
Brusa 21
Brutus 101
Bucoliastae 148
bucrania *see* bulls' heads
Bulgaria 98–9; *see also* Batkoun, Pautalia, Philippopolis
bull: as symbol 6; figurines 7; in myth 2, 149; on coins 28; on terracotas 139; sacrifice of 64, 99, 133, 172, 193, 206; Zeus as 2, 6
*Bulletin de correspondence hellénique* from: Athens 93, 106, 165, 198, 202, 204, 206; Caria 118; Cos 94; Crete 34; Cyzicus 161; Delos 183; Olympia 141;

Oropus 101; Tegea 138; Thasos 17, 185, 187, 188
*Bulletin de la Société Royale archaéologique d'Alexandrie* 132
bulls: and healing 99, 102; on artefacts 2, 21, 23, 73
bulls': heads 35, 80, 129; horns 6, 8–9, 129, 169
Bundalish 155
burial ch. 9 *passim*; individual 123 ff.; legislation 128–9; multiple 122–213; *see also* dead, death, funeral, funerary
burial places 26
burials 26
Byblos 65, 156
Bybon 141
Byron 212
Byzantine period 23, 27, 46, 56, 60, 66, 112, 182
Byzantium 56

Cabeiri, Mysteries of 35, 110–16
Cabeirion 116
Cadmilos 111–12
caduceus 17, 21, 169
Caesar, Julius 171
Caesareum 172
Cagnat, R., *et al.*: *Inscriptiones Graecae ad res Romanas pertinentes* 136, 146, 171
cairn 17; *see also* herm
Caistris 185
Calauria 49, 166
caldron 26, 40, 68, 75, 93, 122, 126
calendar: cult- 96, 173–4, 175; sacred 198; sacrificial 198, 205, 208
Callatis 114
Callichorus spring 104
Callicles 14
Callicrates 191
Calligeneia 200
Callimachus 174; *Hymn to Zeus* 3
Calliste (Loveliest) 131

Callisto 212
Callynteria 206
Calydon 16, 44
Camarina 20
Cameiros 15, 19, 26, 152
*canephorus* 52
Capitolea 65
Cappadocia 176
Capua, Aphrodite of 19
Carales 133
Caria 118, 160
Carneia 164
Carpathos 114
Carthaea 171
Carthage 75, 153
caryatids 106, 191
Casmilos 111
Castalia, spring of 70, 72–3
Castor and Pollux 168
*cathemerothytes* 52
cave *see* sanctuaries: cave; oracular caves
Cecrops 75, 193
cella 39, 41, 42, 44, 46, 81, 102, 178
Centaurs v. Lapiths 44, 55, 58, 192, 213
century: AD: fifth 95, 123, first 75, 100, 157, 183, 187, fourth 28, 85, 95, 135, second 22, 28, 61, 72, 82, 120, 146, 157, 160, 196, seventh 46, sixth 95, third 22, 83
BC: eighth: Attica in 196 death and burial in 124, 128 games and festivals in 54, 57, 64 Mysteries in 111 sanctuaries and temples in 23, 25, 26, 28, 31, 34–5, 36 votives in 137
fifteenth 9, 25,
fifth: ancient Crete in 3 Attica in 190, 191, 195, 197, 198, 203, 211, 213 death and burial in 127–8, 132, 133 games and festivals in 55–6, 60, 62, 63, 64 healing in

229

# INDEX

Century – *cont.*
88, 92–3, 94 island cults in 177, 178, 181, 186, 187, 188 magic in 151, 153 Mysteries in 103, 105, 108, 111, 114, 116 oracles in 69, 71, 73, 77 Pantheon in 11–12, 14, 20, 22 politics in 160, 162, 163, 166 sanctuaries and temples in 28, 30, 32, 35, 37, 44, 45
first: Attica in 198 healing in 100, 102 island cults in 176, 177, 186, 187 Mysteries in 115 oracles in 75 Pantheon in 13, 14, 19 politics in 166, 170 priesthood in 52
fourth: Ancient Crete in 4 Attica in 194, 195, 199, 207, 208, 211 death and burial in 127, 132, 134, 135 games and festivals in 55, 56, 61 healing in 88, 92, 93, 94, 96 island cults in 173, 181, 186, 187, 189 magic in 148, 153 Mysteries in 105, 108, 109, 114 oracles in 68, 74, 75, 76, 80, 83 Pantheon in 12, 14 politics in 160, 162, 163, 166, 169 sanctuaries and temples in 28, 30, 32, 45 votives in 143, 145
ninth 26, 38, 40
second: Attica in 191, 195, 196, 203 games and festivals in 65 healing in 97 island cults in 181 Mysteries in 108, 118 oracles in 69, 75, 83 Pantheon in 12
politics in 160, 166, 170 sanctuaries and temples in 32, 34, 43, 46 votives in 145
seventh: Attica in 211 death and burial in 126, 131, 134 games and festivals in 64 island cults in 176, 178, 181, 185, 187, 189 Mysteries in 113 oracles in 71, 76, 79, 81 Pantheon in 11, 16 politics in 166 sanctuaries and temples in 28, 31, 35, 38, 39, 41, 42, 43, 44 votives in 139
sixth: Attica in 195, 201, 213 death and burial in 126 games and festivals in 55, 56, 57, 58, 59, 61, 62, 64, 65 healing in 88 island cults in 173, 176, 179, 181, 182, 183, 187, 188, 189 magic in 152 Mysteries in 105, 111, 113, 114 oracles in 74, 76, 79, 81, 86 Pantheon in 11, 12, 13, 17, 19, 21, 23 politics in 163, 164, 166 sanctuaries and temples in 27, 34–5, 39–40, 41, 42 votives in 139, 140
tenth 5–26, 37
third: Attica in 205, 211, 213 death and burial in 128 games and festivals in 65 healing in 96, 97 island cults in 175, 180, 188 Mysteries in 109, 113, 114, 117–18 oracles in 68, 82 Pantheon in 17, 19 politics in 165, 170 sanctuaries and temples in 27, 28
twelfth 123

Ceos 25–6, 163–4
Cephalus 24
Cerberus 79, 134
Cercopes 23, 45
Ceryneian hind 23
Chaerestratus 213
Chalce 29
Chalcedon 48, 49–50, 114
Chalceia 200
Chalcis 125, 126, 163–4, 171
Chalkotheke 191
Chamalières 100
chariot-racing 55–6, 57, 58, 62, 63, 65, 199
Charitesia 65
charms 148
Charon 126, 134
Charonion 101–2
Chatillon, Musée de 100
Cheramyes 41
Chersonesus 97
child: burial 124, 126–7; initiates 118, 121
childbirth 2, 21, 33, 212; goddess of 2, 27, 187; temple to 55; motherless 13
children: as guardians 159; holy 118; introduced into cult 143–4; on artefacts 130, 139, 142; respect for 121
Chios 50, 65, 76–7
*chiton* 21, 53
Choreia 185, 187
*chous* 201
*chresmographeion* 81
Christian period 46, 56, 61, 63, 64, 93, 95, 110, 133, 182, 186, 195, 211
Chromius of Aetna 62
chryselephantine statue: of Athene 191–2; of Zeus 55, 196
chthonic powers 110, 139–40, 196
Chrysaor 45
Chytrai 201
Cicero: *De Divinatione* 162; *Laws* 104; *Verrine Orations* 170
Cicero, Quintus 83
Cimon 105

230

# INDEX

*cistai* 106
Cithaeron, Mt 31
Citharoedus 83
Cition 145
citizen status of priesthood 48
City: Guardian of 187, 192, 206; Protector of 188
civilization v. barbarism 160, 192
Cladeus, river 56
*Clara Rhodos* 174
Claria 65
Claros 28, 83–4
classical period: Ancient Crete in 3; Attica in 213; death and burial in 126, 129; games and festivals in 54–6, 58, 61; magic in 147–8; oracles in 71; Pantheon in 13; pre- 34–5, 44; sanctuaries and temples in 25–6, 27, 28, 30, 32, 35, 44, 45
Claudius 95
*cleidophorus* 52
*cleiduchi* 52
Clement of Alexandria: *Protrepticus* 41, 106
Cleo, healing of 89
Cleonae 61
Clermont-Ferrand 100
cliffs, goddess of 38
Cnidos 74, 141, 151, 152; Aphrodite of 19; sanctuary of Underworld Deities 20
Cnossos 2, 5, 6–7, 9, 97, 133, 137
Coccygion, Mt 31
cock symbol 155
Codrus 196, 203
Cohn-Haft, L.: *The Public Physicians of Ancient Greece* 95
coins: from Aphytis 87; from Arcadia 12; from Argos 13, 62; from Athens 14; from Attica 28; from Byzantium 23; from Claros 84; from Cos 95, 175, 176; from

Crannon 147; from Crete 2–3, 5; from Cyprus 18–19; from Delphi 15; from Eleusis 109; from Elis 12; from Gaul 100; from Lesbos 167, 183, 184; from Lycia 85; from Macedonia 169; from Magnesia 28; from Metapontum 175; from Naxos 21; from Nemea 63; from Olympia 11; from Oropus 101; from Pantalia 98; from Pergamon 46; from Poseidonia 20; from Rhodes 24; from Samos 41; from Samothrace 111; from Thasos 159, 187; from Thessaly 29; of Alexander the Great 167; of Gallienus 106; of Hellenistic Age 167–9; of Ptolemaic period 167–8
Colaeus 40
Cole, Susan 112, 114
Collitz, H., Bechte, F., et al.: *Sammlung des griechischen Dialektinschriften* 140, 141, 161
colonization 162
Colophon 83, 148
colonnade 40, 46, 56, 180; circular 60; Doric 43, 212; Ionic 213; to palaestra 58
columns: clay bases 36; Corinthian 89; Doric 39, 43, 55, 60, 62, 76, 88, 191, 196, 213; entasis in 44; in other buildings 105; in temples 40, 42, 93, 180; Ionic 41, 80, 184, 191; supporting roof 37
Comba (Gombe) 22
Commagene 170
competitions 96, 101, 173,

207; *see also* contests, games
Comedy, statue of 187
*Comptes rendus de l'Academie d'Inscriptions* 83
Concord 175; temple of 46
confession of sin 112, 114
Constantine 75, 149
contests 44, 51, 55, 58, 60, 62, 63, 64, 66, 125, 165
continuity 3, 25–8, 46, 176; absence of 166
Cook, John 41
Copenhagen museum 23, 152
Coptic names 157
Corbusier, Le 191
Corcyra 45, 65, 68, 69, 73, 163
Corfu 11
Corinth 12, 17, 18, 33, 44, 59–60, 61, 63, 74, 80, 91–2, 124, 126, 132, 138; League of 163; museum 60, 141
Corinthian: coins 60; helmet 184; order 44, 45, 62, 80, 89; period 30; ware 27, 39
corn: and Mysteries 106; maiden 103; mother 20; seed, underground 104
cornucopiae 53, 131, 167–9, 180
*Corpus Inscriptionum Atticarum*: I 65, 141; II 51, 65, 106, 140, 142, 145; III 32, 65, 101, 141, 146, 153; IV 106, 141, 142; app. 153
*Corpus Inscriptionum Graecarum* 2, 51, 65, 101, 142, 145, 171, 183, 184
Croesus 42
*corythale* 147
Cos 30, 34, 49, 52, 65, 82, 93–6, 97, 173–6; museum 28, 130, 141
Cosmos and Damien 93
*cosmeteira* 52
Cottiaeum 135
council chamber 68; *see also bouleuterion*
crab (of Heracles) 175
crafts, patron of 14

231

# INDEX

Crannon 147
Craterus 77
cremation 123–4, 126–7
Cretan bull 23
Cretans: liars 3
Crete: ancient ch. 1 *passim*, 26, 34, 37–8, 52, 82, 97, 123, 141, 182; in classical times 3; in historical times 3; *see also* Aptera, Astypalaea, Ayia Triadha, Chersonesus, Cnossos, Dreros, Gortyna, Gournia, Iraklion museum, Itanos, Lasaea, Lato, Lebena, Mallia, Olous, Phaestos, Pylorus
Creusa 193
crimson colour 149–50
Cronos 153, 202, 205
Ctesileos and Theano 131
cuckoo, Zeus in form of 38
cult: calendar 96, 173–4, 175; drama 116; houses 39; imperial 171–2, 176, 186; island ch. 14 *passim*; of dead 123, 131; private ch. 11 *passim*; prostitution 149; regulations 107; rooms 9, 31, 116, 120; ruler 167–72, 175–6; scenes 5; society 13, 116, 143–6; state- 96, ch. 13 *passim*, 183; statues 13–14, 20–1, 24, 27, 32, 37, 40–1, 43–5, 55, 60, 87–8, 106, 108, 181, 187, 191, 193–4, 213; temple 165; titles *see under individual gods and goddesses*
cults: foreign 48; of Aphrodite 174, 184, 193, of Apollo 5, 43–4, 177–9, 183, of Artemis 182, 187–8, of Asclepius 174, of Athene 173, 184, 188,
of Cybele 146, of Demeter 2, 20, 174, of Dionysus 5, 21, 174, 183, 187, of Hecate 175, of Hera 173, of Heracles 81, 188, of Hermes 174, of heroes 144–5, 188, of Hestia 175, of mother-goddess 9, of Poseidon 64, 174, 184, of Sarapis 180, of Twelve Gods 22, 179, 185, 194, of Zeus 12–13, 28–31, 173
culture: god of 15; with religion and politics 160
cupbearer, Hermes as 184
Cureotis 200
cures, records of 89–91, 92, 93, 95, 97
Curetes 149
Curotrophus 51
curses 62, 134, 150, 152–4, 164, 170
Curtius, Quintus 87
Cybele 24, 101, 142, 146, 189; Demeter- 138
Cydonia 2, 5
Cyme 19, 126
Cynosarges 196
Cynthus, Mt 29, 176
cypress 61, 94–5, 110, 127, 173
Cyprus 18–19, 31, 65, 139, 149, 153; *see also* Ayia Irini, Kourion, Meniko, Palapaphos
Cypselus 15, 125
Cyrene 18, 66, 74, 86, 97
Cyrrhus 29
Cythera 18
Cyzicus 161, 171

*daduchus* 52
*daemon* 134
Dakaris, Sotiris 78
Damianus 83
Damnameneus 155
dance 2, 6, 105, 114, 119–20, 160, 207
dancing girls 75
Daphne (Antioch) 168
Daphni 212

Dardanus 112
Darius 80
Dark Ages 25–6, 55, 123–4, 138
darkness, power of 157
Daryngo 155
Datis 14, 160
dawn goddess 24
dead: banquet of 131; beliefs about 9, 33, 36, 123; festival of 143, 203; god(s) of 103, 111; guide of 17; power of 6; protection of 123; recovery of 163, 201, 202; souls of 109; spirits of 201
Dead, House of 122
death ch. 9 *passim*; and games 57; and new life 104, 117–18, 120; attitudes to 125, 129; forbidden on Delos 177; gods of 183; of gods 2, 5; spirit of 125
Deceleia 143–4
decree 207
Deidamas 133
*deipnophoria* 211
Delia 64–5
Delos: Athenian domination of 166, 181; Greek Pantheon on 12, 15, 22; healing on 97; island cult 176–82, 183; magic on 152; sacred palm on 68; sanctuaries on 25, 28, 29, 35, 36, 38, 39, 65, 114
Delos, Confederation of 177, 185
*Délos, Guide de* 29
Delphi: burial at 128; Greek Pantheon at 13, 15, 23; oracle at 70–7, 161; Pythian games at 58–9, 190; temple of Apollo at 25, 45, 165, 177; votives at 140–1
Delphic: Theoxenia 36; tripod 23, 71–3
deme, membership of

232

# INDEX

143–4, 197; *see also* Archia, Marathon, Myrrhinus, Teithras
Demeter: and island cults 174, 186; and Kore 182, 185, contest in honour of 165, sanctuary of 117, 138, 173, 178, 194, 195, 213; and magic 152–3; and Mysteries 103–9, 111, 115, 174; and oracle 83; and politics 169; and priests 51; cult titles: Cabeiria 116, Europa 2, of Cnidos 103, 152, Soteira 174, Thesmophorus 82, 138; -Cybele 138; identified with Isis 124; in Attica 193, 196, 200, 201, 206, 210; in Pantheon 20, 22; oath to 163; on coins 183, 185; on Crete 3; sanctuaries and temples of 29, 35, 107, 151, 165, 194; votives 146
Demetrieia 185
Demetrius I Poliorcetes 14, 160, 169; II 168
demigod: Alexander 167; shrines to 145; status of 129, 133
Democratia 203
Demonax 195
Demophoon 103–4
Demos 194
Demosthenes 48, 143, 197, 200, 202
Demotionidae 143–4
*dendrophoroi* 146
*Denkschriften der Akademie der Wissenschaften* 118, 135
Dentheletai 98
Dero, cave of 27
destruction: by eruption 182; by fire 60; god of 15; power of 177
Dexileos 131
*diabateria* 164
*diaconus* 52

Dia(i)sia 29, 185, 201
Dicte, Mt 2, 9
Dictynna 2, 3
Didyma 33, 43, 80–3
Dike (Justice) 120
Dinsmoor, W. B. 37, 46
Diocletian 83
Diodorus 64, 87
Diogenes Laertius 149
Diognetus 145
Dione 67, 69
Dionysia 65, 184, 185, 187, 193, 200–1, 202
Dionysios 5
Dionysopolis 114
Dionysus: and island cults 174, 176, 183–4, 186; and magic 152; and Mysteries 52, 109, 110, 107–21, 174, 178, 187; and oracles 75, 84; and politics 159; and priests 53; and the Nymphs 184; doublet of Orpheus 116; in Pantheon 21–2; in the Marshes 196; on coins 183; on Crete 2, 5; sacrifices to 202; sanctuaries of 26, 178, 187; shrine of 77; son of Zeus 21; temple of 182; theatre of 51, 193; votives 146
Diophantus 188
Dioscuri 98, 112, 141, 189, 205, 210; sanctuary of 166, 181
Dioscuria 186
Dipoleia 29, 206
Dirphya 39; *see also* Hera
Dirphys, Mt 39
disease, types of, treated 89–91, 93
Dithyramb 187
Dittenberger, W. and Purgold, K.: *Olympia 5 Die Inschriften* 141, 164
Dittenberger, W.: *Sylloge Inscriptionum Graecorum*: 100s 164; 200s 199, 208; 300s 160, 175; 500s 17, 48, 49, 50, 166; 600s 48,

49, 50; 900s 32, 33; 1000s 36, 50, 165, 173, 174, 175, 176, 198, 207; 1100s 152, 161, 176
Dodona 24, 65, 67–70, 87, 140–1; *see also* oracle
Doedalsas 19
dolphin: of Aphrodite 19; of Poseidon 20, 61, 182, 186
dolphins in myth 22, 59
Dorpia 200
Dove Goddess 137
dove: of Aphrodite 18–19, 68, 87; of Hera 40
drama: of initiation 119; ritual 114; sacred 112
Drerians 3, 82
Dreros 34, 36, 37
dromos 122–3
Duodecathea 185
Duris of Samos 169
*dyaus* 11

eagle (of Zeus) 11–12, 13, 120, 182
earrings, gold 124, 181
earth 1, 6, 153; and new life 104; goddess 25, 55, 71; mother 10, 15, 16, 18, 20, 24, 38, 39–40, 42, 54, 80, 192; oracle of 67, 71; power of 13, 15, 148, 155; sanctuary of 70; union of, with sky 13, 39, 204
earthquakes 25, 27, 70, 76, 95, 174
eclipses 150, 165
Edelstein, E. J. and L.: *Asclepius* 99
Edessa 12
Eetioneia 144
egg: cosmic 117, 121; in burials 126
Egretes 145
Egypt 13, 41, 122, 148, 153–4, 157, 169–70; oracles in 85–7; Pharaohs of 80; Ptolemies of 24, 101, 114, 154, 167, 169–70, 176, 179–80, 182

233

# INDEX

Egyptian gods 35, 91, 124, 154, 169–70, 180, 182
Eilithyia (Eleuthyia) 2–3, 6, 27, 55, 137
*eiresione* 147, 198
Eitrem, S.: *Papyri Osloenses* 157
*ekphora* 128
Elaphebolion 199, 202, 205, 208
elections, phratry 143
Electra 112
Eleusinia 65, 199
Eleusis 20, 37, 52, 91, 92, 103–9, 112, 124, 147, 150, 198, 204, 209, 212; Grand Relief of 108
Eleutheria 165
Eleutherna 3, 5
elevation, power of 116
Elis 12, 31, 55, 163–4; temple of Aphrodite 19
Elymnion, bridal 39
Empedo 193
Empedocles 116
*enagismos* 32
*encoemeterion* 89, 97
Enna 110
entablature 41, 43, 62
entasis 44
Eos 24
ephebes 144, 147, 160–1, 182
*Ephemeris Archaiologike* 104
Ephesia 64, 65
Ephesian writings 148
Ephesus 16, 34, 40, 42–3, 52, 54, 64, 80, 114, 171
Ephyra 78
Epicteta 145–6
Epicureanism 135–6
Epidauria 106, 203
Epidaurus 26, 31, 52, 56, 68, 88–91, 95, 97, 99, 142, 165
Epie 17
epigram 94, 118
epigraphic evidence 144, 197; *see also* inscriptions
Epione 91, 96, 98
epiphany: of god(dess) 5, 8, 14–15, 17, 52, 76, 160, 166, 171; on coinage 168–9
Epirus 68, 78, 111
*epispondorchestes* 52
Epitaphia 65
epitaphs 24, 131–6
Epops 210
*epopteia* 106
*epoptes* 112
Eranistai 205
*eranos* 146
Erasinos, river 212
Erchia 198, 202–6, 210
Erechteum *see* Athens
Erechtheus 191
Ereschigal (Ereshkigal) 155
Eresus 182–4
Eretria 40, 135, 160
Eriboea 185; altar of 199, 207
Erymanthian boar 23
Erysichthon 174
Erythrae 49, 99, 163
Eryx 18
Essarois 100
Etionidae 144
Etruscans 74
*Etymologicum Magnum* 2, 30
*euandria* 63
Euboea 16, 31, 37, 39, 141, 153, 174; Mt 10, 38, 39
Eubul(e)us 107, 110
Eubulides 194
Eucles 110
Eudocia 142
Eulamo 153
Eumelus 174
Eumenes II 76, 168, 185
Eumolpidae 107
Euripides: *Ion* 73, 77–8, 193; *Iphigeneia in Tauris* 71, 212; *Phoenissae* 72
Europa 2, 6; Demeter 2
Eurotas, river 16, 35
Eurydice 17
Eurysaces 36, 51, 205, 211
Eurystheus 23
Eusebea 65
Eusebius: *Vita Constantini* 149
Euthymus 141
Eutychides 167
Evans, Sir Arthur 3, 5, 9
*exegetes* 52
Exekias 22
*Exploration archéologique de Délos* 179, 181
eye magic 156

faience artefacts 124
family cult 176
Fates 134, 175
father-god 22
Father (of gods and men) 11, 22, 170
fertility 3, 6, 16, 43, 104, 118, 129, 147–9, 151, 167–8, 174; festivals 200, 201; god of 111, 152; magic 200; male, bull as 6; ritual 206
festivals ch. 5 *passim*; all-night 118, 199; at Eleusis 106–7; at healing sanctuaries 101; calendar of 185–6; in Messenia 115; of Apaturia 143; of Asclepieia, Great 91, 96–7; of Athene 173; of Attaleia 176; of Attica 197–208; of Diaisia 29; of Dionysia 160, 184; of Dipoleia 29; of Eleutheria 165; of Poseidon 174; of Roman rulers 170–1; of Zeus 173; on Samothrace 112–13; panhellenic 77, 125; symbol of 129; Terrace of the 182; with animal sacrifice 32; with public banquets 50; *see also* Alexandreia, Anthesteria, Boedromia, Callynteria, Carneia, Chalceia, Choreia, Demetrieia, Dioscuria, Duodecathea, Eleusinia, Eleutheria, Genesia, Great

234

## INDEX

Heracleia, Great Romaia, Gymnopaediae, Hadrianeia, Haloa, Hecatombaia, Heroxeinia, Hyacinthia, Lenaea, Maimakteria, Noumenia, Panathenaea, Panionia, Plerosia, Plynteria, Pompaia, Poseideia, Proerosia, Pyanopsia, Soteria, Synoecia, Thalysia, Theodaisia, Theogamia, Theseia, Thesmophoria
figurines 1, 2, 25, 27, 39, 122, 124, 134, 138–9, 170
fire: and creation 117; and immortality 103; ceremonial 34; destruction by 60, 79; god 207; spirit of 20; St Elmo's 166
fish and oracles 84–5
flagellation 119
Flamininus 171
flocks, associations with 5
Florence: Museo Archaeologico 125; Uffizi museum 19, 103, 126
flowers: as offerings 142; as ornamentation 138, 140; as symbols 1, 6–7
Fortune *see* Tyche
*Fouilles de Delphes* 70, 73
fountain-house 195
fountains 15, 113
Franchthi, cave of 27
Frazer, Sir James 58
freedom, festival of 165
Freistadt 128
fresco 1, 6, 9
friezes 23, 44, 45, 74, 114, 160, 174, 178, 179, 187, 192, 195, 199, 207, 213
funeral: games 57, 60, 62, 125–6; procession 128
funerary: expenditure 126; feasts 125; pollution 33; vases 23, 123
Furies 153

Gaea, priestess 51
Galaxion 185
Galen 96
Gallienus 106
Gambreion 128
Gamelia 204
Gamelion 198, 201, 204, 210
games ch. 5 *passim*, 199; Isthmian 59–61, 63; memorial 54, 60, 125–6; Nemean 59, 61–3; Olympian 54, 57–8, 59, 62–3, 125; Pythian 58, 59, 63, 73, 165
Ganymede 120
Gaul 76, 100, 169, 173, 175; *see also* Nîmes
Ge 49, 70, 70, 163, 203, 205, 208, 210; oracle of 72; sanctuary of 75; *see also* earth
Geffcken, J.: *Griechischen Epigramme* 135
Gela 19, 35, 56, 57
Gell, Sir William 64
gemstones 5, 34, 93, 155
Genesia 203
*gennetai* 144
*genos* 144
Geometric period 34, 37, 55, 123–4, 138, 139, 176; late 29
Geraneia, Mt 30
Glaucon 132
goat-sacrifice 201, 205, 210; to Aphrodite 19; of Dionysus 22
god: dwelling place of 190; high 11, 183; of gods 157; ruler as 167–72; sky- 6, 11–12, 28, 31, 39, 183; supreme 170; union with priestesses 149; v. giants 33, 74, 76, 130, 160, 192, 213; v. goddess 6
goddess: Minoan 1–2, 6; mother 9, 40
Gods: Great 170, sacrifice for 115–16, sanctuary of 111, 113; King of the 86
gold: and magic 151; artefacts 17, 26, 76, 93, 106, 124, 166, 178, 181; bowls 117, 137; curses on 152; figurines 15; masks 122; offerings 137; plates 109; statues 14, 88
Good: Fortune 78, 180; Luck 24, 180, 187, 198, *see also* Agathe Tyche; Shepherd 17; Spirit 68, 187, *see also* Agathos Daemon
*gorgoneion* 184
Gorgons 13, 43–4, 45, 150
Gorgos 55
Gortyna 2, 3, 38, 97
Gortys 97
Gournia 5
Graces 28, 186, 194, 198
Graeco-Roman period 19, 32, 156
graffiti 27, 138, 182, 189
grain: goddess of 106; offering of 142
*grammateus* 52
gratitude 77
grave: cist- 122, 123–5; shaft 122; tile 126
gravestone 118, 124; *see also* stelae
griffins on artefacts 17, 40, 116
grove, sacred 54, 61, 80, 94–115, 116, 173
Guarducci, M.: *Inscriptiones Creticae*: I 2, 3, 5, 97, 98, 133; II 5, 97, 205; III 4, 5, 97; IV 3
gymnasium 56, 65, 82, 91, 182, 195, 196
Gymnopaediae 182
Gytheum 171–2

# INDEX

Hadad 181
Hades 109, 111, 130, 134, 153; *see also* Pluto
Hadran 181
Hadrian 171, 177, 196
Hadrianea 65, 171
Hadrumetum 153
hair, offering of 142
Halicarnassus 48, 49–50, 112, 134, 165
Halios 94
Haloa 201
*halos* 75
Halos 125
Hamera 94
Handmaidens, Two 137
hand symbolism 156
Harmodius 195
Harpocrates 155, 180
*Harpocration* 198, 200, 206
Hathor 168
Head, B. V.: *Historia Nummorum* 109
healing: deities 15, 100, 196, 197, 208; power of 177; sanctuaries ch. 7 *passim*; snakes 24
hearth: boy from the 108; goddess of 21; power of 175; sacred 16, 34, 113, 193; sacrificial 38, 113–14
Heaven and Earth 112
heaven and earth, creation of 117
Hecate: and death ritual 131, 133; and healing 94, 101; and magic 153, 155, 157; and Mysteries 103, 108, 111; and politics 160, 169; and priests 52; cult titles: Megala 175, Pontia 175, Soteira 175, Stratia 175, Zerynthia 113; in Attica 210; island cults 175; representations of 160; sanctuaries and temples of 29, 160
Hecatombaion 185, 198–9, 202–3, 209
Hegeso 131

*hekatompedon* 37, 40
Helicon, Mt 31
Helios 23–4, 45, 60, 76, 117, 163, 170, 176; -Sarapis 186
Helladic period, Middle 122
*Hellenica Oxyrhyncha* 162
Hephaestea 65
Hephaestus 20, 91, 200; on coins 183; temple of 23, 45, 46, 193
Hera: and Attica 204; and festivals 55–6; and island cults 173, 177, 179; and priests 48, 51; as earth mother 39; cult titles: Acraea 36, 38, 138, Argeia Heleia Basileia 173, Dirphya 39, Epilimenia 186, Thelchinia 203, 210; in Crete 3; in Pantheon 13, 22, 23; is Argos 159; is Samos 159; on coins 183; sanctuaries of 13, 25, 31, 32, 33, 34, 38, 39, 138, 181, 185; temples of 34, 35, 36, 39–42, 44, 54; votives 137, 138; Zeus and 169
Heraeum, Argive 33, 38
Heracleia-by-Latmos 82
Heracleia, Great 185
Heracles: and death 130; and festivals 54, 58, 60, 61–2; and healing 95; and Mysteries 109; and oracles 74, 82; and politics 159, 170; and priests 49; at the Ferry 51; Children of 198; club of 175; cult titles: Alexikakos 148, Misogynus 48, Soter 185; Gate of 186; grotto to 182; in Attica 196, 198, 211; in Pantheon 15, 23; in sanctuaries 35, 45; island cults 175, 186; labours of 194; lionskin of 167; Mausolus as 176; on coins 169, 175, 188; sanctuary of 179, 188; shrines of 68, 181; temples of 23, 34
Heraclidae 210
Heraea 163–4
herald 162–3
Hercyna, river 78
herds, associations with 5
Hermaistai 184
herm 17, 53, 118, 130
Hermae, Mutilation of 151, 161, 195
Hermes: and dead 126, 130; and healing 99; and magic 153; and Mysteries 111, 115; and politics 159, 170; and the Graces, Gate of 186; as messenger 162; cakes 50; cult titles: Agoraeus 49, Eumelius 174; in Attica 196, 198, 200, 203, 205; in Pantheon 17, 21, 22; island cults 174, 176, 179, 184, 189; grotto to 182; on coins 183, 184; oracles 69; sanctuaries 27, 28, 42; -Thoth 155, 157; votives 137
Hermione 20
Hermogenes 43
hero: altar to 54; shrine to 62, 194
Herodotus 40, 41, 64, 78, 81, 86–7, 96, 111, 141, 164
heroes 23–4, 36, 45, 73, 132, 140, 145, 167, 208–10; cult of 144–5, 148; death of 125
heroines 203, 204, 208–10
heroon 45, 56, 146, 182
Herostratus 42
Heroxeinia 185
Herzog, R.: *Heilige Geschichte von Cos* 94, 174, 175, 176; *Koische Forschungen und Funde* 173, 175
Hesiod: fragment apud Strabo 67; *Theogony* 31,

# INDEX

32; *Works and Days* 126, 164, 198
*Hesperia* 3, 36, 106, 108, 144, 193, 197, 198, 202–3, 205, 211
Hestia 21, 55, 175; Boulaea, sanctuary of 16
Hesychius 2, 30, 64, 183, 200, 210
*hiarorgus* 52
Hierapolis 66, 171
*hiereia* 52, 116
*hiereus* 52
Hiero II 33, 35
*hieroduli* 52, 149
*hierokeryx* 52
*hieron* 114, 116
*hierophantes* 52
*hieros gamos see* marriage: sacred
*Hierothytai* 52
Himera 56
Hipparchus 195
Hippocrates 93
Hippocratic corpus 187
hippodrome 65, 75
Hippolytus: *Philosophumena* 106
historical period 3, 14; pre- 93
Hittites 29, 177
holocaust 36, 125, 210
holy places 31–2, 41, 55, 179–80, 181
Homer 18, 134; *Hymn to Demeter* ix, 3, 8, 64, 103; *Iliad* 2, 38, 67, 125, 185; *Odyssey* 2, 3, 27, 67
Homonoia 175
horns of consecration 6, 8, 9
horseback 206, 207
horseracing 57, 58, 63, 65, 66, 199
horses: and burials 122; as symbols 11, 14; as votive offerings 139; on reliefs 196; on votive offerings 140
Horus 55, 170, 180; -lion 154

hotel 91, 95
hunting scenes on sarcophagi 129–30
Hyacinthia 164
Hyacinthus 5, 25
*hydrophorus* 52
Hygieia 51, 92, 96, 97, 98–9, 142; Athene 208; temple of 171
Hymettus, Mt 26, 28, 29–30, 210, 212
*Hymn of the Curetes, The* 3–4, 8
hymns, Orphic 116
Hyperboreans 15; Maidens, Tomb of 178
Hyperoche 178
Hypnos 126
hypocausts 98
Hypsipyle 61

Iacchus 103, 108, 153, 194
Ialysus 32, 123, 125
Iao 153; Sabaoth Abrasax 154
Iasion 3
Iaso 98–9
Iasos 82
Icaria 65
Ictinus 44, 191
Ida, Mt: Crete 9, 27, 28–9; Troy 18
idols 27
Idomeneus 133
Idrias 91
Iecri 153
Ikaria 212
Iliaca 65
Ilium 51
Ilissus 196
Imbrasus 40
Imbros 12
immortality 13, 110, 120, 131–3, 158
imperial cult 171–2, 176, 186
*in antis* 38
incubation 91, 93, 99, 101; place of 89, 92, 96, 100, 181; *see also abaton, encoemeterion*
inhumation 123, 124–9

Initiated, Assembly of the 110
initiates: of Bendis 205; of the Mysteries 104, 105, 106–7, 108–9, 110, 112, 116, 118, 119–20, 186; regulations of 115
initiation 27, 112–14, 116–17, 118; hall of 113
Initiation, power of 120
Ino 59
Inopus, river 180
*Inscriptiones Graecae*: I 63, 94, 107, 132, 162, 163, 190, 202, 203, 210; II 2, 48, 49, 92, 93, 144, 146, 161, 162, 163, 165, 193, 196, 197, 198, 199, 201, 202, 203, 204, 205, 206, 207, 208, 210; III 2, 19, 134, 202; IV 31, 118, 165; V 134, 165; VII 36, 165; IX 2, 134; XI 146, 183; XII 2, 31, 49, 118, 127, 159, 165, 183, 184, 187
*Inscriptiones Graecae Antiquissimae praeter Atticas in Attica repertas* 101, 140, 141
*Inscriptiones Graecae insularum maris Aegaei praeter Delum* 101, 142
inscriptions: from Ancient Crete 2–3, 5; from Attica 193, 194, 207, 211; of death and burial 126, 128, 131; of games and festivals 57, 62, 65; of healing 91, 95, 97, 98; of island cults 173, 174, 177, 178, 179, 181, 183, 184, 186, 187; of Mysteries 106, 107, 112, 114, 115, 120–1; of oracles 74, 75–7, 78, 82, 83–4; of Pantheon 5, 12, 22; of politics 159, 160, 162, 164, 165, 166, 171; of priesthood 51, 52; of sanctuaries and temples 29, 33, 34, 45; of votives 143, 145

237

# INDEX

inspiration 72, 81, 83, 84
Iobacchoi 198, 202, 205
Ioleus 36
Ion 193
Iphigeneia 16, 211–12
Iphimedeia 137
Iraklion museum 6
Iran 157
Iris 159
Iron Age 123
iron: grilles 79; knives 98; ring 195; weapons 30
Isis 124, 154, 170, 176, 180
Ismenion 80
Isopeta 7
Istanbul museum 53, 83, 130, 160, 183, 187
Isthmia 55, 164
Isthmian games 59–61, 190
Istros 114
Itanos 97
Ithaca 79
Ithome, Mt 16
ithyphallic 111, 116, 151, 159, 187
ivory: artefacts 124, 178; doors 88; statues 14, 88; statuettes 1

Jacoby, F.: *Fragmente der griechischen Historiker* 203
*Jahreschrifte des öesterreichischen archäologischen Instituts* 48, 133
jewellery 138, 212
Jews 65
Johannes Lydus: *De Mensibus* 30
Johnson, Dr 136
*Journal of Hellenic Studies* 34
Judaism: influence of 153, 156; links with 155, 157
Juktas, Mt 8, 9, 26
Juliopolis 171
Justice, spirit of 120
Justinian 46, 60

Kahn, Louis 39
Kaibel, G.: *Epigrammata Graeca* 132, 133, 134, 135
Kaisariani 18, 212
Kamares 7, 27
Kamini 123
*kataklyston* 29
*katharma* 147
Keil, J.: *Inscriptiones de Smyrna* 52, 120–1
Kenyon, F. G. and Bell, H. I.: *Greek Papyri in the British Museum* 157, 171
Kerata 31
Keraton 178
Keratovouni 31
Kern, O.: *Die Inschriften von Magnesia am Maeander* 118, 161; *Orphicorum Fragmenta* 108, 109–10
*kerykeion* 111
Kerykes 107, 162
kid (and Dionysiac Mysteries) 110, 119
king, priest- 9
Kings, gift-bearer of 175
kingship, sacred 9
Kinsfolk, Society of 145–6
kinship 143–5
knucklebones 27, 90, 93, 142
*koinon* 94
*korai* 126, 178, 190
Kore 3, 20, 22, 35, 85, 102, 103–9, 111, 152–3, 185, 186; Demeter and 117, 138, 165, 173, 178, 182, 185, 194, 195, 213; temple of 107; the Saviour 83; *see also* Persephone
*koureion* 144
Kourion 139
*kouros* 41, 65, 83, 126, 189, 212
Kourotrophos 198, 203, 204, 206, 208–9, 210, 211
Kronion 54
Kronos 54

*labrys* 6

Labyrinth 41; Lady of the 137
Laconia 86, 133, 140
Lacratides 108
*lada* 3
Lady: of Aswos 137; of Upo 137; our 13, 153; Our, of the Animals 1, 15, 211; Our, the Queen of the Dead 110
Lagina 160
lamps 27, 28, 101, 103, 112, 180; ever-burning 206
land: fertility of 104, 106; sacred 17
Laodice 178
Laodicea: in Asia 171; in Syria 171
Lapiths v. Centaurs 44, 55, 58, 192, 213
Las 2
Lasaea 97
Latin Language 153
Lato 3, 34; Phytia 3
latrines 95, 97
laurel 5, 72, 76, 84, 115, 149, 168
Laurium 32, 146
lawcourt 195, 196
lead: and curses 151, 152, oracular 69–70; artefacts 62, 148
Lebadeia 2
Le Bas, P. and Foucart, P.: *Inscriptions grecques et latines recueillies en Grèce et en Asie Mineur* 51
Lebena 97
Lefkandi 36
legend 23, 32, 61, 80, 205, 211; of flood 182
Lehmann 111
Lemnos 20, 110
Lenaea 201
Lenaeon 201
*leonidaion* 56
Leonteus 141
Lera, cave of 27
Lerna 118
Lesbos 36, 111, 166, 182–5

238

# INDEX

Leto 3, 22, 37, 83–4, 99, 177–8, 179, 198, 205, 210; Rock of 180
Leucaspis 205, 210
Leucothea 182
Levadhia 78
libation 53, 79, 93, 113, 119, 138; vessel 70, 124
libations to dead 106–7, 123, 128, 133
library 95, 97
life: beyond death 126, 135; power of 6, 117–18, 120; v. death 125, 129–30, 133–4
Limyra 85
Linear B tablets 21, 26, 137
Lindos 14, 17, 33, 101, 160
Lion: Gate 10, 34; Nemean 23, 61; of Apollo 182; of Demeter-Cybele 138
lion: -headed god 154; -head gargoyles 89
lioness artefacts 70
lions: carved 28, 65, 80; hunted 77; on amulets 156; on artefacts 1, 8, 15–16, 17, 24; on coins 111; terrace of 179
lionskin of Heracles 167
Lisus 2
literary evidence ix; of Aphrodite 18; of Artemis 17; of Athene 14; of Crete 1, 2; of death 125; of Demeter 20; of Dionysus 21; of festivals 64, 198, 200–3, 205, 206; of Hera 41–2; of island cults 181, 183; of magic 148–51; of Mysteries 106, 112, 113, 116; of oracles 71–3, 76, 78, 84–5; of politics 161–2, 164–5, 169; of Poseidon 60; of priests 48–9, 52; of temples and sanctuaries 14, 17, 18, 20, 40–2, 52, 60; of

Zeus 12, 13, 29–31, 38, 55
Livia 213
living, guide of 17
Livy 105, 148
Locri 103, 165
Longus, romance of 142
*loutrophorus* 52
Loutsa 16
Lucian 79
Lucian: *De Dea Syria* 181; *Philopseudes* 150; *Saltatores* 2
Ludovisi throne 13, 18
lustration 116, 119, 149
lustral bowl 127
Lycabettus, Mt 18
Lycaeon, Mt 147
Lyceum 32
Lycia 20, 22, 45, 84–5, 129, 146; see also Myra, Pinara, Sidyma, Telmessus, Xanthus
Lycophron: *Alexandra* 31
Lycurgus 207
Lydia 13, 33, 42
Lydos 11
Lygos 40
Lykaion, Mt 11, 12, 30
Lysander 185
Lysimachus 168
Lysippus 23

Macedon 65, 111
Macedonia 12, 147, 160, 165, 169
Machaon 94, 98
maenads 21, 28, 116, 117, 174; on coins 187
*mageiros* 52–3
magic ch. 12 *passim*; apotropaic 150, 152; black 149; circle 147–8; contagious 149; familiar 79; fertility 200; hostile 79; love 150; number 151, 155, 162; rain 147; sympathetic 30, 58, 147, 149
magical rites 147
Magna Graecia 35, 56, 62, 109–10
Magnesia-ad-Sipylum 29

Magnesia-on-the-Maeander 17, 28, 42–3, 46, 117, 161, 166
Maimakteria 185
Maimakterion 185, 200, 204
Maiuri, A.: *Nuova Silloge Epigrafico di Rodi e Cos* 173–6
maledictions 107
Malice *see Phthonos*
Mallia 5, 6, 7, 9
Mantinea 51, 164
*mantis* 52, 83
Manto, prophetess 183
Marathon 74, 140, 164, 192, 199, 205, 207, 210; deme of 208–9
marble: altars 34; artefacts 55, 84, 93, 98, 141; heads 27; in temples 42, 52, 95, 112–13, 181, 190–1, 194; monuments 126; reliefs 88; statues 28, 41, 99, 181; tablets 32, 51; treasury 74
Marcellus 170
Marcus Aurelius 29–30
Marcus Julius Apellas 91
*Marmor Parium* 127
Maroneia cave 27
marriage: mystical 120; of Zeus and Hera 13, 23, 204; sacred 13, 39, 69, 106, 149, 201
Martiennsen 192
Massilia 2, 65
*Mater Dolorosa* 20, 108
Mathia, Mt 10
Mausolus 176
maze 150
medicine, scientific 94–5, 98, 101
Medusa 45, 80
Megalo Mavrovouni 31
Megalopolis 142
Megara 30, 56, 74, 133, 141, 165
*megaron* 37, 105, 178
Meiggs, R. and Lewis, D.: *Greek Historical Inscriptions* 163, 164

# INDEX

*meion* 144
Melampus 36
Meleas 99
Melicertes 59
Melite 197
Melos 5, 15, 153; Aphrodite of 19
Memnon 24
memorial, tomb as 134
Men 101, 106
Menander 169
Menedeius 206, 210
Meniko 139
Men Tyrannus 32, 146
Meranda 31
Mesa 184
Mesembria 133
Mesopotamia 3, 79, 157
Messara 7
Messenia 56, 115, 123, 141
messenger of gods 17
Metageitnion 199, 203, 209
Metapontum 12, 56, 164
Methana 147
Methone 140
Methymna 118, 182–4
metopes 13, 16, 23, 33, 43–4, 45, 74, 192, 194
Miamu, cave of 26
Micythus 101
Mikalson, J. D.: *The Sacred and Civil Calendar of the Athenian Year* 197–9
Miletus 12–13, 35, 64, 80–3, 101, 113, 118
military: cult titles 175; service 51
millennia, BC: second 9, 41, 55, 64, 105, 122, 176, 182; third 67, 176
Milles, Carl, collection 53
Milo 141
Miltner, F.: *Anatolia* 16
Minoan period 3, 5, 9, 15, 26, 34, 71, 182; Early 26; Late 8, 27; Middle 1
Minos 2
Minotaur 23, 58
Mios 154
Mithradates 95, 177

Mithraea 105, 182
Mithras 170
*Mithrasliturgy* 158
*Mitteilungen des deutschen archäologischen Instituts, Römische Abteilung* 16, 20, 108, 133, 183
Mnasistratus 115
Mnemosyne 194
Modena 117
Moirai 175
Molossi 69
monsters 11, 14, 44, 125, 150
*Monumenta Asiae Minoris Antiquae* 172
monuments, funeral 126, 129–30
moon 2, 8; symbols 205
moral principles 76–7
Moretti, L.: *Iscrizioni agonistische greche* 165
mosaic 95, 120, 179
Mother, Divine 137
mother: goddess 111, *see also* earth mother; mythical 112; of the gods 55, 153, 194
Mothers 101
mothers, nursing, on artefacts 2
mountain: alignment 9–10; mother 44; sanctuaries 31
mountains: and Zeus 28–31; as symbols 16, 118; dominating sites 16, 114; goddess of 18; god(dess) on 16, 39; god of 17; on artefacts 1, 8, 167
mourners 123, 127–8, 130–1; on vases 126–7, 128
Mummius, L. 101
Munichia 205
Munichion 198, 205, 208
Munich museum 20, 22
Muses 83, 194; hill of 165; of Ilissus 196; temple to 145–6
music, god of 15, 58
musical: ballet 105;

competitions and events 51, 58, 63, 65, 66, 96, 101, 207; instruments 128, 139; notation 74
musicians: dedications from 174; in ceremonies 115; offerings of 141; on artefacts 9, 15, 114, 128
Mycale 64
Mycale, Mt 40
Mycenae 1, 10, 34, 37, 122; Grave Circles 122
Mycenean period: Attica 196; death and burial 122–3; healing sites 88; island cults 176, 177, 178; late 27; oracles 70–1, 78; pantheon in 15, 20; sanctuaries and temples 25–6, 34, 38; votives 137
Myconos 36, 198, 201
Mylasa 91, 114
Myra 84, 129
Myron 23, 56
Myrrhinus 204
Mysia 13
*mystai* 114
Mysteries 52, 92, ch. 8 *passim*, 199, 208; Greater 107, 108; Lesser 107, 108, 201–2; of Agrae 108, 199, 201; of Demeter 174; Profanation of 161, 195; Villa of the 22, 110, 117, 119–21
mystery 27, 46
*mystes* 112
myth 2, 15, 16, 20, 21–2, 54, 58, 71, 109, 112, 116, 121, 150, 177, 178, 191, 193; aetiological 32, 104, 183; Cretan 2, 149; dramatic re-enactment of 105; pre-Greek 5
Mytilene 49, 82, 166, 182–5

Naa 65
*naiskos* 81

# INDEX

*naos* 43, 45
Naples museum 19, 23
narthex 36, 45
nature 3, 15, 21
Naucratis 43
Naupactus 56
Naxos 2, 18, 21, 31, 65, 75, 123, 125, 176, 179
Neapolis 171
necrodeipnon 131
necropoleis 123
Neleus 203
Nemea 23, 31
Nemesis 83, 175, 189, 213
Neocaesarea 171
*neocorus* 50, 52, 101, 171
neolithic period 1, 3, 5, 6, 20, 27
Nero 57, 95, 171
New York, Metropolitan Museum 201
Nicharoplex 155
Nicias 176
Nicias (Athenian) 178; Peace of 164
Nicomedes II 169
Nicomedia 171
Nicopolis 66, 171
Niinnion 103, 108–9, 150
Nike 11, 50, 113, 168, 175, 191, 208; *see also* Athene Nike
Nilsson, Martin 9, 120, 147
Nîmes 133
Niobe, children of 15–16
nirvana 132
Nocturnal Serenade 187
Noumenia 197
number magic 151, 155, 162
Nunnius Nigrinus 106
nymphaeum 195
Nymphe 197
nymphs 177, 186; caves of 27–8
Nymphs 93, 195, 196, 203, 204, 210; Apollo, Pan and the 28; Dionysus and the 184; Hill of the 196; Pan and the 27, 28, 193
Nysa 101–2, 171; queen 203

oaktree and oracles 67–8, 87
oaths 2, 3, 114, 160–1, 163, 173; treaty 3
obelisks 22
Oche, Mt 31, 39
octopus as symbol 7
odeon 66, 195
Odeon of Pericles 63
Odessus 114
Odysseus 79
*oenochous* 52
Oenomaus 55
Oesterreich archäologische Institut: *Forschungen in Ephesos* 171
offerings 27, 29–30, 31, 41, 53, 73–4, 77, ch. 10 *passim*, 178, 180, 197, 198, 208; animal 137, 184; benches for 36, 38; burnt 30, 34; festival 63; individual 30, 32; ritual 119, 125; sacrificial 50, 78, 99; table for 39; thank- 89–90, 101; to dead 114, 122–3, 128, 133; to gods 33, 35, 36, 87; to heroes 36
Olbia 84, 114
olive: boughs 198; crowns 57; symbol 14, 147; tree, sacred 55, 161, 191; -wood vases 212
Olous 97
Olympia 11, 12, 13, 15, 21, 23, 26, 33, 35, 39, 44, 52, 54–7, 77, 101, 125, 140–1, 164, 190
Olympiads 52, 54, 57, 58
Olympias of Epirus 111
Olympic Games 58, 125, 164
Olympieia 205
Olympus: Attic 31; Lycian 85; Mt 20, 31, 132
Olynthus 35
omens 64, 164
omphalos 15, 71, 84, 168
Onomastos 126
Opheltes 61

*opisthodomus* 45
oracle 17, 28, 60, ch. 6 *passim*; at Delphi 63, 67, 70–3, 76, 81, 83, 84, 117, 161–2; at Didyma 80–3, 162; at Dodona 24, 67–70, 73, 87; at Siwah 86–7, 162; at Thebes 80; of Amphiaraus 100; of Earth 67, 71, 72; of the dead 78–9, 133–4; of Trophonius 77–8; political: consultations of 69, 73, 81–2, influence of 161–2, 166; questions to 69, 73, 78, 79, 81, 85–6
oracular caves 72, 78, 80, 83, 84
Orchomenus 65
*orgeones* 197, 203
*Orientis Graeci Inscriptione Selectae* 96, 169, 171, 185
Orontes, god of 167
Oropus 50, 51, 100–1, 140
Oros 30
Orpheus 17, 110, 184
Orphic: hymns 116; Mysteries 110, 116–17, 121
Orthia 141
Ortineus 156
Oschophoria 147, 198
*oschophoria* 211
Osiris 153, 170, 176; -lion 154
owl (of Athene) 13

Pactyes of Lydia 81–2
Paeon 94
Paeonius 56
Paestum *see* Poseidonia
*pais aph' hestias* 108
palaces 5, 6, 9, 57; alignment of 9–10, 27; Mycenaean 10; sacral functions of 9
Palaemon 60–1
palaestra 56, 58, 62, 65, 91

# INDEX

Palaikastro 4, 5, 6, 7
Palapaphos 139
palatial periods 6–8
Palatine Anthology 142
Palermo museum 13
Palestine 155
palindromes 155
Pallas Athene 13; *see also* Athene
palm: leaves of victory 167; tree: bronze 76, 178, sacred 68
Pan 28, 83, 106, 117, 119, 169, 188, 193, 196; and the Nymphs 27, 28, 193, 212; Apollo and the Nymphs 28; cave of 26; sanctuary of 188, 196
Panacea 98–9
Panamara 118
Panathenaea 63, 141, 162, 190, 199, 200, 206
Panathenaic procession 191, 192, 207
Panayia 78
Pancrates 196
*pancratium* 57, 59, 62, 190, 207
Pandia 202
Pandion 193
Pandrosus 51, 206, 211
Panhellenia 65
panhellenism 59, 61, 63, 66, 76–7, 82, 96, 107, 125, 141, 173
Pani 31
Panionia 63–4
Panionion 165
Panisca 119
Panormus 80
*panspermia* 148
pantheon: Delian 22; Greek 2–5, ch. 2 *passim*; Lycian 22
panther (of Dionysus) 187
Panticapaeum 140
Papageorgiu, P. N.: *Rhodos kai Lesbos* 184
Paphos 18
papyrus 13, 150, 156–7
Paralus 36
Paris 142; Bibliothèque

Nationale 12; book 157; Louvre 12, 17, 19, 20, 113
Paris, Judgement of 74
Parnes, Mt 30
*Parola del Passato* 173, 174
*Parium, Marmor* 127
Paros 21, 65, 74, 162, 177, 185, 189
Parpaxin 153
Parso cave 28
parting with dead 130–1
Pasionax 153
Pasiphae 2, 6, 9, 149
Paton, W. R. and Hicks, E. L.: *The Inscriptions of Cos* 30, 82, 96, 141, 173–6
Patrae 140
Patroclus 57, 125
Pausanias ix, 11, 42, 54, 55, 77, 80, 164, 194; I 1, 14, 29, 30, 31, 196, 206; II 20, 30, 31, 38, 49, 88; III 1, 2; IV 30; V 1, 12; VI 1; VII 48, 49, 72; VIII 30, 49; IX 2, 31, 49, 78; X 72
Payne, Humfry 38
peacock symbol 13
Peck, W.: *Griechische Vers-Inschriften* 118, 127, 128, 134
pediments, temple 15, 23, 43, 45, 55, 76, 108, 180, 192, 194, 196
Pegasus 45
Pelasgi 67
Pelion, Mt 30
Pella 169
Pelopion 54
Peloponnese 20, 44, 62, 140, 166; *see also* Lerna, Pylos
Pelops 54–5, 125
pentathlon 57, 62, 207
Pentelicus, Mt 28
Perachora 33, 36, 38
Pergamon 29, 32–3, 41, 46, 52, 75, 76, 96–7, 116, 118, 171, 176, 185; Attalids of 168
Perge 171

Pericles 105, 191
Perinthus 171
*periodonices* 59
*periodos* 59
*peripsema* 147
peristyle 41, 43, 44, 102
perquisites from sacrifices 50, 107, 141, 143, 199, 208
Persephone 79, 110–11, 153, 185, 196, 200; *see also* Kore
Perseus 45, 169
Persia 3, 62, 76, 77, 80–2, 133, 155, 169–70
Persian: expedition 14; War 55, 75, 76, 105, 159, 177, 190
Phaena, priestess 51
Phaestos 2, 5, 6, 9, 27
Phalasarna 2
Phaleron 211
phallus symbol 118, 119–20, 148, 150, 151–2, 156, 162, 178, 193, 200
Phaneromeni 27
Phanes 117
Pharaohs of Egypt 80
*pharmakos* 147
Pheidias 12, 14, 55–6, 191
Pheidon of Cleonae 62
Philadelphia 114; museum 18
Philadelphion 180
Phileremus 24
Philip II of Macedon 111, 114, 163, 165
Philip III 114
Philippides 165
Philippopolis 13, 98, 171
*Philologische Wochenschrift* 174
Phocis 2, 27, 49, 165
Phoebus Apollo 15; *see also* Apollo
Phoenicians 18, 65
Photius 200
*phrateres* 143
*Phratriai* 200
phratry, gods of the 144
Phre 154
Phrygia 13, 21, 156

242

# INDEX

*Phthonos* 134
Phylakopi 5
Phyle 203
Pietrosa 117
pillar symbol 1, 5
pillar-tombs 22, 129
Pinara 129
Pindar 12, 59, 116; *Nemeans* 61; *Olympians* 54
Piraeus 14, 48, 93, 99, 140, 207
Pirithous 55
Pisistratus 105, 177, 205
Pistoxenus painter 19
pit: burials 122, 123; graves 122; of underworld deities 31–2, 35, 78; sacrificial 34, 35, 37, 78; shrines 61, 113, 188
Pithecusae 125
Pithoigia 201
Plataea 75, 164–5
Plato x, 111, 116; *The Republic* 28, 132, 206; *Timaeus* 206
Plerosia 204
Pliny: *Natural History* 72, 84, 85
Plutarch 77; *De Pythiae Oraculis* 49; *De Sollertia Animalium* 84; *Flamininus* 171; *Moralia* 29, 72, 150, 198, 201, 203; *Phocion* 205; *Themistocles* 197; *Theseus* 2, 198
Pluto 101–2, 103–8, 110, 111, 153, 179, 183; -Hades 22; Lord of All 153; *see also* Hades
Plynteria 206
Plyntherion 185
Podalirios 98
political: associations of games 64; consultations of oracle 69, 73, 81–2; life ch. 13 *passim*
pollution 32–3, 48–9, 129, 146
*polos* 13, 16, 131
Polybius 161

Polycharmus 85
Polycleitus 13; the Younger 89
Polycrates 41, 177
polygonal masonry 75, 105
Polyrhenia 2, 5
Polyzalus 77
pomegranate 13, 104
Pompaia 200, 204
Pompeii, Villa of the Mysteries 22, 110, 117, 119–21
Pompeion 194
Pontus 169
Popillius Laenas, C. 148
porch 36–7, 105
Porinos 64
Porphyry: *De Abstinentia* 206
Porthmos 211
portico 94, 96, 145, 178, 180
Poseideia 185
Poseid(e)on (month) 185, 198, 201, 204, 208
Poseidon: and games 59–61; and island cults 173–4, 175, 179, 180, 186; and politics 164, 169; and priests 49, 206; and votives 137; cult titles: Gerastios 174, Heliconius 64; in Attica 192, 198, 204, 206, 210, 212; in Pantheon 12, 20, 22; on coins 169, 183; sanctuary of 186; son of 169; temples of 20, 186, 212
Poseidonia 20, 39
Potidaea 74, 132
*Potnia Theron* 1, 15, 137
pottery: and Artemis 16–17, 25; as votive offerings 138; deposits 37, 67, 100, 113, 126, 179; Geometric period 29; jars for burial 125; Mycenaean period 25, 27, 78; painted 6
power: apotropaic 149–50; numinous 15,

31, 70; of life and death 117–18, 120, 126–7; of nature 3, 15; symbols of 24
Praxitelean school 187
Praxiteles 19
prayers 150, 154, 157, 158, 172
pre-Greek period 40, 42, 67, 111, 176; names 5, 13, 20, 25, 112, 176
Preisendanz, K.: *Papyri Graecae Magicae* 149–51, 157–8
Priapus 53, 152
Priene 35, 43, 46, 64
priestesses 67, 72, 82, 107–8, 115, 118, 119, 133, 147, 186, 191, 206; union of, with priests 149
priesthood 161, 171, 211; hereditary 185; of phratry 144
priest-king 9, 64
priests 30, 45, ch. 4 *passim*, 56, 71–2, 77, 80, 81, 83, 101, 114, 115, 117, 143, 172, 180, 186, 206
Prinias 38
prizes 126, 207
Procris 24
Proerosia 204
Promachus 14
Prometheus 32, 207
*pronaos* 44–5, 81, 84, 178
prophecy: god of 15; weather 30
prophet 83, 84; *see also* oracles
*prophetes* 52, 83
prophetess 71, 81
propylaea 105, 106, 181, 186, 187, 191, 207
prostitution 18, 149
*prothesis* 127
proto-Geometric period 25, 176
*protomystae* 115
Prott, J. de and Ziehen, L.: *Leges Graecorum Sacrae* 32, 49, 50, 129
*proxenia* 164

243

# INDEX

Prusias II 76
*prytaneion* 55, 75
*Psalms* 155
*psyche* 132
Psychro 5–6, 8, 27
Ptolemies of Egypt 24, 180
Ptolemy: I 167; II 114; II Philadelphus 176, 179; III 167, 182; IV 101; V 169–70; VI Philometor 182
punishments 32–3, 50, 57, 81, 107, 115, 163
purchase of priesthood 49
purification, ritual 78–9, 109, 114, 115, 116
Pyanopsia 147, 198
Pyanopsion 198, 200, 204, 210
Pygmas 133
pygmies, ithyphallic 116
Pylorus 97
Pylos 10, 20, 26, 122, 137
pyre, funeral 124–5
Pyrgos 26
*pyrphorus* 52
Pyrrha 182, 184
Pyrrhic dance 63
Pyrrhus, King 68
Pythagorean 121, 149
Pythaists 211
Pythia 83
Pythian Games 58, 59, 63, 73, 165
Pytho (snake) 58, 71

Queen of the Dead, Our Lady, the 110
queen: of the mountains 1; of the sky 2; of the wild 6
Quintilian 12, 55

rain: and fertility 106; god 29–30, 31
ram: and oracular sacrifice 78; and the Mysteries 111, 115; as offering 137, 140, 210; Dionysus on 201
ram's horn of Zeus Ammon 167–8

raven: of Apollo 15; of darkness 117; of death 117
rays (of Helios) 167
*Receuil d'inscriptions grecques supplément* 36, 70, 82, 141
regatta 64, 199, 207
Reggio Calabria museum 103
regulations: for initiates 115, 118; for priests 48–51; for sanctuaries 174
Rehm, A.: *Didyma 11: Die Inschriften* 82
reliefs 27, 29, 35, 53, 63, 72, 83, 88, 93, 106, 108, 117, 141, 178, 182, 184, 189, 196; double 22; grave 129; Hellenistic 22; high 33, 98; low 17, 21, 126; votive 140–1, 187; wooden 13
religion: and fabric of society 161; v. irreligion 160
religious: buildings 9, 26, 30, 31, 36, 47; ceremonies 6, 9; festivals 57, 64, 66, ch. 8 *passim*
revelation 116, 117; *see also epopteia*
*Revelation of St John the Divine, The* 46
*Revue de philologie* 82
*rhabdophori* 52
*Rhamnus* 213
Rhegium 57
Rhodes 16, 23–4, 28, 29, 30, 32, 49, 65, 75, 114, 125, 132, 134, 146, 148, 165, 167; museum 19, 21, 22, 97, 129–30; *see also* Cameiros, Ialysus, Lindos
Rhodos 175
Rhoicus 41
rings: as charms 148; as evidence 8, 34, 63, 93, 111–12, 124, 125

*rites de passage* 147
ritual: activities 191, 192–3; attitudes 119; banquets 112–13, 180; bath 13, 40; breaking 138; civic and political 50; death 8; fertility 3; gestures 7, 127–8; healing 88, 98, 102; mourning 123; offerings 125, 139; prostitution 149; puberty 3; purification 78–9, 181; ruler 9; sacred marriage 3; sacrifice 206, 207; scenes 140; union 2
river gods 164, 167
*Rivista di Filologia* 173
robbers, tomb- 122
Robert, F. 166, 181
Robert, Louis 83, 134
rock: altar 111, 113; -carved throne 182; carving 28; -cut reliefs 196; -cutting 28, 29, 45, 106, 191, 193, 195; tombs 129
Roma, shrine of 171
Romaia, Great 186
Romania 117
Rome 84, 132, 148, 153, 160, 161; Capitoline museum 19; Hadrian's villa 19; national museum 13; Ostia 19; Vatican museum 19, 21; Villa Albani 17, 21, 23; Villa Medici 118
Rosetta stone 169
Rouse, W. H. D. 140–2
ruler worship 167–72, 176

Sabazius 156
sacred: bough 147–8; bronze artefacts 96, 191; crocodiles 180; drama 75, 181, 201, 202; grove 54, 61, 80, 94–5, 116, 173; hearth 16, 34, 113, 193; marriage 13, 39, 69, 106, 149, 201,

# INDEX

204; processions 194; prostitution 149; springs 18, 80, 89, 93, 100, 101, 104, 193, 212; steps 212
Sacred Way: at Delphi 59, 71, 73–5; at Didyma 80; at Eleusis 104; at Epidaurus 91; at Pergamon 96; in Attica 18, 104, 194, 195; on Delos 179; on Thera 182
sacred well 96, 147, 178
sacrifice 32, 36, 50, 51, 52, 53, 82, 106, 113, 129, 146, 162, 198, 199, 200, 202, 203, 205, 206; animal 6, 8, 27, 28, 32, 50, 57, 64, 72, 78–9, 96, 99, 107, 115, 141, 147, 175, 186, 189, 195, 200–1, 205–9; ashes of 54, 62; at festivals 197–208; by Spartans 164; calendar for 198, 205, 208; human 8, 35, 125, 205; mystic 20; perquisites from 50, 107, 141, 143, 199, 208; places for 31, 33–4, 38; regulations 99, 141, 199, 208
sacrificial: offerings 99; scenes 22; *see also* Anarrhysis
sailors: and Dioscuri 166; guardians of 112
Salaminioi 51, 198
Salamis 36, 123, 140, 164, 205, 211
Samos 13, 25, 26, 34, 35, 40–1, 64, 138, 148, 159, 177
Samothrace 35, 110–14, 181
sanctuaries: cave 6, 7, 8, 9, 26–8, 104, 179
Sappho 184; painter 128
Sarapieion 180
Sarapis 24, 83, 85, 154, 176, 180; Helios- 186
sarcophagi 8, 9, 22, 45, 103, 118, 123, 129, 131
Sardinia 84

Sardis 30, 42, 171
Satyra 107
satyrs 21–2, 28, 119, 174; on coins 187
Saviour goddess cult 131
scapegoat 147
Scira 206, 209
Sciras 211
Scirophorion 199, 206, 209
Scopas 19, 114
Scully, Vincent: *The Earth, the Temple and the Gods* 9–10, 39, 44, 46, 68–9, 192
sea: associations 16, 20, 60; birth from 18; god(dess) 182, 183; symbolism 7
sealstone evidence 1, 6, 7, 8, 23, 93, 124
sealstones as magic 148, 154
Sebastoi 172
Selene 151, 153
Seleuceia on Calycadnus 118
Seleucus: I 168; II 82
Selinus 13, 16, 23, 45, 56
Selloi 67
Semele 11, 21, 159, 202, 210
Semitic gods 156, 180
Semnai 193
Serapis 85
Servilius Isauricus, P. 117
Set 157
sexual: relations 33; union 39, 121, 149
Shear, T. L. 193
sherds 27, 29, 31, 64, 79
Sherwin-White, S. M.: *Ancient Cos* 173
ship and death 130–1
ship-cart 199, 201, 207
shipping, protectors of 189
shrines 1, 5, 8, 9, 16, 20, ch. 3 *passim*, 54, 67–8, 76; cave 9; domestic 5; island 16, 18; oracular 78
Sibyl, Rock of the 71, 75

Sicily, 49, 56, 65, 75, 101, 148, 151, 165; *see also* Acragas, Eryx, Palermo, Selinus, Syracuse
Sicyon 16, 49, 56, 74
Side 171
Sidon 2, 65
Sidyma 129
Silenus 21, 119, 159, 187; Gate of 186
Silius Italicus 86–7
silver: artefacts 27, 93, 111; curses on 152; mines 146; offerings 90, 142; prizes 207
Simaetha 149, 151
Sinope 24
Siphnian treasury 23
Siphnos 17, 74
Sipylus, Mt 29
Siren 125, 131
Sisyphus 60
Siwah, Oasis of 86
sky: gods 6, 11–12, 28, 31, 39, 183; symbolism 7, 8, 11; union of, with earth 13, 39, 204
slaves 75, 176
Slavs 63
Smilis 41
Smyrna 36, 52, 120–1, 133, 171
snakes: and death 130–1; and healing 88, 90, 93, 97, 98, 142; and Nemean games 61–2; and Pythian games 58; as symbols 1, 6, 17, 21, 24, 111, 142, 155–6; column 75; on artefacts 1, 11, 71, 117, 139–40, 197; on coins 23, 95
Sokolowski, F.: *Lois Sacrées d'Asie Mineure* 50, 118, 128
soldier-goddess 159
*Solomon, The Testament of* 156
Solon 63, 105, 126, 128
Solygeia 37
Sophia, Santa 46
Sophocles 12, 39;

245

# INDEX

Sophocles – *cont.*
   *Trachiniae* 68
Sophron 148
Soteria 65, 185
Soteriastai 198
Sozomen: *Historia Ecclesiae* 149
Sozon 84
Sparta 2, 16, 26, 35, 55, 57, 63, 74, 140–1, 162, 164–5, 171, 185
spells 150
sphinx 39, 44, 75, 80, 125, 126, 139, 150, 186
spittle 150–1
*spondai* 163
*spondophori* 52
Springs, Apollo of the 100
springs: healing 96, 98; mineral 100; oracles and ch. 6 *passim*; sacred 18, 80, 89, 93, 100, 104, 193, 212; sanctuaries 31, 73
stadia 55, 57, 58, 59, 61, 62–3, 65, 66, 68, 91
Staff, Renewal of the 96
star: and immortality 132; symbols 6–7, 111
starting line 61
stave, sacred 111
*stegonomus* 53
stelae 14, 22, 84, 88, 93, 100, 126, 129–31; *see also* gravestone
Stenia 200
Stephanus of Byzantium 87, 184
stepped buildings 33–4, 35, 46, 62, 80, 83, 84, 95, 180, 187, 212
stoa 75, 93, 100, 113, 178, 188, 191, 194–5, 196, 212; of Attalus 195; Painted 195
stone: altars 33, 35, 41; carvings 100; circle 20; dressed 126; graves 122; in other buildings 105; inscriptions 166, 183; in temples 36, 37, 54, *see also* columns; shrines 100; treaty in 159
Stone Age 20, 27

storage jars 7, 79
Strabo 43, 64, 67, 80, 95, 101
Stratonicea 114, 160
*Studia Pontica* 134
Stymphalia 16
Stymphalian birds 16, 23
Styra 153
*Suda* 94, 198, 200
Sulla 101
sun: god 23, 86, 156, 167, 176, 177, *see also* Helios, Apulunas; in temple 45; power of 155, 157; symbolism 6–7
Sun, Fountain of the 86–7
sun associations 2, 5, 6, 8, 15, 37, 46
sunflower motif 7
Sunion 211, 212
superstition 148, 150
*Supplementum Epigraphicum Graecum* 30, 94, 171, 174, 205, 206
*Sura* 84–5
swastika 7, 16, 138
sword as symbol 1
Sybaris 56
Sybrita 5
synagogue 65
syncretism 169, 170
Synnada 171
Synoecia 202
Syracuse 33, 35, 41, 46, 56, 74, 170
Syria 12, 29, 139, 148, 149, 155–6, 167–8
Syrian gods 181
Syriscus 15

Taylour, Lord William 1
Talthybii 162
Tanagra 123
Tanit 18
Taras 74
Tarentines 140–1
Tarsus 171
Tartarus 134
technology, patrons of 173, 200
Tegea 49, 138
Teiresias 79
Teithras 203

Telemachus of Acharnae 92
Telephus 33
Telesphorus 98
Telestar 62
telesterion 105, 107
*telete* 115
Telete 120, 210
Telmessus 129
*temenos* 31, 92, 152
temple: and burials 128–9; and treaties 164; association with games 55; cults 165; law 50; officials 52–3; orientation 16, 44, 46, 102, 181, 188; prostitutes 18, 149; round 19, 21, 96; sculpture 13, 15, 16, 23; sites 2, 3, 16, 18, 20, 38–9
temples ch. 3 *passim*, 75–6, 80, 83, 84, 87, 178, 190–3, 212; alignment of 37, 38, 76, 80; at healing sanctuaries 88, 91, 92, 93, 97, 100; of Mysteries 114, 116, 118; *see also* cella, friezes, metopes, pediments and individual deities
*templum* 31
Tenos 13, 65
Teos 82, 141, 171
Terpsicles 141
terracotta 43; altars 35; animals 26; figures 5–6, 17, 18, 20, 25, 28, 39, 125, 138; limbs 92; painted 27, 44, 212; plaques 56; tablets 7, 54; votive offerings 138–9, 186
Tetrapolis 209
Thalysia 174
Thargelia 65, 147, 198
Thargelion 185, 198, 205–6, 209
Thasos 16, 34, 159, 164, 185–9

# INDEX

theatres 51, 57, 61, 65, 66, 68, 82, 83; and healing sites 88–9, 91, 97, 100–1; and Mysteries 113, 114, 115, 187; and ritual drama 109, 116, 181; friezes 23; priests' seats in 51
Thebes 12, 35, 65, 75, 80, 100, 116, 118, 142; in Egypt 86–7; Seven against 45, 100
Themis 69, 71, 75, 91, 193, 213
Themistocles 164, 197
Theocritus 148, 174; *Idylls* 149, 150, 151
Theodaisia 184
Theodorus 41, 42
Theodorus, priest 143
Theodotes 88
Theogamia 204
Theoi Patro(i)oi 176, 188
theophant 121
Theophrastus: *Characters* 148, 150; *De Signis Tempestatum* 29
Theos Hypsistos 12–13
Thera 35, 65, 145, 151–2, 182
Theras 182
Thermae 166, 183
Thermi 182
Thermon 37, 43
Thermopylae 164, 165
Thersilochus 189
Thesea 65
Theseia 198
Theseus 2, 23, 36, 55, 58, 60, 74, 118, 178, 198, 213
Thesmophoria 185, 197, 200
Thesmophorion 178
Thespiae 49, 165
Thesprotians 78
Thessalonica 12, 120, 171
Thessalians 165
Thessaly 29, 65, 88, 123, 125, 142, 148
*thiasoi* 117, 144–5, 146, 174, 176
Thiasotae 204, 205

thieves, patron of 17
Thirsty Ones 137
tholos: at Athens 194; at Delphi 45; at Epidaurus 89; at Samothrace 113
Thorikos 213
Thrace 65, 156, 162, 205–6
Thracian horseman 98
Thracians 48
Thrasymedes of Paros 88
throne: Demeter on 108; of Apollo 125; rock-carved 182; Zeus on 12
thrones: of Zeus 29; on artefacts 117
Thucydides 69, 162, 164–5, 177, 183, 196, 201, 202
thunder 174
thunderbolt 6, 11–12, 116, 168, 191
Thurii 140–1
Thyateira 13, 133
Thyiads 75
*thymele* 89
*thyrorus* 52
thyrsus 21, 118
*thysia* 32
tiles 40, 52, 61, 97, 126
Timarista and Crito 130
Timocleides 187
Timotheus 88
Tiryns 10, 34
Titaness 70
Titans 11, 116, 121
Tmolus, Mt 30
Tomb of Hyperborean Maidens 178
tombs 7, 45, 54, 61, 80, 85, 111, 123, 128, 152, 177, 182, 212; as eternal home 133; as memorial 134; beehive 213; chamber 122–3; house 129; Mycenaean 78, 122; pillar- 22, 129; temple 129; tholos 10, 34, 122, 125
Tomis 114, 146, 171
torch: bearer 103, 105, 108, 112, 114, 117, 193; -race 199, 206, 207
totemism 6
traders and Hermes 174
Tragedy, statue of 187
Tralles 101, 171
travellers, protector of 17
treasuries 40, 45, 50, 55, 56, 74, 77, 178
treasury, sacred 107
treaties 163–4
treatment 89–91, 93, 96, 97–8
tree: bearers 146; -cutting ceremony 173; god of 174; of death 110; of life 110; sacred 40, 54, 55, 68; symbol 5, 8
Tricca 96
trickster god 17
trident (of Poseidon) 20, 167
triglyphs 33, 43
tripod: and caldrons 140; dedications 93; of oracle 23, 71–3; on vases 141; -Plataea 75; prizes 126
Tripolis 171
Triptolemus 104, 107–8
Tritopatores 205, 209
Troezen 18
Trojan: Horse 74; v. Greek 192; War 45, 74
Trophonia 65
Trophonius: oracle of 77–8; sanctuary of 30
truce, sacred 54, 57, 107, 164
Tryphon 168
Trysa 45
Tumuli: of cremations 125
tunnels 57, 62–3
Türkomen-Däg 21
Turullius 95
Twelve Gods 22, 179, 185; Altar of 194; dedications to 22, 194; sanctuary of 65
Tyche 24, 134, 166–8; Agathe 24, 180, 187; of Antioch 167; of Mytilene 166

# INDEX

Typhon 11
Tyre 2, 145
Tzetzes: *Historiarum variarum chiliades* 94

underworld deities 20, 31–2, 35–6, 78, 103, 131, 151, 153, 175, 183
universe, view of 132
urn, burial 124

Vari 28
Vase: Chieftain 8, 9; François 125
vegetable stew offering 198, 201
vegetation: associations 5; cycle 2, 3; god(s) of 21, 146, 174; spirits 2
*Vendidad* 155
Venice 75
Venus 18; de Milo 19; Medici 19
*Venus pudica* 19
Vergil: *Ciris* 151; *Eclogues* 151
Victorinus 60
victors: in games 56, 57, 59, 61, 63, 65, 83, 141, 190; in war 56, 66, 140–1, 165
Victory 11, 12, 14, 56, 101, 175, 179, 180, 191, 194; *see also* Nike
Vienna museum 45
vine: magic 147–8; on coins 169; symbol 147, 161, 177
virginity 15, 16, 49, 115, 193, 212
Vitruvius 43
volcanic eruption 182
votaries 108
votive: artefacts 13, 26, 39, 95; deposits 25, 67; inscriptions 12; niche 182, 197; offerings 6, 8, 17, 20, 27, 68, 93, 97, 114, ch. 10 *passim*, 212; pots 195, 197; reliefs 28, 106, 187, 189; statues 107; statuettes 109,

125; storage of 181; tablets 5, 7, 8, 103, 181; terracottas 138–9, 186

wall, polygonal 75
war: -dance 63; god of 18
water-supply 14, 56, 60, 72, 80, 95, 104, 197
wealth, god of 103
weapons: and burials 122, 124; and offerings 140–1; on coins 168
weather: god 29; prophecy 30
well, sacred 96, 147, 178
Wheel-Lake, Sacred 65, 179
wheel symbol 6–7, 138
White Shield, deity of 205, 210
Wiegand, T.: *Milet, Ergebnisse der Ausgabungen und Untersuchungen seit 1899* 81–3
wild, power of 16
Willetts, R. F. 1, 3
wind-gods 205
winds 117, 204
wine: and Dionysiacs 118; and festivals 160, 201, 210; and funerals 125; and healing 98; as offering 137, 142; god of 21; -pourer 52
Wisdom, Holy 46
witchcraft 148
women: and cult of Athene 188; exclusion of 189; festival of 118, 200, 206; offerings reserved for 211
Wonders of the World 42, 55
wooden: altars 31; artefacts 212; columns 36, 40, 44, 181; entablature 62; ex-votos 100; images 41; reliefs 13; temples 36, 100
workshops 1, 16, 20, 139
workers' strike 82
worshippers 32, 45, 50–1,

111, 115, 117, 138, 139, 140
wrestlers 60, 63, 141
wrestling 57, 62, 66, 207
Wycherley, R. E.: *The Stones of Athens* 196

Xanthus: in Lycia 22, 129; slave 32, 146
Xenophanes x, 186
Xenophon: *Anabasis* 164; court doctor 95, 173; *Hellenica* 60
*xyleus* 53
*xystus* 65

Yahweh 12
Yalouris, Nikolaos 55
Yavis, Constantine 34

Zacorus 52
Zagreus 3
Zagron, Mt 3
Zakro 5, 7
Zanes 57
Zara, Mt 10
*Zeitschrift für Numismatik* 106
*Zeitschrift für Papyrologie und Epigraphik* 176
Zeus: altars of 29, 31, 33–4, 41, 46, 179; and Crete 3–5, 10; and festivals 57, 202–6; and Hera 169, Gate of 186; and island cults 176; and magic 147; and mountains 28–31; and Mysteries 103, 117; and politics 159, 170; cult titles: Acraeus 28–9, Actaeus 30, Agoraeos Thasios 186, Agoraeus 194, Alastoros 186, Alseios 173, Ammon 86, 167–8, Anchesmius 28, Anthaleus 209, Apennius 30, Apesantius 31, Aphesius 30, Aslepius 97, Atabyrius 28, 84,

248

# INDEX

Athoius 28, Boulaios 173, Cithaeronius 28, Coryphaeus 29, Cretagenes 3, Ctesios 186, Cynthius 28, 29, 179, Dictaeus 3, 137, Epacrius 29–30, 205, 210, Epoptes 203, 210, Eubuleus 22, 179, 186, Exopsius 196, Exousius 196, Heliconius 28, Horios 173, 204, 210, Hyetius 30, Hymettius 28, 30, Hypatos 208, Hypsistos 12–13, 179, 197, Idaeus 28, Kataibates 29, Lycaeus 30, Machaneus 173, Maenolius 183, Mantellanius 30, Megistos 173, Meilichios 202, 210, Melusius 31, Na(i)os 69, 70, Ombrius 29–31, Panamerius 160, Panhellenius 196, Parnethius 28, Patroos 185, 186, Phatrius 194, Phratrius 143–4, 200, Polieus 173, 175, 179, 192, 206, 210, Sabazius 156, Sarapis 154, Semaleus 30, Semius 29–30, Soter 51, 173, 179, Teleios 204, 212, Tropaeus 140; -Hadad 181; in Attica 191, 193, 200, 205, 212; in Pantheon 11–13, 15, 20, 22, 23; in sculpture 160; Liberator 171; Mt 31; myths of 2, 6, 21, 32, 38, 116, 177; oath to 163; Olympius 31, 163, 171, 195–6, 205; on coins 167–9, 183; oracles of 67–70, 83; priests of 48; sanctuaries of 26, 27–31, 54, 67; son of 167–8; temples of 15, 29, 39, 44, 45, 52, 55–6, 57, 62, 164, 168, 195–6, 205; votives 137, 142
zodiac, signs of 117
Zonnysus 184
Zosime 183
Zuntz, Gunther: *Persephone* 110